Lecture

Cavendish
Publishing
Limited

BUSINESS LAW

David Kelly, BA, BA (Law), PhD
Principal Lecturer
The Law School
Staffordshire University

&

Ann Holmes, BA, MPhil, PGD
Principal Lecturer
The Law School
Staffordshire University

First published in Great Britain 1994 by Cavendish Publishing Limited, The Glass House, Wharton Street, London WC1X 9PX
Telephone: 071-278 8000   Facsimile: 071-278 8080

British Library Cataloguing in Publication Data

Kelly, David
Business Law – (Lecture Notes Series)
I Title II Holmes, Ann E M III Series
344.20666

ISBN 1-85941-041-3
Cover photograph by Jerome Yeats
Printed and bound in Great Britain

Preface

Business and commercial enterprise takes place within a legal context and, in the final analysis, it is governed and regulated by law. One of the problems facing the person studying business activity, and the one that is specifically addressed in this book, is the fact that business enterprise takes place within a general and wide-ranging legal environment; but the student is required to have more than a passing knowledge of the legal rules and procedures which impact on business activity. The difficulty lies in acquiring an *adequate* knowledge of the many areas that govern such business activity. Law students legitimately may be expected to focus their attention on the minutiæ of the law but those studying law within, and as merely a component part of, a wider sphere of study cannot be expected to have the same detailed level of knowledge of law students. Nonetheless they are expected to have a more than superficial knowledge of various legal topics.

For the author of a business law text-book, the difficulty lies in pitching the material considered at the appropriate level so that those studying the subject acquire a sufficient grasp to understand law as it relates *generally* to business enterprise, and of course to equip the student to pass the requisite exams. To achieve this goal the text must not be too specialised and focus on too small a part of what is contained in most business law syllabuses. For example, although contract law is central to any business law course, to study it on its own, or with a few ancillary topics, is not sufficient. Nor, however, should the text be so wide-ranging as to provide the student with no more than a superficial general knowledge of most of the possible interfaces between law and business enterprise. A selection has to be made and it is hoped that this text has made the correct one. No attempt has been made to cover all the areas within the potential scope of business law but it is hoped that attention has been focused on the most important of these without excluding any area of major importance. Additionally, it is hoped that the material provided deals with the topics selected in as thorough a way as is necessary.

The authors would like to express their thanks to Erika Kelsall who assisted in producing the final text and the *Institute of Industrial and Commercial Law* at Staffordshire University for its financial assistance in producing the book.

David Kelly
Ann Holmes
Staffordshire
July 1994

Outline Table of Contents

Detailed Table of Contents

Table of Cases

Table of Statutes

Chapter 1

Domestic Sources of Law

As the title of this chapter implies it does not cover all the possible sources of law operative within the UK. The fact is that ever since the UK joined the European Economic Community, now the European Union (EU), it has progressively passed the power to create laws which have effect in this country to the wider European institutions. It is essential, therefore, that the contemporary student of law be aware of the operation of the legislative and judicial processes of the EU. As a matter of convenience, based on the fact that European Union law does not impact as widely as domestic law, consideration of the effect of the EU on domestic UK law will be postponed until the next chapter. It must be borne in mind, however, that where they do operate, European Union law and legal processes are superior in authority to domestic procedures considered in this chapter.

Although we still refer to our legal system as a common law system and although the courts still have an important role to play in the interpretation of statutes, it has to be recognised that legislation is the predominant method of law making in contemporary society. It is necessary therefore to have a knowledge of the workings of the legislative procedure through which law is made.

As an outcome of various historical political struggles, Parliament, and in particular the House of Commons, has asserted its authority as the ultimate source of law-making in the UK. Parliament's prerogative to make law is encapsulated in the notion of the supremacy of Parliament.

Parliament consists of three distinct elements; the House of Commons, the House of Lords and the Monarch. Before any legislative proposal, known at that stage as a bill, can become an Act of Parliament it must proceed through, and be approved by, both Houses of Parliament and must receive the Royal Assent.

Before the formal law making procedure is started, the government of the day, which in practice decides and controls what actually becomes law, may enter into a process of consultation with concerned individuals or organisations.

Green Papers are consultation documents issued by the government which set out and invite comments from

1.1 Introduction

1.2 Legislation

1.2.1 The legislative process

interested parties on particular proposals for legislation. After considering any response the government may publish a second document in the form of a *White Paper* in which it sets out its firm proposals for legislation.

A bill must be given three readings in both the House of Commons and the House of Lords before it can be presented for the Royal Assent. It is possible to commence the procedure in either House although *money bills* must be placed before the Commons in the first instance.

Before it can become law any bill introduced in the Commons must go through five distinct procedures.

- First reading

  This is purely a formal procedure in which its title is read and a date is set for its second reading.

- Second reading

  At this stage the general principles of the bill are subject to extensive debate. The second reading is the critical point in the process of a bill. At the end a vote may be taken on its merits and if it is approved it is likely that it will eventually find a place in the statute book.

- Committee stage

  After its second reading the bill is passed to a standing committee whose job is to consider the provisions of the bill in detail, clause by clause. The committee has the power to amend it in such a way as to ensure that it conforms with the general approval given by the House at its second reading.

- Report stage

  At this point the standing committee reports the bill back to the House for consideration of any amendments made during the committee stage.

- Third reading

  Further debate may take place during this stage but it is restricted solely to matters relating to the content of the bill; questions relating to the general principles of the bill cannot be raised.

When a bill has passed all these stages it is passed to the House of Lords for its consideration. After consideration by the Lords the bill is passed back to the Commons which must then consider any amendments to the bill that might have been introduced by the Lords. Where one House refuses to agree to the amendments made by the other, bills can be repeatedly passed between them; but since bills must complete their process within the life of a particular parliamentary session, a failure to reach agreement within that period might lead to the total loss of the bill.

Since the Parliament Acts of 1911 and 1949, the blocking power of the House of Lords has been restricted as follows:

- a money bill, ie one containing only financial provisions, can be enacted without the approval of the House of Lords after a delay of one month;

- any other bill can be delayed by one year by the House of Lords.

The Royal Assent is required before any bill can become law. The procedural nature of the Royal Assent was highlighted by the Royal Assent Act 1967 which reduced the process of acquiring Royal Assent to a formal reading out of the short titles of any act in both Houses of Parliament.

An Act of Parliament comes into effect on the date of the Royal Assent, unless there is any provision to the contrary in the act itself.

In contemporary practice the full-scale procedure detailed above is usually only undergone in relation to 'enabling acts'. These acts set out general principles and establish a framework within which certain individuals or organisations are given power to make particular rules designed to give practical effect to the enabling act. The law produced through this procedure is referred to as delegated legislation.	1.2.2 Delegated legislation

As has been stated, delegated legislation is law made by some person or body to whom Parliament has delegated its general law-making power. A validly enacted piece of delegated legislation has the same legal force and effect as the Act of Parliament under which it is enacted; but equally it only has effect to the extent that its enabling act authorises it. Any action taken in excess of the powers granted is said to be *ultra vires* and the legality of such *ultra vires* legislation can be challenged in the courts as is considered below.

The output of delegated legislation in any year greatly exceeds the output of Acts of Parliament. Each year there are over 2,000 sets of rules and regulations made in the form of delegated legislation as opposed to less than 100 public Acts of Parliament. In statistical terms, therefore, it is at least arguable that delegated legislation is actually more significant than primary Acts of Parliament.

There are various types of delegated legislation:

- Orders in Council permit the government through the *Privy Council* to make law. The Privy Council is nominally a non-party-political body of eminent parliamentarians but in effect it is simply a means through which the government, in the form of a committee of ministers, can introduce legislation without the need to go through the full parliamentary process. Although it is usual to cite situations of state emergency as exemplifying occasions when the government will resort to the use of Orders in Council, in actual fact, a great number of acts are brought into operation through Orders in Council;

- Statutory Instruments are the means through which government ministers introduce particular regulations under powers delegated to them by Parliament in enabling legislation.

- Bye-laws are the means through which local authorities and other public bodies can make legally binding rules. Bye-laws may be made by local authorities under such enabling legislation as the Local Government Act (1972) and public corporations, such as British Rail, are empowered to make regulations relating to their specific sphere of operation;

- Court Rule Committees are empowered to make the rules which govern procedure in the particular courts over which they have delegated authority under such acts as the Supreme Court Act 1981, the County Courts Act 1984, and the Magistrates' Courts Act 1980;

- Professional regulations governing particular occupations may be given the force of law under provisions delegating legislative authority to certain professional bodies who are empowered to regulate the conduct of their members. An example is the power given to the Law Society under the Solicitors' Act 1974 to control the conduct of practising solicitors.

1.2.3 The advantages in the use of delegated legislation

The advantages of using delegated legislation are as follows:

- Time-saving

  Delegated legislation can be introduced quickly where necessary in particular cases and permits rules to be changed in response to emergencies or unforeseen problems.

  The use of delegated legislation, however, also saves parliamentary time generally. Given the pressure on debating time in Parliament and the highly detailed nature of typical delegated legislation, not to mention its sheer volume, Parliament would not have time to consider each individual piece of law that is enacted in the form of delegated legislation.

- Access to particular expertise

Related to the first advantage is the fact that the majority of MPs simply do not have sufficient expertise to consider such provisions effectively. Given the highly specialised and extremely technical nature of many of the regulations that are introduced through delegated legislation, it is necessary that those authorised to introduce the legislation should have access to the necessary external expertise required to formulate such regulations. With regard to bye-laws it practically goes without saying that local and specialist knowledge should give rise to more appropriate rules than reliance on the general enactments of Parliament.

- Flexibility

The use of delegated legislation permits ministers to respond on an ad hoc basis to particular problems as and when they arise and provides greater flexibility in the regulation of activity subject to the minister's overview.

Disadvantages in the prevalence of delegated legislation are as follows:

1.2.4 Disadvantages in the prevalence of delegated legislation

- Accountability

A key issue involved in the use of delegated legislation concerns the question of accountability and the erosion of the constitutional role of Parliament. Parliament is presumed to be the source of legislation but with respect to delegated legislation the individual MPs are not the source of the law. Certain people, notably government ministers, and the civil servants who work under them to produce the detailed provisions of delegated legislation, are the real source of such regulations. Even allowing for the fact that they are in effect operating on powers delegated to them from Parliament it is not beyond questioning whether this procedure does not give them more power than might be thought appropriate or indeed constitutionally correct.

- Scrutiny

The question of general accountability raises the need for effective scrutiny, but the very form of delegated legislation makes it extremely difficult for ordinary MPs to fully understand what is being enacted and, therefore, to effectively monitor it.

* Bulk

  The problems faced by ordinary MPs in effectively keeping abreast of delegated legislation is further increased by the sheer mass of such legislation, and if parliamentarians cannot keep up with the flow of delegated legislation the question has to be asked as to how the general public can be expected to do so.

1.2.5   Control over delegated legislation

The foregoing difficulties and potential shortcomings in the use of delegated legislation are, at least to a degree, mitigated by the fact that specific controls have been established to oversee the use of delegated legislation. These controls take two forms:

* Parliamentary control over delegated legislation

  Power to make delegated legislation is ultimately dependent upon the authority of Parliament and Parliament retains general control over the procedure for enacting such law.

  New regulations, in the form of delegated legislation, are required to be laid before Parliament. This procedure take two forms depending on the provision of the enabling legislation. Some regulations require a positive resolution of one or both of the Houses of Parliament before they become law. Most acts, however, simply require that regulations made under their auspices be placed before Parliament. They automatically become law after a period of 40 days unless a resolution to annul them is passed.

  Since 1973 there has been a Joint Select Committee on Statutory Instruments whose function it is to consider statutory instruments. This committee scrutinises statutory instruments from a technical point of view as regards drafting and has no power to question the substantive content or the policy implications of the regulation. Its effectiveness as a general control is therefore limited. European Community legislation is overseen by a specific committee and local authority bye-laws are usually subject to the approval of the Department of the Environment.

* Judicial control of delegated legislation

  It is possible for delegated legislation to be challenged, through the procedure of judicial review, on the basis that the person or body to whom Parliament has delegated its authority has acted in a way that exceeds the limited powers delegated to them. Any provision outwith this authority is *ultra vires* and is void. Additionally, there is a presumption that any power delegated by Parliament is to be used in a reasonable manner and the courts may on occasion hold particular delegated legislation to be void on the basis that it is unreasonable.

The foregoing has highlighted the increased importance of legislation in today's society but even allowing for this, and the fact that case law can be overturned by legislation, the UK is still a common law system and the importance and effectiveness of judicial creativity and common law principles and practices cannot be discounted. Case law is the name given to the creation and refinement of law in the course of judicial decisions.

1.3   Case law

The doctrine of binding precedent, or *stare decisis*, lies at the heart of the English Common Law system. It refers to the fact that within the hierarchical structure of the English courts, a decision of a higher court will be binding on a court lower than it in that hierarchy. In general terms this means that when judges try cases they will check to see if a similar situation has come before a court previously. If the precedent was set by a court of equal or higher status to the court deciding the new case then the judge in that case should follow the rule of law established in the earlier case. Where the precedent is set by a court lower in the hierarchy, the judge in the new case does not have to follow it but will certainly consider it and will not overrule it without due consideration.

1.3.1   The meaning of precedent

The operation of the doctrine of binding precedent depends on the existence of an extensive reporting service to provide access to previous judicial decisions. The earliest summaries of cases appeared in the Year Books but since 1865 cases have been reported by the Council of Law Reporting, which produces the authoritative reports of cases. Modern technology has resulted in the establishment of the Lexis computer-based storage of cases.

Civil   **Criminal**

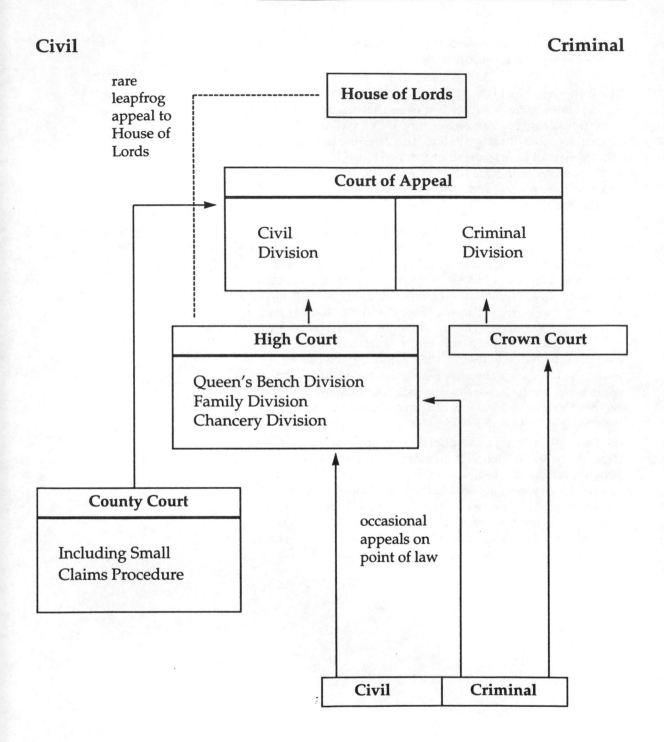

Fig 1. The hierarchy of the courts

The House of Lords stands at the summit of the English court structure and its decisions are binding on all courts below it in the hierarchy. As regards its own previous decisions, up until 1966 the House of Lords regarded itself as bound by its previous decisions. In a Practice Statement (1966), Lord Gardiner indicated that the House of Lords would in future regard itself free to depart from its previous decisions where it appeared right to do so. Given the potentially destabilising effect on existing legal practice based on previous decisions of the House of Lords, this is not a discretion that the House of Lords exercises lightly. There have been, however, a number of cases in which the House of Lords has overruled or amended its own earlier decisions (eg *Conway v Rimmer* (1968); *Herrington v British Rail Board* (1972); *Miliangos v George Frank (Textiles) Ltd* (1976); *R v Shivpuri* (1986)).

In civil cases the Court of Appeal is generally bound by previous decisions of the House of Lords.

The Court of Appeal is also bound by its own previous decisions in civil cases. There are, however, a number of exceptions to this general rule. Lord Greene MR listed these exceptions in *Young v Bristol Aeroplane Co Ltd* (1944). The exceptions arise where:

- There is a conflict between two previous decisions of the Court of Appeal. In this situation the later court must decide which decision to follow and as a corollary which to overrule (*Tiverton Estates Ltd v Wearwell Ltd* (1974));

- A previous decision of the Court of Appeal has been overruled, either expressly or impliedly, by the House of Lords. In this situation the Court of Appeal is required to follow the decision of the House of Lords (*Family Housing Association v Jones* (1990));

- The previous decision was given *per incuriam* or, in other words, that previous decision was taken in ignorance of some authority, either statutory or case law, that would have led to a different conclusion. In this situation the later court can ignore the previous decision in question (*Williams v Fawcett* (1985)).

There is also the possibility that as a consequence of s 3 of the European Communities Act, the Court of Appeal can ignore a previous decision of its own which is inconsistent with European Community law or with a later decision of the European Court.

Although, on the basis of *R v Spencer* (1985), it would appear that there is no difference in principle between the operation of the doctrine of stare decisis between the criminal

1.3.2   The hierarchy of the courts and the setting of precedent

and civil divisions of the Court of Appeal, it is generally accepted that in practice, precedent is not followed as strictly in the former as it is in the latter. Courts in the criminal division are not bound to follow their own previous decisions which they subsequently consider to have been based on either a misunderstanding or a misapplication of the law. The reason for this is that the criminal courts deal with matters involving individual liberty and therefore require greater discretion to prevent injustice.

The divisional court is bound by the doctrine of *stare decisis* in the normal way and must follow decisions of the House of Lords and the Court of Appeal. It is also normally bound by its own previous decisions, although in civil cases it may make use of the exceptions open to the Court of Appeal in *Young v Bristol Aeroplane Co Ltd* and in criminal appeal cases the Queen's Bench Divisional Court may refuse to follow its own earlier decisions where it feels the earlier decision to have been wrongly made.

The High Court is also bound by the decisions of superior courts. Decisions by individual High Court Judges are binding on courts inferior in the hierarchy, but such decisions are not binding on other High Court Judges although they are of strong persuasive authority and tend to be followed in practice.

Crown Courts cannot create precedent and their decisions can never amount to more than persuasive authority.

County courts and magistrates' courts do not create precedents.

1.3.3   The nature of precedent

Previous cases establish legal precedents which later courts have to either follow or, if the decision was made by a court lower in the hierarchy, at least consider. It is essential to realise, however, that not every part of the case as reported in the law reports is part of the precedent. In theory it is possible to divide cases into two parts: the *ratio decidendi* and *obiter dicta*.

- *Ratio decidendi*

  The *ratio decidendi* of a case may be understood as the statement of the law applied in deciding the legal problem raised by the concrete facts of the case. It is essential to establish that it is not the actual decision in a case that sets the precedent. It is the rule of law on which that decision is founded that sets the precedent. This rule, which is an abstraction from the facts of the case, is known as the *ratio decidendi* of the case.

- *Obiter dictum*

  Any statement of law that is not an essential part of the *ratio decidendi* is, strictly speaking, superfluous; and any such statement is referred to as *obiter dictum* (*obiter dicta* in the plural), ie said by the way. Although *obiter dicta* statements do not form part of the binding precedent they are persuasive authority and can be taken into consideration in later cases.

The division of cases into these two distinct parts is a theoretical procedure. It is the general misfortune of all those who study law that judges do not actually separate their judgments into the two clearly defined categories. It is the particular misfortune of a student of business law, however, that they tend to be led to believe that case reports are divided into two distinct parts: the ratio, in which the judge states what he takes to be the law; and *obiter* statements, in which the judge muses on alternative possibilities. Such is not the case: there is no such clear division and anyway it is actually later courts which effectively determine the ratio in any particular case. Indeed later courts may declare *obiter* what was previously felt to part of the *ratio*. One should never overestimate the objective scientific nature of the legal process.

The foregoing has set out the doctrine of binding precedent as it operates in theory to control the ambit of judicial discretion. It has to be recognised, however, that the doctrine does not operate as stringently as it appears at first sight and that there are particular shortcomings in the system that have to be addressed in weighing up the undoubted advantages with the equally undoubted disadvantages.	1.3.4 Evaluation

There are numerous perceived advantages of the doctrine of *stare decisis*; amongst which are:	1.3.5 Advantages of case law

- Certainty

  Once the legal rule has been established in one case, individuals can orient their behaviour with regard to that rule relatively secure in the knowledge that it will not be changed by some later court.

- Time saving

  This particular advantage follows from the preceding one. As the judiciary are bound by precedent, lawyers and their clients can be reasonably certain as to the likely outcome of any particular case on the basis of established precedent. As a consequence most disputes do not have to be re-argued before the courts. With regard to potential litigants it saves them money in court expenses because they can apply to their solicitor/barrister for guidance as to how their particular case is likely to be decided in the light of previous cases on the same or similar points.

- Flexibility

  This refers to the fact that various mechanisms enable the judges to manipulate the common law in such a way as to provide then with an opportunity to develop law in particular areas without waiting for Parliament to enact legislation. It should be recognised that judges do have a considerable degree of discretion in electing whether to be bound or not by a particular authority.

  Flexibility is achieved through the possibility of previous decisions being either overruled, or distinguished, or the possibility of a later court extending or modifying the effective ambit of a precedent. The main mechanisms through which judges alter or avoid precedents are:

- Overruling

  This is the procedure whereby a court higher up in the hierarchy sets aside a legal ruling established in a previous case.

  It is somewhat anomalous that, within the system of *stare decisis*, precedents gain increased authority with the passage of time. As a consequence, courts tend to be reluctant to overrule long-standing authorities even though they may no longer accurately reflect contemporary practices. In addition to the wish to maintain a high degree of certainty in the law, the main reason for judicial reluctance to overrule old decisions would appear to be the fact that overruling operates retrospectively and the principle of law being overruled is held never to have been law. Overruling a precedent, therefore, might have the consequence of disturbing important financial arrangements made in line with what were thought to be settled rules of law. It might even, in certain circumstances, lead to the imposition of criminal liability on previously lawful behaviour. It has to be emphasised, however, that the courts will not shrink from overruling authorities where they see them as no longer representing an appropriate statement of law. The recent legal recognition of the possibility of rape within marriage is simply one example of this process.

  Overruling should not be confused with reversing which is the procedure whereby a court higher in the hierarchy reverses the decision of a lower court in the same case.

- Distinguishing

  The main device for avoiding binding precedents is distinguishing. As has been previously stated, the *ratio decidendi* of any case is an abstraction from the material facts of the case. This opens up the possibility that a court may regard the facts of the case before it as significantly different from the facts of a cited precedent and thus consequentially it will not find itself bound to follow that precedent. Judges use the device of distinguishing where, for some reason, they are unwilling to follow a particular precedent and the law reports provide many examples of strained distinctions where a court has quite evidently not wanted to follow an authority that it would otherwise have been bound by.

It should be noted that the advantage of flexibility, at least, potentially contradicts the alternative advantage of certainty, but there are other disadvantages in the doctrine which have to be considered. Amongst these are:

1.3.6   Disadvantages of case law

*   Uncertainty

    This refers to the fact that the degree of certainty provided by the doctrine of *stare decisis* is undermined by the absolute number of cases that have been reported and can be cited as authorities. This uncertainty is compounded by the ability of the judiciary to select which authority to follow through use of the mechanism of distinguishing cases on their facts.

*   Fixity

    This refers to possibility that the law, in relation to any particular area, may become ossified on the basis of an unjust precedent with the consequence that previous injustices are perpetuated. An example of this is the long delay in the recognition of the possibility of rape within marriage, which has only recently been recognised.

*   Unconstitutionality

    This is a fundamental question that refers to the fact that the judiciary are in fact overstepping their theoretical constitutional role by actually making law, rather than restricting themselves to the role of simply applying it. It is now probably a common place of legal theory that judges do make law. Due to their position in the constitution, however, judges have to be circumspect in the way in which and the extent to which they use their powers to create law and impose values. To overtly assert or exercise the power would be to challenge the power of the legislature. For an unelected body to challenge a politically supreme Parliament would be unwise, to say the least.

1.4	**Statutory interpretation**	

The two previous sections have tended to present legislation and case law in terms of opposition: legislation being the product of Parliament and case law the product of the judiciary in the courts. Such stark opposition is of course misleading for the two processes come together when consideration is given to the necessity for judges to interpret statute law in order to apply it.

1.4.1   Problems in interpreting legislation

In order to apply legislation judges must ascertain its meaning and in order to ascertain that meaning they are faced with the difficulty of interpreting the legislation. Legislation, however, shares the general problem of uncertainty inherent in any mode of verbal communication. Words can have more than one meaning and the meaning of a word can change depending on its context.

One of the essential requirements of legislation is generality of application, the need for it to be written in such a way as to ensure that it can be effectively applied in various circumstances without the need to detail those situations individually. This requirement, however, can give rise to particular problems of interpretation; the need for generality can only really be achieved at the expense of clarity and precision of language.

Legislation, therefore, involves an inescapable measure of uncertainty that can only be made certain through judicial interpretation. To the extent, however, that the interpretation of legislative provisions is an active process, it is equally a creative process; and inevitably involves the judiciary in creating law through determining meaning and effect to being given to any particular piece of legislation.

1.4.2   Rules of interpretation

In attempting to decide upon the precise meaning of any statute judges use well established rules of interpretation, of which there are three primary ones, together with a variety of other secondary aids to construction.

The three rules of statutory interpretation are:

• The literal rule

Under this rule the judge is required to consider what the legislation actually says rather than considering what it might mean. In order to achieve this end the judge should give words in legislation their literal meaning; ie their plain, ordinary, every day meaning; even if the effect of this is to produce what might be considered an otherwise unjust or undesirable outcome.

A classic example of this approach from the area of contract law is *Fisher v Bell* (considered in detail in

Chapter 6) where, in line with the general contract law principles, it was decided that the placing of an article in a window did not amount to offering but was merely an invitation to treat, and thus the shopkeeper could not be charged with 'offering the goods for sale'. In this case the court chose to follow the 'contract law' literal interpretation of the meaning of offer in the act in question and declined to consider the usual 'non-legal' literal interpretation of the word offer.

A problem in relation to the literal rule, arises from the difficulty judges face in determining the literal meaning of even the commonest of terms. In *R v Maginnis* judges differed amongst themselves as to the literal meaning of the common word 'supply'.

• The golden rule

This rule is generally considered to be an extension of the literal rule. It is applied in circumstances where the application of the literal rule is likely to result in an obviously absurd result.

An example of the application of the golden rule is *Adler v George* (1964). In this case the court held that the literal wording of the statute 'in the vicinity of' covered the action committed by the defendant who carried out her action 'within' the area concerned.

Another example of this approach is to be found in *Re Sigsworth* (1935) in which the court introduced common law rules into legislative provisions, which were silent on the matter, to prevent the estate of a murderer from benefiting from the property of the party he had murdered.

• The mischief rule

This rule, sometimes known as the rule in *Heydon's case* (1584), operates to enable judges to interpret a statute in such a way as to provide a remedy for the mischief the statute was enacted to prevent. Contemporary practice is to go beyond the actual body of the legislation to determine what mischief a particular Act was aimed at redressing.

In addition to the three main rules of interpretation there are a number of secondary aids to construction. These can be categorised as either intrinsic or extrinsic in nature.

• Intrinsic assistance

This is help actually derived from the statute which is the object of interpretation. The judge uses the full statute to understand the meaning of a particular part of it.

1.4.3   Aids to construction

Assistance may be found from various parts of the statute such as: the title, long or short; any preamble, which is statement preceding the actual provisions of the act; schedules, which appear as detailed additions at the end the act. Section headings or marginal notes may also be considered where they exist.

• Extrinsic assistance

Sources outside of the act itself, may on occasion be resorted to in determining the meaning of legislation. For example, judges have always been entitled to refer to dictionaries in order to find the meaning of non-legal words. The Interpretation Act 1978 is also available for consultation with regard to the meaning of particular words used generally in statutes.

Judges are also allowed to use extrinsic sources to determine the mischief at which particular legislation is aimed. For example, they are able to examine earlier statutes and they have been entitled for some time to look at Law Commission reports, Royal Commission reports, and the reports of other official commissions.

• *Pepper v Hart* (1993)

Until very recently Hansard, the verbatim report of parliamentary debate, literally remained a closed book to the courts. In *Pepper v Hart* (1993), however, the House of Lords decided to overturn the previous rule. In a majority decision, it was held that, where the precise meaning of legislation was uncertain or ambiguous, or where the literal meaning of an act would lead to a manifest absurdity, the courts could refer to Hansard's reports of parliamentary debates and proceedings as an aid to construing the meaning of the legislation.

1.4.4   Presumptions

In addition to the rules of interpretation the courts may also make use of certain presumptions. As with all presumptions they are rebuttable, which means that the presumption is subject to being overturned in argument in any particular case. The presumptions operate:

• Against the alteration of the common law

Parliament can alter the common law whenever it decides to do so. In order to do this, however, Parliament must expressly enact legislation to that end. If there is no express intention to that effect it is assumed that statute does not make any fundamental change to the common law. With regard to particular provisions, if there are alternative interpretations, one of which will maintain the existing common law situation, then that interpretation will be preferred.

- Against retrospective application

  As the War Crimes Act 1990 shows, Parliament can impose criminal responsibility retrospectively, where particular and extremely unusual circumstances dictate the need to do so; but such effect must be clearly expressed.

- Against the deprivation of an individual's liberty, property or rights

  Once again the presumption can be rebutted by express provision and it is not uncommon for legislation to deprive people of their rights to enjoy particular benefits. Nor is it unusual for individuals to be deprived of their liberty under the Mental Health Act 1983.

- Against application to the Crown

  Unless the legislation contains a clear statement to the contrary it is presumed not to apply to the Crown.

- Against breaking international law

  Where possible, legislation should be interpreted in such a way as to give effect to existing international legal obligations.

- In favour of the requirement that mens rea (a guilty mind) be a requirement in any criminal offence

  The classic example of this presumption is *Sweet v Parsley* (1969). Offences which do not require the presence of *mens rea* are referred to as strict liability offences.

- In favour of words taking their meaning from the context in which they are used

  This final presumption refers back to, and operates in conjunction with, the major rules for interpreting legislation considered previously. The general presumption appears as three distinct sub-rules, each of which carries a Latin tag.

  (a) The *noscitur a sociis* rule is applied where statutory provisions include a list of examples of what is covered by the legislation. It is presumed that the words used have a related meaning and are to be interpreted in relation to each other (see *IRC v Frere* (1965)).

  (b) The *eiusdem generis* rule applies in situations where general words are appended to the end of a list of specific examples. The presumption is that the general words have to be interpreted in line with the prior restrictive examples. Thus a provision which referred to a list that included, 'horses, cattle, sheep and other animals' would be unlikely to apply to domestic animals such as cats and dogs (see *Powell v Kempton Park Racecourse*(1899)).

(c) The *expressio unius exclusio alterius* rule simply means that where a statute seeks to establish a list of what is covered by it provisions, then anything not expressly included in that list is specifically excluded (see *R v Inhabitants of Sedgley* (1831)).

1.5   Custom

The traditional view of the development of the common law tends to adopt an overly romantic view as regards its emergence. This view suggests that the common law is no more than the crystallisation of ancient common customs; the distillation being accomplished by the judiciary in the course of their historic travels round the land in the middle-ages. This view, however, tends to ignore the political process that gave rise to this procedure. The imposition of a common system of law represented the political victory of a state that had fought to establish and assert its central authority. Viewed in that the light, the emergence of the common law perhaps can better be seen to be the invention of the judges as representatives of the state and to represent what they wanted the law to be, rather than what people generally thought it was.

One source of customary practice that undoubtedly did find expression in the form of law was business and commercial practice. These customs and practices were originally constituted in the distinct form of the Law Merchant but gradually this became subsumed under the control of the common law courts and ceased to exist apart from the common law.

Notwithstanding the foregoing it is still possible for specific local customs to operate as a source of law. In certain circumstances parties may assert the existence of customary practices in order to support their case. Such local custom may run counter to the strict application of the common law and where they are found to be legitimate they will effectively replace the common law. Even in this respect, however, reliance on customary law as opposed to common law, although not impossible, is made unlikely by the stringent tests that have to be satisfied (see *Egerton v Harding* (1974)). The requirements that a local custom must satisfy in order to be recognised are that:

• It must have existed from 'time immemorial' ie 1189;

- It must have been exercised continuously within that period;

- It must have been exercised peacefully without opposition;

- It must also have been felt as obligatory;

- It must be capable of precise definition;

- It must have been consistent with other customs;

- It must be reasonable.

Given this list of requirements it can be seen why local custom is not an important source of law.

1.5.1   Books of authority

In the very unusual situation where a court is unable to locate a precise or analogous precedent it may refer to legal textbooks for guidance. Such books are subdivided, depending on when they were written. In strict terms only certain works are actually treated as authoritative sources of law. Legal works produced after Blackstone's Commentaries of 1765 are considered to be of recent origin, and although they cannot be treated as authoritative sources the courts may consider what the most eminent works by accepted experts in particular fields have said in order to help determine what the law is or should be.

Sources of Domestic Law

Legislation is the law produced through the parliamentary system. The passage of a bill through each House of Parliament involves five distinct stages; first reading, second reading, committee stage, report stage, and third reading. Then it is given Royal Assent. The House of Lords only has limited scope to delay legislation.

Delegated legislation is a sub-classification of legislation which appears in the form of: Orders in Council; Statutory Instruments; bye-laws; professional regulations.

The main advantages of delegated legislation relate to: speed of implementation; the saving of parliamentary time; access to expertise; flexibility.

The main disadvantages relate to: the lack of accountability of those making such law; the lack of scrutiny of proposals for such legislation; the sheer amount of delegated legislation.

Controls over delegated legislation are: in Parliament, the Joint Select Committee on Statutory Instruments; and in the courts, *ultra vires* provisions may be challenged through judicial review.

Case law is the law created by judges in the course of deciding cases. The doctrine of *stare decisis* or binding precedent refers to the fact that courts are bound by previous decisions of courts equal or above them in the court hierarchy. The House of Lords can now overrule its own previous rules; the Court of Appeal cannot.

It is the reason for a decision, the *ratio decidendi*, that binds. Everything else is obiter dictum and not bound to be followed.

Judges avoid precedents through either overruling or distinguishing them.

The advantages of the doctrine are: saving the time of all parties concerned; certainty; flexibility.

The disadvantages relate to: uncertainty; fixity; unconstitutionality.

Statutory interpretation refers to the process through which judges give practical meaning to legislative provisions. Communication is inherently uncertain, but legislation has

Legislation

Delegated legislation

Case law

Statutory interpretation

particular problems that arise from the contradictory nature of the various ends it tries to achieve.

The rules of interpretation

The Literal rule gives words in legislation their plain, ordinary, every day meaning, even if this leads to an apparent injustice.

The Golden rule is used in circumstance where the application of the literal rule is likely to result in an obviously absurd result. The court will not apply the literal meaning but will instead interpret the provision in such a way as to avoid the absurdity.

The Mischief rule permits the court to go beyond the words of the statute in question to consider the mischief at which it was aimed.

Aids to construction

Intrinsic assistance relies on such internal evidence as the statute under consideration can provide through reference to: the title of the act, any preamble, or any schedules to it.

Extrinsic assistance permits the judge to go beyond the act in question in order to ascertain its meaning. Amongst possible sources are; dictionaries, text-books, other statutes including the Interpretation Act, reports, other parliamentary papers, and since *Pepper v Hart*, Hansard may also be consulted.

Presumptions

In addition to the rules of interpretation there are also various presumptions that will be applied, unless rebutted. The most important of these are presumptions: against the alteration of the common law; retrospective application; the deprivation of an individual's liberty, property or rights; and application to the Crown. In addition there are presumptions in favour of; the requirement for *mens rea* in relation to criminal offences; and deriving the meaning of words from their contexts.

Custom

Custom is of very limited importance as a contemporary source of law although it was important in the establishment of business and commercial law in the form of the old Law Merchant.

Chapter 2

UK Law within the European Union

As stated in the previous chapter it is unrealistic and indeed impossible for any student of UK law, and especially a student of business and business law, to ignore the EU as a source of law and legal regulation. What follows is no more than a basic introduction to the institutions of the Union.

Before the UK joined the European Economic Community (EEC) in 1973, as it was titled then, its law was just as foreign as law made under any other jurisdiction. On joining the Community, however, the UK and its citizens accepted, and became subject to, EC law. This subjection to European law remains the case even where the parties to any transaction are themselves both UK subjects. In other words in areas where it is applicable, the law of the EU supersedes any existing UK law to the contrary.

An example of Community law invalidating the operation of UK legislation can be found in the *Factortame* case (1989 and 1991). The Common Fishing Policy established by the EEC had placed limits on the amount of fish that any member country's fishing fleet was permitted to catch. In order to gain access to British fish stocks and quotas Spanish fishing-boat owners formed British companies and re-registered their boats as British. In order to prevent what it saw as an abuse, and an encroachment on the rights of indigenous fishermen, the British government introduced The Merchant Shipping Act 1988 which provided that any fishing company seeking to register as British would have to have its principal place of business in the UK, and at least 75% of its shareholders would have to be British nationals. This effectively debarred the Spanish boats from taking up any of the British fishing quota. Some 95 Spanish boat-owners made applications in the British courts for judicial review of the Merchant Shipping Act on the basis that it was contrary to Community law. The case went from the High Court through the Court of Appeal to the House of Lords who referred the case to the European Court of Justice. There it was decided that the Treaty of Rome required domestic courts to give effect to the directly enforceable provisions of Community law and in doing so such courts are required to ignore any national law that runs counter to Community law.

2.1   Introduction

2.2 Sources of European Union law

The sources of Union law are fourfold: internal treaties and protocols; international agreements; secondary legislation; and decisions of the European Court of Justice.

2.2.1 Internal treaties

Internal treaties govern the member states of the Union and anything contained therein supersedes domestic legal provisions. The primary treaty is the Treaty of Rome as amended by such legislation as the Single European Act 1986 or the Maastricht treaty.

2.2.2 International treaties

International treaties are negotiated with other nations by the European Commission on behalf of the Union as a whole and are binding on the individual members of the Union.

2.2.3 Secondary legislation

Secondary legislation is provided for under Article 189 of the Treaty of Rome. It provides for the three types of legislation to be introduced by the European Council and the Commission:

- Regulations apply to, and within, member states generally without the need for those states to pass their own legislation. They are binding and enforceable from the time of their creation and individual states do not have to pass any legislation to give effect to regulations.

- Directives, on the other hand, state general goals and leave the precise implementation to the individual member states in the appropriate form. Directives, however, tend to exemplify the means as well as the ends to which they are aimed and the European Court of Justice will give direct effect to directives which are sufficiently clear and complete.

- Decisions on the operation of European laws and policies, are aimed at particular states or individuals and have the force of law under Article 189.

2.2.4 The European Court of Justice

The Court of Justice is the judicial arm of the EU, and in the field of Union law its judgments overrule those of National Courts. Under Article 177, National Courts have the right to apply to the ECJ for a preliminary ruling on a point of Union law before deciding a case.

2.3 The institutions of the EU

The major institutions of the EU are the Council of Ministers, the European Parliament, the Commission, and the European Court of Justice; all of which can have direct impact on the operation of law within the UK.

2.3.1 The Council of Ministers

The Council is made up of ministerial representatives of each of the 12 member states of the Union. When considering economic matters the various states will be represented by their finance ministers or if the matter before the Council relates to agriculture, the various agricultural ministers will attend. The Council of Ministers is the supreme decision-making body of the EU and as such it has the final say in deciding upon Union legislation. Although it acts on recommendations and proposals made to it by the Commission, it has the power to instruct the Commission to undertake particular investigations and to submit detailed proposals for its consideration.

Council decisions are taken on a mixture of voting procedures. Some measures only require a simple majority, in others a procedure of qualified majority voting is used, and yet in others unanimity is required. Qualified majority voting is the procedure in which the votes of the 12 members countries are weighted in proportion to their population from 10 down to three votes each. The Single European Act extended the use of qualified majority voting.

Since the format of particular councils fluctuates, much of its day-to-day work is delegated to a committee of permanent representatives which operates under the title of Coreper.

The European Parliament is the directly elected European institution and to that extent it can be seen as the body which exercises democratic control over the operation on the EU. As in National Parliaments, members are elected to represent constituencies, the elections being held every five years. There are a total of 518 members divided amongst the 12 members approximately in proportion to the size of their various populations. MPs do not sit in national groups but operate within political groupings.

2.3.2   The European Parliament

The Parliament's general secretariat is based in Luxembourg and although the Parliament sits in plenary session in Strasbourg for one week in each month, its detailed and preparatory work is carried out through 18 permanent committees which usually meet in Brussels. These permanent committees consider proposals from the Commission and provide the full Parliament with reports of such proposals for discussion.

The powers of the European Parliament, however, should not be confused with those of National Parliaments, for the European Parliament is not a legislative institution and in that respect it plays a subsidiary role to the Council of Ministers. Originally its powers were merely advisory and supervisory.

In pursuance of its advisory function the Parliament always had the right to comment on the proposals of the

Commission and since 1980 the Council has been required to wait for the Parliament's opinion before adopting any law. In its supervisory role the Parliament scrutinises the activities of the Commission and has the power to remove the Commission by passing a motion of censure against it by a two-thirds majority.

The legislative powers of the Parliament were substantially enhanced by the Single European Act in 1987. Since that enactment it has had a more influential role to play particularly in relation to the completion of the internal market. It can now negotiate directly with the Council as to any alterations or amendments it wishes to see in proposed legislation. It can also intervene to question and indeed alter any 'joint position' adopted by the Council on proposals put to it by the Commission. If the Council then insists on pursuing its original 'joint position' it can only do so on the basis of unanimity.

The Single European Act also required the assent of Parliament to any international agreements to be entered into by the Union. As a consequence it has ultimate control, not just in relation to trade treaties, but also with regard to any future expansion in the Union's membership.

The European Parliament is, together with the Council of Ministers, the budgetary authority of the EU. The budget is drawn up by the Commission and is presented to both the Council and the Parliament. With regard to what is known as 'obligatory' expenditure the Council has the final say, but in relation to 'non-obligatory' expenditure Parliament has the final decision whether to approve the budget or not. Such budgetary control places the Parliament in an extremely powerful position to influence Union policy and it has not failed to make use of such power. Indeed in 1979 and 1984 it rejected the proposed budgets which had to be redrafted.

If the Parliament represents the directly elected arm of the Union then the Economic and Social Committee represents a collection of unelected but nonetheless influential interest groups throughout the Union. This committee is a consultative institution and its opinion must be sought prior to the adoption by the Council of any Commission proposal.

2.3.3   The Commission

The Commission is the executive of the EU and in that role is responsible for the administration of Union policies. There are 17 Commissioners chosen from the various member countries to serve for renewable terms of four years. Commissioners are appointed to head departments with specific responsibility for furthering particular areas of Union policy. Once appointed,

Commissioners are expected to act in the general interest of the Union as a whole rather than in the partial interest of their own home country.

In pursuit of Union policy the Commission is responsible for ensuring that treaty obligations between the member states are met, and that Union laws relating to individuals are enforced. In order to fulfil these functions the Commission has been provided with extensive powers both in relation to the investigation of potential breaches of Union law and the subsequent punishment of offenders. The classic area in which these powers can be seen in operation is in the area of competition law. Under Articles 85 and 86 of the Treaty of Rome the Commission has substantial powers to investigate and control potential monopolies and anti-competitive behaviour and it has used these powers to levy, what in the case of private individuals, would amount to huge fines where breaches of Union competition law has been discovered. In February 1993 the Commission imposed fines totalling more than £80 million on 17 steel producers for what was described as 'a very serious, illegal price-fixing cartel'. The UK company British Steel suffered the greatest individual imposition of £26.4 million.

The Commission also acts, under instructions from the Council, as the negotiator between the Union and external countries.

In addition to these executive functions the Commission also has a vital part to play in the Union's legislative process. The Council can only act on proposals put before it by the Commission. The Commission, therefore, has a duty to propose to the Council measures that will advance the achievement of the Union's general policies.

As has been stated above the European Court of Justice is the judicial arm of the EU and in the field of Union law its judgments overrule those of National Courts. It consists of 13 judges, assisted by six advocates general, and sits in Luxembourg. The role of the advocate general is to investigate the matter submitted to the court and to produce a report together with a recommendation for the consideration of the court. The actual court is free to accept the report or not as they see fit.

2.3.4   The Court of Justice

The Single European Act (1986) provided for a new Court of First Instance to be attached to the existing Court of Justice. The jurisdiction of the Court of First Instance is limited mainly to internal claims by employees of the Union and to claims against fines made by the Commission under Union competition law. The aim is to reduce the burden of work on the Court of Justice but there is a right of appeal, on points of law only, to the full Court of Justice.

The Court of Justice performs two key functions:

Firstly, it decides whether any measures adopted, or rights denied, by the Commission, Council or any national government are compatible with treaty obligations. Such actions may be raised by any Union institution, government or individual. A member state may fail to comply with its treaty obligations in a number of ways. It might fail or indeed refuse to comply with a provision of the treaty or a regulation; or alternatively it might refuse to implement a directive within the allotted time provided. Under such circumstances the state in question will be brought before the European Court of Justice, either by the Commission or another member state or, indeed, individuals within the state concerned.

Secondly, it provides authoritative rulings, at the request of National Courts under Article 177 of the Treaty of Rome, on the interpretation of points of Union law. When an application is made under Article 177, the national proceedings are suspended until such time as the determination of the point in question is delivered by the European Court. Whilst the case is being decided by the European Court, the National Court is expected to provide appropriate interim relief, even if this involves going against a domestic legal provision, as in the Factortame case.

This procedure can take the form of a preliminary ruling where the request precedes the actual determination of a case by the National Court.

Summary of Chapter 2

UK Law within the European Union

UK law is now subject to Union law in particular areas. This has led to the curtailment of parliamentary sovereignty in those areas.

The EU

The sources of Union law are: internal treaties and protocols; international agreements; secondary legislation; and decisions of the European Court of Justice.

Secondary legislation takes three forms: regulations which are directly applicable; directives which have to be given statutory form; decisions are directly applicable.

Union law

The major institutions of the EU are: the Council of Ministers; the European Parliament; the Commission; the European Court of Justice.

The institutions of the EU

Chapter 3

The Criminal and Civil Courts

In the UK the structure of the court system is divided into two distinct sectors following the division between criminal and civil law. This chapter locates particular courts within the general hierarchical structure in ascending order of authority (see the diagram on p 8). It is essential to be aware not just of the role and powers of the individual courts but also to know the paths of appeal from one court to another within the hierarchy.

3.1   Introduction

Crimes are offences against the law of the land and are usually prosecuted by the State. Criminal cases are normally cited in the form *R v Brown*. Cases are heard in different courts depending on their seriousness.

3.2   The criminal court structure

The office of magistrate or Justice of the Peace (JP) dates from 1195 when King Richard I appointed 'keepers of the peace' to deal with those who were accused of breaking 'the King's peace'. The JP's originally acted as local administrators for the King in addition to their judicial responsibilities.

Nowadays there are some 29,000 unpaid part-time lay magistrates and about 60 full-time professional stipendiary magistrates operating within approximately 700 magistrates' courts in England. Magistrates are empowered to hear and decide a wide variety of legal matters and the amount and importance of the work they do should not be underestimated. It has been estimated that 97% of all criminal cases are dealt with by the magistrates' court.

Lay magistrates are not usually legally qualified and sit as a bench of three. Stipendiary magistrates are legally qualified and decide cases on their own.

A bench of lay magistrates is legally advised by a justices' clerk who is legally qualified and guides the justices on matters of law, sentencing and procedure, even when not specifically invited to do so. The clerk should not give any opinion on matters of fact. Magistrates are independent of the clerks and clerks should not instruct the magistrates as to what decision they should reach.

3.3   Magistrates' courts

Magistrates' courts have considerable power. In relation to criminal law they are empowered to try summary cases, ie

3.3.1   Powers of magistrates' courts

cases which are triable without a jury. Additionally, with the agreement of the accused, they may deal with cases triable either way cases, ie cases which can either be tried summarily by the magistrates, or which can be tried on indictment before a jury in the Crown Court.

The maximum sentence that magistrates can impose is a £5,000 fine and/or a six month prison sentence. The maximum sentences for many summary offences, however, are much less than these limits. Where a defendant is convicted of two or more offences at the same hearing, consecutive sentences amounting to more than six months are not permitted although this can rise to 12 months in cases involving offences triable either way. If the magistrates feel that their sentencing powers are insufficient to deal with the defendant then the offender may be sent to the Crown Court for sentencing.

Magistrates can impose alternative sentences, such as community service orders, or probation orders. They can also discharge offenders either conditionally or absolutely. In addition they can issue Compensation Orders. Such orders are not used as a means of punishing the offender but as a way of compensating the victims of the offender without them having to sue the offender in the civil courts. The maximum payment under any such order is £5,000.

Where magistrates decide that an offence triable either way should be tried in the Crown Court, they hold committal proceedings. These proceedings are also held where the defendant has been charged with an indictable offence. Acting in this way, the justices become 'examining magistrates'. The object of these proceedings is to determine whether there is a *prima facie* case against the defendant. If the justices decide there is a *prima facie* case they must commit the defendant to a Crown Court for trial; if not they must discharge the accused.

Magistrates sit in Youth Courts to try children and young persons. These private tribunals sit separately from the ordinary magistrates' court in order to protect the young defendants from publicity.

The Crown Court is not a local court like the magistrates' court but a single court which sits in over 90 centres. The Crown Court is part of the Supreme Court which is defined as including the Court of Appeal, the High Court of Justice and the Crown Court. For the purposes of the operation of the Crown Court, England and Wales are divided into six circuits, each with its own headquarters and staff. The centres are divided into three tiers. In first-tier centres High Court judges hear civil and criminal cases whereas circuit judges and recorders hear only criminal cases. Second-tier centres are served by the same types of judge but hear criminal cases only. At third-tier centres, recorders and circuit judges hear criminal cases only.

The Crown Court hears all cases involving trial on indictment. It also hears appeals from those convicted summarily in the magistrates' courts. At the conclusion of an appeal hearing the Crown Court has the power to confirm, reverse or vary any part of the decision under appeal (Supreme Court Act 1981 s 48(2)). If the appeal is decided against the accused, the Crown Court has the power to impose any sentence which the magistrates could have imposed, including one which is harsher than originally imposed on the defendant.

3.4   Jurisdiction

The process of appeal depends upon how a case was originally tried, whether summarily or on indictment. The following sets out the various routes and procedures involved in appealing against the decisions of particular courts.

3.5   Criminal appeals

Two routes of appeal are possible. The first route allows only a defendant to appeal. The appeal is to a judge, and between two and four magistrates, sitting in the Crown Court and can be:

3.5.1   Appeals from magistrates' courts

- Against conviction (only if the defendant pleaded not guilty) on points of fact or law; or

- Against sentence.

  Such an appeal will take the form of a new trial (a trial *de novo*).

  Alternatively, either the defendant or the prosecution can appeal 'by way of case stated' to the High Court (the divisional court of the Queen's Bench Division). This court consists of two or more judges (usually two) of whom one will be a Lord Justice of Appeal. This appeal is limited to matters relating to:

- Points of law; or

- The fact that the magistrates acted beyond their jurisdiction.

  Appeal from the divisional court is to the House of Lords. Either side may appeal but only on a point of law and only if the divisional court certifies the point to be one of general public importance. Leave to appeal must also be granted either by the Court of Appeal or the House of Lords.

Appeals from this court lie to the Court of Appeal (criminal division) which hears appeals against conviction and sentence.

3.5.2   Appeals from the Crown Court

The Court hears about 6,000 criminal appeals and applications per year.

Appeals may be made by the defence against conviction but the prosecution cannot appeal against an acquittal. Under s 36 Criminal Justice Act 1972, the Attorney-General can refer a case which has resulted in an acquittal to the Court of Appeal where he believes the decision to have been questionable on a point of law. The Court of Appeal only considers the point of law and even if its finding is contrary to the defendant's case the acquittal is not affected. This procedure merely clarifies the law for future cases.

Leave to appeal is not required against conviction on a point of law but leave is required for appeals on points of fact or mixed fact and law. In the case of an appeal against conviction, the court may confirm or quash the original conviction or, where previously unavailable evidence has emerged, it may order a retrial. Under s 2 Criminal Appeal Act 1968, the Court of Appeal may uphold the appellant's technical argument but nevertheless decline to set aside the conviction on the ground that no miscarriage of justice has occurred.

Leave is required for appeals against sentence. In such cases the court may confirm or alter the original sentence by way of changing the terms or substituting a new form of punishment. It cannot increase the sentence on appeal. However, under the Criminal Justice Act 1988, the Attorney-General may refer indictable-only cases to the Court of Appeal where the sentence at trial is regarded as unduly lenient. In such circumstances the court may impose a harsher sentence.

3.6   House of Lords

Following the determination of an appeal by the Court of Appeal or by the divisional court, either the prosecution or the defence may appeal to the House of Lords. Leave from the court below or the House of Lords must be obtained and two other conditions fulfilled according to s 33 Criminal Appeal Act 1968:

- The court below must certify that a point of law of general public importance is involved; and

- Either the court below or the House of Lords must be satisfied that the point of law is one which ought to be considered by the House of Lords.

3.7   Judicial Committee of the Privy Council

The Committee is the final court of appeal for certain Commonwealth countries which have retained this option and from some independent members and associate members of the Commonwealth. The committee comprises Privy Councillors who hold (or have held) high judicial office. The Committee comprises five Lords of Appeal in Ordinary, sometimes assisted by a judge from the country concerned.

Most of the appeals heard by the Committee are civil cases. In the rare criminal cases it is only on matters involving legal questions that appeals are heard, the Committee does not hear appeals against criminal sentence.

Civil actions are between individuals. The state merely provides the legal framework within which they determine and seek to enforce their mutual rights and obligations. Civil cases are cited in the form *Smith v Jones*.	**3.8 The civil court structure**

Although they deal mainly with criminal matters, the magistrates' courts have a significant civil jurisdiction. They hear family proceedings under the Domestic Proceedings and Magistrates' Courts Act 1978 and the Children Act 1989. Under such circumstances the court is termed a 'family proceedings court'. A family proceedings court must normally be composed of not more than three justices, including, as far as is practicable, both a man and a woman. Justices who sit on such benches must be members of the 'family panel' which comprises people specially appointed and trained to deal with family matters. Under the Children Act the court deals with adoption proceedings, applications for residence and contact orders, and maintenance relating to spouses and children. Under the 1978 Act the court also has the power to make personal protection orders and exclusion orders in cases of matrimonial violence.

3.9   Magistrates' courts

The magistrates' courts have powers of recovery in relation to the community charge and its replacement, the council tax. They also have the power to enforce charges for water, gas and electricity. Magistrates' courts also function as licensing courts under which guise they grant, renew or revoke licences for selling liquor, betting, or operating a taxi service.

There are approximately 400 county courts served by some 420 circuit judges and 225 district judges; every county court has at least one specifically assigned circuit judge. District judges can try cases where the amount involved is £5,000 or less. A Practice Direction (1991) has stated that any case involving issues of particular importance or complexity should, as far as possible, be heard by a circuit judge. An appeal from the district judge's decision lies to the circuit judge.

3.10   County courts

The Courts and Legal Services Act 1990 introduced major changes in the operation of the county courts. By virtue of s 3 of that act, county courts were given virtually the same powers as the High Court. As a consequence most cases are now tried in the county courts. Under the Act and statutory instrument the High Court and County Court Jurisdiction Order (1991) the county courts have jurisdiction in relation to:

- All personal injury claims under £50,000;

- All actions in relation to land where the capital value of the land, or the interest concerned in the land, is not greater than £30,000;

- Equity and probate cases involving assets under £30,000;

- Undefended divorce actions;

- Insolvency matters and the winding up on companies where the paid-up share capital does not exceed £5,000, or where the case is undefended;

- There is now no specific financial limitation in relation to contract or tort cases that can be heard by the county court. However, actions worth less than £25,000, should be tried by the county court unless the court thinks that the action should be heard by the High Court. Equally it is presumed that actions worth more than £50,000 should be heard by the High Court.

Thus, either the county court or the High Court can try cases in the region of £25,000–£50,000. Cases should be allocated according to the following criteria:

- The financial substance of the action;

- The importance of the action, in particular, whether it raises issues relevant to third parties or points of general public interest;

- The complexity of the facts, the law, remedies or procedures involved;

- Whether a transfer is likely to result in a quicker resolution of the dispute.

Proceedings commenced in the High Court are transferable to a county court under s 40 of the County Courts Act 1984. The High Court can do this on its own motion or on that of one of the parties. Section 4 of the Courts and Legal Services Act allows the court to penalise a party bringing an action in the High Court which it considers should have been commenced in the county court. Costs may be reduced by up to 25%.

A Practice Direction (1991) states that certain types of actions set down for trial in the High Court are considered too important for transfer to a county court. These are cases involving:

- Professional negligence;

- Fatal accidents;

- Allegations of fraud or undue influence;

- Defamation;

- malicious prosecution or false imprisonment;

- Claims against the police.

The county courts have an important role to play in the resolution of small claims through their operation of an arbitration scheme. Consideration of the detailed operation of this scheme will be undertaken in the following chapter.

The High Court has three administrative divisions: the Court of Chancery, the Queen's Bench Division and the Family Division. In addition, each division has a confusingly named divisional court which hears appeals from other legal forums.	**3.11** **The High Court of Justice**

High Court judges sit mainly in the Courts of Justice in the Strand in London, although it is possible for the High Court to sit anywhere in England or Wales.

The main civil work of the Queen's Bench Divisional Court is in contract and tort cases. The Commercial Court is part of this division. It is staffed by judges with specialist experience in commercial law.	3.11.1 The Queen's Bench Division

The Queen's Bench Divisional Court, as distinct from the QBD (above) exercises appellate jurisdiction. Here two, or sometimes three, judges sit to hear cases relating to the following circumstances:	3.11.2 The Queen's Bench Divisional Court

- Appeals on a point of law by way of case stated from magistrates' court's, tribunals and the Crown Court;

- Applications for judicial review of the decisions made by governmental and public authorities, inferior courts and tribunals;

- Applications for the writ of habeas corpus from persons who claim they are being unlawfully detained.

The Chancery Division is the modern successor to the old Court of Chancery, the Lord Chancellor's court from which	3.11.3 The Chancery Division

equity was developed. Its jurisdiction includes matters relating to:

- The sale or partition of land and the raising of charges on land;

- The redemption or foreclosure of mortgages;

- The execution or declaration of trusts;

- The administration of the estates of the dead;

- Bankruptcy;

- Contentious probate business eg the validity and interpretation of wills;

- Company law and partnerships;

- Revenue law.

Like the QBD, Chancery contains specialist courts; these are the patents court and the companies court.

| 3.11.4 | The Chancery Divisional Court | Comprising of one or two Chancery judges, the Chancery Divisional Court hears appeals from the Commissioners of Inland Revenue on income tax cases, and from county courts on certain matters like bankruptcy. |

| 3.11.5 | The Family Division | The Family Division of the High Court deals with all matrimonial matters both first instance and on appeal. It also considers proceedings relating to minors under the Children Act 1989. |

| 3.11.6 | The Family Divisional Court | The Family Divisional Court, consisting of two High Court judges, hears appeals from decisions of magistrates' courts and county courts in family matters. Commonly these involve appeals against orders made about financial provision under the Domestic Proceedings and Magistrates' Courts Act 1978. |

In addition to the divisions within the High Court there also are two specialist courts which although not actually part of the High Court are equivalent in status. These are:

- The Restrictive Practices Court, established by statute in 1956, hears cases relating to the area of commercial law concerned with whether an agreement is unlawful owing to the extent to which it restricts the trading capabilities of one of the parties. One QBD judge sits with specialist lay persons to hear these cases.

- The Employment Appeal Tribunal is presided over by similar panels, hearing appeals from Industrial Tribunals.

Appeals from decisions made by a judge in one of the three High Court divisions will usually go to the Court of Appeal (Civil Division). An exception to this rule allows an appeal to miss out or 'leapfrog' a visit to the Court of Appeal and go straight to the House of Lords. In order for this to happen, the trial judge must grant a 'certificate of satisfaction' and the House of Lords must give leave to appeal. For the judge to grant a certificate he must be satisfied that the case involves a point of law of general public importance either concerned mainly with statutory interpretation or is one where the court was bound by a previous Court of Appeal or House of Lords decision. Also, both parties must consent to the procedure.

The Court of Appeal hears appeals from the three divisions of the High Court; the divisional courts; the county courts; and various tribunals (considered below). Usually three judges will sit to hear an appeal although for very important cases five may sit.

The appeal procedure takes the form of a re-hearing of the case through the medium of the transcript of the case together with the judges notes. Witnesses are not re-examined and fresh evidence is not usually allowed.

3.12   Court Of Appeal (Civil Division)

Acting in its judicial capacity, as opposed to its legislative one, the House of Lords is the final court of appeal in civil as well as criminal law. For most cases, five Lords will sit to hear the appeal but seven are sometimes convened to hear very important cases.

3.13   House of Lords

As with criminal law so the Committee is the final court of appeal for certain Commonwealth countries which have retained this option and from some independent members and associate members of the Commonwealth. In practice most of the appeals heard by the Committee are civil cases.

The decisions of the Privy Council are very influential in English courts because they concern points of law that are applicable in this jurisdiction and they are pronounced upon by Lords of Appeal in Ordinary, in a way which is thus tantamount to a House of Lords ruling. Technically, however, these decisions are of persuasive precedent only, although they are normally followed by English courts.

3.14   Judicial Committee of the Privy Council

The function of the European Court of Justice, which sits in Luxembourg, is to 'ensure that in the interpretation and application of this treaty [the EEC Treaty 1957] the law is observed' (Article 164). The Court is the ultimate authority on the law of the EU. As the treaty is often composed in general

3.15   The European Court of Justice

terms, the court is often called upon to provide the necessary detail for EU law to operate. By virtue of the European Communities Act 1972, EU law has been enacted into English law so the decisions of the court have direct authority in the English jurisdiction.

The Court hears disputes between nations and between nations and the institutions of the EU such as the European Commission. Individuals, however, can only bring an action if they are challenging a decision which affects them personally.

3.16 The European Court of Human Rights

The European Convention on Human Rights is not related to the EU as such. The Convention, which seeks to regulate matters relating to human and political rights, and to which the UK is a signatory, establishes two institutions:

- The European Commission of Human Rights

  This body is charged with the task of examining, and if need be investigating the circumstances of, petitions submitted to it. If the Commission is unable to reach a negotiated solution between the parties concerned it may refer the matter to the Court of Human Rights.

- The European Court of Human Rights

  This body, which sits in Strasbourg, is responsible for all matters relating to the interpretation and application of the current convention. The European Convention on Human Rights provides that the judgment of the court shall be final and that parties to it will abide by the decisions of the court.

  Signatories to the convention agree to ensure a range of human and political rights to the citizens within their jurisdictions. The European Commission on Human Rights investigates claims that states are in violation of the Convention and any such case may be taken to the court if the state concerned has accepted the compulsory jurisdiction of the court. Perhaps unfortunately, however, there is no mechanism for enforcement of a court ruling within the jurisdiction of a particular signatory.

The Civil and Criminal Courts

Trials take place in either magistrates' courts or the Crown Court depending on the nature of the offence.

Summary offences cover less serious criminal activity and are decided by the magistrates. Indictable offences are the most serious and are tried before a jury in the Crown Court.

Offences triable either way may be tried by magistrates with the agreement of the defendant otherwise they go to the Crown Court.

The sentencing powers of magistrates is limited but they may commit an accused to the Crown Court if they think their powers will be inadequate to deal with the offence in question.

Appeals from magistrates' courts are to the Crown Court or the High Court, QBD divisional court, by way of case stated procedure.

Appeal from the Crown Court is to the Court of Appeal and may be as to sentence or conviction.

Appeals from the Court of Appeal or the QBD divisional court are to the House of Lords, but only in relation to a point of law of general public importance. Leave to appeal must be granted.

Magistrates' courts have limited but important civil jurisdiction in licensing and especially as a 'family proceedings court' under the Children Act 1989.

County courts

County courts try personal injuries cases worth up to £50,000. Other actions up to £25,000 should normally be heard by them.

Whether actions between £25,000 and £50,000 are heard in the county court or the High Court depends upon the substance, importance and complexity of the case.

The High Court consists of three divisions:

- The Queen's Bench Division deals with contract and tort amongst other things. Its divisional court hears applications for judicial review.

- Chancery deals with matters relating to commercial matters, land, bankruptcy, probate etc. Its divisional court hears taxation appeals.

- The Family Division hears matrimonial and child-related cases and its divisional court hears appeals from lower courts on these issues.

The Court of Appeal (Civil Division)

The Court of Appeal, consisting usually of three judges, hears appeals from the High Court and county court and in most cases it is the ultimate court of appeal.

The House of Lords

The House of Lords hears appeals on points of law of general importance. Appeals are heard from the Court of Appeal and may rarely, under the 'leapfrog' provision, hear appeals from the High Court.

The Judicial Committee of the Privy Council

The Judicial Committee of the Privy Council is the final court of appeal for those Commonwealth countries which have retained at the head of their national legal systems.

The European Court of Justice

The European Court of Justice interprets and determines the application of EU law throughout the community. In such matters its decisions bind all national courts.

The European Court of Human Rights

The European Court of Human Rights decides cases in the light of the European Convention on Human Rights. It has no mechanism for directly enforcing its decisions against member countries.

Chapter 4

Alternatives to the Courts

Although attention tends to be focused on the courts as the forum for resolving conflicts when they arise, the court system is not necessarily the most effective way of deciding disputes; especially those which arise between people, or indeed businesses, which have enjoyed a close relationship. The problem with the court system is that it is essentially an antagonistic process designed ultimately to determine a winner and a loser in any particular dispute. As a consequence, court procedure tends to emphasise and heighten the degree of conflict between the parties rather than seek to produce a compromise solution. For various reasons, considered below, it is not always in the best long-term interests of the parties to enter into such hostile relations as are involved in court procedure. In recognition of this fact a number of alternative procedures to court action have been developed for dealing with such disputes.

4.1   Introduction

The first and oldest of these alternative procedures is arbitration. Because businesses seek to establish and maintain long-term relationships with other concerns, which court action tends to sever or at best disrupt, it is often the case that businesses will only seek recourse to the courts as a last resort where other mechanisms have failed to produce a resolution to the dispute. Arbitration is the procedure whereby parties in dispute refer the issue to a third party for resolution, rather than take the case to the ordinary law courts. In contemporary business practice it is common, if not standard, practice for commercial contracts to contain express clauses referring future disputes to arbitration. This practice is well established and its legal effectiveness has long been recognised by the law.

4.2   Arbitration

Where the reference to arbitration is itself in writing, the arbitration procedure is governed by the Arbitration Acts of 1950 and 1979. It is possible for arbitration agreements to specify in advance the person who will act as arbitrator in the event of any later dispute. Alternatively, if the parties are members of a common trade association they may refer the dispute to that body for resolution. In addition, there are specialist arbitration bodies and it is quite common for the agreement simply to refer the dispute to such a body and allow it to select an appropriate arbitrator. The arbitrator does

4.2.1   Procedure

not have to be a legal practitioner and indeed the very point of the exercise is to ensure that it is considered by an expert in the particular commercial field to which the contract relates. There is, of course, no rule against legally qualified arbitrators and judges from the Commercial Court do sit, on occasion, in such a capacity.

Where there is no specific mention of the matter, a reference to arbitration is treated under s 6 of the 1950 Act as a reference to a single arbitrator. Where there is a provision for the appointment of two arbitrators, one being appointed by each party concerned, then where the two original arbitrators fail to reach an agreement, a third arbitrator must be appointed as umpire to make the final decision.

The Arbitration Acts provide that the procedure must be carried out in a judicial manner, in line with natural justice. At the conclusion of the hearing the arbitrator is required to provide reasons for any award given. A failure to comply with these requirements opens the decision to a possible challenge for judicial review in the High Court. Any award decided on at the conclusion of arbitration is enforceable in the ordinary courts without the requirement for the case to be argued again.

4.2.2	Relationship to ordinary courts

In general terms the courts have no objection to individuals settling their disputes on a voluntary basis, but, at the same time, they are careful to maintain their supervisory role in such procedures. Arbitration agreements are no different from other terms of a contract, and, in line with the normal rules of contract law (see Chapter 8), courts will strike out any attempt to oust their ultimate jurisdiction, as being contrary to public policy.

Under the Arbitration Act (1979) the decision of the arbitrator as to findings of fact are conclusive and cannot be appealed against. Appeals can be taken on points of law, subject to the prior approval of the court hearing the appeal, but normally such leave to appeal will not be granted unless the question of law involved would substantially affect the rights of one of the parties.

4.2.3	Advantages of arbitration over court procedure

There are numerous advantages to be gained from using arbitration rather than the court system. Amongst them are the following:

• Privacy
  Arbitration is a private procedure. This has the twofold advantage that outsiders do not get access to any potentially sensitive information and further, the parties to the arbitration do not run the risk of any damaging publicity arising out of reports of the proceedings.

- Informality

  The proceedings do not involve the degree of formality that accompanies a court case. The proceedings can also be scheduled more flexibly than court proceedings.

- Speed

  Arbitration is generally much quicker than taking a case through the courts. Where, however, one of the parties makes use of the available grounds to challenge an arbitration award the prior costs of the arbitration will have been largely wasted.

- Cost

  Arbitration is generally a much cheaper procedure than taking a case to the normal courts. None the less the costs of arbitration and the use of specialist arbitrators may be substantial and should not be underestimated.

- Expertise

  The use of a specialist arbitrator ensures that the person deciding the case has expert knowledge of the actual practice within the area under consideration and can form his conclusion in line with accepted practice in that area of business or commerce.

Since 1973 an arbitration service has been available within the county court specifically for the settlement of relatively small claims. This small claims procedure, known as arbitration, is operated by county court district judges. When it was first established the small claims procedure was seen as a mechanism through which consumers could enforce their rights against traders. In practice the arbitration procedure has proved to be just as useful for, and to have been used just as much by, traders and businesses, as consumers.	4.2.4 Small claims procedure in the county court

Reference to arbitration is normally automatic in cases involving sums of money up to £1,000, and arbitration proceedings may be used in situations involving more than £1,000, where the parties concerned agree. The district judge can refuse to deal with a case in arbitration and may refer it for trial in the county court. The grounds for this action depend on:

- The case involving a difficult of law or fact, or involving a charge of fraud;

- The agreement of the parties;

- Whether the district judge considers that it would to be unreasonable to decide the case in arbitration on the basis of the subject matter, or the circumstances of the parties, or the interests of any of person likely to be affected by any award made (see *Pepper v Healey* (1982)).

4.2.5   Procedure

Arbitration proceedings begin with an individual filing 'statements of claim' at the county court. This document details the grounds of their dispute and requests the other party to be summonsed to appear. There may be preliminary hearings at which the issues involved are clarified, but it is possible for the dispute to be settled at such hearings. If no compromise can be reached at this stage a date is set for the hearing of the arbitration.

Arbitration hearings are usually heard by the district judge, although the parties to the dispute may request that it be referred to the circuit judge or even an outside arbitrator. The arbitrator, hearing the case, may at any time before or after the hearing, with the agreement of the parties, consult an expert on the matter under consideration and, again with the approval of the parties, may invite an expert to sit on the arbitration in the role of assessor.

If one of the parties fails to appear at the hearing the dispute can be decided in their absence. Alternatively, the parties may agree to the case being decided by the arbitrator, solely on the basis of documents and written statements.

As the arbitration procedure is intended to be a less formal forum than that provided by the ordinary courts the County Court Rules provide that the strict rules of evidence shall not be applied in such hearings. Parties are encouraged to represent themselves rather than make use of the services of professional lawyers although they may be legally represented if they wish. Under the Courts and Legal Services Act (1990) the Lord Chancellor extended the right of audience to lay representatives in small claims courts. This decision had the effect of allowing individuals access to non-professional, but expert, advice and advocacy. Members of such organisations as Citizens Advice Bureau and Legal Advice Centres are now permitted to represent their clients in arbitration proceedings.

The County Court Rules gives arbitrators wide discretion to adopt any procedure they consider helpful to ensure that the parties have an equal opportunity to put their case. This discretion is not limitless, however, and it does not remove the normal principles of legal procedure, such as the right of direct cross-examination of one of the parties by the legal representative of the other party (see *Chilton v Saga Holidays plc* (1986)).

On the basis of the information provided the arbitrator decides the case and, if the plaintiff is successful, makes an award for appropriate compensation. A no-costs rule operates to ensure that the costs of legal representation cannot be recovered, although the losing party may be instructed to pay court fees and the expenses of witnesses. Judgments are legally enforceable.

Arbitration schemes are usually run under the auspices of particular trade associations and are designed to deal with the problems encountered by consumers in the specific area of enterprise covered by the trade association. As part of the regulation of trade practices and in the pursuit of effective measures of consumer protection the Office of Fair Trading has encouraged the establishment of voluntary codes of practice within particular areas. It is usual to find that such codes of practice provide arbitration schemes to resolve particularly intractable problems between individual consumers and members of the association. Such schemes are never compulsory and do not seek to replace the consumer's legal rights but they do provide a relatively inexpensive mechanism for dealing with problems without the need even to bother the county court. Such schemes are numerous: the most famous is probably the travel industry scheme operated under the auspices of the Association of British Travel Agents, but other associations run similar schemes in such areas as car sales, shoe retailing, dry-cleaning, and many other areas.

4.2.6   Arbitration under codes of conduct

Although attention tends to be focused on the operation of the courts as the forum within which legal decisions are taken, it is no longer the case that the bulk of legal and quasi-legal questions are determined within that court structure. There are, as an alternative to the court system, a large number of tribunals which have been set up under various Acts of Parliament to rule on the operation of the particular schemes established under those acts. There are at least 60 different types of administrative tribunal, and within each type there may well be hundreds of individual tribunals operating locally all over the country to hear particular cases. Over 250,000 cases are dealt with by tribunals each year.

4.3   Administrative tribunals

The precise distinction between tribunals and courts is a matter of uncertainty but what is certain is that tribunals are inferior to the normal courts. One of the main purposes of the tribunal system is to prevent the ordinary courts of law from being overburdened by cases, but tribunals are still subject to

4.3.1   Tribunals and courts

judicial review on the basis of breach of natural justice or where it acts in an ultra vires manner, or where it goes wrong in relation to the application of the law when deciding cases.

In addition to the control of the courts tribunals are also subject to the supervision of the Council on Tribunals originally established under the Tribunals and Inquiries Act 1958, as subsequently amended by the Acts 1971 and 1992 which is the current legislation. Members of the Council are appointed by the Lord Chancellor and its role is to keep the general operation of the system under review.

4.3.2   Composition of tribunals

Tribunals are usually made up of three members, only one of whom, the chair, is expected to be legally qualified. The other two members are lay representatives. The lack of legal training is not considered a drawback given the technical, administrative, as opposed to specifically legal, nature of the provisions they have to consider. Indeed, the fact of there are two lay representatives on tribunals provides them with one of their perceived advantages over courts. The non-legal members may provide specialist knowledge and thus they may enable the tribunal to base its decision on actual practice as opposed to abstract legal theory or mere legal formalism. An example of this can be seen in regard to the tribunals having responsibility for determining issues relating to employment, which usually have a trade union representative and a employers' representative sitting on the panel and are therefore able to consider the immediate problem from both sides of the employment relationship.

The procedure for nominating tribunal members is set out in the statute establishing the tribunal, but generally it is the Minister of State with responsibility for the operation of the statute in question, who ultimately decides the membership of the tribunal.

4.3.3   Statutory tribunals

There are a number of tribunals which have considerable power in their areas of operation and it is necessary to have some detailed knowledge of a selection of the most important of these. Examples of such tribunals are:

- Industrial tribunals

  These are governed by the Employment Protection (Consolidation) Act 1978 which sets out their composition, major areas of competence and procedure. In practice such tribunals are normally made up of a legally qualified chairperson, a representative chosen from a panel representing employers and another representative chosen from a panel representing the interests of employees.

Industrial tribunals have jurisdiction in relation to a number of statutory provisions relating to employment issues. The majority of issues arise from the Employment Protection (Consolidation) Act in relation to matters such as: disputes over the meaning and operation of particular terms of employment; disputes relating to redundancy payments; disputes involving issues of unfair dismissal; and disputes as to the provision of maternity pay.

They also deal with complaints about racial discrimination in the employment field under the Race Relations Act 1976: complaints about sexual discrimination in employment under the Sex Discrimination Act 1975; complaints about equal pay under the Equal Pay Act 1970 as amended by the Sex Discrimination Act; complaints about unlawful deductions from wages under the Wages Act 1986; and appeals against the imposition of improvement notices under the Health and Safety at Work Act 1974.

- Social Security Appeal tribunal

  Various Social Security Acts have provided for safety-net provisions for the disadvantaged in society to ensure that they at least enjoy a basic standard of living. The function of the Social Security Appeal tribunals, of which there are some 200 in England and Wales, is to hear and decide upon the correctness of decisions made by adjudication officers, who are the people who actually determine the level of benefit individuals are entitled to receive.

- Mental Health Review tribunals

  These operate under the Mental Health Act 1983. The tribunals have wide powers to decide whether or not individuals should be subject to compulsory treatment. They can also dispose of the property of such individuals. Given the particular area within which the Mental Health Review tribunal operates it is essential that there are medical experts present to decide on medical issues.

- The Lands tribunal

  Established under the Lands Tribunal Act 1949, its essential function is to determine the legality of, and the levels of compensation in relation to, compulsory purchase orders over land. It also considers matters relating to planning applications.

- Rent Assessment Committee

  This tribunal deals with matters specifically relating to the rent charged for property. It resolves disputes between landlords and tenants of private accommodation, hears appeals from decisions of rent officers and has the power to fix rent in relation to furnished and unfurnished residential tenancies.

4.3.4   Domestic tribunals

The foregoing has focused on public administrative tribunals set up under particular legislative provisions to deal with matters of public relevance. The term tribunal, however, is also used in relation to the internal, disciplinary procedures of particular institutions. Whether these institutions are created under legislation or not is immaterial, the point is that domestic tribunals relate mainly to matters of private rather than public concern although at times the two can overlap. Examples of domestic tribunals are the disciplinary committees of professional institutions such as the Bar, the Law Society, or the British Medical Association, Trade Unions, and universities. The power that each of these tribunals has may be very great and it is controlled by the ordinary courts through ensuring that the rules of natural justice are complied with and that the tribunal does not act *ultra vires* ie beyond its powers.

4.3.5   Advantages of tribunals

Advantages of tribunals over courts relate to such matters as:

- Speed
  The ordinary court system is notoriously dilatory in hearing and deciding cases. Tribunals are much quicker to hear cases. A related advantage of the tribunal system is the certainty that it will be heard on a specific date and not subject to the vagaries of the court system.

- Cost
  Tribunals are a much cheaper way of deciding cases than using the ordinary court system. One factor that leads to a reduction in cost is the fact that no specialised court building is required to hear the cases. Also the fact that those deciding the cases are less expensive to employ than judges, together with the fact that complainants do not have to rely on legal representation makes the tribunal procedure considerably less expensive than using the traditional court system. These reductions are further enhanced by the additional facts that there are no court fees involved in relation to tribunal proceedings and that costs are not normally awarded against the loser.

- Informality
  Tribunals are supposed to be informal in order to make them less intimidating than full-blown court cases. The strict rules relating to evidence, pleading and procedure

which apply in courts, are not binding in tribunal proceedings. The lack of formality is strengthened by the fact that proceedings tend not to be inquisitorial or accusatorial but are intended to try to encourage and help participants to express their views of the situation before the tribunal.

- Flexibility

  Tribunals are not bound by the strict rules of precedent although some pay more regard to previous decisions than others. It should be remembered that, as tribunals are inferior and subject to the courts, they are governed by the precedents made in the courts.

- Expertise

  Reference has already been made to the advantages to be gained from the particular expertise that is provided by the lay members of tribunals as against the more general legal expertise of the chairperson.

- Accessibility

  The aim of tribunals is to provide individuals with a readily accessible forum in which to air their grievances, and gaining access to tribunals is certainly not as difficult as getting a case into the ordinary courts.

- Privacy

  The final advantage is the fact that proceedings can be taken before a tribunal without triggering the publicity that might follow from a court case.

There are particular weaknesses in the system of tribunal adjudication. Some of these relate to:

4.3.6   Disadvantages of tribunals

- Appeals procedures

  There is ground for confusion in lack of uniformity in relation to appeals from tribunals. Rights of appeal from decisions of tribunals and the route of such appeals, depend on the provision of the statute under which a particular tribunal operates. Where such rights exist, they may be exercised variously, to a further tribunal, a minister or a court of law. A more consistent approach would improve the system.

- Publicity

  It was stated above that lack of publicity in relation to tribunal proceedings was a potential advantage of the system. A lack of publicity, however, may be a distinct disadvantage because it has the effect that cases involving issues of general public importance are not given the publicity and consideration that they might merit.

- The provision of legal aid

  Except for Lands tribunal and the Commons Commissioners, legal aid is not available to people pursuing cases at tribunals. They may be entitled to legal advice and assistance under the 'green form' system but such limited assistance is unlikely to provide potential complainants with sufficient help to permit them to pursue their case with any confidence of achieving a satisfactory conclusion.

4.4   Mediation and conciliation

The final alternative dispute mechanisms to be considered, mediation and conciliation, are the most informal of all.

Mediation is the process whereby a third party acts as the conduit through which two disputing parties communicate and negotiate in an attempt to reach a common resolution of a problem.

Conciliation takes mediation a step further and gives the mediator the power to suggest grounds for compromise and the possible basis for an conclusive agreement. Both mediation and conciliation have been available in relation to industrial disputes under the auspices of the government funded Advisory Conciliation and Arbitration Service (ACAS). One of the statutory functions of ACAS is to try to resolve industrial disputes by means of discussion and negotiation or if the parties agree the Service might take a more active part as arbitrator in relation to a particular dispute. Conciliation also has an important part to play in family matters, where it is felt that the adversarial approach of the traditional legal system has tended to emphasise, if not increase, existing differences of view between individuals and has not been conducive to amicable settlements. Thus in divorce cases conciliation places the emphasis on the parties themselves working out an agreed settlement rather than having one imposed on them from outside.

The essential weakness in these two procedures, however, lies in the fact that, although they may lead to the resolution of a dispute, they do not necessarily achieve that end. Where they operate successfully they are excellent methods of dealing with problems, since, essentially, the parties to the dispute determine their own solutions and therefore feel committed to the outcome. The problem is that they have no binding power and do not always lead to an outcome.

Alternatives to the Courts

ADR has many features that make it preferable to the ordinary court system in many areas.

Its main advantage is that it is less antagonistic than the more normal legal system, and is designed to achieve agreement between the parties involved.

Alternative Dispute Resolution (ADR)

Arbitration is the procedure whereby parties in dispute refer the issue to a third party for resolution, rather than take the case to the ordinary law courts.

Arbitration procedures can be contained in the original contract or agreed after a dispute arises.

The procedure is governed by the Arbitration Acts 1950 and 1979.

Arbitration awards are enforceable in the ordinary courts.

It must be carried out in a judicial manner and is subject to judicial review.

Advantages over the ordinary court system are: privacy, informality, speed, lower cost, expertise, and the fact that it is less antagonistic.

Small claims procedure in the county court is a distinct process although referred to as arbitration.

Arbitration

Administrative tribunals deal with cases involving conflicts between the state, its functionaries, and private citizens. Domestic tribunals deal with private internal matters within institutions.

Tribunals may be seen as administrative but they are also adjudicative in that they have to act judicially when deciding particular cases.

Tribunals are subject to the supervision of the Council on Tribunals but are subservient to, and under the control of, the ordinary courts.

Usually only the chair of a tribunal is legally qualified.

Examples of tribunals are: industrial tribunals, social security appeals tribunal, mental health review tribunal, lands tribunal, rent assessment committee.

Advantages of tribunals over ordinary courts relate to: speed, cost, informality, flexibility, expertise, accessibility, and privacy.

Administrative tribunals

Disadvantages relate to: appeals procedure, lack of publicity and the lack of legal aid in most cases.

Mediation and conciliation

Mediation means that the third party only acts as a go-between.

Conciliation means the third party is more active in facilitating a reconciliation or agreement between the parties.

Chapter 5

The Nature and Function of Contract Law

Ours is a market system. This means that economic activity takes place through the exchange of commodities. Individual possessors of commodities meet in the market place and freely enter into negotiations to determine the terms on which they are willing to exchange those commodities.

Although people have always exchanged goods, market transactions really only came to be the dominant form of economic activity, even in the UK, in the course of the 19th century. The general law of contract, as it now operates, is essentially the product of the common law and emerged in the course of the 19th century. It has been suggested that the general principles of contract law, or the classical model of contract as they are known, are themselves based on an idealised model of how the market operates. It should be noted that statutory inroads have been made into the common law, particularly in the area of consumer protection. For example one notable piece of legislation that will require close attention is the Unfair Contract Terms Act 1977.

The purpose of this short chapter is to introduce contract law as the mechanism through which such market activity is conducted and regulated.

The simplest possible description of a contract is 'a legally binding agreement'. It should be noted, however, that although all contracts are the outcome of agreements; not all agreements are contracts; ie not all agreements are legally enforceable. In order to be in a position to determine whether a particular agreement will be enforced by the courts one must have an understanding of the rules and principles of contract law.

The emphasis placed on agreement highlights the consensual nature of contracts. It is sometimes said that contract is based on consensus *ad idem*, a meeting of minds. This is slightly misleading, however, for the reason that English contract law applies an objective test in determining whether or not a contract exists. It is not so much a matter of what the parties actually had in mind as to what their behaviour would lead others to conclude as to their state of mind.

There is no general requirement that contracts be made in writing. They can be created by word of mouth, or by action,

| 5.1 | Introduction |

| 5.2 | Definition |

| 5.3 | Formalities |

as well as in writing. Contracts made in any of these ways are known as parol or simple contracts, whereas those made by deed are referred to as speciality contracts. It is generally left to the parties to decide on the actual form that the contract has to take, but in certain circumstances formalities are required:

- Contracts that must be made by deed

  Essentially this requirement applies to conveyances of land and leases of property extending over a period of more than three years. Agreements, which would not otherwise be enforceable as contracts, will be implemented by the courts where they have been made by deed.

- Contracts that must be in writing (but not necessarily by deed)

  Amongst this group are : bills of exchange, cheques and promissory notes (by virtue of Bills of Exchange Act 1882); consumer credit agreements such as hire-purchase agreements (by virtue of Consumer Credit Act 1972); contracts of marine insurance (by virtue of Marine Assurance Act 1906).

- Contracts that must be evidenced in writing

  The sole remaining member of this category are contracts of guarantee, derived from s 4 of the Statute of Frauds Act 1677. It should be noted that the previous other example relating to the sale or other disposition of land under s 40 of the Law of Property Act 1925 has been removed by the Law of Property (Miscellaneous Provisions) Act 1989. The new Act requires all such contracts to be made in writing and thus they come within the second group considered above.

5.4   The legal effect of agreement

It has already been pointed out that not all agreements are recognised as contracts in law, it also has to be borne in mind that even where agreements do constitute contracts they may not be given full effect by the courts. The legal effect of particular agreements may be distinguished as follows:

- Valid contracts

  These are agreements which the law recognises as binding in full. The court will enforce the contract by either insisting on performance or awarding damages to the innocent party.

- Void contracts

  This is actually a contradiction in terms, for this type of agreement does not constitute a contract: it has no legal effect. Agreements may be void for a number of reasons including mistake, illegality, public policy, or the lack of a necessary requirement such as consideration. The ownership of property exchanged does not pass under a void contract and remains with the original owner. The legal owner may recover it from the possession of the other party or indeed any third party if it has been passed on to such a person. This is so even where the third party has acquired the property in good faith and has provided consideration for it.

- Voidable contracts

  These are agreements which may be avoided, ie set aside, by one of the parties. If, however, no steps are taken to avoid the agreement then a valid contract ensues. Examples of contracts which may be voidable are those which have been entered into on the basis of fraud, misrepresentation or duress. Goods which have been exchanged under a voidable contract can be sold to an innocent third party, who will receive good title.

- Unenforceable contracts

  These are agreements which, although legal, cannot be sued upon for some reason. One example would be where the time limit for enforcing the contract has lapsed. The title to any goods exchanged under such a contract is treated as having been validly passed and cannot, therefore, be reclaimed.

The following four chapters will consider the major substantive rules relating to contracts, but first it is necessary to issue a warning in relation to examinations. Contract forms the main component in most syllabuses. It is not possible to select particular areas as more important than others and, therefore, more likely to be examined. Unfortunately, any aspect of contract may be asked about, and therefore candidates must be familiar with most, if not all, aspects of the subject. For example, it may be legitimate to expect a question on the vitiating factors in relation to contracts (see Chapter 8). It is not possible, however, to predict with any confidence which particular vitiating factor will be selected. To restrict one's study would be extremely hazardous. The candidate may well know mistake and misrepresentation very well, but that will be to no avail if the question asked actually relates to duress, as it might very well do. The warning, therefore, is to study contract thoroughly.

The Nature and Function of Contract Law

The simplest possible description of a contract is 'a legally binding agreement'. The rules of contract law determine whether or not an agreement is legally enforceable.

Definition

There is no formal requirement that contracts are to be made in writing.

Formalities

Speciality contracts are agreements made by deed; others are referred to as simple or parol contracts.

Some contracts must be made by deed. Conveyances of land and leases of property extending over a period of more than three years are examples.

Some contracts must be in writing. Bills of exchange, consumer credit agreements and contracts of marine insurance are examples.

Some contracts must be evidenced in writing, contracts of guarantee are now the only example of this requirement.

The legal effect of agreements are:

The legal effect of agreements

- Valid contracts which are agreements which the law recognises as binding in full.

- Void contracts which have no legal effect. Agreements may be void for a number of reasons; including mistake, illegality, public policy, or the lack of a necessary requirement such as consideration.

- Voidable contracts which are agreements which may be set aside by one of the parties to it. If, however, no steps are taken to avoid the agreement then a valid contract ensues. Contracts entered into on the basis of fraud, misrepresentation or duress are voidable.

Unenforceable contracts which are agreements which, although legal, cannot be sued upon for some reason. One example would be where the time limit for enforcing the contract has lapsed.

Chapter 6

The Formation of a Contract

As has been seen not every agreement, let alone every promise, will be enforced by the law. But what distinguishes the enforceable promise from the unenforceable one? The essential elements of a binding agreement, and the constituent elements of the classical model of contract, are as follows:

- Offer;
- Acceptance;
- Consideration;
- Privity;
- Capacity;
- Intention to create legal relations;
- There must be no vitiating factors present.

The first six of these elements must be present, and the seventh one absent, for there to be a legally enforceable contractual relationship. This chapter will consider the first five elements in turn. Vitiating factors will be considered separately in Chapter 8.

6.1   Introduction

An offer is a promise which is capable of acceptance, to be bound on particular terms. The person who makes the offer is the *offeror*; the person who receives the offer is the *offeree*. The offer sets out the terms upon which the offeror is willing to enter into contractual relations with the offeree.

6.2   Offer

The offer must be capable of acceptance, thus it must not be too vague.

In *Scammel v Ouston* (1941) Ouston ordered a van from Scammel on the understanding that the balance of the purchase price could be paid on 'hire-purchase terms over two years'. Scammel used a number of different hire-purchase terms and the actual terms of Ouston's agreement were never actually fixed. When Scammel failed to deliver the van, Ouston sued for breach of contract. It was held that the action failed on the basis that no contract could be established due to the uncertainty of the terms.

An offer may, through acceptance by the offeree, result in a legally enforceable contract. It is important to be able to distinguish what the law will treat as an offer from other

6.2.1   Distinguishing factors of an offer

statements which will not form the basis of an enforceable contract. An offer must be distinguished from the following:

- A mere statement of intention

  Such a statement cannot form the basis of a contract even though the party to whom it was made acts on it. See, for example, *Re Fickus* (1900) where a father informed his prospective son-in-law that his daughter would inherit under his will. It was held that the father's words were simply a statement of present intention which he could alter as he wished in the future. They were not an offer, and therefore the father could not be bound by them.

- A mere supply of information

  The case *Harvey v Facey* (1893) demonstrates this point. The plaintiff telegraphed the defendants 'Will you sell us Bumper Hall Pen? Telegraph lowest cash price'. The defendant answered 'Lowest price for Bumper Hall Pen £900'. The plaintiff then telegraphed 'We agree to buy Bumper Hall Pen for £900', and sued for specific performance when the defendants declined to transfer the property. It was held that the defendant's telegram was not an offer capable of being accepted by the plaintiff. It was simply a statement of information.

- An invitation to treat

  This is an invitation to others to make offers. The person extending the invitation is not bound to accept any offers made to them. The following are examples of common situations involving invitations to treat:

  (a) The display of goods in a shop window. The classic case in this area is *Fisher v Bell* (1961) in which a shopkeeper was prosecuted for offering offensive weapons for sale, by having flick-knives on display in his window. It was held that the shopkeeper was not guilty as the display in the shop window was not an offer for sale but only an invitation to treat.

  (b) The display of goods on the shelf of a self-service shop. In this instance the exemplary case is *Pharmaceutical Society of Great Britain v Boots Cash Chemists* (1953). The defendants were charged with breaking a law which provided that certain drugs could only be sold under the supervision of a qualified pharmacist. They had placed the drugs on open display in their self-service store and, although a qualified person was stationed at the cash desk, it was alleged that the contract of sale had been formed when the customer removed the goods from the shelf. It was held that Boots were not guilty. The display of goods on the shelf was only an invitation to treat. In law, the customer offered to buy the goods at the cash desk where the pharmacist was stationed. This decision is clearly practical, as the alternative would mean that once customers had placed goods in their shopping baskets they would be bound to accept them and could not change their minds and return the goods to the shelves.

(c)   A public advertisement. Once again this does not amount to an offer. This can be seen from *Partridge v Crittenden* (1968) in which a person was charged with 'offering' a wild bird for sale contrary to Protection of Birds Act 1954, after he had placed an advert relating to the sale of such birds in a magazine. It was held that he could not be guilty of offering the bird for sale as the advert amounted to no more than an invitation to treat.

(d)   A share prospectus. Contrary to common understanding, such a document is not an offer; it is merely an invitation to treat, inviting people to make offers to subscribe for shares in a company.

It can be seen that the decisions in both *Fisher v Bell* and *Partridge v Crittenden* run contrary to the common, non-legal, understanding of the term offer. It is interesting to note that later legislation, such as the Trades Descriptions Act 1968, has been specifically worded in such a way as to ensure that invitations to treat are subject to the same legal regulation as offers.

An offer may be made to a particular person or to a group of people or to the world at large. If the offer is restricted then only the people to whom it is addressed may accept it; but if the offer is made to the public at large, it can be accepted by anyone.

6.2.2   Offers to particular people

In *Carlill v Carbolic Smoke Ball Co* (1893) the company advertised that they would pay £100 to anyone who caught influenza after using their smoke ball as directed. Carlill used the smoke ball but still caught influenza and sued the company for the promised £100. Amongst the many defences argued for the company, it was suggested that the advert could not have been an offer as it was not addressed to Carlill. It was held that the advert was an offer to the whole world which Mrs Carlill had accepted by her conduct. There was, therefore, a valid contract between her and the company.

A person cannot accept an offer that they do not know about. Thus if a person offers a reward for the return of a lost watch

6.2.3   Acceptance of offers

and someone returns it without knowing about the offer, they cannot claim the reward. Motive for accepting is not important as long as the person accepting knows about the offer. See *Williams v Carwadine* (1883) where a person was held to be entitled to receive a reward although that was not the reason they provided the information requested. (Acceptance generally will be considered in detail in para 6.3 below.)

6.2.4   Rejection of offers

Express rejection of an offer has the effect of terminating the offer. The offeree cannot subsequently accept the original offer. A *counter-offer*, where the offeree tries to change the terms of the offer has he same effect.

In *Hyde v Wrench* (1840) Wrench offered to sell his farm for £1,000. Hyde offered £950, which Wrench rejected. Hyde then informed Wrench that he accepted the original offer. It was held that there was no contract. Hyde's counter-offer had effectively ended the original offer and it was no longer open to him to accept it.

A counter-offer must not be confused with a request for information. Such a request does not end the offer, which can still be accepted after the new information has been elicited. See *Stevenson v McLean* (1880) where it was held that a request by the offeree as to the length of time the offeror would give for payment did not terminate the original offer, which he was entitled to accept prior to revocation.

6.2.5   Revocation of offers

Revocation, the technical term for cancellation, occurs when the offeror withdraws their offer. There are a number of points that have to be borne in mind in relation to revocation:

- An offer may be revoked at any time before acceptance

    Once revoked it is no longer open to the offeree to accept the original offer.

    In *Routledge v Grant* (1828) Grant offered to buy Routledge's house and gave him six weeks to accept the offer. Within that period, however, he withdrew the offer. It was held that Grant was entitled to withdraw the offer at any time before acceptance and upon withdrawal Routledge could no longer create a contract by purporting to accept it.

- Revocation is not effective until it is actually received by the offeree

    This means that the offeror must make sure that the offeree is made aware of the withdrawal of the offer, otherwise it might still be open to the offeree to accept the offer.

    In *Byrne v Tienhoven* (1880) the defendant offerors carried out their business in Cardiff, the plaintiff offerees in New

York. On 1 October an offer was made by post. On 8 October a letter of revocation was posted, seeking to withdraw the offer. On 11 October the plaintiffs telegraphed their acceptance of the offer. On 20 October the letter of revocation was received by the plaintiffs.

It was held that the revocation did not take effect until it arrived and the defendants were bound by the contract which had been formed by the plaintiffs' acceptance. (See also the consideration of the postal rule in para 6.3.2 below.)

- Communication of revocation may be made through a reliable third party

Where the offeree finds out about the withdrawal of the offer from a reliable third party the revocation is effective and the offeree can no longer seek to accept the original offer.

In *Dickinson v Dodds* (1876) Dodds offered to sell property to Dickinson and told him that the offer would be left open until Friday. On the Thursday the plaintiff was informed by a reliable third party, who was acting as an intermediary, that Dodds intended selling the property to someone else. Dickinson still attempted to accept the offer on the Friday, by which time the property had already been sold. It was held that the sale of the property amounted to revocation which had been effectively communicated by the third party.

- A promise to keep an offer open is only binding where there is a separate contract to that effect

This is known as an option contract, and the offeree/promisee must provide consideration for the promise to keep the offer open.

- In relation to unilateral contracts revocation is not permissible once the offeree has started performing the task requested

A unilateral contract is one where one party promises something in return for some action on the part of another party. Reward cases are examples of such unilateral promises. There is no compulsion placed on the party undertaking the action but it would still seem to be unfair if the promisor were entitled to revoke their offer just before the offeree was about to complete their part of the contract.

In *Errington v Errington* (1952) a father promised his son and daughter-in-law that he would convey a house to them when they had paid off the outstanding mortgage. After the father's death his widow sought to revoke the promise. It was held that the promise could not be withdrawn as long as the mortgage payments continued to be met.

6.2.6   Lapsing of offers

Offers will lapse and will no longer be capable of acceptance in the following circumstances:

- At the end of a stated period

  It is possible for the parties to agree, or the offeror to set, a time limit within which acceptance has to take place. If the offeree has not accepted the offer within that period the offer lapses and can no longer be accepted.

- After a reasonable time

  Where no set time limit is set, then an offer will lapse after the passage of a reasonable time. What amounts to a reasonable time is of course dependent upon the particular circumstances of each case.

- Where the offeree dies

  This automatically brings the offer to a close.

- Where the offeror dies and the contract was one of a personal nature

  In such circumstances the offer automatically comes to an end but the outcome is less certain in relation to contracts that are not of a personal nature. See *Bradbury v Morgan* (1862) for an example of a case where it was held that the death of an offeror did not invalidate the offeree's acceptance.

  It should be noted that the effect of death *after acceptance* also depends on whether the contract was one of a personal nature or not. In the case of a non-personal contract the contract can be enforced by and against the representatives of the deceased. On the other hand, if performance of the contract depended upon the personal qualification or capacity of the deceased then the contract will be frustrated (see para 9.4).

6.3   **Acceptance**

Acceptance is necessary for the formation of a contract. Once the offeree has assented to the terms offered, a contract comes into effect. Both parties are bound: the offeror can no longer withdraw their offer, nor can the offeree withdraw their acceptance.

6.3.1   Form of acceptance

In order to form a binding agreement the acceptance must correspond with the terms of the offer. Thus the offeree must not seek to introduce new contractual terms into their acceptance.

In *Neale v Merritt* (1830) one party offered to sell property for £280. The other party purported to accept the offer by sending £80 and promising to pay the remainder by monthly instalments. It was held that this purported acceptance was ineffective as the offeree had not accepted the original offer as stated.

As has been seen in *Hyde v Wrench*, such a counter-offer does constitute acceptance. Analogously it may also be stated that a conditional acceptance cannot create a contract relationship. Thus any agreement 'subject to contract' is not binding but merely signifies the fact that the parties are in the process of finalising the terms on which they will be willing to be bound. The case of *Winn v Bull* (1877) provides authority for this point.

Acceptance may be in the form of express words, either oral or written; or it may be implied from conduct.

In *Brogden v Metropolitan Railway Co* (1877) the plaintiff, having supplied the company with coal for a number of years, suggested that they should enter into a written contract. The company agreed and sent Brogden a draft contract. He altered some points and returned it marked approved. The company did nothing further about the document, but Brogden continued to deliver coal on the terms included in the draft contract. When a dispute arose Brogden denied the existence of any contract. It was held that the draft became a full contract when both parties acted on it.

The general rule is that acceptance must be communicated to the offeror. As a consequence of this rule, silence cannot amount to acceptance. The classic case in this regard is *Felthouse v Bindley* (1863) where an uncle had been negotiating the purchase of his nephew's horse and he eventually wrote offering to buy it at a particular price stating 'If I hear no more about him I shall consider the horse mine'. When the horse was mistakenly sold by an auctioneer the uncle sued the auctioneer in conversion. It was held that the uncle had no cause of action as the horse did not belong to him. Acceptance could not be imposed on the offeree on the basis of his silence.	6.3.2 Communication of acceptance

There are, however, exceptions to the general rule that acceptance must be communicated which arise in the following cases:

• Where the offeror has waived the right to receive communication

In unilateral contracts, such as *Carlill v Carbolic Smoke Ball Co* or general reward cases, acceptance occurs when the offeree performs the required act. Thus in the Carlill case Mrs Carlill did not have to inform the Smoke Ball Co that she had used their treatment. Nor, in reward cases, do those seeking to benefit have to inform the person offering the reward that they have begun to perform the task that will lead to the reward.

* Where acceptance is through the postal service

In such circumstances acceptance is complete as soon as the letter, properly addressed and stamped, is posted. The contract is concluded even if the letter subsequently fails to reach the offeror.

In *Adams v Lindsell* (1818) on 2 September the defendant made an offer to the plaintiff. Due to misdirection the letter was delayed. It arrived on 5 September and Adams immediately posted an acceptance. On 8 September Lindsell sold the merchandise to a third party. On 9 September the letter of acceptance from Adams arrived. It was held that valid acceptance occurred when Adams posted the letter and Lindsell was therefore liable for breach of contract.

As has already been seen in *Byrne v Van Tienhoven* the postal rule applies equally to telegrams. It does not apply, however, when means of instantaneous communication are used (see *Entores v Far East Corp* (1955) for a consideration of this point). It follows that when acceptance is made by means of telephone, fax, or telex, the offeror must actually receive the acceptance.

It should be noted that the postal rule will only apply where it is in the contemplation of the parties that the post will be used as the means of acceptance. If the parties have negotiated either face to face, in a shop for example, or over the telephone, then it might not be reasonable for the offeree to use the post as a means of communicating their acceptance and they would not gain the benefit of the postal rule.

In order to expressly exclude the operation of the postal rule the offeror can insist that acceptance is only to be effective on receipt (see *Holwell Securities v Hughes* (1974)). The offeror can also require that acceptance be communicated in a particular manner. Where the offeror does not actually insist that acceptance can only be made in the stated manner, then acceptance is effective if it is communicated in a way no less advantageous to the offeror (see *Yates Building Co v J Pulleyn & Sons* (1975)).

These arise where one party wishes particular work to be done and issues a statement asking interested parties to submit the terms on which they are willing to carry out the work. In the case of tenders the person who invites the tender is simply making an invitation to treat. The person who submits a tender is the offeror and the other party is at liberty to accept or reject the offer as they please.

The effect of acceptance depends upon the wording of the invitation to tender. If the invitation states that the potential purchaser will require to be supplied with a certain quantity of goods, then acceptance of a tender will form a contract and they will be in breach if they fail to order the stated quantity of goods from the tenderer.

If, on the other hand, the invitation states only that the potential purchaser may require goods, acceptance gives rise only to a *standing offer*. There is no compulsion on the purchaser to take any goods but they must not deal with any other supplier. Each order given forms a separate contract and the supplier must deliver any goods required within the time stated in the tender. The supplier can revoke the standing offer but they must supply any goods already ordered.

In *Great Northern Railway v Witham* (1873) the defendant successfully tendered to supply the company with 'such quantities as the company may order from time to time'. After fulfilling some orders Witham refused to supply any more goods. It was held that he was in breach of contract in respect of the goods already ordered, but once those were supplied he was at liberty to revoke his standing order.

The foregoing has presented the legal principles relating to offer and acceptance in line with the Classical Model of Contract. As has been stated, underlying that model is the operation of the market in which individuals freely negotiate the terms on which they are to be bound. The offeror sets out terms to which they are willing to be bound and if the offeree accepts those terms then a contract is formed. If, however, the offeree alters the terms then the parties reverse their roles: the former offeree now becomes the offeror and the former offeror now becomes the offeree, able to accept or reject the new terms as they choose. This process of role reversal continues until an agreement is reached or the parties decide that there are no grounds on which they can form an agreement. Thus the Classical Model of Contract insists that there must be a correspondence of offer and acceptance, and that any failure to match acceptance to offer will not result in a binding contract.

6.3.3 Tenders

6.4 Offer, acceptance and the classical model of contract

Commercial reality, however, tends to differ from this theoretical model and lack of genuine agreement as to terms in a commercial contract can leave the courts with a difficult task in determining whether there was actually a contract in the first place and, if there was, upon precisely which, or whose, terms was it entered into. This difficulty may be seen in relation to what is known as 'the battle of the forms' in which the parties do not actually enter into real negotiations but simply exchange standard form contracts, setting out their usual terms of trade, with one another. The point is that the contents of these standard form contracts might not agree and indeed might actually be contradictory. The question then arises as to whose terms are to be taken as forming the basis of the contract if indeed a contract has actually been concluded.

Some judges, notably Lord Denning, have felt themselves to be too restricted by the constraints of the Classical Model of Contract and have argued that rather than being required to find, or construct, a correspondence of offer and acceptance they should be able to examine the commercial reality of the situation in order to decide whether the parties had or had not intended to enter into contractual relations. As Lord Denning would have had it judges should not be restricted to looking for a precise matching of offer and acceptance but should be at liberty to: '... look at the correspondence as a whole, and at the conduct of the parties, and see therefrom whether the parties have come to an agreement on everything that was material.'

The above opinion was expressed in *Gibson v Manchester City Council* (1979). This case concerned the sale of a council house to a tenant. The tenant had entered into negotiations with his local council about the purchase of his house. Before he had entered into a binding contract the political make-up of the council changed and the policy of selling houses was reversed. It is clear that under the Classical Model of contract there was no correspondence of offer and acceptance but the Court of Appeal nonetheless decided that the tenant could insist on the sale.

The status quo was restored by the House of Lords, which overturned the Court of Appeal's decision. In doing so Lord Diplock expressed the view that:

'... there may be certain types of contract, though they are exceptional, which do not easily fit in to the normal analysis of a contract as being constituted by offer and acceptance, but a contract alleged to have been made by an exchange of correspondence by the parties in which the successive communications other than the first are in reply to one another is not one of these.'

Subsequent to this clear re-affirmation of the Classical Model even Lord Denning was cowed in deciding *Butler Machine Tool Co Ltd v Ex-Cell-O Corporation (England) Ltd* (1979). Although he did not hesitate to repeat his claim as to the unsuitability of the traditional offer/acceptance analysis in the particular case, which involved a clear battle of the forms, he did feel it necessary to frame his judgment in terms of the traditional analysis.

It is perhaps possible that Lord Denning's questioning of the Classical Model has been revitalised by the recent decision of the Court of Appeal in *Trentham Ltd v Archital Luxfer* (1993), another battle of the forms case, in which Lord Justice Steyn stated that he was:

'... satisfied that in this fully executed contract transaction a contract came into existence during performance *even if it cannot be precisely analysed in terms of offer and acceptance.*'

It must be pointed out, however, that the case involved a completed contract and that the court was, therefore, faced with the problem of giving retrospective commercial effect to the parties' interactions and business relationship. It must also be emphasised that in reaching its decision the Court of Appeal relied on the authority of *Brogden v Metropolitan Railway Co*. The case may not, therefore, be as significant in the attack on the Classical Model of Contract as it appears at first light and its full scope remains to be seen.

6.5 Consideration

English law does not enforce gratuitous promises unless they are made by deed. Consideration can be understood as the price paid for a promise. The element of bargain implicit in the idea of consideration is evident in the following definition by Sir Frederick Pollock, adopted by the house of Lords in *Dunlop v Selfridge* (1915), as:

'An act or forbearance of one party, or the promise thereof, is the price for which the promise of the other is bought, and the promise thus given for value is enforceable.'

It is sometimes said that consideration consists of 'some benefit to the promisor or detriment to the promisee'. It should be noted that both elements stated in that definition are not required to be present to support a legally enforceable agreement; although in practice they are usually present. If the promisee acts to their detriment it is immaterial that the action does not directly benefit the promisor.

6.5.1 Forbearance

Forbearance involves non-action, or the relinquishing of some right. An example is forbearance to sue. If two parties, A and B, believe that A has a cause of legal action against B, then if B promises to pay a sum of money to A if he will give up his right to pursue the action, there is a valid contract to that effect: A has provided consideration by giving up his recourse to law. Such action would not amount to consideration if A knew that the claim was either hopeless or invalid.

6.5.2   Types of consideration

Consideration can be divided into the following categories:

• Executory consideration

This is the promise to perform an action at some future time. A contract can be made on the basis of an exchange of promises as to future action. Such a contract is known as an *executory contract*.

• Executed consideration

In the case of unilateral contracts, where the offeror promises something in return for the offeree's doing something, the promise only becomes enforceable when the offeree has actually performed the required act. If A offers a reward for the return of their lost watch the reward only becomes enforceable once it has been found and returned to them.

• Past consideration

This category does not actually count as valid consideration sufficient to make any agreement based on it a binding contract. Normally consideration is provided either at the time of the creation of a contract or at a later date. In the case of past consideration, however, the action is performed before the promise that it is supposed to be the consideration for. Such action is not sufficient to support a promise as consideration cannot consist of any action already wholly performed before the promise was made.

In *Re McArdle* (1951) a number of children were entitled to a house on the death of their mother. Whilst the mother was still alive her son and his wife had lived with her, and the wife made various improvements to the house. The children later promised that they would pay the wife £488 for the work she had done. It was held that as the work was completed when the promise was given, it was past consideration and the later promise could not be enforced.

There are exceptions to the rule that past consideration will not support a valid contract:

• Under s 27 of the Bills of Exchange Act 1882 past consideration can create liability on a bill of exchange;

• Under s 29 of the Limitation Act 1980 a time barred debt becomes enforceable again if it is acknowledged in writing;

- Where the plaintiff performed the action at the request of the defendant and payment was expected, then any subsequent promise to pay will be enforceable.

  In *Casey's Patents* (1892) the joint owners of patent rights asked Casey to find licensees to work the patents. After he had done as requested they promised to reward him. When one of the patent holders died his executors denied the enforceability of the promise made to Casey on the basis of past consideration. It was held that the promise made to Casey was enforceable. There had been an implied promise to reward him before he had performed his action and the later payment simply fixed the extent of that reward.

It has already be seen that consideration must not be past. But that is only one of the many rules that govern the legal definition and operation of consideration. Other rules are as follows:

6.5.3   Rules relating to consideration

- Performance must be legal

  The courts will not countenance a claim to enforce a promise to pay for any criminal act.

- Performance must be possible

  It is generally accepted that a promise to perform an impossible act cannot form the basis of a binding contractual agreement.

- Consideration must move from the promisee

  If A promises B £1,000 if B gives his car to C, then normally C cannot enforce B's promise, because C is not the party who has provided the consideration for the promise.

  In *Tweddle v Atkinson* (1861) on the occasion of the marriage of A and B their respective fathers entered in to a contract to pay money to A. When one of the parents died without having made the payment A tried to enforce the contract against his estate. It was held that A could not enforce the contract as he personally had provided no consideration for the promise. (This point should be considered in relation to the rules in relation to privity of contract. See later at para 6.6.)

- Consideration must be sufficient but need not be adequate

  It is up to the parties themselves to decide the terms of their contract. The court will not intervene to require equality in the value exchanged, as long as the agreement has been freely entered into.

In *Thomas v Thomas* (1842) the executors of a man's will promised to let his widow live in his house in return for rent of £1 per year. It was held that £1 was sufficient consideration to validate the contract, although it did not represent an adequate rent in economic terms.

In *Chappell & Co v Nestle Co* (1959) it was held that a used chocolate wrapper was consideration sufficient to form a contract, even although it had no economic value whatsoever to Nestle and was in fact thrown away after it was returned to them.

6.5.4   Performance of existing duties

Although it has generally been accepted that performance of an existing duty does not provide valid consideration, the recent authority of *Williams v Roffey Bros* (1990) has indicated a contrary possibility. The rules relating to existing duty are as follows:

• The discharge of a public duty

As a matter of public policy, to forestall the possibility of corruption or extortion, it has long been held that those required to perform certain public duties cannot claim the performance of those duties as consideration for a promised reward.

In *Collins v Godefroy* (1831) the plaintiff was served with a subpoena which meant that he was legally required to give evidence in the court case in question. Additionally, however, the defendant promised to pay him for giving his evidence. When the plaintiff tried to enforce the promised payment it was held that there was no binding agreement as he had provided no consideration by simply fulfilling his existing duty.

Where, however, a promisee does more than their duty, they are entitled to claim on the promise. See for example *Glassbrook v Glamorgan CC* (1925), where the police authority provided more protection than their public duty required; and the similar case of *Harris v Sheffield United FC* (1987) where the football club was held liable to pay police costs for controlling crowds at their matches.

In cases where there is no possibility of corruption and no evidence of coercion the courts have stretched the understanding of what is meant by consideration in order to fit the facts of the case in question within the framework of the Classical Model of Contract. See for example *Ward v Byham* (1956) in which a mother was held to provide consideration by looking after her child well and *Williams v Williams* (1957) in which the consideration for a husband's promise of maintenance to his estranged wife seemed to be the fact of her staying away from him. In both of these cases Lord Denning introduced *obiter dicta* which directly questioned the reason why the performance of an existing duty should not amount to consideration but the cases were ultimately decided on the basis that sufficient consideration was provided.

- The performance of a contractual duty

  Lord Denning's challenge to the formalism of the Classical Model of Contract is particularly pertinent when considered in the context of commercial contracts, where the mere performance of a contract may provide a benefit, or at least avoid a loss, for a promisor. The long-established rule, however, was that the mere performance of a contractual duty already owed to the promisor cannot be consideration for a new promise.

  In *Stilk v Myrick* (1809) when two members of his crew deserted, a ship's captain promised the remaining members of the crew that they would share the deserter's wages if they completed the voyage. When the ship was returned to London the owners refused to honour the promise and it was held that it could not be legally enforced since the sailors had only done what they were already obliged to do by their contracts of employment.

  Although *Stilk v Myrick* is cited as an authority in relation to consideration, it would appear that the public policy issue in the perceived need to preclude even the possibility of sailors in distant parts exerting coercive pressure to increase their rewards was just as important. Thus although the *reason* for the decision was a matter of public policy its legal *justification* was in terms of consideration.

  As in the case of a public duty, so performance of more than the existing contractual duty will be valid consideration for a new promise. Thus in *Hartley v Ponsonby* (1857), the facts of which were somewhat similar to those in *Stilk and Myrick*, it was decided that the crew had done more than they previously had agreed to do because the number of deserters had been so great as to make the return of the ship unusually hazardous. On that basis they were entitled to enforce the agreement to increase their wages. Once again in this case one finds a reluctance to deny the theoretical application of the Classical Model of Contract whilst at the same time undermining its operation in practice.

The continued relevance and application of *Stilk v Myrick* in commercial cases has been placed in no little doubt in recent years by a potentially extremely important decision of the Court of Appeal.

In *Williams v Roffey Bros* (1990) Roffey Bros had entered into a contract to refurbish a block of flats and subcontracted with Williams to carry out carpentry work for a fixed price of £20,000. It became apparent that Williams was in such financial difficulties that he might not be able to complete his work on time with the consequence that Roffey Bros would be subject to a penalty clause in the main contract. As a result Roffey Bros offered to pay Williams an additional £575 for each flat he completed. On that basis Williams carried on working, but when it seemed that Roffey Bros were not going to pay him, he stopped work and sued for the additional payment in relation to the eight flats he had completed after the promise of additional payment. The Court of Appeal held that Roffey Bros had enjoyed practical benefits as a consequence of their promise to increase Williams payment: the work would be completed on time; they would not have to pay any penalty; and they would not suffer the bother and expense of getting someone else to complete the work. These benefits were sufficient *in the circumstances* to provide consideration for the promise of extra money and Williams was held to be entitled to recover the extra money owed to him.

It should be emphasised that the Court of Appeal in *Williams v Roffey Bros* made it clear that they were not to be understood as disapproving the ratio in *Stilk v Myrick*. They distinguished the present case but in so doing they effectively limited the application of the ratio in *Stilk v Myrick*. As the owners in *Stilk v Myrick* would appear to have enjoyed similar practical benefits to those enjoyed by Roffey Bros it would seem that the reason for distinguishing the cases rests on the clear absence of any fraud, economic duress or other improper pressure, as emphasised by the Court of Appeal in *Williams v Roffey*.

The legal situation would now seem to be that *the performance of an existing contractual duty can amount to consideration for a new promise* in circumstances where there is no question of fraud or duress, and where practical benefits accrue to the promisor. Such a conclusion not only concurs with the approach suggested earlier by Lord Denning in *Ward v Byham* and *Williams v Williams* but also reflects commercial practice where contracts are frequently renegotiated in the course of their performance.

The foregoing has considered the situation that operates between the parties to an existing contract. It has long been recognised that the performance of a contract duty owed to one person can amount to valid consideration *for the promise made by another person.*

In *Shadwell v Shadwell* (1860) the plaintiff had entered into a contract to marry. His uncle promised that if he went ahead with his marriage he would pay him £150 per year, until his earnings reached a certain sum. When the uncle died owing several years' payment, the nephew successfully sued his estate for the outstanding money. It was held that going through with the marriage was sufficient consideration for the uncle's promise, even although the nephew was already contractually bound to his fiancée.

At common law, if A owes B £10 but B agrees to accept £5 in full settlement of the debt, B's promise to give up existing rights must be supported by consideration on the part of A. In *Pinnel's case* (1602) it was stated that a payment of a lesser sum cannot be any satisfaction for the whole. This opinion was approved in *Foakes v Beer* (1884) where Mrs Beer had obtained a judgment in debt against Dr Foakes for £2,091. She had agreed in writing to accept payment of this amount in instalments. When payment was finished she claimed a further £360 as interest due on the judgment debt. It was held that Beer was entitled to the interest as her promise to accept the bare debt was not supported by any consideration from Foakes.

It can be appreciated that there are some similarities between the rule in *Foakes v Beer* and the rule in *Stilk v Myrick* in the way in which promisors escape subsequent liability for their promises. In the former case, however, the promisor was being asked to give up what she was legally entitled to insist on; whereas in the latter the promisors were being asked to provide more than they were legally required to.

As has been considered above the rule in *Stilk v Myrick* has been subsequently modified and made less strict in its application by *Williams v Roffey Bros.* However, no corresponding modification has taken place in relation to *Foakes v Beer*; indeed the Court of Appeal has recently rejected the argument that it should be so modified.

In *Re Selectmove Ltd* (1994) in negotiations relating to money owed to the Inland Revenue the company had agreed with the collector of taxes that it would pay off the debt by

6.5.5   Consideration in relation to the waiver of existing rights

instalments. The company started paying off the debt only to be faced with a demand from the Revenue that the total be paid off immediately on the threat of liquidation. It was argued for the company, on the basis of *Williams v Roffey Bros*, that its payment of the debt was sufficient consideration for the promise of the Revenue to accept it in instalments. It was held that situations relating to the payment of debt were distinguishable from those relating to the supply of goods and services, and that in the case of the former the court was bound to follow the clear authority of the House of Lords in *Foakes v Beer*.

The practical validity of the distinction drawn by the Court of Appeal is, to say the least, arguable. It ignores the fact that payment by instalments, and indeed part payment, is substantially better than no payment at all, which is a possible, if not likely, outcome of liquidating businesses in an attempt to recover the full amount of a debt. It is surely unnecessarily harsh to deny legal enforceability to re-negotiated agreements in relation to debt where the terms have been re-negotiated freely without any suggestion of fraud, or coercion. Nonetheless the Court of Appeal clearly felt itself constrained by the doctrine of binding precedent and had less scope to distinguish *Foakes v Beer* than it had with regard to *Stilk v Myrick*. It remains to be seen whether the House of Lords will be asked to reconsider the operation of *Foakes v Beer* in the light of current commercial practice.

In any case there are a number of situations in which the rule in *Foakes v Beer* does not apply. The following will operate to fully discharge an outstanding debt:

* Payment in kind

  Money's worth is just as capable of satisfying a debt as is money. So A may clear a debt if B agrees to accept something instead of money.

  As considered previously, consideration does not have to be adequate, thus A can discharge a £10 debt by giving B £5 and a chocolate sweet. Payment by cheque is no longer treated as substitute payment in this respect. (*See D & C Builders Ltd v Rees* (1966)).

* Payment of a lesser sum before the due date of payment

  The early payment has, of course, to be acceptable to the party to whom the debt is owed.

* Payment at a different place

  As in the previous case this must be at the wish of the creditor.

- Payment of a lesser sum by a third party
  See *Welby v Drake* (1825)).

- A composition arrangement

  This is an agreement between creditors to the effect that they will accept part-payment of their debts. The individual creditors cannot subsequently seek to recover the unpaid element of the debt (see *Good v Cheesman* (1831)).

It has been seen that English law generally will not enforce gratuitous promises, ie promises not supported by consideration by the promisee. The equitable doctrine of promissory estoppel, however, can sometimes be relied upon to prevent promisors from going back on their promises. The doctrine first appeared in *Hughes v Metropolitan Railway Co* (1877) and was revived by Lord Denning in the High Trees case.

6.5.6   Promissory estoppel

In *Central London Property Trust Ltd v High Tress House Ltd* (1947) the plaintiffs let a block of flats to the defendants, in 1937, at a fixed rent. Due to the war it became difficult to let the flats and the parties renegotiated the rent to half the original amount. No consideration was provided for this agreement. By 1945 all the flats were let and the plaintiffs sought to return to the terms of the original agreement. They claimed they were entitled to the full rent in the future and enquired whether they were owed additional rent for the previous period. It was held that the plaintiffs were entitled to the full rent in the future but were estopped from claiming the full rent for the period from 1941 to 1945.

The precise scope of the doctrine of promissory estoppel is far from certain. There are a number of conflicting judgments on the point, with some judges adopting a wide understanding of its operation, whilst others prefer to keep its effect narrowly constrained. However, the following points may be made:

- It arises from a promise made by a party to an existing contractual agreement

  The promise must have been made with the intention that it be acted upon and must actually have been acted on. It was once thought that the promisee must have acted to their detriment but such detriment is no longer considered necessary (see *WJ Alan & Co v El Nasr Export & Import Co* (1972)).

- It only varies or discharges of rights within a contract

  Promissory estoppel does not apply to the formation of

contract and therefore it does not avoid the need for consideration to establish a contract in the first instance. This point is sometimes made by stating that promissory estoppel is 'a shield and not a sword' (see *Combe v Combe* (1951)).

* It normally only suspends rights

  It is usually open to the promisor, on the provision of reasonable notice, to retract the promise and revert to the original terms of the contract (see *Tool Metal Manufacturing Co v Tungsten Electric Co* (1955)). Rights may be extinguished, however, in the case of a non-continuing obligation, or where the parties cannot resume their original positions. (Consider *D & C Builders v Rees* (1966) below). It is clear that had the builders been able to reply on promissory estoppel the Rees family would have *permanently* lost their right to recover the full amount of the original debt.)

* The promise relied upon must be given voluntarily

  As an equitable remedy the benefit of promissory estoppel will not be extended to those who have behaved in an inequitable manner. Thus, if the promise has been extorted through fraud, duress, or any other inequitable manner it will not be relied on and the common law rules will apply.

  In *D & C Builders v Rees* (1966) the defendants owed the plaintiffs £482, but would agree to pay only £300. As the builders were in financial difficulties they accepted the £300 in full settlement of the account. The plaintiffs later successfully claimed the outstanding balance on the grounds that they had been forced to accept the lesser sum. As the defendants themselves had not acted in an equitable manner they were denied the protection of the equitable remedy and the case was decided on the basis of the rule in *Pinnel's case*.

6.5.7   Promissory estoppel
         after *Williams v Roffey*

It is likely that the decision in *Williams v Roffey* will reduce the need for reliance on promissory estoppel in cases involving the re-negotiation of contracts for the supply of goods or services since performance of existing duties may now provide consideration for new promises. As was stated previously with regard to *Re Selectmove*, however, the same claim cannot be made in relation to partial payments of debts. Those situations are still subject to the rule in *Foakes v Beer* as, uncertainly, modified by the operation of promissory estoppel. As estoppel is generally only suspensory in effect, it is always open to the promisor, at least in the case of continuing debts, to re-impose the original terms by withdrawing their new promise. Although it is at least arguable that *Foakes and Beer* would itself be decided differently on the basis of promissory estoppel, on the grounds that it involved a one-off debt, it is unlikely that the same would be true in regard to *Re Selectmove* which involved a continuing debt.

There is some debate as to whether privity is a principle in its own right, or whether it is simply a conclusion from the more general rules relating to consideration. In any case it is a general rule that a contract can only impose rights or obligations on persons who are parties to it. This is the doctrine of privity and its operation may be seen in *Dunlop v Selfridge* (1915). In this case Dunlop sold tyres to a distributor, Dew & Co, on terms that the distributor would not sell them at less than the manufacturer's list price, and that they would extract a similar undertaking from anyone they supplied with tyres. Dew & Co resold the tyres to Selfridge who agreed to abide by the restrictions and to pay Dunlop £5 for each tyre they sold in breach of them. When Selfridge sold tyres at below Dunlop's list price, Dunlop sought to recover the promised £5 per tyre sold. It was held that Dunlop could not recover damages on the basis of the contract between Dew and Selfridge to which they were not a party.

There are, however, a number of ways in which consequences of the application of strict rule of privity may be avoided to allow a third party to enforce a contract. These occur where:

- The beneficiary sues in some other capacity

  Although an individual may not originally be party to a particular contract they may, nonetheless, acquire the power to enforce the contract where they are legally appointed to administer the affairs of one of the original parties. An example of this can be seen in *Beswick v Beswick* (1967) where a coal merchant sold his business to his nephew in return for a consultancy fee of £6.10s during his lifetime, and thereafter an annuity of £5 per week payable to his widow. After the uncle died the nephew stopped paying the widow. When she became administratrix of her husband's estate she sued the nephew for specific performance of the agreement in that capacity as well as in her personal capacity. It was held that, although she was not a party to the contract and therefore could not be granted specific performance in her personal capacity, such an order could be awarded to her as the administratrix of the deceased person's estate.

6.6   Privity of contract

- The situation involves a collateral contract

  A collateral contract arises where one party promises something to another party if that other party enters into a contract with a third party eg A promises to give B something if B enters into a contract with C. In such a situation the second party can enforce the original promise ie B can insist on A complying with the original promise. It may be seen from this that, although treated as an exception to the privity rule, a collateral contract conforms with the requirements which relate to the establishment of any other contract: consideration for the original promise being the making of the second contract. An example of the operation of a collateral contracts will demonstrate, however, the way in which the courts tend to 'construct' collateral contracts in order to achieve what they see as fair dealing.

  In *Shanklin Pier v Detel Products Ltd* (1951) the plaintiffs contracted to have their pier repainted. On the basis of promises as to its quality, the defendants persuaded the pier company to insist that a particular paint produced by Detel be used. The painters used the paint but it proved unsatisfactory. The plaintiffs sued for breach of the original promise as to the paint's suitability. The defendants countered that the only contract they had entered into was between them and the painters to whom they had sold the paint, and that as the pier company were not a party to that contract they had no right of action against Detel. The pier company were successful. It was held that in addition to the contract for the sale of paint, there was a second collateral contract between the plaintiffs and the defendants by which the latter guaranteed the suitability of the paint in return for the pier company specifying that the painters used it.

- There is a valid assignment of the benefit of the contract

  A party to a contract can transfer the *benefit* of that contract to a third party through the formal process of assignment. The assignment must be in writing, and the assignee receives no better rights under the contract than the assignor possessed. The *burden* of a contract cannot be assigned without the consent of the other party to the contract.

- One of the parties has entered the contract as a trustee for a third party

  There exists the possibility that a party to a contract can create a contract specifically for the benefit of a third party.

In such limited circumstances the promisee is considered as a trustee of the contractual promise for the benefit of the third party. In order to enforce the contract the third party must act through the promisee by making them a party to any action. For a consideration of this possibility see *Les Affreteurs Reunis SA v Leopold Walford (London) Ltd* (1919).

The other main exception to the privity rule is agency, where the agent brings about contractual relations between two other parties even where the existence of the agency has not been disclosed.

In the area of motoring insurance statute law has intervened to permit third parties to claim directly against insurers, but much wider statutory intervention has been proposed by a recent Law Commission Report (1991) which recommended that third parties should be entitled to enforce contracts entered into for their benefit. At present if someone buys a present for someone else and it turns out to be faulty then, due to the operation of the privity rule, the recipient of the present has no contractual rights against the supplier. The Law Commission's proposal would remove this legal technicality by permitting the third party to take action against the supplier.

Capacity refers to a person's ability to enter into a contract. In general, all adults of sound mind have full capacity. The capacity of certain individuals, however, is limited.	**6.7 Capacity**

A minor is a person under the age of 18 (the age of majority was reduced from 21 to 18 by the Family Reform Act (1969)). The law tries to protect such persons by restricting their contractual capacity and thus preventing them from entering into disadvantageous agreements. The rules which apply are a mixture of common law and statute, and depend on when the contract was made. Contracts entered into after 9 June 1987 are subject to the Minors' Contracts Act (1987) which replaced the Infants Relief Act (1874). Agreements entered into by minors may be classified within three possible categories.	**6.8 Minors**

Contracts can be enforced against minors where they relate to the following:	6.8.1 Valid contracts

• Contracts for necessaries

A minor is bound to pay for necessaries, ie things necessary to maintain the minor. Necessaries are defined in the Sale of Goods Act s 3 as goods suitable to the condition in life of the minor and their actual requirements at the time of sale. The operation of this section is demonstrated in Nash v Inman (1908) where a tailor sued a minor to whom he had supplied clothes, including 11 fancy waistcoats. The minor was an undergraduate at Cambridge University at the time. It was held that, although the clothes were suitable according to the minor's station in life, they were not necessary, as he already had sufficient clothing.

The minor is, in any case, only required to pay a reasonable price for any necessaries purchased.

- Beneficial contracts of service

  A minor is bound by a contract of apprenticeship or employment, as long as it is, on the whole, for their benefit.

  In *Doyle v White City Stadium* (1935) Doyle, a minor, obtained a professional boxer's licence, which was treated as a contract of apprenticeship. The licence provided that he would be bound by the rules of the Boxing Board of Control, who had the power to retain any prize money if he was ever disqualified in a fight. He claimed that the licence was void as it was not for his benefit; but it was held that the conditions of the licence were enforceable. In spite of the penal clause it was held that, taken as whole, it was beneficial to him.

  There has to be an element of education or training in the contract and ordinary trading contracts will not be enforced. See for example *Mercantile Union Guarantee Corp v Ball* (1937) where a minor, who operated a haulage business, was not held liable on a hire-purchase contract he had entered into in relation to that business.

6.8.2   Voidable contracts

Voidable contracts are binding on the minor, unless they are repudiated during the period of minority or within a reasonable time after reaching the age of majority. These are generally transactions in which the minor acquires an interest of a permanent nature with continuing obligations. Examples are contracts for shares, or leases of property, or partnership agreements.

If the minor has made payments prior to repudiation of the contract, such payment cannot be recovered unless there is a total failure of consideration, and the minor has received no benefit whatsoever. An example is the case of *Steinberg v Scala (Leeds)* (1923). A Miss Steinberg, while still a minor, applied for, and was allotted, shares in the defendant company. After paying some money on the shares she defaulted on payment and repudiated the contract. The company agreed that her name be removed from its register of members, but refused to return the money she had already paid. It was held that Steinberg was not entitled to the return of the money paid. She had benefitted from membership rights and thus there had not been a complete failure of consideration.

Under the Infants Relief Act (1874) the following contracts were stated to be absolutely void:

- Contracts for the repayment of loans;
- Contracts for goods other than necessaries;
- Accounts stated ie admissions of money owed.

6.8.3   Void contracts

In addition, no action could be brought on the basis of the ratification, made after the attainment of full age, of an otherwise void contract.

The main effect of the Minors' Contracts Act 1987 was that the contracts set out in the Infants Relief Act were no longer to be considered as absolutely void. As a consequence, unenforceable, as well as voidable, contracts may be ratified on the minor attaining the age of majority.

Although the Infants Relief Act stated that such contracts were absolutely void, in effect, this simply meant that they could not be enforced against the minor. The other party could not normally recover goods or money transferred to the minor. Where, however, the goods had been obtained by fraud on the part of the minor, and where they were still in the minor's possession, the other party could rely on the doctrine of restitution to reclaim them. The minor, on the other hand, could enforce the agreement against the other party. Specific performance would not be available, however, on the grounds that it would be inequitable to grant such an order to minors while it could not be awarded against them.

The Minors' Contracts Act has given the courts wider powers to order the restoration of property acquired by a minor. They are no longer restricted to cases where the minor has acquired the property through fraud but can order restitution where they think it 'just and equitable' to do so.

As there is no minimum age limit in relation to actions in tort, minors may be liable under a tortious action. The courts, however, will not permit a party to enforce a contract indirectly by substituting an action in tort, or quasi-contract, for an action in contract.

6.8.4   Minors liability in tort

In *Leslie v Shiell* (1914) Shiell, whilst a minor, obtained a loan from Leslie by lying about his age. Leslie sued to recover the money as damages in an action for the tort of deceit. It was held, however, that the action must fail as it was simply an indirect means of enforcing the otherwise void contract.

6.9 Mental incapacity and intoxication

A contract by a person who is of unsound mind or under the influence of drink or drugs is *prima facie* valid. In order to avoid a contract such a person must show:

- That their mind was so affected at the time that they were incapable of understanding the nature of their actions; and

- That the other party either knew or ought to have known of their disability.

The person claiming such incapacity, nonetheless, must pay a reasonable price for necessaries sold and delivered to them. The Sale of Goods Act specifically applies the same rules to such people as applies to minors.

6.10 Intention to create legal relations

All of the aspects considered previously may well be present in a particular agreement, and yet there still may not be a contract. In order to limit the number of cases that might otherwise be brought, the courts will only enforce those agreements which the parties intended to have legal effect. Although expressed in terms of the parties' intentions, the test for the presence of such intention is once again an objective, rather than a subjective, one. For the purposes of this topic, agreements can be divided into three categories, in which different presumptions apply.

6.10.1 Domestic and social agreements

In this type of agreement there is a presumption that the parties do not intend to create legal relations.

Balfour v Balfour (1919)

When a husband returned from Ceylon to take up his employment he promised his wife, who could not return with him due to health problems, that he would pay her £30 per month as maintenance. When the marriage later ended in divorce the wife sued for the promised maintenance. It was held that the parties had not intended the original promise to be binding and therefore it was not legally enforceable.

It is essential to realise that the intention not to create legal relations in such relationships is only a presumption and that, as with all presumptions, it may be rebutted by the actual facts and circumstances of a particular case. A case in point is *Merritt v Merritt* (1970). After a husband had left the matrimonial home he met his wife and promised to pay her £40 per month, from which she undertook to pay the outstanding mortgage on their house. The husband, at the wife's insistence, signed a note agreeing to transfer the house into the wife's sole name when the mortgage was paid off. The wife paid off the mortgage but the husband refused to transfer the house. It was held that the agreement was enforceable as in the circumstances the parties had clearly intended to enter into a legally enforceable agreement.

In commercial situations the strong presumption is that the parties intend to enter into a legally binding relationship in consequence of their dealings.

6.10.2 Commercial agreements

In *Edwards v Skyways* (1964) employers undertook to make an *ex gratia* payment to an employee they had made redundant. It was held that in such a situation the use of the term *ex gratia* was not sufficient to rebut the presumption that the establishment of legal relations had been intended. The former employee, therefore, was entitled to the payment promised.

As with other presumptions this one is open to rebuttal. In commercial situations, however, the presumption is so strong that it will usually take express wording to the contrary to avoid its operation. An example can be found in *Rose & Frank Co v Crompton Bros* (1925) in which it was held that an express clause stating that no legal relations were to be created by a business transaction was effective. Another example is *Jones v Vernon's Pools Ltd* (1938) where the plaintiff claimed to have submitted a correct pools forecast, but the defendants denied receiving it and relied on a clause in the coupon which stated that the transaction was 'binding in honour' only. Under such circumstances it was held that the plaintiff had no cause for an action in contract as no legal relations had been created.

Agreements between employers and trade unions may be considered as a distinct category of agreement, for although they are commercial agreements, they are presumed not to give rise to legal relations, and, therefore, are not normally enforceable in the courts. Such was the outcome of *Ford Motor Co v AUEFW* (1969) in which it was held that Ford could not take legal action against the defendant trade union which had ignored previously negotiated terms of a collective agreement.

6.10.3 Collective agreements

Once again this presumption can be rebutted if the circumstances of the particular case make it clear that the parties intend legal relations to be created.

Such documents are generally used by parent companies to encourage potential lenders to extend credit to their subsidiary companies by stating their intention to provide financial backing for those subsidiaries. It is generally the case that such letters of comfort merely amount to statements of present

6.10.4 Letters of comfort

intention on the part of the parent company and therefore they do not amount to offers that can be accepted by the creditors of any subsidiary companies. Given the operation of the doctrine of separate personality this effectively leaves the creditors with no legal recourse against the parent company for any loans granted to the subsidiary (see para 15.2.2).

In *Kleinwort Benson v Malaysian Mining Corp* (1989) the defendant company had issued a letter of comfort to the plaintiffs in respect of its subsidiary company MMC Metals. However, when MMC Metals went into liquidation the defendants failed to make good its debts to the plaintiffs.

At first instance the judge decided in favour of the plaintiffs, holding that in such commercial circumstances the defendants had failed to rebut the presumption that there had been an intention to create legal relations. On appeal it was held that, *in the circumstances of the instant case*, the letter of comfort did not amount to an offer but a statement of intention which could not bind the defendants contractually. Malaysian Mining Corp, therefore, was not legally responsible for the debt of its subsidiary.

It is important to note that the *Kleinwort Benson* case opens up the possibility that, *under different circumstances*, letters of comfort might be considered to constitute offers capable of being accepted and leading to contractual relations. Under such circumstances the presumption as to the intention to create legal relations as they normally apply in commercial situations will operate; although it is almost inconceivable that a court would decide that a letter of comfort amounted to an offer without also finding an intention to create legal relations.

The Formation of a Contract

In order to create a contract the following factors have to be present.

An offer is a promise, which is capable of acceptance, to be bound on particular terms.

Offer

An offer may be made to a particular person or to a group of people or to the world at large. If the offer is restricted then only the people to whom it is addressed may accept it; but if the offer is made to the public at large, it can be accepted by anyone.

A person cannot accept an offer that they do not know about.

An offer may be revoked at any time before acceptance but cannot be revoked after acceptance.

An offer must be distinguished from an invitation to treat which is an invitation to others to make offers. The person extending the invitation is not bound to accept any offers made to them. Examples are goods in windows and goods on the shelves of supermarkets.

In order to form a binding agreement the acceptance must correspond with the terms of the offer.

Acceptance

The general rule is that acceptance must be communicated to the offeror. Exceptions are where; the offeror has waived the right to receive communication, or acceptance is through the postal service.

English law does not enforce gratuitous promises unless they are made by deed. Consideration consists of 'some benefit to the promisor *or* detriment to the promisee'.

Consideration

Consideration is provided either at the time of the creation of a contract (executed) or at a later date (executory). Past consideration, performed before the promise it seeks to bind, is normally not sufficient, although there are specific exceptions to this where the action was requested by the promisor and payment was expected by the promisee.

Consideration must be sufficient but need not be adequate. The courts will not enquire into the economics of a transaction as long as some consideration is provided.

It generally has been accepted that performance of an existing duty does not provide valid consideration, however, the recent authority of *Williams v Roffey Bros* (1990) has indicated a contrary possibility. The situation would now seem to be that the performance of an existing contractual duty can amount to consideration for a new promise in circumstances where there is no question of fraud or duress, and where practical benefits accrue to the promisor.

Promissory estoppel

The equitable doctrine of promissory estoppel can sometimes be relied upon to prevent promisors from going back on their promises.

Promissory estoppel does not apply to the formation of contract and therefore it does not avoid the need for consideration to establish a contract in the first instance. It only varies or discharges of rights within a contract. It normally only suspends rights. The promise relied upon must be given voluntarily.

Privity

A contract can only impose rights or obligations on persons who are parties to it. Third parties cannot therefore enforce contracts unless they can sue in some other capacity or they can show the existence of a collateral contract, or a trust, or there has been a valid assignment of the benefit of the contract.

Capacity

People under the age of 18 have only a limited capacity to enter into binding agreements. Contracts can be enforced against minors where they relate to contracts for necessaries or beneficial contracts of service. Other commercial contracts are unenforceable against a minor.

Voidable contracts are binding on a minor, unless they are repudiated during the period of minority or within a reasonable time after reaching the age of majority.

As a consequence of the Minors' Contracts Act 1987, unenforceable, as well as voidable, contracts may be ratified on the minor attaining the age of majority.

The courts will not permit a party to enforce a contract indirectly by substituting an action in tort, or quasi-contract, for an action in contract.

A contract by a person who is of unsound mind or under the influence of drink or drugs is prima facie valid. The person claiming incapacity must show that they were incapable of understanding the nature of their action and that the other party was aware of this. Nonetheless, they must pay a reasonable price for necessaries sold to them.

The courts will only enforce those agreements which the parties intended to have legal effect.

In social and domestic agreements there is a rebuttable presumption that the parties do not intend to create legal relations.

In commercial and business agreements there is a rebuttable presumption that the parties intend to create legal relations.

Agreements between employers and trade unions, although commercial in nature, are presumed not to give rise to legal relations.

Letters of comfort usually amount to statements of present intention and do not amount to offers capable of acceptance.

Intention to create legal relations

Chapter 7

Contents of a Contract

The previous chapter dealt with how a binding contractual agreement comes to be formed; this chapter will consider what the parties have actually agreed to do.

As the parties will normally be bound to perform any promise that they have contracted to undertake, it is important to decide precisely what promises are included in the contract. Some statements do not form part of a contract, even though they might have induced the other party to enter into the contract. These pre-contractual statements are called representations. The consequences of such representations being false will be considered in Chapter 8, but for the moment it is sufficient to distinguish them from contractual terms, which are statements which do form part of the contract. There are four tests for distinguishing a contractual term from a mere representation:

- Where the statement is of such major importance that the promisee would not have entered into the agreement without it, then it will be construed as a term. In *Bannerman v White* (1861) as the defendant wanted to buy hops for brewing purposes, he asked the plaintiff if they had been treated with sulphur. On the basis of the plaintiff's false statement that they had not been so treated, he agreed to buy the hops. When he discovered later that they had been treated with sulphur, he refused to accept them. It was held that the plaintiff's statement about the sulphur was a fundamental term of the contract, and since it was not true, the defendant was entitled to repudiate the contract.

- Where there is a time gap between the statement and the making of the contract, then the statement will most likely be treated as a representation.

  In *Routledge v McKay* (1954) on 23 October the defendant told the plaintiff that a motorcycle was a 1942 model. On 30 October a written contract for the sale of the bike was made, without reference to its age. The bike was actually a 1930 model. It was held that the statement about the date was a pre-contractual representation, and the plaintiff could not sue for damages for breach of contract. However, this rule is not a hard and fast one. In *Schawell v Reade* (1913), the court held that a statement made three months before the final agreement was part of the contract.

- Where the statement is oral, and the agreement is subsequently drawn up in written form, then the exclusion from the written document will suggest that the statement was not meant to be a contractual term. *Routledge v McKay* may also be cited as authority for this proposition.

- Where one of the parties to an agreement has special knowledge or skill, then statements made by them will be terms, but statements made to them will not.

  In *Dick Bentley Productions Ltd v Harold Smith (Motors) Ltd* (1965) the plaintiff bought a Bentley car from the defendant after being assured that it had only travelled 20,000 miles since its engine and gearbox had been replaced. When this statement turned out to be untrue the plaintiff sued for breach of contract. It was held that the statement was a term of the contract and the plaintiff was entitled to damages.

  In *Oscar Chess Ltd v Williams* (1957) Williams traded in one car when buying another from the plaintiffs. He told them that his trade-in was a 1948 model; whereas it was actually a 1939 model. The company unsuccessfully sued for breach of contract. The statement as to the age of the car was merely a representation, and the right to sue for misrepresentation had been lost due to delay.

7.2 Conditions, warranties, and innominate terms

Once it is decided that a statement is a term, rather than merely a pre-contractual representation, it is necessary to determine which type of term it is, in order to determine what remedies are available for its breach.

Terms can be classified as one of three types.

7.2.1 Conditions

A condition is a fundamental part of the agreement – it is something which goes to the root of the contract. Breach of a condition gives the innocent party the right either to terminate the contract and refuse to perform their part of it, or to go through with the agreement and sue for damages.

7.2.2 Warranties

A warranty is a subsidiary obligation which is not vital to the overall agreement, and does not totally destroy its efficacy. Breach of a warranty does not give the right to terminate the agreement. The innocent party has to complete their part of the agreement, and can only sue for damages.

The difference between the two types of term can be seen in the following cases:

In *Poussard v Spiers & Pond* (1876) the plaintiff had contracted with the defendants to sing in an opera they were producing. Due to illness she was unable to appear on the first night, or for some nights thereafter. When Mme Poussard recovered, the defendants refused her services as they had hired a replacement for the whole run of the opera. It was held that her failure to appear on the opening night had been a breach of a condition, and the defendants were at liberty to treat the contract as discharged.

In *Bettini v Gye* (1876) the plaintiff had contracted with the defendants to complete a number of engagements. He had also agreed to be in London for rehearsals six days before his opening performance. Due to illness, he only arrived three days before the opening night, and the defendants refused his services. On this occasion it was held that there was only a breach of warranty. The defendants were entitled to damages, but could not treat the contract as discharged.

The distinction between the effects of a breach of condition as against the effects of a breach of warranty was enshrined in s 11 of the Sale of Goods Act 1893 (now SGA 1979). For some time it was thought that these were the only two types of term possible, the nature of the remedy available being prescribed by the particular type of term concerned. This simple classification has subsequently been rejected by the courts as too restrictive, and a third type of term has emerged: the innominate term.

In this case, the remedy is not prescribed in advance simply by whether the term breached is a condition or a warranty, but depends on the consequence of the breach.	7.2.3 Innominate terms

If the breach deprives the innocent party of 'substantially the whole benefit of the contract', then the right to repudiate will be permitted even if the term might otherwise appear to be a mere warranty.

If, however, the innocent party does not lose 'substantially the whole benefit of the contract', then they will not be permitted to repudiate but must settle for damages, even if the term might otherwise appear to be a condition.

In *Cehave v Bremer (The Hansa Nord)* (1976) a contract for the sale of a cargo of citrus pulp pellets, to be used as animal feed, provided that they were to be delivered in good condition. On delivery, the buyers rejected the cargo as not complying with this provision, and claimed back the price paid from the sellers. The buyers eventually obtained the pellets when the cargo was sold off, and used them for their original purpose. It was held that since the breach had not been serious, the buyers had not been free to reject the cargo, and the sellers had acted lawfully in retaining the money paid.

7.3	**Express and implied terms**	So far, all the cases considered have involved express terms: statements actually made by one of the parties, either by word of mouth or in writing. Implied terms, however, are not actually stated, but are introduced into the contract by implication. Implied terms can be divided into three types.

7.3.1 Terms implied by statute

For example, under the Sale of Goods Act 1979, terms relating to description, merchantable quality, and fitness for purpose are all implied into sale of goods contracts. (For consideration of these implied terms see Chapter 10.)

7.3.2 Terms implied by custom

An agreement may be subject to customary terms, not actually specified by the parties. For example, in *Hutton v Warren* (1836) it was held that customary usage permitted a farm tenant to claim an allowance for seed and labour on quitting his tenancy. It should be noted, however, that custom cannot override the express terms of an agreement (*Les Affreteurs v Walford* (1919)).

7.3.3 Terms implied by the courts

Generally it is a matter for the parties concerned to decide the terms of a contract, but on occasion the court will presume that the parties intended to include a term which is not expressly stated. They will do so where it is necessary to give business efficacy to the contract.

Whether a term may be implied can be decided on the basis of 'the officious bystander' test. Imagine two parties, A and B, negotiating a contract. A third party, C, interrupts to suggest a particular provision. A and B reply that that particular term is understood. In just such a way the court will decide that a term should be implied into a contract.

In *The Moorcock* (1889) the appellants, owners of a wharf, contracted with the respondents to permit them to discharge their ship at the wharf. It was apparent to both parties that when the tide was out the ship would rest on the river bed. When the tide was out the ship sustained damage by settling on a ridge. It was held that there was an implied warranty in the contract that the place of anchorage should be safe for the ship. As a consequence the shipowner was entitled to damages for breach of that term.

7.4 The parol evidence rule

If all the terms of a contract are in writing, then there is a strong presumption that no evidence supporting a different oral agreement will be permitted to vary those terms.

In *Hutton v Watling* (1948) on the sale of a business together with its goodwill, a written agreement was drawn up and signed by the vendor. In an action to enforce one of the clauses in the agreement the vendor claimed that it did not represent the whole contract. It was held that the vendor was not entitled to introduce evidence on this point as the written document represented a true record of the contract.

The presumption against introducing contrary oral evidence can be rebutted, however, where it is shown that the document was not intended to set out all of the terms agreed on by the parties.

In *Re SS Ardennes* (1951) a ship's bill of lading stated that it might proceed 'by any route ... directly or indirectly ...'. The defendants promised that the ship would proceed directly to London from Spain with its cargo of tangerines. However, the ship called at Antwerp before heading for London, and as a result the tangerines had to be sold at a reduced price. The shippers successfully sued for damages as it was held that the bill of lading did not constitute the contract between the parties, but merely evidenced their intentions. The verbal promise was part of the final contract.

In a sense, an exemption clause is no different from any other clause, in that it seeks to define the rights and obligations of the parties to a contract. However, an exemption clause is a term in a contract which tries to exempt, or limit, the liability of a party in breach of the agreement. Exclusion clauses give rise to most concern when they are included in 'standard form' contracts, in which one party, in a position of commercial dominance, imposes their terms on the other party, who has no choice (other than to take it or leave it) as far as the terms of the contract go. Such standard form contracts are contrary to the ideas of consensus and negotiation which underpin contract law; for this reason they have received particular attention from both the judiciary and the legislature, in an endeavour to counteract their perceived unfairness.

The actual law relating to exclusion clauses is complicated by the interplay of the common law, the Unfair Contract Terms Act 1977, and the various Acts which imply certain terms into particular contracts. However, the following questions should always be asked with regard to exclusion clauses:

- Has the exclusion clause been incorporated into the contract?

- Does the exclusion clause effectively cover the breach?

- What effect does the Unfair Contract Terms Act have on the exclusion clause?

7.5 Exemption or exclusion clauses

7.5.1   Has the exclusion
         clause been
         incorporated into the
         contract?

An exclusion clause cannot be effective unless it is actually a term of a contract. There are three ways in which such a term may be inserted into a contractual agreement, by:

• Signature

  If a person signs a contractual document, then they are bound by its terms, even if they did not read it.

  In *L'Estrange v Graucob* (1934) a café owner bought a vending machine, signing a contract without reading it, which took away all her rights under the Sale of Goods Act 1893. When the machine proved faulty she sought to take action against the vendors, but it was held that she had no cause of action as she had signified her consent to the terms of the contract by signing it.

  The rule in *L'Estrange v Graucob* may be avoided where the party seeking to rely on the exclusion clause misled the other party into signing the contract (*Curtis v Chemical Cleaning & Dyeing Co* (1951)).

• Notice

  Apart from the above, an exclusion clause will not be incorporated into a contract unless the party affected actually knew of it, or was given sufficient notice of it. In order for notice to be adequate, the document bearing the exclusion clause must be an integral part of the contract, and given at the time the contract is made.

  In *Chapleton v Barry UDC* (1940) the plaintiff hired a deck-chair and received a ticket which stated on the back that the council would not be responsible for any injuries arising from the hire of the chairs. After he was injured because his chair collapsed, Chapleton successfully sued the council. It was held that the ticket was merely a receipt, and could not be used effectively to communicate the exclusion clause.

  In *Olley v Marlborough Court Ltd* (1949) a couple arrived at a hotel and paid for a room in advance. On reaching their room they found a notice purporting to exclude the hotel's liability in regard to thefts of goods not handed in to the manager. A thief later stole the wife's purse. It was held that the hotel could not escape liability since the disclaimer had only been made after the contract had been formed.

  Whether the degree of notice given has been sufficient is a matter of fact, but in *Thornton v Shoe Lane Parking Ltd* (1971) it was stated that the greater the exemption, the greater the degree of notice required.

- Custom

  Where the parties have had previous dealings on the basis of an exclusion clause, that clause may be included in later contracts (*Spurling v Bradshaw* (1956)), but it has to be shown that the party affected had actual knowledge of the exclusion clause.

  In *Hollier v Rambler Motors* (1972) on each of the previous occasions when the plaintiff had his car repaired at the defendant's garage he had signed a form containing an exclusion clause. On the last occasion he had not signed such a form. When the car was damaged by fire through negligence the defendants sought to rely on the exclusion clause. It was held that there was no evidence that Hollier had been aware of the clause to which he had been agreeing and, therefore, it could not be considered a part of his last contract.

As a consequence of the disfavour with which the judiciary have looked on exclusion clauses, they have developed a number of rules of construction which operate to restrict the effectiveness of exclusion clauses. These are:

7.5.2   Does the exclusion clause effectively cover the breach?

- The *contra proferentum* rule

  This requires that any uncertainties or ambiguities in the exclusion clause be interpreted against the meaning claimed for it by the person seeking to rely on it.

  In *Andrews v Singer* (1934) the plaintiffs contracted to buy some 'new Singer cars' from the defendant. A clause excluded 'all conditions, warranties and liabilities implied by statute, common law, or otherwise'. One car supplied was not new. It was held that the requirement that the cars be new was an express condition of the contract and therefore was not covered by the exclusion clause which only referred to implied clauses.

  In *Hollier v Rambler* it was stated that as the exclusion clause in question could be interpreted as applying only to non-negligent accidental damage, or alternatively to include damage caused by negligence; it should be restricted to the former, narrower, interpretation. As a consequence, the plaintiff could recover for damages caused to his car by the defendant's negligence.

- The doctrine of fundamental breach

  In a series of complicated and conflicting cases, ending with the House of Lords decision in *Photo Production v Securicor*, some courts attempted to develop a rule that it was impossible to exclude liability for breach of contract if a fundamental breach of the contract had occurred ie the party in breach had failed altogether to perform the contract.

In *Photo Production v Securicor Transport* (1980) the defendants had entered into a contract with the plaintiffs to guard their factory. An exclusion clause exempted Securicor from liability even if one of their employees caused damage to the factory. One of the guards later deliberately set fire to the factory. Securicor claimed the protection of the exclusion clause. It was ultimately decided by the House of Lords that whether an exclusion clause could operate after a fundamental breach was a matter of construction. There was no absolute rule that total failure of performance rendered such clauses inoperative. The exclusion clause in this particular case was wide enough to cover the events that took place and so Photo Production's action failed.

7.5.3 What effect does the Unfair Contract Terms Act 1977 have on the exclusion clause?

This act represents the statutory attempt to control exclusion clauses. In spite of its title, it is really aimed at unfair exemption clauses, rather than contract terms generally. It also covers non-contractual notices which purport to exclude liability under the Occupiers' Liability Act 1957. The controls under the Act relate to two areas:

* Negligence

  There is an absolute prohibition on exemption clauses in relation to liability in negligence resulting in death or injury (ss 2 and 5). Exemption clauses relating to liability for other damage caused by negligence will only be enforced to the extent that they satisfy the 'requirement of reasonableness' (s 5).

  In *Smith v Bush* (1989) the plaintiff bought a house on the basis of a valuation report carried out for her building society by the defendant. The surveyor had included a disclaimer of liability for negligence in his report to the building society and sought to rely on that fact when the plaintiff sued after the chimneys of the property collapsed. The House of Lords held that the disclaimer was an exemption clause and that it failed the requirement that such terms should be reasonable.

* Contract

  These provisions apply in consumer transactions. They also apply in non-consumer transactions, where one party deals on the other's standard terms. Any exclusion clause which seeks to avoid liability for breach of contract is only valid to the extent that it complies with the 'requirement of reasonableness' (s 2). This test also applies where a clause seeks to permit a party to avoid performing the contract completely, or to permit performance less than reasonably expected.

The implied term relating to title, under s 12 of the Sale of Goods Act, cannot be excluded in any contract (s 6(1)).

The other implied terms as to description, fitness, merchantable quality, and sample, cannot be excluded in a consumer contract (s 6(2)); and in a non-consumer transaction any restriction is subject to the 'requirement of reasonableness' (s 6(3)).

A person deals as a consumer if they do not make the contract in the course of business, nor hold themselves out as so doing, and the other party does make the contract in the course of business, the goods being supplied normally for private consumption (s 12).

The requirement of reasonableness means 'fair and reasonable ... having regard to the circumstances ...' (s 11). The second schedule of the Act provides guidelines for the application of the reasonableness test in regard to non-consumer transactions, but it is likely that similar considerations will be taken into account by the courts in consumer transactions. Amongst these considerations are:

• The relative strength of the parties' bargaining power;

• Whether any inducement was offered in return for the limitation on liability;

• Whether the customer knew, or ought to have known, about the existence or extent of the exclusion;

• Whether the goods were manufactured or adapted to the special order of the customer.

In *George Mitchell (Chesterhall) Ltd v Finney Lock Seeds Ltd* (1983) the respondents planted 63 acres with cabbage seed supplied by the appellants. The crop failed, due partly to the fact that the wrong type of seed had been supplied, and partly to the fact that the seed supplied was of inferior quality. When the respondents claimed damages, the sellers relied on the protection of a clause in their standard conditions of sale limiting their liability to replacing the seeds supplied or refunding payment. It was held, however, that the respondents were entitled to compensation for the loss of the crop. The House of Lords decided that although the exemption clause was sufficiently clear and unambiguous to be effective at common law, it failed the test of reasonableness under the Unfair Contract Terms Act.

It is likely that many of the situations in the cases considered under the common law prior to the UCTA would now be decided under the Act. It is still important, however, to understand the common law principles for the very good reason that the UCTA does not apply in many important situations. Amongst these are transactions relating to insurance, interests in land, patents and other intellectual property, the transfer of securities, and the formation of companies or partnerships.

Contents of a Contract

There are four tests for distinguishing a contractual term from a mere representation:

- Where the statement is of such major importance that the promisee would not have entered into the agreement without it, then it will be construed as a term.

- Where there is a time gap between the statement and the making of the contract, then the statement will most likely be treated as a representation.

- Where the statement is oral, and the agreement is subsequently drawn up in written form, then the exclusion from the written document will suggest that the statement was not meant to be a contractual term.

- Where one of the parties to an agreement has special knowledge or skill, then statements made by them will be terms, but statements made to them will not.

Contract terms and mere representations

Terms can be classified as one of three types:

- A condition is a fundamental part of the agreement – it is something which goes to the root of the contract.

- A warranty is a subsidiary obligation which is not vital to the overall agreement, and does not totally destroy its efficacy.

- In the case of an innominate term if the innocent party is deprived of 'substantially the whole benefit of the contract', then the right to repudiate will be permitted even if the term might otherwise appear to be a mere warranty.

Terms

Express terms are the terms which the parties themselves state are to be in the contract.

Express terms

Implied terms are terms which are not expressly stated but which are nonetheless treated as part of the contractual agreement.

Implied terms

Terms may be implied by:

- Statute;

- Custom;
- The courts.

The parol evidence rule

If all the terms of a contract are in writing, then there is a strong presumption that no evidence supporting a different oral agreement will be permitted to vary those terms.

Exemption or exclusion clauses

An exemption clause is a term in a contract which tries to exempt, or limit, the liability of a party in breach of the agreement.

The following questions should always be asked with regard to exclusion clauses:

- Has the exclusion clause been incorporated into the contract?

- Does the exclusion clause effectively cover the breach?

- What effect does the Unfair Contract Terms Act have on the exclusion clause?

There are three ways in which such a term may be inserted into a contractual agreement:

- By signature;

- By notice;

- By custom.

The judiciary have developed rules of construction which operate to restrict the effectiveness of exclusion clauses. Foremost amongst these is the *contra proferentum* rule.

The Unfair Contracts Terms Act

The controls under the Unfair Contracts Terms Act relate to two areas:

- There is an absolute prohibition on exemption clauses in relation to liability in negligence resulting in death or injury;

- Any exclusion clause which seeks to avoid liability for breach of contract is only valid to the extent that it complies with the 'requirement of reasonableness'.

Chapter 8

Vitiating Factors

In this chapter it is intended to consider the vitiating factors –
those elements which will render any agreement either void,
or voidable, depending on which vitiating factor is present.
The vitiating factors are:

- Mistake;

- Misrepresentation;

- Duress;

- Undue influence;

- Contracts void or illegal for reasons of public policy.

8.1 Mistake

Generally speaking, the parties to a contract will not be
relieved from the burden of their agreement simply because
they have made a mistake. If one party makes a bad bargain,
that is no reason for setting the contract aside. Very few
mistakes will affect the validity of a contract at common law,
but where a mistake is operative, it will render the contract
void. This has the effect that property transferred under
operative mistake can be recovered, even where it has been
transferred to an innocent third party.

It is usual to divide mistakes into the following three
categories:

- Common mistake;

- Mutual mistake;

- Unilateral mistake.

8.1.2 Common mistake

This is where both parties to an agreement *share the same
mistake* about the circumstances surrounding the transaction.
In order for the mistake to be operative, it must be of a
fundamental nature.

In *Bell v Lever Bros Ltd* (1932) Bell had been employed as
chairman of the company by Lever Bros. When he became
redundant they paid off the remaining part of his service
contract. Only then did they discover that Bell had been guilty
of offences which would have permitted them to dismiss him
without compensation. They claimed to have the payment set
aside on the basis of the common mistake that neither party

had considered the possibility of Bell's dismissal for breach of duty. It was held that the action must fail. The mistake was only as to quality and not sufficiently fundamental to render the contract void.

The cases suggest that a mistake as to quality can never render an agreement void for mistake, and that the doctrine of common mistake is restricted to the following two specific areas:

- *Res extincta*

  In this case, the mistake is as to the existence of the subject matter of the contract.

  In *Couturier v Hastie* (1856) a contract was made in London for the sale of corn being shipped from Salonica. Unknown to the parties, however, the corn had already been sold. It was held that the London contract was void, since the subject matter of the contract was no longer in existence.

  It should be recognised, however, that in *Associated Japanese Bank v Credit du Nord* (1988) a contract was treated as void for common mistake on the basis of the non-existence of some gaming machines, although the agreement in point actually related to a contract of guarantee in relation to the non-existent machines.

- *Res sua*

  In this case, the mistake is that one of the parties to the contract already owns what they are contracting to receive.

  In *Cooper v Phibbs* (1867) Cooper agreed to lease a fishery from Phibbs. It later transpired that he actually owned the fishery. The court decided that the lease had to be set aside at common law . In equity, however, Phibbs was given a lien over the fishery in respect of the money he had spent on improving it, permitting him to hold the property against payment.

  Cooper v Phibbs is an example of one possible way in which equity may intervene in regard to common mistake, namely setting an agreement aside on particular terms. Alternatively, the agreement may even be set aside completely in equity.

- *Magee v Pennine Insurance Co Ltd* (1969)

  A proposal form for car insurance had been improperly filled in by the plaintiff. When the car was subsequently written off, the insurance company offered Magee £375 as a compromise on his claim. After he had accepted this offer, the defendants discovered the error in the proposal form, and sought to repudiate their agreement. It was held that although not void at common law, the agreement could be set aside in equity.

This occurs where the parties are at cross-purposes. They have *different views on the facts* of the situation, but they do not realise it. However, an agreement will not necessarily be void simply because the parties to it are at cross-purposes. In order for mutual mistake to be operative ie to make the contract void, it must comply with an objective test. The court will try to decide which of the competing views of the situation a reasonable person would support, and the contract will be enforceable on such terms.

8.1.3   Mutual mistake

In *Smith v Hughes* (1871) the plaintiff offered to sell oats to the defendant. Hughes wrongly believed that the oats were old, and on discovering that they were new oats, he refused to complete the contract. It was held that the defendant's mistake as to the age of the oats did not make the contract void.

In *Scriven Bros v Hindley & Co* (1913) at an auction, the defendants bid for two lots believing both to be hemp. In fact one of them was tow, an inferior and cheaper substance. Although the auctioneer had not induced the mistake, it was not normal practice to sell hemp and tow together. It was decided that in such circumstances, where one party thought he was buying hemp while the other thought he was selling tow, the contract was not enforceable.

If the court is unable to decide the outcome on the basis of an objective 'reasonable person test', then the contract will be void.

In *Raffles v Wichelhaus* (1864) the defendants agreed to buy cotton from the plaintiffs. The cotton was to arrive 'ex *Peerless* from Bombay'. There were, however, two ships called *Peerless* sailing from Bombay; the first in October, the second in December. Wichelhaus thought he was buying from the first but Raffles thought he was selling from the second. Under the exceptional circumstances it was impossible for the court to decide which party's view was the correct one. It was decided, therefore, that the agreement was void for mutual mistake.

In respect of mutual mistake, equity follows the common law.

In *Tamplin v James* (1880) James purchased a public house at auction. He had believed wrongly that the property for sale included a field which the previous publican had used. The sale particulars stated the property for sale correctly, but James did not refer to them. When he discovered his mistake James refused to complete the transaction. It was held that, in spite of his mistake, an order of specific performance would be granted against James.

8.1.4   Unilateral mistake

This occurs where only *one of the parties to the agreement is mistaken* as to the circumstances of the contract, and the other party is aware of that fact.

Most cases of unilateral mistake also involve misrepresentation, although this need not necessarily be so. It is important to distinguish between these two elements – whereas unilateral mistake makes a contract void, and thus prevents the passing of title in any property acquired under it, misrepresentation merely makes a contract voidable, and good title can be passed before the contract is avoided. This distinction will be seen in *Ingram v Little* and *Phillips v Brooks*.

The cases involving unilateral mistake mainly relate to mistakes as to identity. A contract will only be void for mistake where the seller intended to contract with a different person from the one with whom they did actually contract.

In *Cundy v Lindsay* (1878) a crook named Blenkarn ordered linen handkerchiefs from Cundy. His order, from 37 Wood Street, was signed to look as if it were from Blenkiron & Co, a reputable firm known to Cundy, who carried on business at 123 Wood Street. The goods were sent to Blenkarn, who sold them to Lindsay. Cundy successfully sued Lindsay in the tort of conversion. It was held that he had intended only to deal with Blenkiron & Co. Since there was no contract with Blenkarn, he received no title whatsoever to the goods, and therefore could not pass title on to Lindsay.

Although *King's Norton Metal Company v Edridge, Merrit & Co* (1897) appears to be similar it was decided differently on the grounds that the crook had made use of a completely fictitious company to carry out his fraud. The mistake therefore was with regard to the attributes of the company rather than its identity.

Where the parties enter into a contract face to face, it is generally presumed that the seller intends to deal with the person before them, and therefore they cannot rely on unilateral mistake to avoid the contract.

In *Phillips v Brooks* (1919) a crook selected a number of items in the plaintiff's jewellery shop, and proposed to pay by cheque. On being informed that the goods would have to be retained until the cheque was cleared, he told the jeweller that he was Sir George Bullough of St James's Square. On checking in a directory that such a person did indeed live at that address, the jeweller permitted him to take away a valuable ring. The crook later pawned the ring to the defendant. Phillips then sued the defendant in conversion. It was decided that the contract between Phillips and the crook was *not void for mistake*. There had not been a mistake as to identity, but only as to the creditworthiness of the buyer. The contract had been *voidable for misrepresentation*, but the crook had passed title before Phillips took steps to avoid the contract.

A similar decision was reached by the Court of Appeal in *Lewis v Avery* (1971), in which a crook obtained possession of a car by misrepresenting who he was to the seller. The court declined to follow its earlier decision in *Ingram v Little* (1960), a very similar case. It is generally accepted that *Lewis v Avery* represents the more accurate statement of the law.

Here again equity follows the common law, and considers contracts tainted by unilateral mistake to be void.

There are two mechanisms for dealing with mistakes in written contracts.

8.1.5 Mistake in respect of documents

- Rectification

    Where the written document fails to state the actual intentions of the parties, it may be altered under the equitable doctrine of rectification.

    In *Joscelyne v Nissen* (1970) the plaintiff agreed to transfer his car-hire business to his daughter in return for her agreeing to pay certain household expenses, although this was not stated in a later written contract. The father was entitled to have the agreement rectified to include the terms agreed.

- *Non est factum*

    Where a party signs a contract they will usually be bound by the terms as set out. It is assumed that the signatory has read, understood and agreed to the terms as stated and the courts are generally reluctant to interfere in such circumstances.

    Where, however, someone signs a document under a misapprehension as to its true nature, the law may permit them to claim *non est factum* ie that the document is not their deed. Originally, the mistake relied on had to relate to the type of document signed, but now it is recognised that the defence is open to those who have made a fundamental mistake as to the content of the document they have signed. However, the person signing the document must not have been careless in regard to its content.

    In *Saunders v Anglia Building Society* (1970) Mrs Gallie, a 78-year-old widow, signed a document without reading it whilst her glasses were broken. She had been told, by a person named Lee, that it was a deed of gift to her nephew, but in fact it was a deed of gift to Lee. Lee later mortgaged the property to the respondent building society. Mrs Gallie sought to repudiate the deed of gift on the basis of non est factum. Her action failed. Although it was accepted that she had not been careless, the document was not fundamentally different from what she expected to sign.

This decision can be contrasted with a later successful reliance on the defence in *Lloyd's Bank Plc v Waterhouse* (1990) where the defendant, who was illiterate, intended to provide a guarantee in relation to his son's purchase of a farm. In actual fact the document he signed was a guarantee in relation to all of his son's liabilities. In the Court of Appeal it was decided that the father could rely on *non est factum*. He had not been careless, he had questioned the extent of his liability; and the document was fundamentally different from what he expected to sign.

8.2   Misrepresentation

As was seen in Chapter 7, a statement which induces a person to enter into a contract, but which does not become a term of the contract, is a representation. A false statement of this kind is a *misrepresentation*, and renders the contract *voidable*. The innocent party may rescind the contract, or in some circumstances claim damages (see para 8.2.7).

Misrepresentation can be defined as a false statement of fact, made by one party before or at the time of the contract, which induces the other party to enter into the contract. The following points follow from this definition.

8.2.1   There must be a statement

There is no general duty to disclose information, and silence does not generally amount to a representation. There are exceptions to this rule:

- Where the statement is a half-truth. It may be true, but misleading none the less.

  In *Notts Patent Brick & Tile Co v Butler* (1886) the buyer of land asked the seller's solicitor whether the land was subject to any restrictive covenants. The solicitor said that there were none that he knew of, but did not mention that he had not read the documents to find out. It was held that the solicitor's statement was a misrepresentation, and the buyer could rescind the contract.

- Where the statement was true when made, but has subsequently become false before the contract is concluded.

In *With v O'Flanagan* (1936) in January the seller of a doctor's practice told the prospective buyer that it was worth an income of £2,000 per annum. By the time the contract was concluded its value had dropped substantially to only £5 per week. The court held that the representation was of a continuing nature, and as it was false when it induced the contract, the buyer was entitled to rescind.

• Where the contract is *uberrimae fidei* ie it is based on utmost good faith. In contracts of this nature, such as those involving insurance, there is a duty to disclose all material facts.

The following statements will not amount to a representation:

• Mere sales puffs

    The statement must have some meaningful content. Thus in *Dimmock v Hallett* (1866), it was held that a statement that land was 'fertile and improvable' was not actionable as a misrepresentation.

• Statements of law

    Everyone is presumed to know the law, and therefore, in theory, no one can be misled as to what the law is.

• Statements of opinion

    These are not actionable, because they are not statements of fact.

    In *Bisset v Wilkinson* (1927) the vendor of previously ungrazed land in New Zealand stated that it would be able to support 2,000 sheep. This turned out to be untrue but it was held that the statement was only an expression of opinion and as such was not actionable.

    If, however, the person does not actually believe the truth of the opinion they express, then an action for misrepresentation will be possible (*Edgington v Fitzmaurice* (1884)).

That the statement must actually induce the contract means that:

• The statement must have been made by one party to the contract to the other, and not by a third party;

• The statement must have been addressed to the person claiming to have been misled;

• The person claiming to have been misled must have been aware of the statement;

8.2.2 The statement must actually induce the contract

- The person claiming to have been misled must have relied on the statement.

In *Horsfall v Thomas* (1962) Horsfall made and sold a gun to Thomas. He concealed a fault in it by means of a metal plug, but Thomas never even examined the gun. After short usage, the gun blew apart. Thomas claimed that he had been misled, by the plug, into buying the gun. It was held that the plug could not have misled him as he had not examined the gun at the time of purchase.

Whether the reliance was reasonable or not is not material once the party claiming misrepresentation shows that they did in fact rely on the statement. See *Museprime Properties Ltd v Adhill Properties Ltd* (1990), in which an inaccurate statement contained in auction particulars, and repeated by the auctioneer, was held to constitute a misrepresentation, in spite of the claims that it should have been unreasonable for anyone to allow themselves to be influenced by the statement.

8.2.3	Types of misrepresentations	Misrepresentation can be divided into three types, each of which involves distinct procedures and provides different remedies.
8.2.4	Fraudulent misrepresentations	In the case of fraudulent misrepresentation the statement is made, knowing it to be false, or believing it to be false, or recklessly careless whether it is true or false. The difficulty with this type of misrepresentation is proving the necessary mental element; it is notoriously difficult to show the required *mens rea*, or guilty mind, to demonstrate fraud.

In *Derry v Peek* (1889) the directors of a company issued a prospectus, inviting the public to subscribe for shares. The prospectus stated that the company had the power to run trams by steam power, but in fact it only had power to operate horse-drawn trams; it required the permission of the Board of Trade to run steam trams. The Directors assumed that permission would be granted, but in fact it was refused. When the company was wound up, the directors were sued for fraud. It was held that there was no fraud since the directors had honestly believed the statement in the prospectus. They may have been negligent but they were not fraudulent.

8.2.5	Negligent misrepresentation	With negligent misrepresentation the false statement is made in the belief that it is true, but without reasonable grounds for that belief. (It follows that the directors in *Derry v Peek* would be liable for negligent misrepresentation.) There are two categories of negligent misrepresentation:

- At common law

  Prior to 1963, the law recognised no such concept as negligent misrepresentation. The possibility of liability in negligence for misstatements arose from *Hedley Byrne & Co v Heller* (1964). In *Hedley Byrne & Co v Heller*, however, the parties were not in a contractual or a pre-contractual relationship, so there could not have been an action for misrepresentation. But in *Esso Petroleum v Mardon* (1976), Mardon succeeded in an action for negligent misstatement, on the basis that he had been wrongly advised as to the amount of petrol he could expect to sell from a garage.

- Under the Misrepresentation Act 1967 (MA)

  Although it might still be necessary, or beneficial, to sue at common law, it is more likely that such actions would now be taken under the statute. The reason for this is that s 2(1) of the MA reverses the normal burden of proof. In an action in negligence the burden of proof is on the party raising the action to show that the other party acted in a negligent manner. However, where a misrepresentation has been made, then under s 2(1) of the MA it is up to the party who made the statement to show that they had reasonable grounds for believing it to be true.

Innocent misrepresentation occurs where the false statement is made by a person who not only believes it to be true, but also has reasonable grounds for that belief.

8.2.6   Innocent misrepresentation

For fraudulent misrepresentation, the remedies are rescission, and/or damages for any loss sustained. Rescission is an equitable remedy which is designed to return the parties to their original position. The action for damages is in the tort of deceit.

8.2.7   Remedies for misrepresentation

For negligent misrepresentation, the remedies are rescission, and/or damages. The action for damages is either in the tort of negligence, at common law or under s 2(1) of the MA 1967. Under the statute, the measure of damages will still be determined as in a tort action (see *Royscot Trust Ltd v Rogerson* (1991) where the Court of Appeal confirmed this approach).

For innocent misrepresentation, the common law remedy is rescission. Under the MA, however, the court may award damages instead of rescission, in cases where it is considered equitable to do so (s 2(2)).

With regard to s 2(2), it should be noted that the court can only award damages, instead of rescission, where the remedy of rescission is still available. The importance of this lies in the fact that the right to rescind can be lost:

- By affirmation, where the innocent party, with full knowledge of the misrepresentation, either expressly states that they intend to go on with the agreement, or does some action from which it can be implied that they intend to go on with the agreement. Affirmation may be implied from lapse of time (see *Leaf v International Galleries* (1950));

- Where the parties cannot be restored to their original positions;

- Where third parties have acquired rights in the subject matter of the contract (see *Phillips v Brooks* above).

Section 3 of the MA provides that any exclusion of liability for misrepresentation must comply with the requirement of reasonableness.

The following diagram shows how statements may be classified and the consequence of such classification.

Fig 2:   Forms of
misrepresentation

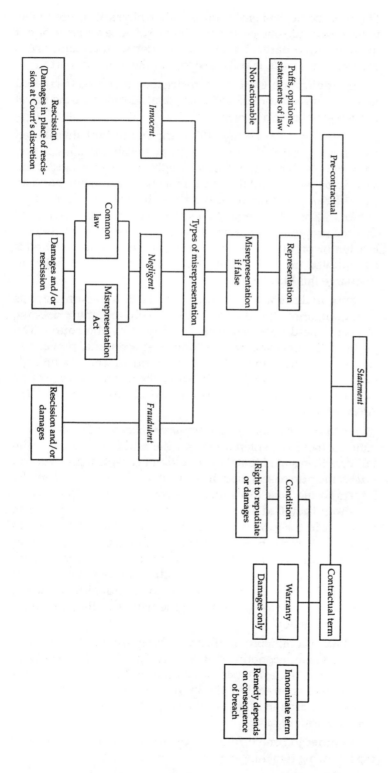

8.3   Duress

Duress is some element of force, either physical or economic, used to override one party's freedom to choose whether or not to enter into a particular contract. Under such circumstances the contract is *voidable* at the instance of the innocent party.

Its application used to be restricted to contracts entered into as a consequence of actual physical violence, or the threat of such violence to a person.

In *Barton v Armstrong* (1975) the defendant threatened Barton with death if he did not arrange for his company to buy Armstrong's shares in it. Barton sought to have the agreement set aside. It was found that the threats had been made but that, in addition, Barton thought that the transaction was a favourable one. Barton nonetheless succeeded. The court held that the proper inference was that duress was present, and the burden of proof was on Armstrong to show that the threats had played no part in Barton's decision. He had failed to discharge this burden.

Originally it was held that threats to a person's goods could not amount to duress, but relatively recently a doctrine of economic duress has been developed by the courts. The germ of the doctrine, that an abuse of economic power can render a contract invalid, can be found in Lord Denning's decision in *D & C Builders Ltd v Rees* (1966), and was developed in later cases such as *The Siboen & The Sibotre* (1976); and *The Atlantic Baron* (1979).

In *North Ocean Shipping Company v Hyundai Construction* a contract had been entered into for the building of a ship. The builders then stated that they would not complete construction unless the purchasers paid an extra 10%. Without the ship, the buyers would have lost a lucrative contract with a third party, to whom they had already agreed to charter the ship. The buyers paid the extra money and then, at a later date, sued to recover it, on the basis of economic duress, amongst other things. It was held that the threat to terminate the contract did constitute economic duress, which rendered the contract voidable. In the event, the buyers' delay in bringing the action acted as an affirmation of the agreement and they lost their right to rescission.

There is a difficulty in distinguishing ordinary commercial pressure from economic duress (see *Pao On v Lau Yiu Long* (1979)), but the existence of economic duress as a distinct principle of contract law finally received the approval of the House of Lords in *Universe Tankships Inc v ITWF* (1982), the *Universe Sentinel* case.

In order to benefit from the doctrine, plaintiffs must show the following two things:

- That pressure, which resulted in an absence of choice on their part, was brought to bear on them; and

- That the pressure was of a nature considered illegitimate by the courts.

Only under such circumstances will the court permit rescission of an agreement as can be seen in *Atlas Express v Kafco* (1990). The defendant company had secured a highly profitable contract with Woolworths, the large retail outlet, and employed the plaintiffs as their carriers. After beginning to perform the contract Atlas sought to increase their price. Although they protested, Kafco felt they had no option but to agree to the demand rather than break their contract with Woolworths which would have proved economically disastrous for them. When Atlas sued to recover the increased charges they failed as it was held that the attempt to increase the charge was a clear case of economic duress.

8.4   Undue influence

Transactions, either contract or gifts, may be avoided where they have been entered into as a consequence of the undue influence of the person benefiting from them. The effect of undue influence is to make a contract voidable, but delay may bar the right to avoid the agreement. There are two possible situations relating to undue influence.

8.4.1   Special relationships

Where there is a special relationship between the parties, there is a presumption that the transaction is the consequence of undue influence. The burden of proof is on the person receiving the benefit to rebut the presumption.

In *Re Craig* (1971) after the death of his wife Mr Craig, then aged 84, employed a Mrs Middleton as his secretary-companion. In the course of six years for which she was employed, he gave her money to the extent of some £30,000. An action was taken to have the gifts set aside. The action succeeded as it was held that the circumstances raised the presumption of undue influence, which Mrs Middleton had failed to rebut.

Examples of special relationships are:

- Parent and child while still a minor;

- Guardian and ward;

- Religious adviser and follower;

- Doctor and patient;

- Solicitor and client.

The list is not a closed one, however, and other relationships may be included within the scope of the special relationship (as in *Re Craig*).

Where a special relationship exists, then an important way in which the presumption of undue influence can be rebutted is to show that independent advice was taken by the other party, although all that is necessary is to show that the other party exercised their will freely.

Even where a special relationship exists, a transaction will not be set aside unless it is shown to be manifestly disadvantageous.

In *National Westminster Bank v Morgan* (1985) when a couple named Morgan fell into financial difficulties the plaintiff bank made financial arrangements which permitted them to remain in their house. The refinancing transaction secured against the house was arranged by a bank manager who called at their home. Mrs Morgan had no independent legal advice. When the husband died, the bank obtained a possession order against the house in respect of outstanding debts. Mrs Morgan sought to have the refinancing arrangement set aside, on the grounds of undue influence. The action failed on the grounds that the doctrine of undue influence had no place in agreements which did not involve any manifest disadvantage, and Mrs Morgan had actually benefited from the transaction by being able to remain in her home for a longer period.

The key element in deciding whether a relationship was a special one or not was whether one party was in a position of dominance over the other. *National Westminster Bank v Morgan* also decided that a normal relationship between a bank manager and his client is not a special relationship.

8.4.2   No special relationship

Where no special relationship exists between the parties, the burden of proof is on the party claiming the protection of the undue influence doctrine. It is of interest to note that relationships which are not included as special relationships include the relationships of husband and wife and bank and customer yet these are precisely the relationships that are likely to generate the most problems.

The rule relating to manifest disadvantage, considered above in relation to special relationships, does not apply in the case where no such special relationship applies.

In *CIBC Mortgages plc v Pitt* (1993) Mrs Pitt sought to set aside a mortgage she had signed against her home in favour of the plaintiffs on the basis that her husband had exerted undue influence over her. Whereas the Court of Appeal had rejected her plea on the grounds that the agreement was not to her manifest disadvantage, the House of Lords declared that such a principle did not apply in cases where undue influence was actual rather than presumed. They did, however, recognise the validity of the mortgage on the grounds that the creditor had no knowledge, either actual or constructive, of the exercise of undue influence in relation to the transaction.

It is of interest to note in relation to this last case that the House of Lords, in *Barclays Bank plc v O'Brien* (1993), referred to an implied duty on creditors, in particular circumstances which certainly included a marital relationship, to ensure that parties had not entered into agreements on the basis of misrepresentation or undue influence.

It has been suggested that undue influence and duress are simply examples of a wider principle, based on inequality of bargaining power. The existence of such a principle was suggested in a number of decisions involving Lord Denning. It was intended to provide protection for those who suffered as a consequence of being forced into particular agreements due to their lack of bargaining power. This doctrine, however, was considered, and firmly rejected by the House of Lords in *National Westminster Bank v Morgan*. It could be suggested that the very idea of inequality of bargaining power is incompatible with the reality of today's economic structure with its domination by large scale, if not monopolistic, organisations. It should be recognised, however, that, as considered in Chapter 7, the idea of inequality of bargaining power has found a place in determining how the Unfair Contract Terms Act is to operate.	**8.4.3 Inequality of bargaining power**
It is evident that some agreements will tend to be contrary to public policy. The fact that some are considered more serious than others is reflected in the distinction drawn between those which are said to be illegal and those which are simply void.	**8.5 Contracts and public policy**
A contract which breaks the law is illegal. The general rule is that no action can be brought by a party to an illegal contract. The contract may be expressly prohibited by statute, or implicitly prohibited by the common law. The following is a list of illegal contracts:	**8.6 Illegal contracts**

• Contracts prohibited by statute;

• Contracts to defraud the Inland Revenue;

• Contracts involving the commission of a crime or a tort;

- Contracts with a sexually immoral element;

- Contracts against the interest of the UK or a friendly state;

- Contracts leading to corruption in public life;

- Contracts which interfere with the course of justice.

8.7   Void contracts

A void contract does not give rise to any rights or obligations. The contract is only void so far as it is contrary to public policy, thus the whole agreement may not be void. *Severance* is the procedure whereby the void part of a contract is excised, permitting the remainder to be enforced. Contracts may be void under statute, or at common law.

8.7.1   Contracts void by statute

- Wagering contracts

  A wagering contract is an agreement that, upon the happening of some uncertain event, one party shall give something of value to the other, the party who has to pay being dependent on the outcome of the event. Such contracts are governed by the Gaming Acts.

- Restrictive trading agreements

  Certain restrictive trading agreements are subject to registration and investigation under the Restrictive Trade Practices Act 1976. If the agreements cannot be justified by the parties to them, as required under s 10 of that Act, then they are void and unenforceable.

- Resale price maintenance agreements

  Agreements which seek to enforce minimum prices for goods through resale price maintenance agreements are void, and the enforcement of such agreements is prohibited under the Resale Prices Act 1976. It is possible, however, for particular classes of goods to qualify for exemption from the provisions of the Act.

8.7.2   Contracts void at common law

- Contracts to oust the jurisdiction of the court

  Any contractual agreement which seeks to deny the parties the right to submit questions of law to the Courts are void, as being contrary to public policy. Agreements which provide for compulsory arbitration are enforceable.

- Contracts prejudicial to the status of marriage

  It is considered a matter of public policy that the institution of marriage be maintained. Hence any contract which seeks to restrain a person's freedom to marry, or undermines the institution in any way, will be considered void.

One area of particular importance subject to the control of the common law are contracts in restraint of trade. A contract in restraint of trade is an agreement whereby one party restricts their future freedom to engage in their trade, business, or profession. The general rule is that such agreements are *prima facie* void but they may be valid if it can be shown that they meet the following requirements:

8.7.3   Contracts in restraint of trade

- The person who imposes the restrictions has a legitimate interest to protect;

- The restriction is reasonable as between the parties;

- The restriction is not contrary to the public interest.

  The doctrine of restraint of trade is flexible in its application, and may be applied to new situations when they arise. Bearing this in mind, however, it is usual to classify the branches of the doctrine as follows:

- Restraints on employees

  Employers cannot protect themselves against competition from an ex-employee, except where they have a legitimate interest to protect. The only legitimate interests recognised by the law are trade secrets and trade connection.

  Even in protecting those interests the restraint must be of a reasonable nature. What constitutes 'reasonable' in this context depends on the circumstances of the case.

  In *Lamson Pneumatic Tube Co v Phillips* (1904) the plaintiffs manufactured specialised equipment for use in shops. The defendant's contract of employment stated that, on ceasing to work for the plaintiffs, he would not engage in a similar business, for a period of five years, anywhere in the Eastern hemisphere. It was held that such a restriction was reasonable, bearing in mind the nature of the plaintiff's business.

  This has to be compared with *Empire Meat Co Ltd v Patrick* (1939) where Patrick had been employed as manager of the company's butcher's business in Mill Road, Cambridge. The company sought to enforce the defendant's promise that he would not establish a rival business within five miles of their shop. In this situation it was held that the restraint was too wide and could not be enforced.

  The longer the period of time covered by the restraint the more likely it is to be struck down, but in *Fitch v Dewes* (1921) it was held that a life-long restriction placed on a solicitor was valid.

- Restraints on vendors of business

  The interest to be protected in this category is the *goodwill* of the business ie its profitability. Restrictions may legitimately be placed on previous owners to prevent them from competing, in the future, with new owners. Again, the restraint should not be greater than is necessary to protect that interest.

  In *British Concrete v Schelff* (1921) the plaintiffs sought to enforce a promise given by the defendant, on the sale of his business to them, that he would not compete with them in the manufacturer of road reinforcements. It was held that given the small size and restricted nature of the business sold, the restraint was too wide to be enforceable.

  However in *Nordenfeld v Maxim Nordenfeld Guns & Ammunition Co* (1894), a world-wide restraint on competition was held to be enforceable, given the nature of the business sold.

- Restraints on distributors/solus agreements

  This category of restraint of trade is usually concerned with solus agreements between petrol companies and garage proprietors, by which a petrol company seeks to prevent the retailer from selling its competitors' petrol. It is recognised that petrol companies have a legitimate interest to protect, and the outcome depends on whether the restraint obtained in protection of that interest is reasonable.

  In *Esso Petroleum v Harper's Garage* (1968) the parties had entered into an agreement whereby Harper undertook to buy all of the petrol to be sold from his two garages from Esso. In return Esso lent him £7,000, secured by way of a mortgage over one of the garages. The monopoly right in regard to one garage was to last for four and a half years, and in regard to the other garage for 21 years. When Harper broke his undertaking Esso sued to enforce it. It was held that the agreements in respect of both garages were in restraint of trade. But whereas the agreement which lasted for four and a half years was reasonable, the one which lasted for 21 years was unreasonable and void.

  Until fairly recently it was thought that *Esso v Harper's* case had set down a rule that any solus agreement involving a restriction which was to last longer than five years would be void, as being in restraint of trade. In *Alec Lobb (Garages) Ltd v Total Oil Ltd* (1985), however, the Court of Appeal made it clear that the outcome of each case depended on its own particular circumstances, and in that case approved a solus agreement extending over a period of 21 years.

- Exclusive service contracts

This category relates to contracts which are specifically structured to exploit one of the parties by controlling and limiting their output, rather than assisting them. The most famous cases involve musicians.

In *Schroeder Music Publishing Co v Macauley* (1974) an unknown songwriter, Macauley, entered into a five year agreement with Schroeder. Under it, he had to assign any music he wrote to them, but they were under no obligation to publish it. The agreement provided for automatic extension of the agreement if it yielded £5,000 in royalties but the publishers could terminate it at any time with one month's notice. It was decided that the agreement was so one-sided as to amount to an unreasonable restraint of trade, and hence was void.

Since the above case numerous artists have made use of this ground for avoiding their contracts.

Vitiating Factors

Operative mistake renders a contract void ab initio. There are three kinds of operative mistake:

Mistake

- Common mistake

  Where both parties to an agreement *share the same error* about the circumstances surrounding the transaction. Examples usually involve either *res sua* or *res extincta*.

- Mutual mistake

  This occurs where the parties *believe different versions of the facts* of the situation, but they do not realise it. In order for mutual mistake to be operative it must comply with an objective test.

- Unilateral mistake

  This occurs where *only one of the parties to the agreement is mistaken* as to the circumstances of the contract, and the other party is aware of that fact. Where parties enter into a contract face to face, it is generally presumed that the seller intends to deal with the person before them, and therefore they cannot rely on unilateral mistake to avoid the contract.

There are two mechanisms for dealing with mistakes in written contracts.

Mistake in respect of documents

- Rectification

  This allows the contract to be altered where it does not accurately represent the intentions of the parties.

- *Non est factum*

  This may operate where someone, without carelessness, signs a document under a misapprehension as to its true nature or content. If the document is fundamentally different from what they thought they were signing they may avoid its effect.

Misrepresentation can be defined as a false statement of fact, made by one party before or at the time of the contract which induces the other party to enter into the contract.

Misrepresentation

Some statements will not amount to a representation ie sales puffs, statements of opinion, statements of law. The statement must actually induce the contract.

Types of misrepresentations

In *fraudulent misrepresentation* the statement is made, knowing it to be false, or believing it to be false, or recklessly careless whether it is true or false.

In *negligent misrepresentation* the false statement is made in the belief that it is true, but without reasonable grounds for that belief. There are two categories of negligent misrepresentation:

- At common law;

- Under the Misrepresentation Act 1967.

The latter is preferable in most cases as it reverses the burden of proof.

Innocent misrepresentation occurs where the false statement is made by a person who not only believes it to be true, but also has reasonable grounds for that belief.

Remedies for misrepresentation

Initially rescission was the main remedy for misrepresentation. Damages were only available for fraud.

The possibility of damages in negligence was opened after *Hedley Byrne v Heller*.

The Misrepresentation Act 1967 provides the possibility of damages under s 2(1) for negligent misrepresentation and under s 2(2) for innocent misrepresentation.

Duress

Duress is some element of force used to override a party's freedom to choose whether or not to enter into a particular contract. Duress renders a contract *voidable* at the instance of the innocent party. This concept used to be restricted to contracts entered into as a consequence of actual physical violence, or the threat of such violence to a person, but has been extended so far as to include economic duress.

In order to benefit from the doctrine of economic duress, plaintiffs must show the following two things:

- That pressure, which resulted in an absence of choice on their part, was brought to bear on them; and

- That the pressure was of a nature considered illegitimate by the courts (*Atlas Express v Kafco* (1990)).

Undue influence

The effect of undue influence is to make a contract *voidable*, but delay may bar the right to avoid the agreement.

Where there is a *special relationship* between the parties, there is a presumption that the transaction is the consequence of undue influence. The presumption is open to rebuttal.

Examples of special relationships are:

- Parent and child while still a minor;

- Guardian and ward;

- Religious adviser and follower;

- Doctor and patient;

- Solicitor and client.

The above list is not a closed one.

Where *no special relationship exists* between the parties, the burden of proof is on the party claiming the protection of the undue influence doctrine.

A contract which breaks the law is *illegal*. Contracts may be expressly prohibited by statute, or implicitly prohibited by the common law. The general rule is that no action can be brought by a party to an illegal contract.

A *void* contract does not give rise to any rights or obligations. Contracts are only void so far as they are contrary to public policy.

Severance is the process whereby the void part of a contract is excised, permitting the remainder to be enforced.

- Wagering contracts;

- Restrictive trading agreements;

- Resale price maintenance agreements.

- Contracts to oust the jurisdiction of the court;

- Contracts prejudicial to the status of marriage.

The general rule is that such agreement are *prima facie* void but they may be valid if it can be shown that they meet the following requirements:

- The person who imposes the restrictions has a legitimate interest to protect;

- The restriction is reasonable as between the parties;

- The restriction is not contrary to the public interest.

There are four distinct areas in relation to restraint of trade and the application of the law differs in each:

- Restraints on employees;

- Restraints on vendors of business;

- Restraints on distributors/solus agreements;

- Exclusive service contracts.

Contracts and public policy

Contracts void by statute

Contracts void at common law

Contracts in restraint of trade

Chapter 9

Discharge of a Contract

Discharge of contract means that the parties to an agreement are freed from their contractual obligations. A contract is discharged in one of four ways:

- agreement;
- performance;
- frustration;
- breach.

9.1 Introduction

Emphasis has been placed on the consensual nature of contract law, and it follows that what has been made by agreement can be ended by agreement. The contract itself may contain provision for its discharge, by either the passage of a fixed period of time, or the occurrence of a particular event. Alternatively, it may provide, either expressly or by implication, that one or other of the parties can bring it to an end, as in a contract of employment.

9.2 Discharge by agreement

Where there is no such provision in a contract, another contract would be required to cancel it before all of the obligations have been met. There are two possible situations:

- *Where the contract is executory*, the mutual exchange of promises to release one another from future performance will be sufficient consideration.

- *Where the contract is executed*, ie one party has performed, or partly performed, their obligations, the other party must provide consideration in order to be released from performing their part of the contract (unless the release is made under seal). The provision of this consideration discharges the original contract, and there is said to be *accord and satisfaction*.

This occurs where the parties to a contract perform their obligations under it. It is the normal way in which contracts are discharged. As a general rule, discharge requires complete and exact performance of the obligations in the contract.

9.3 Discharge by performance

In *Cutter v Powell* (1795) Cutter was employed as second mate on a ship sailing from Jamaica to Liverpool. The agreement was that he was to receive 30 guineas when the journey was completed. Before the ship reached Liverpool, Cutter died and his widow sued Powell, the ship's master, to recover a proportion of the wages due to her husband. It was held that the widow was entitled to nothing as the contract required complete performance.

There are four exceptions to the general rule requiring complete performance:

• Where the contract is divisible

  In an ordinary contract of employment, where it is usual for payment to be made periodically, the harshness of the outcome of *Cutter v Powell* is avoided.

  In *Bolton v Mahadeva* (1972) the plaintiff had contracted to install central heating for the defendant for £560. It turned out to be defective and required a further £179 to put right. It was held that Bolton could not claim any of the money as he had failed to perform the contract. An agreement to supply a bathroom suite was divisible from the overall agreement, however, and had to be paid for.

• Where the contract is capable of being fulfilled by substantial performance

  This occurs where the essential element of an agreement has been performed, but some minor part remains to be done, or some minor fault remains to be remedied. The party who performed the act can claim the contract price, although they remain liable for any deduction for the work outstanding.

  In *Hoenig v Isaacs* (1952) Hoenig was employed by Isaacs to decorate his flat. The contract price was £750, to be paid as the work progressed. Isaacs paid a total of £400, but refused to pay the remainder as he objected to the quality of the work carried out. Hoenig sued for the outstanding £350. It was held that Isaacs had to pay the outstanding money less the cost of putting right the defects in performance. These latter costs amounted to just under £56.

  This should be compared with *Bolton v Mahadeva*, above, in which no payment was allowed for work done in a totally unsatisfactory manner.

• Where performance has been prevented by the other party

  Under such circumstances, the party prevented from performance can sue for breach of contract, or on a *quantum meruit* basis (see below).

• Where partial performance has been accepted by the other party

This occurs in the following circumstances: A orders a case of 12 bottles of wine from B. B only has 10, and delivers those to A. A is at liberty to reject the 10 bottles if he wants to, but if he accepts them he must pay a proportionate price for them.

Tender of performance simply means an offer to perform the contractual obligations. For example, if a buyer refuses to accept the goods offered, but later sues for breach of contract, the seller can rely on the fact that they tendered performance as discharging their liability under the contract. The seller would also be entitled to claim for breach of contract.

9.3.1   Tender of performance

In *Macdonald v Startup* (1843) Macdonald promised to deliver 10 tons of oil to the defendant 'within the last 14 days of March. He tried to deliver on Saturday 31 March at 8.30 pm, and Startup refused to accept the oil. It was held that the tender of performance was equivalent to actual performance, and Macdonald was entitled to claim damages for breach of contract.

Section 29(5) of the Sale of Goods Act now provides that tender is ineffectual unless made at a reasonable hour. It is unlikely that 8.30 pm on a Saturday evening would be considered reasonable.

Where it is impossible to perform an obligation from the outset, no contract can come into existence. Early cases held that subsequent impossibility was no excuse for non-performance. In the 19th century, however, the doctrine of frustration was developed to permit a party to a contract, in some circumstances, to be excused performance on the grounds of impossibility arising subsequently to the formation of the contract.

9.4   Discharge by frustration

A contract will be discharged by reason of frustration in the following circumstances:

- Where destruction of the subject matter of the contract has occurred

  In *Taylor v Caldwell* (1863) Caldwell had agreed to let a hall to the plaintiff for a number of concerts. Before the day of the first concert the hall was destroyed by fire. Taylor sued for breach of contract. It was held that the destruction of the hall had made performance impossible, and therefore the defendant was not liable under the contract.

- Where government interference, or supervening illegality, prevents performance

The performance of the contract may be made illegal by a change in the law. The outbreak of war, making the other party an enemy alien, will have a similar effect.

In *Re Shipton, Anderson & Co etc* (1915) a contract was made for the sale of wheat stored in a warehouse in Liverpool. Before the seller could deliver, it was requisitioned by the government, under wartime emergency powers. It was held that the seller was excused from performance. Due to the requisition, it was no longer possible to lawfully deliver the wheat.

- Where a particular event, which is the sole reason for the contract, fails to take place

In *Krell v Henry* (1903) Krell let a room to the defendant for the purpose of viewing the coronation procession of Edward VII. When the procession was cancelled due to the King's ill health, Krell sued Henry for the due rent. It was held that the contract was discharged by frustration, since its purpose could no longer be achieved.

This only applies where the cancelled event was the sole purpose of the contract.

In *Herne Bay Steamboat Co v Hutton* (1903) a naval review, which had been arranged as part of Edward VII's coronation celebrations, also had to be cancelled due to illness. Hutton had contracted to hire a boat from the plaintiffs for the purpose of seeing the review. It was held that Hutton was liable for breach of contract. The sole foundation of the contract was not lost as the ship could still have been used to view the assembled fleet.

- Where the commercial purpose of the contract is defeated

This applies where the circumstances have so changed that to hold a party to their promise would require them to do something which, although not impossible, would be radically different from the original agreement.

In *Jackson v Union Marine Insurance Co* (1874) the plaintiff's ship was chartered to proceed to Newport to load a cargo bound for San Francisco. On the way, it ran aground. It could not be refloated for over a month, and needed repairs. The charterers hired another ship and the plaintiff claimed under an insurance policy he had taken out to cover the eventuality of his failure to carry out the contract. The insurance company denied responsibility on the basis that the plaintiff could claim against the charterer for breach of contract. The court decided, however, that the delay had put an end to the commercial sense of the contract. As a consequence the charterers had been released from their obligations under the contract and were entitled to hire another ship.

* Where, in the case of a contract of personal service, the party dies or becomes otherwise incapacitated

In *Condor v Barron Knights* (1966) Condor contracted to be the drummer in a pop group. After he became ill he was medically advised that he could only play on four nights per week, not every night as required. It was decided that the contract was discharged by the failure in the plaintiff's health preventing him from performing his duties under it, and thus any contractual obligations were unenforceable.

In *Tsakiroglou & Co v Noblee & Thorl* (1960) it was stated that frustration is a doctrine only too often invoked by a party to a contract who finds performance difficult or unprofitable, but it is very rarely relied on with success. It is, in fact, a kind of last resort, and it is a conclusion which should be reached rarely and with reluctance. A contract will not be discharged by reason of frustration in the following circumstances:

9.4.1   Situations in which doctrine of frustration does not apply

* Where the parties have made express provision in the contract for the event which has occurred

In this case, the provision in the contract will be applied.

* Where the frustrating event is self-induced

An example of such a situation is the case of *Maritime National Fish Ltd v Ocean Trawlers Ltd* (1935). Maritime were charterers of a ship, equipped for 'otter' trawling, owned by Ocean Trawlers. Permits were required for 'otter' trawling, and Maritime, who owned four ships of their own, applied for five permits. They were only granted three permits, however, and they assigned those permits to their own ships. They claimed that their contract with Ocean Trawlers was frustrated, on the basis that they could not lawfully use the ship. It was held, however, that the frustrating event was a result of their action in assigning the permits to their own ships, and therefore they could not rely on it as discharging their contractual obligations.

* Where an alternative method of performance is still possible

In such a situation the person performing the contract will be expected to use the available alternative method.

In *Tsakiroglou & Co v Noblee & Thorl* (1962) a contract was entered into to supply 300 tons of Sudanese groundnuts cif Hamburg. It had been intended that the cargo should go via the Suez canal, and the appellants refused to deliver the nuts when the canal was closed. It was argued that the contract was frustrated, as to use the Cape of Good Hope route would make the contract commercially and fundamentally different from that which was agreed. The court decided that the contract was not fundamentally altered by the closure of the canal, and, therefore was not discharged by frustration. The appellants therefore were liable for breach of contract.

• Where the contract simply becomes more expensive to perform

In such circumstances the court will not allow frustration to be used as a means of escaping from a bad bargain.

In *Davis Contractors v Fareham UDC* (1956) the plaintiff's contracted to build 78 houses in eight months, at a total cost of £94,000. Due to shortage of labour it actually took 22 months to build the houses, at a cost of £115,000. They sought to have the contract set aside as frustrated, and to claim on a *quantum meruit* basis. The court determined that the contract had not been frustrated by the shortage of labour, and the plaintiffs were thus bound by their contractual undertaking with regard to the price.

9.4.2	The effect of frustration	At common law, the effect of frustration was to make the contract void as from the time of the frustrating event. It did not make the contract void *ab initio*, ie from the beginning. The effect of this was that each party had to perform any obligation which had become due before the frustrating event, and was only excused from obligations which would arise after that event. On occasion this could lead to injustice. For example, in *Krell v Henry* the plaintiff could not claim the rent, as it was not due to be paid until after the coronation event had been cancelled. The outcome was different in a similar case, however, where the rent had to be paid immediately on the making of the contract.

In *Chandler v Webster* (1904) the plaintiff had already paid £100 of the total rent of £141 15s for a room from which to watch the coronation procession, before it was cancelled. He sued to recover his money. It was decided that not only could he not recover the £100, but he also had to pay the outstanding £41 15s as the rent had fallen due before the frustrating event had taken place.

9.4.3	Law Reform (Frustrated Contracts) Act 1943	Statute intervened to remedy the potential injustice of the Common Law in 1943 with the introduction of Law Reform (Frustrated Contracts) Act. The position is now as follows:

• Any money paid is recoverable;

- Any money due to be paid ceases to be payable;

- The parties may be permitted, at the discretion of the court, to retain expenses incurred from any money received; or recover those expenses from money due to be paid before the frustrating event. If no money was paid, or was due to be paid, before the event, then nothing can be retained or recovered.

  The Act does not apply to the following types of contract:

- Contracts for the carriage of goods by sea;

- Contracts of insurance;

- Contracts for perishable goods.

Breach of a contract occurs where one of the parties to the agreement fails to comply, either completely or satisfactorily, with their obligations under it. A breach of contract may occur in three ways:

9.5   Discharge by breach

- Where a party, prior to the time of performance, states that they will not fulfil their contractual obligation;

- Where a party fails to perform their contractual obligation;

- Where a party performs their obligation in a defective manner.

Any breach will result in the innocent party being able to sue for damages. In addition, however, some breaches will permit the innocent party to treat the contract as discharged. In this situation they can refuse either to perform their part of the contract, or to accept further performance from the party in breach. The right to treat a contract as discharged arises in the following instances:

9.5.1   Effect of breach

- Where the other party has repudiated the contract before performance is due, or before he has completed performance;

- Where the other party has committed a fundamental breach of contract. As has already been pointed out in Chapter 7 there are two methods of determining whether a breach is fundamental or not; one relying on the distinction between conditions and warranties, the other relying on the seriousness of the consequences that flow from the breach.

Anticipatory breach arises where one party, prior to the actual due date of performance, demonstrates an intention not to

9.5.2   Anticipatory breach

perform their contractual obligations. The intention not to fulfil the contract can be either express or implied.

- Express

  This occurs where a party actually states that they will not perform their contractual obligations.

  In *Hochster v De La Tour* (1853) De La Tour engaged Hochster, in April, to act as courier on his European tour, starting on 1 June. On 11 May De La Tour wrote to Hochster stating that he would no longer be needing his services. The plaintiff started proceedings for breach of contract on 22 May, and the defendant claimed that there could be no cause of action until 1 June. It was held, however, that the plaintiff was entitled to start his action as soon as the anticipatory breach occurred (ie when De La Tour stated he would not need Hochster's services).

- Implied

  This occurs where a party carries out some act which makes performance impossible.

  In *Omnium D'Enterprises v Sutherland* (1919) the defendant had agreed to let a ship to the plaintiff. Prior to the actual time for performance, he sold the ship to another party. It was held that the sale of the ship amounted to repudiation of the contract and the plaintiff could sue from that date.

  With regard to anticipatory breach, the innocent party can sue for damages immediately, as in *Hochster v De La Tour*. Alternatively, they can wait until the actual time for performance before taking action. In the latter instance, they are entitled to make preparations for performance, and claim the agreed contract price, even though this apparently conflicts with the duty to mitigate losses (see below).

  In *White & Carter (Councils) v McGregor* (1961) McGregor contracted with the plaintiffs to have advertisements placed on litter bins which were supplied to local authorities. The defendant wrote to the plaintiffs asking them to cancel the contract. The plaintiffs refused to cancel, and produced, and displayed, the adverts as required under the contract. They then claimed payment. It was held that the plaintiffs were not obliged to accept the defendant's repudiation. They were entitled to perform the contract and claim the agreed price.

  Where the innocent party elects to wait for the time of performance, they take the risk of the contract being discharged for some other reason, such as frustration, and thus of losing their right to sue.

In *Avery v Bowden* (1955) Bowden chartered the plaintiff's ship in order to load grain at Odessa within a period of 45 days. Although Bowden later told the ship's captain that he no longer intended to load the grain, the ship stayed in Odessa in the hope that he would change his mind. Before the end of the 45 days, the Crimean war started and thus the contract was discharged by frustration. Avery then sued for breach of contract. It was held that the action failed. Bowden had committed anticipatory breach, but the captain had waived the right to discharge the contract on that basis. The contract continued and was brought to an end by frustration, not by breach.

The principle remedies for breach of contract are:

- Damages;
- Quantum meruit;
- Specific performance;
- Injunction.

9.6   Remedies for breach of contract

The estimation of what damages are to be paid by a party in breach of contract can be divided into two parts: remoteness and measure.

9.7   Damages

What kind of damage can the innocent party claim? This involves a consideration of causation, and the remoteness of cause from effect, in order to determine how far down a chain of events a defendant is liable. The rule in *Hadley v Baxendale* states that damages will only be awarded in respect of losses which *arise naturally*, ie in the natural course of things; or which both parties may *reasonably be supposed to have contemplated,* when the contract was made, as a probable result of its breach.

In *Hadley v Baxendale* (1845) Hadley, a miller at Gloucester, had engaged the defendant to take a broken mill-shaft to Greenwich so that it could be used as a pattern for a new one. The defendant delayed in delivering the shaft, thus causing the mill to be out of action for longer than it would otherwise have been. Hadley sued for loss of profit during that period of additional delay. It was held that it was not a natural consequence of the delay in delivering the shaft that the mill should be out of action. The mill might, for example, have had a spare shaft. So the first part of the rule stated above did not apply. In addition, Baxendale was unaware that the mill would be out of action during the period of delay, so the

9.7.1   Remoteness of damage

second part of the rule did not apply, either. Baxendale, therefore, although liable for breach of contract was not liable for the loss of profit caused by the delay.

The effect of the first part of the rule in *Hadley v Baxendale* is that the party in breach is deemed to expect the normal consequences of the breach, whether they actually expected them or not.

Under the second part of the rule, however, the party in breach can only be held liable for abnormal consequences where they have actual knowledge that the abnormal consequences might follow.

In *Victoria Laundry Ltd v Newham Industries Ltd* (1949) the defendants contracted to deliver a new boiler to the plaintiffs, but delayed in delivery. The plaintiffs claimed for normal loss of profit during the period of delay, and also for the loss of abnormal profits from a highly lucrative contract which they could have undertaken, had the boiler been delivered on time. In this case it was decided that damages could be recovered in regard to the normal profits, as that loss was a natural consequence of the delay. The second claim failed, however, on the grounds that the loss was not a normal one, but was a consequence of an especially lucrative contract, about which the defendant knew nothing.

The decision in the *Victoria Laundry* case was confirmed by the House of Lords in *The Heron II*, although the actual test for remoteness was reformulated in terms of whether the consequence should have been 'within the reasonable contemplation of the parties' at the time of the contract.

In *The Heron II (Czarnikow v Koufos)* (1967) the defendants contracted to carry sugar from Constanza to Basra. They knew that the plaintiffs were sugar merchants, but did not know that they intended to sell the sugar as soon as it reached Basra. During a period when the ship was delayed, the market price of sugar fell. The plaintiffs claimed damages for the loss from the defendants. It was held that the plaintiffs could recover. It was common knowledge that the market value of such commodities could fluctuate, therefore the loss was within the reasonable contemplation of the parties.

As a consequence of the test for remoteness, a party may be liable for consequences which, although within the reasonable contemplation of the parties, are much more serious in effect than would be expected of them.

In *H Parsons (Livestock) Ltd v Uttley Ingham & Co* (1978) the plaintiffs who were pig farmers, bought a large food hopper from the defendants. While erecting it, the plaintiffs failed to unseal a ventilator on the top of the hopper. Because of lack of ventilation, the pig food stored in the hopper became mouldy. The pigs which ate the mouldy food contracted a rare intestinal disease and died. It was held that the defendants were liable for the loss of the pigs. The food affected by bad storage caused the illness as a natural consequence of the breach, and the death from such illness was not too remote.

Damages in contract are intended to compensate an injured party for any financial loss sustained as a consequence of another party's breach. The object is not to punish the party in breach, so the amount of damages awarded can never be greater than the actual loss suffered. The aim is to put the injured party in the same position they would have been in had the contract been properly performed. There are a number of procedures which seek to achieve this end:

9.7.2   Measure of damages

- The market rule

  Where the breach relates to a contract for the sale of goods, damages are usually assessed in line with the market rule. This means that if goods are not delivered under a contract, the buyer is entitled to go into the market and buy similar goods, and pay the market price prevailing at the time. They can then claim the difference in price between what they paid and the original contract price as damages. Conversely, if a buyer refuses to accept goods under a contract, the seller can sell the goods in the market, and accept the prevailing market price. Any difference between the price they receive and the contract price can be claimed in damages.

- The duty to mitigate losses

  The injured party is under a duty to take all reasonable steps to minimise their loss. So in the above examples, the buyer of goods which are not delivered has to buy the replacements as cheaply as possible; and the seller of goods which are not accepted has to try to get as good a price as they can when they sell them.

  In *Payzu v Saunders* (1919) the parties entered into a contract for the sale of fabric, which was to be delivered and paid for in instalments. When the purchaser, Payzu, failed to pay for the first instalment on time, Saunders refused to make any further deliveries unless Payzu agreed to pay cash on delivery. The plaintiff refused to accept this and sued for breach of contract. The court decided that the delay in payment had not given the defendant the right to repudiate the contract. As a consequence, he had breached the contract by refusing further delivery. The buyer, however, should have mitigated his loss by accepting the offer of cash on delivery terms. His damages were restricted, therefore, to what he would have lost under those terms, namely, interest over the repayment period.

- Non-pecuniary loss

    At one time, damages could not be recovered where the loss sustained through breach of contract was of a non-financial nature. The modern position is that such non-pecuniary damages can be recovered.

    In *Jarvis v Swan Tours Ltd* (1973) the defendant's brochure stated that various facilities were available at a particular ski resort. The facilities available were in fact much inferior to those advertised. The plaintiff sued for breach of contract. The court decided that Jarvis was entitled to recover, not just the financial loss he suffered, which was not substantial, but also for loss of entertainment and enjoyment. The Court of Appeal stated that damages could be recovered for mental distress in appropriate cases, and this was one of them.

9.7.3   Liquidated damages and penalties

It is possible, and common in business contracts, for the parties to an agreement to make provisions for possible breach by stating in advance the amount of damages that will have to paid in the event of any breach occurring. Damages under such a provision are known as *liquidated damages*. They will only be recognised by the court if they represent a genuine pre-estimate of loss, and are not intended to operate as a penalty against the party in breach. If the court considers the provision to be a penalty, it will not give it effect, but will award damages in the normal way.

In *Dunlop v New Garage & Motor Co* (1915) the plaintiffs supplied the defendants with tyres, under a contract designed to achieve resale price maintenance. The contract provided that the defendants had to pay Dunlop £5 for every tyre they sold in breach of the resale price agreement. When the garage sold tyres at less than the agreed minimum price, they resisted Dunlop's claim for £5 per tyre, on the grounds that it represented a penalty clause. On the facts of the situation the court decided that the provision was a genuine attempt to fix damages, and was not a penalty. It was therefore enforceable.

9.8   *Quantum meruit*

Quantum meruit means that a party should be awarded 'as much as he had earned', and such an award can be either contractual or quasi-contractual (see below) in nature. If the parties enter into a contractual agreement without determining the reward that is to be provided for performance, then in the event of any dispute, the court will award a reasonable sum.

Payment may also be claimed on the basis of *quantum meruit*, where a party has carried out work in respect of a void contract.

In *Craven-Ellis v Canons Ltd* (1936) the plaintiff had acted as the managing director of a company under a deed of contract. However, since he had not acquired any shares in the company, as required by its articles, his appointment was void. He sued to recover remuneration for the service he had provided prior to his removal. The court decided that, although he could not claim under contract, he was entitled to recover a reasonable sum on the basis of *quantum meruit*.

It will sometimes suit a party to break their contractual obligations, and pay damages; but through an order for *specific performance* the party in breach may be instructed to complete their part of the contract. The following rules govern the award of such a remedy.

9.9   Specific performance

- *An order of specific performance will only be granted in cases where the common law remedy of damages is inadequate.* It is not usually applied to contracts concerning the sale of goods where replacements are readily available. It is most commonly granted in cases involving the sale of land, where the subject matter of the contract is unique.

- *Specific performance will not be granted where the court cannot supervise its enforcement.* For this reason it will not be available in respect of contracts of employment or personal service.

  In *Ryan v Mutual Tontine Westminster Chambers Association* (1893) the landlords of a flat undertook to provide a porter, who was to be constantly in attendance to provide services such as cleaning the common passages and stairs, and delivering letters. The person appointed spent much of his time working as a chef at a nearby club. During his absence his duties were performed by a cleaner or by various boys. The plaintiff sought to enforce the contractual undertaking. It was held that, although the landlords were in breach of their contract, the court would not award an order of specific performance. The only remedy available was an action for damages.

- *Specific performance is an equitable remedy which the court grants at its discretion.* It will not be granted where the plaintiff has not acted properly on their part. Nor will it be granted where mutuality is lacking; thus a minor will not be granted specific performance, because no such order would be awarded against them.

9.10   Injunction

This is also an equitable order of the court, which directs a person not to break their contract. It can have the effect of indirectly enforcing contracts for personal service.

In *Warner Bros v Nelson* (1937) the defendant, the actress Bette Davis, had entered a contract which stipulated that she was to work exclusively for the plaintiffs for a period of one year. When she came to England the plaintiffs applied for an injunction to prevent her from working for someone else. The court granted the order to Warner Bros. In doing so the court rejected Nelson's argument that granting it would force her either to work for the defendants, or not to work at all.

An injunction will only be granted to enforce negative covenants within the agreement, and cannot be used to enforce positive obligations.

In *Whitwood Chemical Co v Hardman* (1891) the defendant had contracted to give the whole of his time to the plaintiffs, who were his employers, but he occasionally worked for others. The plaintiffs applied for an injunction to prevent him working for anyone else. No injunction was granted; Hardman had said what he would do, not what he would not do; and, therefore, there was no negative promise to enforce.

9.11   Quasi-contractual remedies

Quasi-contractual remedies are based on the assumption that a person should not receive any undue advantage from the fact that there is no contractual remedy to force them to account for it. An important quasi-contractual remedy is an action for money paid and received.

If no contract comes into existence for reason of a total failure of consideration, then under this action, any goods or money received will have to be returned to the party who supplied them.

Discharge of a Contract

Where the contract is *executory*, the mutual exchange of promises to release one another from future performance will be sufficient consideration.

Where the contract is executed the other party must provide consideration in order to be released from performing their part of the contract: this amounts to *accord and satisfaction*.

Discharge by agreement

As a general rule, discharge by performance requires complete and exact performance of the obligations in the contract. Except where:

Discharge by performance

- The contract is divisible;

- The contract is capable of being fulfilled by substantial performance;

- Performance has been prevented by the other party;

- Partial performance has been accepted by the other party.

Tender of performance simply means an offer to perform the contractual obligations. Acceptable tender of performance discharges liability under a contract.

Tender of performance

A contract will be discharged by reason of frustration in the following circumstances where:

Frustration

- Destruction of the subject matter of the contract has occurred;

- Government interference, or supervening illegality, prevents performance;

- A particular event, which is the sole reason for the contract, fails to take place;

- The commercial purpose of the contract is defeated;

- In the case of a contract of personal service, the party dies or becomes otherwise incapacitated.

  Frustration will not apply where:

- The parties have made express provision in the contract for the event which has occurred;

- The frustrating event is self-induced;

- An alternative method of performance is still possible;

- The contract simply becomes more expensive to perform.

At common law, the effect of frustration was to make the contract void as from the time of the frustrating event. Under the Law Reform (Frustrated Contracts) Act:

- Money paid is recoverable;

- Money due to be paid ceases to be payable;

- The parties may be permitted, at the discretion of the court, to retain expenses incurred from any money received; or recover those expenses from money due to be paid before the frustrating event;

- Where a party has gained a valuable benefit under the contract he may, at the discretion of the court, be required to pay a reasonable sum in respect of it.

Breach of contract

A breach of contract may occur in three ways:

- Where a party, prior to the time of performance, states that they will not fulfil their contractual obligation;

- Where a party fails to perform their contractual obligation;

- Where a party performs their obligation in a defective manner.

Any breach will result in the innocent party being able to sue for damages.

Where breach gives the right to treat the agreement as discharged the innocent party can refuse either to perform their part of the contract, or to accept further performance from the party in breach.

Anticipatory breach

Anticipatory breach arises where one party, prior to the actual due date of performance, demonstrates an intention not to perform their contractual obligations. Anticipatory breach may be express or implied.

The innocent party can sue for damages immediately or wait until the actual time for performance before taking action.

Damages

The estimation of what damages are to be paid by a party in breach of contract can be divided into two parts: remoteness and measure.

Remoteness of damage

The rule in *Hadley v Baxendale* states that damages will only be awarded in respect of losses which arise naturally or which both parties may reasonably be supposed to have contemplated, when the contract was made, as a probable result of its breach.

Measure of damages

The aim of damages is to put the injured party in the same position they would have been in had the contract been properly performed.

There are a number of procedures which seek to achieve this end:

- The market rule;

- The duty to mitigate losses.

The parties to an agreement may make provisions for the amount of damages that will have to paid in the event of any breach occurring. The court will only enforce the terms where they represent a genuine pre-estimate of loss, and not a penalty against the party in breach.

If the parties enter into a contractual agreement without determining the reward that is to be provided for performance, then in the event of any dispute, the court will award a reasonable sum.

Quantum meruit

Through an order for specific performance, a party in breach may be instructed to complete their part of the contract.

Specific performance

- An order of specific performance will only be granted in cases where the common law remedy of damages is inadequate;

- Specific performance will not be granted where the court cannot supervise its enforcement;

- Specific performance is an equitable remedy which the court grants at its discretion.

This is also an equitable order of the court, which directs a person not to break their contract.

Injunction

These are based on the assumption that a person should not receive any undue advantage from the fact that there is no contractual remedy to force them to account for it.

Quasi-contractual remedies

Chapter 10

Sale of Goods

Commercial transactions involving the sale of goods and the supply of goods and services are an essential activity in our society. The law relating to the sale of goods was first codified in the Sale of Goods Act 1893. This Act has now been consolidated in the Sale of Goods Act 1979. A further extension to the law in this field arises out of the Supply of Goods and Services Act 1982 which, whilst similar in content to the Sale of Goods Act 1979, applies to contracts where goods are supplied under an agreement which does not fall within the definition laid down in s 2(1) Sale of Goods Act 1979 eg where a plumber carries out repairs.

10.1　Introduction

The Act supplies the following definition:

> 'It is a contract through which the seller agrees to transfer property in the goods for a money consideration, called the price'.

The Act is primarily concerned with the relationship between the seller and buyer and implies a number of important terms into the contract for the protection of the buyer.

10.2　What is a contract for the sale of goods?

The 1979 Act defines the type of goods covered by the Act (s 61(1)). In general the word 'goods' includes personal property of a moveable type ie anything which can be physically possessed in some way and is not attached to the land eg crops become goods if they are about to be harvested; money can become goods when it is antique or collectable. However, there are specific exclusions relating to real property eg land and buildings; chattels real – leaseholds; choses in actions eg debts, cheques and currency in circulation.

10.2.1　What are 'goods' under the Act?

Such agreements can be formed orally or in writing. As such there are no formal requirements, although the essentials in forming any contract must be met.

10.2.2　Form of the agreement

It is important to determine exactly when property (ie ownership) passes in the goods between the seller and the buyer, since this usually determines where the risk lies if anything should go wrong eg if goods are destroyed by fire. As a general rule, risk passes with property (s 20), although this rule may be varied by agreement or custom. In such

10.2.3　Transfer of property in goods

circumstances it will become necessary to ascertain who bears the financial risk of loss of the goods, the seller or the buyer. Various possibilities can complicate the situation. It is possible that the title to the goods has passed to the buyer and yet he still does not have possession. Similarly, it is possible that the buyer has the goods in his possession, but the title to the goods and therefore the risk has not yet passed. There are three types of goods that need to be considered separately:

- Specific goods

  These are goods identified and agreed upon at the time of the contract of sale eg the purchase of a bar of chocolate.

- Ascertained goods

  These are goods identified and agreed upon after the making of the contract eg I buy and pay for 20 sacks of flour; however, I do not collect them until they have been identified in the warehouse as mine, that is, separated from the bulk and labelled as mine. Once this is done the goods become ascertained.

- Unascertained goods

  These are goods which have not been specified eg goods which the buyer has agreed to purchase, but which are still part of a larger bulk.

- Future goods

  These are goods to be manufactured or acquired by the seller after the making of the contract of sale.

10.2.4   The passing of property in specific goods

The general rule for passing of property in specific goods is that if a contract of sale is unconditional, property passes to the buyer when the contract is made (s 18 r 1). This is subject to the intention of the parties. In *Re Anchor Line (Henderson Bros Ltd)* (1937) a crane was sold to buyers who agreed to pay annual sums for depreciation. It was held that the buyers would not have paid depreciation on their own goods so the intention must be inferred that the property in the goods remained with the sellers until the price was fully paid.

For property to pass the goods must be in a deliverable state ie they are in such a state as a buyer would, under the contract, be bound to take delivery.

In *Dennant v Skinner & Collam* (1948) a gentleman bought a car at an auction and afterwards he signed a form to the effect that the ownership of the vehicle would not pass to him until the cheque had been cleared. He sold the car to a third party and there followed a dispute about the ownership of the car. It was held that the contract was complete and ownership passed as the auctioneer's hammer fell. The third party therefore acquired a good title to the car.

If the contract is for the sale of specific goods but the owner is bound to do something to them to put them in a deliverable state, then ownership does not pass until that thing is done and the buyer has notice that it is done (s 18, r 2).

In *Underwood v Burgh Castle Brick & Cement Syndicate* (1922) the parties entered a contract for the sale of an engine weighing 30 tons. At the time the contract was made the engine was embedded in a concrete floor. Whilst it was being removed and loaded onto a truck it was damaged. The seller still sued for the price. It was held that the engine was not in a deliverable state when the contract was made and applying r 2, property would not pass until the engine was safely loaded on the truck; the seller must therefore bear the risk.

If the goods are to be weighed, tested or measured, the property will not pass until the process is complete and the buyer is informed, unless there is a specific agreement to the contrary (s 18 r 3).

Where goods are supplied on sale or return or on approval, property passes to the buyer when:

* He signifies his approval or acceptance to the seller;

* He does any other act adopting the transaction; or

* He, whilst not giving approval or acceptance, retains the goods beyond the agreed time or, if no time is agreed, beyond a reasonable time (s 18 r 4). In *Poole v Smith's Car Sales (Balham) Ltd* (1962) where following several requests by the seller for the return of his car which had been left on a garage on a sale or return basis, the car was returned damaged. It was held that as the car had not been returned within a reasonable time, property had passed to the defendant who would then be liable for the price.

The general rule is that the property passes to the buyer when parties intend it to pass. This is usually when the goods have been specified and the buyer is informed of this. This general rule can be rebutted by the particular circumstances of the case.

10.2.5   The passing of property in ascertained goods

No property passes in unascertained or future goods unless, and until, the goods become ascertained. The goods must be in a deliverable state and unconditionally appropriated to the contract by one party with the express or implied assent of the other. This is illustrated by the case of *McDougall v Aeromarine of Emsworth Ltd* (1958) in which the seller agreed to build a

10.2.6   The passing of property in unascertained goods

yacht for the buyer. As part of the agreement after the first instalment was paid the yacht and all the materials were meant to become the 'absolute property' of the buyer. It was held that no property could pass to the buyer since the goods were not physically in existence at that time.

In *Healy v Howlett* (1917) 190 boxes of fish were carried by rail. The buyer was to purchase 20 boxes and the seller directed the railway company to set aside 20 boxes. However, before this could be done the fish went rotten. The seller had sent the buyer an invoice stating that the fish were carried at the buyer's sole risk. It was held that since the fish had gone rotten before the goods were ascertained property could not pass to the buyer who was therefore entitled to reject the goods.

Obviously, the critical factor in this case was the failure on the part of the railway company to identify the 20 boxes by setting them aside for the buyer. It would have been untenable for future buyers if the courts had made the buyer 'bear the loss' in these circumstances.

10.2.7	The perishing of goods	In the event of goods perishing due to delayed delivery through the fault of either the buyer or the seller, then the loss falls on the party at fault. In *Demby Hamilton Co v Barden Ltd*, the seller agreed to sell the buyer 30 tons of crushed apple. The buyer failed to give proper delivery instructions and as a result the apple went bad before it could be delivered. It was held that the loss would fall on the buyer.
10.2.8	The definition of 'perish'	There has been some confusion about the meaning of the word 'perish'. Goods must become unrecognisable before they can be held to have 'perished'. Goods that never existed cannot perish. If a portion of a consignment of goods is destroyed then the goods have been described as having 'perished' within the meaning of the Act. An example of the wide meaning of the word can be seen in the case of *Barrow Lane & Ballard v Phillips* (1929) in which one-seventh of the goods ordered by the buyer disappeared, presumed stolen. It was held that the goods had 'perished' within the meaning of the Act.
10.2.9	Perishing of specific goods	As a general rule, in a contract for specific goods, if it transpires that the goods have perished before the contract is made, the contract can be avoided.

In *Couturier v Hastie* (1856) there was a contract to sell a cargo of corn, but unknown to the seller the ship's master had already sold it in Tunisia because it had begun to ferment. It was held that the contract was void.

However, in *McRae v Commonwealth Disposals Commission* (1951), the seller agreed to sell the buyer a specific shipwrecked oil tanker which did not exist. It was held that the seller was liable to the buyer because he had impliedly warranted that it did exist.

If goods perish after the contract has been made, the contract can be avoided if the risk has not yet passed to the buyer. If the risk has passed, then the buyer must bear the loss. In *Asfar v Blundell* (1896), the parties entered into a contract for the sale of dates. It transpired that the dates had become impregnated with sewage. It was held that the contract was void since the goods had perished within the meaning of the Act.

A contract for unascertained goods may be void if it is established that some goods have perished and it is therefore impossible to carry out the contract. This depends upon whether the unascertained goods are to be ascertained from a specific bulk or whether there was simply a general description of a type of goods eg the buyer may ask for 12 jars of honey from Mr Hayes' clover fed bees or just 12 jars of honey. In the latter case the contract is not void because the goods can be obtained from another source.

10.2.10 Perishing of unascertained goods

It is open to the parties to include a clause in the agreement which stipulates that title to the goods remains with the seller until the buyer has paid for the goods. Such clauses provide some protection for the seller, where goods are sold on credit, in the event of the buyer going bankrupt. Following *Aluminium Industrie Vaasen v Romalpa Aluminium Ltd* (1976), a reservation clause which extends the protection of the seller's title to subsequent dispositions of the goods by the buyer, where the seller remains unpaid, may also be valid. This allows the unpaid seller's claim to take precedence over the buyer's other creditors. Such clauses are known as *Romalpa* clauses.

10.3 Reservation of title

When it becomes impossible to carry out a contract originally conceived through the fault of neither party, a wider principle of common law can be applied, that of frustration of contract. This can occur because goods perish or because the contract becomes impossible to carry out legally.

In *Avery v Bowden* (1855) there was a contract to bring goods from Russia. The Crimean war broke out and it became illegal to trade with Russia. It was held that no claim could be brought against the defendant for failure to load the goods because the contract had been frustrated by illegality.

10.3.1 Frustration of the contract

If the contract is frustrated under the Law Reform (Frustrated Contracts)Act 1943 then the buyer can recover his money, but the court can deduct expenses incurred by the seller in performance of the contract. The law puts into effect what it assumes the parties would have intended, had they considered the circumstances.

In *Sainsbury v Street* (1972) there was a contract for 275 tons of barley to be grown by the seller on his farm. The crop was only 140 tons. The buyer argued that the seller should not be excused performance. It was held that there was an implied term that the buyer had an option of accepting reduced quantities at pro rata rates. Hence the seller was liable for the non-delivery of the 140 tons.

10.4 Sale by a person who is not the owner

There is an implied condition in s 12 of the Act that the seller has a right to sell the goods ie pass on a good title to them. The rule *nemo dat quod non habet* means that a person cannot give what he has not got, so that, in general, ownership is protected. The general rule is that where goods are sold by a person who is not the owner, the buyer acquires no better title than the seller (s 21). However, there are exceptions and the law may often have to choose between the rights of two innocent parties; the innocent purchaser and the real owner of the goods. Generally, the buyer will have to return the goods to the true owner, usually without any recompense, although where he has 'improved' the goods he may be entitled to some reimbursement. The exceptions to the nemo dat rule are as follows.

10.4.1 Estoppel

If the seller or buyer, by their conduct, make the other party believe that a certain fact is true, and the other party alters his position, then that same party will later be estopped (or prevented) from saying that the fact is untrue. For example, this has arisen where a party has, for complicated reasons, signed a statement that their own property belongs to someone else and then ends up 'buying back' their own property. They may be estopped from denying the statement they made falsely about the ownership of the property (*Eastern Distributors Ltd v Goldring* (1957)).

To be claimed successfully, estoppel can only be raised against a person who had actual knowledge of the facts and actually agreed to them knowing that a third party may rely on the 'apparent' authority.

10.4.2 Agency

If a principal appoints an agent to sell his goods to a third party, then any sale by the agent, in accordance with the instructions given, will pass on a good title to the third party.

If, however, the agent has exceeded his instructions in some way, then no title would pass to the third party unless the agent had apparent authority (*Central Newbury Car Auctions v Unity Finance* (1957)).

A third party has an even stronger claim to the title of the goods where the agent is a mercantile agent. A mercantile agent is one 'having in the customary course of business as such agent, authority either to sell goods or to consign goods for the purposes of sale or to buy goods, or to raise money on the security of goods' (Factors Act 1889 s 1(1)). So, for example, where the third party as a consumer buys a car from an agent who is in the car trade, this provision may apply.

10.4.3   Mercantile agency

The Act states that the owner is bound by the actions of a mercantile agent in the following circumstances:

- If the agent has possession of the goods or the documents of title, with the owner's consent and makes any sale, pledge or other disposition of them in the ordinary course of business, whether or not the owner authorised it (s 2(1), *Folkes v King* (1923)). Any third party claiming against the owner in this situation must prove *inter alia*, that at the time of the sale he had no notice of the lack of authority on the part of the agent.

  In *Pearson v Rose & Young* (1951) the owner of a car took it to the dealer and asked him to obtain offers. The owner did not intend to hand over the registration book, but left it with the dealer by mistake. The dealer sold the car with the book to an innocent buyer. The question of the true ownership of the car was raised. It was held that the dealer had obtained the car 'with the consent of the owner' but this consent did not extend to the registration book, hence the sale must be treated as a sale without registration book and the buyer could not get a good title to the car.

- If the mercantile agent pledges goods as security for a prior debt, the pledgee acquires no further right to the goods than the factor has against his principal at the time of the pledge (s 4).

- If the mercantile agent pledges goods in consideration of the delivery of other goods, or of a document of title to goods or of a negotiable security, the pledgee acquires no right in the goods pledged beyond the value of the goods, documents or security when so delivered in exchange (s 5).

- If the mercantile agent has received possession of goods from their owner for the purpose of consignment or sale and the consignee has no notice that he is not the owner, the consignee has a lien on the goods for any advances he has made to the agent (s 7).

| 10.4.4 | Sales authorised by law |

There are cases in which the title does not pass directly from the owner, because the sale is authorised by the Court eg the sale of goods which are the subject matter of legal proceedings. Similarly, in common law or statute, it is sometimes declared that a non-owner is entitled to sell goods eg an agent of necessity or an unpaid seller.

| 10.4.5 | Sale in market overt |

This is an old rule relating to well established open public markets in England and shops within the City of London. These rules do not apply in Scotland and Wales. When goods are sold in such 'markets', at business premises in the normal hours of business between sun rise and sunset, the buyer will obtain a good title as long as he buys the goods in good faith and without notice of the defect in title on the part of the seller (s 22(1)).

In *Reid v Metropolitan Police Commissioner* (1973) a pair of glass candelabras were stolen from Reid. Subsequently, an art dealer bought them in the New Caledonian market for £200. The market normally commenced business at 7 am, but it was normal for dealers to buy earlier and the candelabra had been purchased in half light. The goods were seized by the police. It was held that Reid could recover the goods. The sale must take place within the usual hours of the market, but it must also be 'between the rising of the sun and the going down of the same'. Thus, the dealer did not acquire a good title because the latter requirements were not satisfied.

Whether a market is recognised as being 'overt' will depend on charter or custom. The Sale of Goods (Amendment) Bill 1994 will abolish the market overt exception to the *nemo dat* rule. It should come into force in 1995 although its effect will not be retrospective.

| 10.4.6 | Sale under a voidable title |

If at the time of the sale the seller's title has not been avoided, the buyer can acquire a good title to the goods, provided that he did not know of the seller's defect of title and bought the goods in good faith (s 23).

In this case the sale by the original owner is fully binding until he takes steps to have it set aside. In *Car & Universal Finance Co v Caldwell* (1965) a car was sold to a rogue who supplied a cheque as payment. The cheque was dishonoured. The owner went to the police. It was held that by this action the owner had avoided the contract with the rogue.

Clearly the situation before an owner takes steps to avoid the contract is that someone who does not have a good title eg the rogue can pass on a good title to the innocent third party who pays good value for the goods.

A contract of sale can be complete and valid even where the goods are still in the possession of the seller (s 24) eg awaiting delivery. If in this scenario the seller sells the goods to a second buyer, the second buyer will get a good title to those goods if he takes delivery of them. However, he must take the goods in good faith and without notice of the original sale. This leaves the first buyer in the position of having to sue the seller for breach of contract (see *Worcester Works Finance v Cooden Engineering* (1971).

10.4.7   Disposition by a seller in possession

Disposition by a buyer in possession is a corresponding situation, where the buyer possesses the goods but the seller has retained property in them. Then, if the buyer has the goods and any necessary documents of title with the consent of the seller, and he transfers these to an innocent transferee (second buyer), that transferee will obtain a good title to the goods; again this is subject to the proviso that the second buyer takes the goods in good faith and without notice of any lien or other claim on the goods by the original seller (s 25(1); *Cahn v Pockett's Bristol Channel Co* (1899)).

Section 25 does not extend to hire purchase agreements or regulated conditional sale agreements.

10.4.8   Disposition by a buyer in possession

The law changed in 1964 to protect 'private purchasers' of motor vehicles which were subject to a hire-purchase agreement. The original hirer will still have the same obligation to the finance company. The final purchaser should have taken the car in good faith, without notice of the hire-purchase agreement.

These nine exceptions summarise the cases in which the private purchaser may get a good title to the goods from someone who is not the owner of those goods. In all other cases, the title remains with the true owner who can sue in tort for the conversion of the goods. The true owner can sue the person who possesses the goods currently and anyone who has possessed those goods before that person.

10.4.9   Sale of motor vehicles which are the subject of a hire-purchase agreement

There are some terms which are implied into every contract for the sale of goods by the 1979 Act. It is important to understand the legal effect of such terms as the remedy in the event of a breach may differ. The most important implied terms are *conditions*. A condition is a fundamental term of the contract, any breach of which will allow the injured party to treat the contract as repudiated. This means that the parties are returned to their original positions. The buyer may bring an action for damages instead of repudiating the contract, and, if he has been deemed to have accepted the goods, he will have

10.5   Implied terms

no choice but to sue for damages rather than repudiate the contract.

A *warranty* is a lesser term of the contract and is not seen as being as important as a condition. A breach of warranty will allow the buyer to claim damages, but not to reject the goods. Apart from the implied terms which stipulate the nature of the term, whether any other term is a condition or warranty will depend on the construction of the contract and the intentions of the parties. As a general rule, terms relating to the time of payment are not regarded as conditions whereas terms relating to the time of delivery are to be treated as conditions. A term which is not a condition is an 'innominate' term, a breach of which may result in repudiation if it goes to the root of the contract.

The implied conditions and warranties are as follows:

• The seller must give a good title to the goods (s 12);

• The goods must correspond with any description applied to them (s 13);

• The goods must be of merchantable quality (s 14);

• The goods must be reasonably fit for their normal purpose or for a purpose which was specified by the buyer (s 14);

• If the sale is a sale by sample the goods must correspond with the sample shown (s 15).

10.5.1   Title (s 12)

There is an implied condition that the seller has the right to sell the goods and the ability to transfer a good title to the buyer.

In *Niblett Ltd v Confectioners' Materials Co* (1921) the labels on a number of tins containing condensed milk infringed Nestle's trademark. These tins were being imported from America and were seized by customs and not released to the buyer. It was held that although the American company had a right to transfer title in these goods, the goods were not what they purported to be. The buyer could, therefore, claim damages and breach of condition, as he would not be obtaining a trouble-free title to the goods ie what the law calls 'quiet enjoyment' of the goods. His title would clearly be challenged as sale of the goods infringed Nestle's trademark.

In cases brought under s 12, the buyer can recover the full purchase price, even though he may have used the goods for some time – if he does not receive a good title to the goods there is a total failure of consideration. In *Rowland v Divall* (1923) the buyer had used a car for four months. The title to the car had not been transferred to him. It was held that since he had not received what he had bargained for he could recover the full price paid.

There are also implied warranties that the goods are free from any charge or encumbrance not disclosed or known to the buyer before the contract is made and that the buyer will have quiet possession of the goods (s 12(2)).

In *Microbeads AC v Vinhurst Road Markings* (1975) the seller sold some road marking machines to the buyers. Unknown to the seller at the time of the sale another firm was in the process of patenting this type of equipment, although rights to enforce the patent did not commence until after the contract between the seller and buyer was made. A patent action was subsequently brought against the buyer who then claimed that the seller was in breach of the implied condition as he had no right to sell and was in breach of the warranty of quiet possession. It was held that at the time of sale the seller had every right to sell the goods, but was in breach of the warranty of quiet possession, because that amounted to an undertaking as to the future.

Where the sale of goods is by description, the goods must accord with any description applied to them. Goods are sold by description either where the buyer does not see the goods but relies on a description of them, or where he sees the goods, but he relies on terms describing features of the goods or self description. It must be proved that there was such a description and that the buyer relied on it (*Leinster Enterprises v Christopher Hull Fine Art* (1991)). It can then be determined whether the goods complied with it. A contractual description consists of any words, oral or written, which can be relied upon as identification of the goods that are being bought.

In *Beale v Taylor* (1967) the buyer read an advertisement offering for sale a 'Herald convertible 1961'. He went to see the car. On the back of the vehicle was a plate which stated '1200'. He bought the car and later discovered that it was the back half of a 1961 model welded to the front half of an earlier model. It was held that since the buyer bought the car with reference to the description he was entitled to damages for breach of the implied condition under s 13.

The description may be very simple, as in the case of *Grant v Australian Knitting Mills* (1970) in which 'underpants' was held to be a contractual description as it was the way in which the buyer identified the item he was purchasing. Not all the words used by the seller will be part of the contractual description.

In *Ashington Piggeries v Christopher Hill Ltd* (1972) there was a written contract which stated that the sellers would make a

10.5.2   Description (s 13)

'vitamin-fortified' mink food to be called 'King Size'. The food was made up to a formula specified by the buyers which was also in the contract. It was stated that the formula was the description which specified what the buyers wanted. One of the ingredients was herring meal which was contaminated, but which was still identifiable as herring meal. It was held that the sellers had made up the food correctly so that there was no breach relating to the description of the goods. As we shall see, however, there may be potentially more than one breach of the implied terms.

Section 13 may be broken even if the goods themselves are of merchantable quality and fit for the purpose (*Arcos v Ronaasen* (1933)) and the implied term extends to the packaging of the goods if that is part of the description, as illustrated in *Re Moore & Co and Landauer & Co* (1921), in which the buyer was allowed to reject the goods because he had bought tinned fruit in cases containing 30 tins and the seller delivered the correct tinned fruit in cases some of which contained 30 tins and some 24 tins. It was held that as the goods delivered did not correspond with those ordered, the whole consignment could be rejected.

Where the sale of goods is by sample the goods must correspond to the description as well as the sample. If there is no reliance on the description then s 13 is inapplicable (*Leinster Enterprises Ltd v Christopher Hull Fine Art Ltd* (1991)).

10.5.3	Merchantable quality (s 14(2))

There is an implied condition that the goods shall be of merchantable quality according to s 14(2) of the Act. Unlike s 13, s 14 does not apply to private sales. Once the seller has sold the goods in the normal course of business, the law inserts an implied term that the goods are of merchantable quality with two exceptions:

• There is no claim for a defect in the goods if the defect is specifically brought to the buyer's attention at the time of the contract of sale;

• There can be no claim when the buyer has examined the goods as regards any defects which should have been revealed by that examination (see *Thornett Fehr v Beers* (1919)). The buyer may lose his rights under s 14(2), either by waiving his right to carry out an examination or by carrying out a limited examination in respect of those particular type of goods. It very much depends on the nature of the goods.

The goods which come within s 14(2) include not only goods sold in the normal course of business but also goods sold as part of a business to the consumer eg the sale of a van which has been used in a grocery business.

The Sale of Goods Act s 14(6) defines merchantable quality as:

> '... fit for the purpose for which goods of that kind are commonly bought as it is reasonable to expect having regard to any description applied to them, the price (if relevant) and all other relevant circumstances.'

Obviously, second hand goods will not necessarily be of the same standard as brand new goods, but will still be subject to the definition in s 14(6). The price of the goods may be very relevant in the case of second hand goods (*Business Application Specialists Ltd v Nationwide Credit Ltd* (1988)).

In *Rogers v Parish (Scarborough) Ltd* (1987) a Range Rover was sold as new. It was discovered that within a short time of the purchase it had a defective engine, gearbox, bodywork and oil seals, none of which rendered it incapable of being driven or insufficiently roadworthy, but each of which necessitated the carrying out of repairs. It was held that the vehicle was not of merchantable quality. As the vehicle had been sold as new, the performance and finish should have been equal to that of a model of average standard with no mileage. Deficiencies which might be acceptable with a secondhand vehicle were not to be expected in one purchased as new.

With regard to new cars, the court in *Bernstein v Pamsons Motors (Golders Green) Ltd* (1987) felt that the buyer of a new car was entitled to expect more than the buyer of a secondhand car, although how much more was dependent upon the nature of the defect, length of time of repairs and the price of the vehicle. The court distinguished between 'the merest cosmetic blemish on a new Rolls Royce which might render it unmerchantable whereas on a humbler car it might not'.

The goods need not be suitable for all purposes, but for the majority of their common purposes (*Aswan Engineering Establishment v Lupdine* (1987)).

In *Kendall (Henry) & Sons v William Lillico & Sons Ltd* (1968) the buyer and seller entered into a contract for the sale of groundnut extract for feeding to cattle and poultry. It contained a poison which killed the poultry but did not affect the cattle. As a result the buyer's pheasants were killed. It was held that the goods were of merchantable quality because the test to be applied was:

> '... goods are of merchantable quality if they are fit for one of their normal purposes (regardless of whether they are fit for the buyer's particular purpose) and are saleable

under their contractual description for one of their normal purposes without a reduction in price'.

In this case, the goods were of merchantable quality because they were for cattle, since there was evidence that the buyers of the goods for cattle would have been willing to buy the goods as groundnut extract without any reduction in price.

Had the buyers made known their particular purpose to the seller, they may have had a successful case under s 13 and s 14(3) – description and fitness for the purpose respectively. This last case also creates a potential loophole, in that buyers who made a bad bargain and therefore paid too much for the goods would be able to claim that they were not of merchantable quality.

In *Brown & Son Ltd v Craiks Ltd* (1970) the buyers supplied specifications for cloth to be made for use in dressmaking. The sellers did not know that it was to be used for dressmaking and the specifications were more like those for industrial cloth. The sellers complied with the instructions and the cloth proved suitable only for industrial purposes. The buyers tried to reject the goods on the grounds that they were not of merchantable quality as the price was too expensive for industrial cloth. They argued that no one would be willing to buy the cloth except with a reduction in price. It was held that the cloth was of merchantable quality as it complied with the specifications given. The goods would only have been held to be not of merchantable quality if the reduction in price was really substantial.

The 1979 Act gave the court discretionary powers to reach a fair decision in cases of 'price reduction' (s 14(b)). This discretion would formerly have been used in the case of *Kendall v Lillico* but not in a case such as *Brown v Craiks* where the correct specifications had been supplied.

10.5.4	Reasonable fitness for the purpose

There is an implied condition in a contract for the sale of goods that the goods supplied are reasonably fit for any purpose expressly or impliedly made known to the seller under s 14(3) of the Act. Where goods have a normal purpose, the law implies that you buy those goods for that purpose eg in the case of *Grant v Australian Knitting Mills* where the purpose of 'underpants' was to be worn and *Godley v Perry* (1960) where in purchasing a toy catapult the buyer did not have to state specifically the purpose. If the purpose or use is unusual or the goods have several normal but distinct uses eg timber for paper or for furniture, then the purpose must be made known expressly – that is it must be spelt out clearly either verbally or in writing, to the seller before the buyer can rely on this section. An example of this is illustrated by the case of *Ashington Piggeries v Hill* (above) where the buyers made it clear to the seller that the end product would be fed to mink, even though they supplied the formula.

The question of whether goods are reasonably fit for the purpose is a question of fact. In *Griffiths v Peter Conway Ltd* (1939) the buyer bought a Harris tweed coat. It transpired that she was allergic to the fabric. It was held that there was no breach of s 14(3) as the coat was fit for wear by any normal person and she had failed to make any reference to her condition or sensitivity when she made her purchase.

It is clear that this condition does not apply where the buyer does not rely on the seller's skill and judgment eg if he chooses a brand other than that recommended by the seller or where it is unreasonable for him to have relied on that skill and judgment if, for example, he had greater expertise.

This section applies only if there is a term of the contract which states that it is a contract of sale by sample. This could be an oral term, but if it is in writing, then the term about sale by sample must be written into the contract. The mere act of showing a sample of the goods during negotiations does not make the sale one of sale by sample unless the parties agree to do so. In *Drummond v Van Ingen* (1887), Lord MacNaughten explained the function of a sample in stating that:

> 'the office of a sample is to present to the eye the real meaning and intention of the parties with regard to the subject matter of the contract, which, owing to the imperfection of language, it may be difficult or impossible to express in words. The sample speaks for itself.'

It is no defence under s 15(2) to say that the bulk can easily be made to correspond with the sample.

In *E & S Ruben Ltd v Faire Bros & Co Ltd* (1949) a material known as Linatex was sold which was crinkly, whereas the sample had been soft and smooth. The seller argued that by a simple process of warming, the bulk could have been made as soft as the sample. It was held that there had been a breach of s 15(2) and the sellers were therefore liable to pay damages to the buyer.

A buyer may not be able to claim damages under s 15(2) for defects he could reasonably have discovered upon examination of the goods. He may still have an action under s 14(2) and (3). It is important to remember that the implied conditions under s 15 are:

10.5.5   Sale by sample (s 15)

- That the bulk shall correspond with the sample;

- That the buyer shall have a reasonable opportunity to compare the goods with the sample;

- That the goods will be free from any defect rendering them unmerchantable which would not be apparent on reasonable examination of the sample.

| 10.5.6 | Exclusion clauses | The effect of exclusion clauses on the operation of the Sale of Goods Act is limited not only by the Act itself, but also by the Unfair Contracts Terms Act 1977. The limitations are as follows: |

- Section 12 cannot be excluded ie the seller must pass on a good title.

- In the case of a consumer purchaser (ie where the purchaser is a private individual dealing with a trader eg an individual in a shop) it is impossible to exclude liability under ss 13-15.

- In the case of a non-consumer contract (ie where the buyer is not a private individual and/or the seller is not acting in the course of business as eg in a private sale) it is possible to exclude liability under ss 13-15, but only if the exclusion clause satisfies the test of 'reasonableness'.

- Any other liability for breach of contract can be excluded or restricted only to the extent that it is reasonable.

- It is impossible to exclude liability for death and personal injury.

- It is possible to exclude liability for other loss or damage arising from negligence or misrepresentation only to the extent that the clause is deemed to be reasonable.

    The requirement of 'reasonableness' means that the exclusion clause 'shall be a fair and reasonable one to be included, having regard to the circumstances which were or ought to have been known to or in the contemplation of the parties when the contract was made' (Schedule 2 to the Unfair Contract Terms Act 1977).

| 10.5.7 | Performance of the contract | Normally, it is the duty of the seller to deliver the goods and the duty of the buyer to accept the goods and pay the agreed price for them. Disputes arise most frequently at significant times in the performance of the contract, such as the time of delivery of the goods and the acceptance of those goods or the time of payment. |

Delivery is 'the voluntary transfer of possession from one person to another' according to the Act. It is the duty of the seller to deliver the goods and the duty of the buyer to accept them and pay for them (s 27). Payment and delivery are concurrent conditions unless otherwise agreed (s 28). Delivery by instalment is not acceptable, unless the contract specifically states that delivery is going to take place by this method (s 31).

If delivery is late, the buyer may reject or accept the goods – in the latter case, the buyer cannot repudiate the contract. The buyer loses the right to reject the goods if he accepts late delivery, but is still able to claim damages. Where the seller delivers the contract goods mixed with other goods the buyer may reject the whole or accept the correct goods; he cannot accept the incorrect goods unless the seller offers to sell them to him (s 30).

The buyer may also lose the right to reject the goods by waiver of that right. This could happen where the seller is in breach of a condition before the goods are delivered and the buyer has knowledge of this. If the buyer then indicates that, under the new circumstances, he would still accept the goods, that could amount to a waiver of his right to reject.

Acceptance occurs when either :

* The buyer states to the seller that he has accepted the goods eg he signs an acceptance note; or

* The goods are delivered and the buyer retains the goods for a reasonable length of time without rejecting them or he does an act inconsistent with the seller's ownership such as sell the goods or process them (s 35).

Section 34 states that the buyer is not deemed to have accepted the goods until he has examined them or has had reasonable opportunity to do so. Section 35 follows this by stating that the buyer must have reasonable opportunity to examine the goods even if he does an act inconsistent with the ownership of the seller or keeps the goods a reasonable length of time.

In *Bernstein v Pamsons Motors* (1987) the plaintiff bought a new car from the defendants which on delivery had a minor defect which if not repaired was likely to cause the engine to seize up. The engine seized within three weeks of delivery after the plaintiff had driven 140 miles. The defendants carried out repairs free of charge but the plaintiff refused to take the car back and asked for the return of his money. It was held that the car was not of merchantable quality nor fit for the purpose. However, the plaintiff was deemed to have accepted the car under s 35 and therefore could only treat the breach of

10.6   Delivery and acceptance of the goods

condition as a warranty and claim damages. The court felt that 'reasonable time' meant a reasonable time to try out the goods, not a reasonable time to discover the defect.

10.7 Price

The price is usually considered to be a basic part of the contract for the sale of goods and so it is normally expressly agreed. Section 8 states that the price may be fixed or determined by an agreed procedure. If not, then the buyer must pay a reasonable price, which will be a question of fact depending on the circumstances of the case.

In *May v Butcher* (1934) there was an agreement for the purchase of government tentage which provided that the price, manner of delivery and dates of payment were to be agreed upon from time to time. If the contract had failed to mention those items the matter could have been resolved by applying the provisions of the Act, but the contract expressly stated that the items were to be the subject of a later agreement. It was held that the parties had not intended to make a contract. They were simply agreeing to agree and therefore there was no contract.

It is interesting to note that if there had been no mention of the price, the contract may well have been valid under the 1893 Act and the price could have been determined as a 'reasonable' price. In contrast to this case, the following case illustrates a situation where the price was a less important element of the contract and provision was made for determining the sum in the event of controversy.

In *Foley v Classique Coaches Ltd* (1934) the defendants bought some land from the plaintiffs. It was a condition of the contract that the defendants agreed to purchase petrol from the plaintiffs for the coach business, at a price 'to be agreed by the parties from time to time'. Failing agreement, the price was to be settled by arbitration. It was argued that there was insufficient basis for a contract. It was held that there was a binding contract; the price to be paid being a 'reasonable' price.

Valuation by a third party is one method whereby the parties can stipulate for ascertainment of the price. The Act stresses that where he cannot, or does not, make the valuation, the contract is avoided. If, however, the buyer has already appropriated the goods or if lack of valuation is caused by the fault of either party, then damages are payable.

10.8 Time of payment and delivery

There is a presumption that time of payment is not a fundamental condition, although the parties can expressly agree otherwise. A stipulated time for delivery, however, will be considered to be 'of the essence' of the contract. Similarly, if a date is specified for shipment of the goods by the seller, this may give the buyer grounds for repudiating the contract if it is not fulfilled.

In *Rickards v Oppenheim* (1950) the seller contracted to build a car for the buyer, to be built by 20 March; it was not ready by that date. The buyer did not repudiate the contract, but pressed for early delivery. When it was still not finished by the end of June, the buyer informed the seller that if it was not ready in another four weeks, he would regard the contract as repudiated. At the end of four weeks the car was still not ready. It was held that the buyer had acted within his rights. He lost the right to regard the contract as repudiated on 20 March by his waiver, but it was a condition of that waiver, under those circumstances, that delivery should take place as soon as possible. The buyer could therefore revive his right to repudiate the contract by giving reasonable notice. The buyer was under no obligation, after four weeks, to buy the car.

It is important to consider the remedies that are available to the seller or buyer in the event of a breach of contract. The contract will not always be completely avoided by doing so and it may be in the interests of the other party to accept damages and continue the legal relationship.	**10.8.1** Remedies for breach of contract
If things go wrong for the seller of the goods, he has two types of remedy available to him. The first type of remedy is concerned with the money or the price of the goods and the other type with the goods themselves. The seller has two possible legal actions to recover the price of the goods if things go wrong.	**10.8.2** Seller's remedies
The seller can bring an action for the price of the goods in either of the following circumstances:	**10.8.3** Action for the price of the goods

- The buyer has wrongfully refused or neglected to pay for the goods according to the terms of the contract; or

- The property has passed to the buyer or 'the price is payable on a day certain irrespective of delivery'.

This does not include the circumstances in which the buyer has rightfully rejected the goods for breach of condition.

The seller cannot, in fact, sue unless he is ready and willing to deliver at the time of the refusal to pay. If the seller has granted the buyer credit, then he cannot sue until the end of the credit period. If there is no certain, agreed date, then the action will only succeed when the property has passed to the buyer.

10.8.4	Damages for non-acceptance of the goods	If the seller cannot maintain an action for the price, he may still have a claim for damages for non-acceptance, but usually such damages will be much less than the price and the seller has the inconvenience of trying to find another buyer.
10.8.5	Remedies with respect to the goods	• Lien (ss 41-43)

• Lien (ss 41-43)

The seller has the right to retain possession of the goods, even though the property has passed to the buyer. The Act assumes that delivery and payment are normally concurrent events, except where sales are on credit. The lien or right to keep the goods is based on possession of the goods and is only available for the price of the goods and not for other damages, such as storage charges. It may be a useful remedy in times of economic stress where there are rumours of bankruptcies and liquidations. The unpaid seller may well be financially better off with the goods in his possession than if he had simply become a creditor in the bankruptcy.

Delivery of part of the goods will not destroy the unpaid seller's lien unless the circumstances show an intention to waive the lien. The unpaid seller will lose his lien if he delivers the goods for carriage to the buyer and does not reserve the rights of disposal over them or if the buyer lawfully obtains possession of the goods.

• Stoppage in transit (ss 44-46)

If the buyer becomes insolvent and the goods are still in transit between the seller and the buyer, the unpaid seller is given the right of stoppage in transit and he can recover the goods from the carrier. The cost of redelivery must be borne by the seller in this case.

• *Romalpa* clause

This arose from the case of *Aluminium Industrie Vassen BV v Romalpa Aluminium Ltd* (1976) which established that the manufacturer or supplier of goods had rights to retain some proprietary interest over the goods until he was paid, even when the goods supplied had been processed or sold. Furthermore, proprietary rights could be maintained even after a subsale of the goods (sale by the buyer to another party) so that debts owed to the buyer could be transferred to the manufacturer or supplier, if an appropriate *Romalpa* clause had been inserted.

• Right of resale

An unpaid seller can pass a good title to the goods to a second buyer after exercising his right of lien or stoppage in transit. In these cases the contract with the first buyer is automatically rescinded so that the property in the goods reverts to the seller, who can keep any further profit made from the resale and any deposit put down by the buyer. If he makes a loss on the resale then he can claim damages from the original buyer. There is no requirement that the second purchaser takes delivery or buys in good faith (ie without knowledge of the first sale).

In *Ward (RV) Ltd v Bignall* (1967) two cars were being sold for £850. After paying a deposit of £25, the buyer refused to pay the rest. The seller informed the buyer in writing that if he did not pay the balance by a given date, he would resell the cars. The buyer did not pay. The seller sold one car at £350 but failed to find a purchaser for the other. He bought a claim against the purchaser for the balance of the price and advertising expenses. It was held that the seller could not recover any of the price since the ownership had reverted back to him but he could recover damages. The remaining car was worth £450, so that his total loss on resale would be £50, minus the £25 deposit originally paid. He was entitled to this £25 plus advertising expenses.

• Action for specific performance

The court can make an order of specific performance against the seller in the case of a contract to deliver specific or ascertained goods. This order cannot be made for unascertained or future goods. The seller is required to deliver the goods and he is not given the option of paying damages instead. The courts will not make the order for such a remedy unless damages for non-delivery would not be adequate. Damages will generally be adequate except where the goods are in some way unique or rare.

• Rejection of the goods

If there is a breach of condition by the seller, the buyer has a right to reject the goods and may also have a claim for damages. The buyer can exercise this right by refusing to take delivery and informing the seller he has rejected the goods. He is under no duty, in such circumstances, to return them to the seller who may have to collect them. Under s 35, the seller will have a right of action against the buyer if the buyer's rejection means repudiation of the contract or if the buyer has kept the goods for an unreasonable length of time. The buyer does not have a lien over the rejected goods and must hand them back even if his purchase money has not been returned. He can bring an action against the seller to recover the price on the grounds of failure of consideration. It is important to

10.8.6   Buyer's remedies

consider the meaning of 'acceptance' of the goods in this context, because it is usually at this point that the contract is made and the risk associated with ownership of the goods is transferred.

Acceptance is made in one of the following ways:

(a) the buyer informs the seller that he has accepted the goods;

(b) the buyer has had reasonable opportunity to examine the goods and he does some act inconsistent with the seller being owner of those goods;

(c) the buyer retains the goods for a reasonable length of time without informing the seller that he has rejected the goods.

• Action for damages

The buyer can claim damages for non-delivery or for breach of condition or warranty. The buyer may also be trying to recover the purchase price and/or reject the goods.

Section 11(4) of the Act states that 'where a contract of sale is not severable and the buyer has accepted the goods or part of them', the buyer cannot reject the goods but can only claim damages for breach of condition. This is an important limitation on the buyer's right of rejection.

• Recovery of the purchase price

The buyer can recover all payments made if consideration has failed. This may apply to cases of non-delivery, but also where there had been a breach of condition of the sale. If the contract is severable (eg separate delivery times and instalments for different parts of the goods) the buyer can accept part and reject part of the goods and recover the price paid on the rejected goods.

10.9   Supply of Goods and Services Act 1982

The Supply of Goods and Services Act 1982 provides protection in respect of agreements which do not fulfil the definition of the Sale of Goods Act 1979 but under which goods are supplied, usually along with a service. The Act itself mirrors the 1989 Act in that it implies conditions with respect to goods supplied. These implied conditions are contained in ss 2-5 and are very similar to ss 12-15 Sale of Goods 1989 ie there is an implied condition re title, description, quality and fitness for the purpose as well as sample.

Furthermore the Supply of Goods and Services Act provides protection for the victims of poor quality workmanship, including the time it takes to provide services and the price for such services. The Act applies to all contracts where a 'person agrees to carry out a service in the course of a business'. The implied terms as to services can be found in ss 13-15.

Section 13 states that there is an implied term that where the supplier is acting in the course of a business, he will carry out the service with reasonable skill and care.

Section 14 states that where the supplier is acting within the course of a business and the time for the service to be carried out is not fixed by the contract or determined by a course of dealings between the parties, the supplier will carry out the service within a reasonable time.

Section 15 states that where the consideration is not determined by a contract or in a manner agreed in the contract or by the course of dealing between the parties, the party contracting with the supplier will pay a reasonable price.

These are governed by the Unfair Contract Terms Act 1977 with respect to contracts for the supply of services.	10.9.1 Exclusion clauses

Title cannot be excluded and any attempt to exclude renders the clause void. In consumer sales any attempt to exclude the terms contained in ss 2-5 will render the clause void. If the buyer does not deal as a consumer any attempt to exclude these terms will be subject to the test of reasonableness.

Where an exclusion clause relates to s 13, it must satisfy the test of reasonableness. Liability for death or personal injury cannot be excluded.

10.10   Product liability

The Consumer Protection Act 1987 was passed to implement the EC Directive on product liability. The Act provides a means of redress for a consumer against the manufacturer of a product for injury caused by that product. Although a consumer would have had an action against the manufacturer in negligence (*Donoghue v Stevenson* (1932)), this would involve establishing fault; the Consumer Protection Act does not require such evidence in order to establish liability.

In order to succeed in a claim, the plaintiff must show:

• That the product contained a defect;

• That the plaintiff suffered damage;

• That the damage was caused by the defect;

• That the defendant was a producer, own brander, or importer of the product.

A 'producer' of a product is defined as including the manufacturer of a finished product or of a component; any person who won or abstracted the product; where goods are not manufactured or abstracted, any person responsible for an industrial or other process to which any essential characteristic of the product is attributable eg a person who processes agricultural produce (s 1(2)(a)).

Although a supplier of a defective product does not have primary liability, he will be liable if he fails to identify the producer or importer when requested to do so (s 2(2)).

A person may be deemed to be a 'producer' of a defective product if he holds himself out as a producer by putting his name or trade mark on the product.

10.10.1 'Defective' product

A product will be 'defective' within the meaning of s 3 CPA if the safety of the product is not such as persons generally are entitled to expect, taking all circumstances into account, including the marketing of the product, the presentation of the product including instructions and warnings, the use to which it might reasonably be expected to be put, and the time when it was supplied ie the state of the art at the time of supply.

A 'product' is anything which has undergone an industrial process and it must be moveable.

10.11 Defences

Although the Consumer Protection Act 1987 imposes strict liability, there are a number of defences provided by s 4.

Any person has a defence if it can be shown that:

- The defect is attributable to compliance with an domestic or EC enactment;

- He was not at any time the supplier of the product;

- The supply was not in the course of business;

- The defect did not exist in the product at the time it was supplied;

- The state of scientific and technical knowledge at the relevant time was not such that the producer might be expected to have discovered the defect;

- the defect was in a product in which the product in question had been comprised and was wholly attributable to the design of the subsequent product;

- more than 10 years has elapsed since the product was first supplied.

The 'development risks' defence allows the producer to show that the defect was not discoverable at the time he supplied the product. What is required of a producer for this defence to operate is an area of contention awaiting clarification by the courts. Should the producer make sure he is aware of all available knowledge related to the product and then ensure he applies it or will it suffice to do limited research bearing in mind the cost of development and the potentially small risk to the consumer ?

Any person injured by the product can claim; this includes personal injury or damage to private property, the latter cannot be brought where the amount claimed is less than £275. No claim can be made for 'pure' economic loss or for damage to the product itself.	**10.11.1** Liability cannot be excluded or limited (s 7)

There is a three year limitation period for claims, the date of which runs from the date of the injury. Where the damage is not apparent, the date runs from the time the plaintiff knew or could reasonably have known of the claim.

The CPA 1987 also provides protection for the public from unsafe consumer goods. This part of the statute imposes criminal liability rather than civil liability. It enables the Secretary of State to make safety regulations, which has been done with respect to certain products such flammable materials in furniture, children's nightclothes etc.	**10.12 Consumer safety**

It creates a criminal offence of 'supplying consumer goods which are not reasonably safe' (s 10). It allows the Secretary of State to serve a 'prohibition notice' on a supplier, prohibiting him from supplying goods which are unsafe or a notice to warn which requires the supplier to publish warnings about the unsafe goods.

A consumer may have a civil action for breach of statutory duty against the supplier of unsafe goods under this part of the Act.

The CPA 1987 (s 20) provides that a person is guilty of an offence if, in the course of a business, he gives consumers an misleading indication as to the price at which any goods, services, accommodation or facilities are available. Evidence of an offence is provided by compliance or non-compliance with the Code of Practice published by the Office of Fair Trading.	**10.13 Misleading indications about price**

A number of defences are provided. The defendant must prove that he took all reasonable precautions and exercised all due diligence to avoid the commission of an offence; or that he was an innocent publisher/advertiser who was unaware and who had no ground for suspecting that the advertisement contained a misleading price indication.

10.14   Trade Descriptions Act 1968

The Trade Descriptions Act 1968 provides criminal sanctions for offences relating to the sale of goods, involving the use of false or misleading descriptions. It also provides facilities for the court to make a compensation order for the consumer who has suffered loss.

Under the Act it is a criminal offence to apply, in the course of a trade or business, a false description to goods or to sell goods where such a description is applied. 'False' means 'false to a material degree', therefore, in effect, any deviation from the description must be significant. The meaning of 'trade description' is indicated in s 2(1) as including statements about quantity, size, method of manufacture, fitness for purpose, other physical characteristics, testing and the results of such tests, approvals by any person, place, date and name of manufacturer, producer or processor and any history, including ownership and use.

The Act provides two defences (s24):

- That the misdescription was due to a mistake or to reliance on information supplied by a third party or to the act or default of a third party or some other cause beyond the control of the defendant;

- That all reasonable precautions were taken and due diligence exercised to avoid the commission of an offence.

It is also open to a 'trader' who is supplying goods to issue a disclaimer. This will provide a defence as long as it is sufficiently bold to equal that of the description supplied (*Norman v Bennett* (1974)). Such a disclaimer is not available where the trader is actually applying the trade description himself.

Sale of Goods

A contract for the sale of goods is defined as a contract through which the seller agrees to transfer property in the goods for a money consideration, called the price. Such contracts are governed by the Sale of Goods Act 1979.

The time at which property in the goods is transferred needs to be determined as risk of loss passes with property (s 20). The application of the rules is determined by the type of goods ie specific, ascertained, or unascertained.

Transfer of property in the goods

- The property passes when the contract is made (s 18 r 1):

  Re Anchor Line (Henderson Bros) Ltd (1937)

  Dennant v Skinner & Collam (1948)

Specific goods

- Where the seller of the goods is bound to put them in a deliverable state, property does not pass until this is done and the buyer notified (s 18 r 2):

  Underwood v Burgh Castle Brick & Cement Syndicate (1922)

- Where the goods are to be weighed, tested or measured, property does not pass until this is complete and the buyer notified (s 18 r 3)

- Where goods are supplied on sale or return or approval, property passes when the buyer signifies his approval or does any other act adopting the transaction (s 18 r 4):

  Poole v Smith's Car Sales (Balham) Ltd (1962)

Property passes when the parties intend it to pass.

Ascertained goods

No property passes until the goods are ascertained, in a deliverable state and unconditionally appropriated to the contract (s 18 r 5):

Unascertained goods

  McDougall v Aeromarine of Emsworth Ltd (1958)

  Healy v Howlett (1917)

Any loss incurred for perished goods is generally at the expense of the owner, subject to the apportionment of fault:

Perishing of goods ss 6 and 7

  Demby Hamilton Co v Barden Ltd (1949)

  Where, unknown to the parties, the goods have perished before the contract was made, the contract may be avoided:

Couturier v Hastie (1856)

Asfar v Blundell (1896)

Sale by non-owners

Generally a person who is not the owner of the goods cannot pass a good title to them (s 21), subject to the following exceptions:

- Estoppel;

- Agency;

- Mercantile agent
  Pearson v Rose & Young (1951);

- Sales authorised by law;

- Sale in market overt
  Reid v Metropolitan Police Commissioner (1974);

- Sale under a voidable title;

- Disposition by a seller in possession;

- Sale of motor vehicles which are the subject of a hire-purchase agreement.

Implied terms

A breach of a condition allows the injured party to repudiate the contract.

A breach of a warranty allows a claim for damages.

Title (s 12):

There is an implied condition that the seller has the right to sell the goods (*Niblett Ltd v Confectioners' Materials Co* (1921)); and an implied warranty of quiet possession and that the goods are free from any charge or encumbrance (*Microbeads AC v Vinhurst Road Markings* (1975))

Description (s 13):

There is an implied condition that goods will correspond with their description:

Beale v Taylor (1967)

Ashington Piggeries v Christopher Hill Ltd (1972)

Re Moore & Co & Landauer & Co (1921)

Merchantable Quality (s 14(2)):

There is an implied condition that goods shall be of merchantable quality as defined (s 14(6)), subject to defects specifically brought to the buyer's attention and defects revealed by examination.

Rogers v Parish (Scarborough) Ltd (1987)

Kendall (Henry) & Sons v William Lillico & Sons Ltd (1968)

Brown & Craiks Ltd (1970)

Fitness for the purpose (s 14(3))

Griffiths v Peter Conway Ltd (1939)

Sale by sample (s 15)

E & S Ruben Ltd v Faire Bros & Co Ltd (1949)

Exclusion of liability for breach of the implied terms:

• s 12 cannot be excluded;

• ss 13-15 cannot be excluded in consumer sales;

• ss 13-15 can only be excluded in non-consumer sales if the test of reasonableness is satisfied;

• liability for death or personal injury cannot be excluded (UCTA 1977);

• any other loss can only be excluded subject to the test of reasonableness.

• It is the duty of the seller to deliver the goods and the duty of the buyer to pay for the goods on delivery, subject to agreement (s 27). **Performance**

• In the event of late delivery, the goods may be rejected or accepted by the buyer.

• The buyer has a reasonable time to examine the goods before accepting them (*Bernstein v Pamsons Motors Ltd* (1987)).

• Retention of the goods by the buyer for a reasonable length of time without rejecting them will amount to acceptance.

The price may be determined by the parties or if not the buyer must pay a reasonable price (*Foley v Classique Coaches Ltd* (1934)). **Price**

The time of delivery is 'of the essence'; failure to meet the delivery date may allow the buyer to repudiate the contract (*Rickards v Oppenheim* (1950)). **Delivery**

Seller's remedies: **Remedies**

• Action for the price;

• Damages for non-acceptance;

• Lien;

- Stoppage in transit;
- *Romalpa* clause;
- Right of resale.

Buyer's remedies:

- Specific performance;
- Rejection of the goods;
- Action for damages;
- Recovery of the purchase price.

Further consumer protection

Supply of Goods and Services Act 1982

Consumer Protection Act 1987

Consumer Safety Act 1987

Trade Descriptions Act 1968

Chapter 11

Negligence

Negligence is a tort. It is, however, necessary to define what is meant by a tort before considering the essentials of negligence. A tort is a wrongful act against an individual or body corporate and his or her property, which gives rise to a civil action (usually for damages, although other remedies are available). Principally, liability is based on fault, although there are exceptions eg the tort of *Rylands v Fletcher*, breach of statutory duty, vicarious liability. The motive of the defendant in committing the tort is generally irrelevant.

Negligence is the most important of all the torts, not only because an understanding of it is vital to the comprehension of other torts, such as employer's liability and occupiers liability, but also because it is the one tort which is constantly developing in the light of social and economic change. This can be seen by reference to product liability, professional negligence and economic loss, all of which were originally only compensated if there was in existence a valid contract; in other words, no contract, no claim. After a period of continual development in the scope and application of this tort, the signs are that the Courts are beginning to be more cautious. They are aware of the economic implications on the public and private sector if they continue to extend the scope of actions in negligence. Whether this should be an issue for the Courts is always open to debate, but if the courts are to be pragmatic, then they may have no choice but to be restrained in the current economic climate.

The prime object of the tort of negligence is to provide compensation for the injured person. It has also been suggested that liability in tort provides a deterrent and that negligence is no exception ie it helps to define what is or is not acceptable conduct and therefore sets the boundaries of such behaviour. Unfortunately, people rarely act by reference to the civil law and the only real deterrent is through market forces ie the economic impact being passed on to those who have a higher risk of causing injury. Alternative compensation systems have been considered as this would largely eradicate the need of the injured party to pursue legal action. The alternatives on offer are no fault compensation schemes – see the Pearson Commission Report on Civil Liability and Compensation for Personal Injury (Cmnd 7054, 1978) and extending public and private insurance schemes.

11.2 Elements of the tort

There are specific elements of the tort of negligence which have to be established in the correct order if a claim by an injured party is to succeed. The burden of proof is on the plaintiff, to show on a balance of probabilities, that the following exist:

11.2.1 Duty of care

A person is not automatically liable for every negligent act he commits. The need to establish the essentials and, in particular, duty of care sets a legal limit on who can bring an action as a duty is not owed to the world at large. The onus is on the plaintiff to establish that the defendant owes him a duty of care. Unless this first hurdle is crossed, no liability can arise. The test for establishing whether a duty of care exists arises out of the case of *Donoghue v Stevenson* (1932). Prior to this case the duty of care was only owed in limited circumstances. Now, it is said that the categories of negligence are never closed, in that the law can change to take into account new circumstances and social or technical change. Where, therefore, there is unintentional damage, there is, potentially, an action in negligence.

In *Donoghue v Stevenson* (1932) a lady went into a cafe with her friend who, bought her a bottle of ginger beer. After she had drunk half from the bottle she poured the remainder into a glass. She then saw the remains of a decomposed snail at the bottom. She suffered nervous shock. She sued the manufacturer as the snail must have got into the bottle at the manufacturer's premises since the bottle top was securely sealed when her friend bought it. It was held that a manufacturer owes a duty of care to the ultimate consumer of his goods. He must therefore exercise reasonable care to prevent injury to the consumer. The fact that there is no contractual relationship between the manufacturer and the consumer is irrelevant to this action.

The most important aspect of this case is the test laid down by Lord Atkin. He stated that:

'You must take reasonable care to avoid acts and omissions which you could reasonably foresee would be likely to injure your neighbour. Who then in law is my neighbour? ... any person so closely and directly affected by my act that I ought reasonably to have them in contemplation as being so affected when I am directing my mind to the acts and omissions which are called in question.'

This test forms the basis for deciding the existence of a duty. It follows that if a duty of care is to exist the question for the court is somewhat hypothetical in that the court does not look at the reality ie did you contemplate the effect on the injured party of your actions, but should you have done so ie it is objective rather than subjective. This does not require specific identity of the injured person, merely of the class of person eg pedestrians, children etc.

The test in *Donoghue v Stevenson* was qualified in *Anns v Merton London Borough Council* (1978). Lord Wilberforce in this case introduced the two stage test for establishing the existence of a duty :

• Is there between the alleged wrongdoer and the person who has suffered damage a sufficient relationship of proximity or neighbourhood such that, in the reasonable contemplation of the former, carelessness on his part may be likely to cause damage to the latter?

• If the first question is answered in the affirmative, are there then any considerations which ought to negate, reduce or limit the scope of the duty or the class of persons to whom it is owed or the damages to which a breach of duty may give rise?

The first question clearly corresponds with the neighbour test in *Donoghue v Stevenson*, although it is referred to as the proximity test. The second question introduces the consideration of public policy issues which may be grounds for limiting the situations where a duty of care is found to exist. As far as new situations are concerned, the following are some of the policy arguments which, if justified, may prevent a duty of care from being actionable:

• The 'floodgates' argument ie will an extension of duty to cover this situation lead to a flood of litigation?

• Will it lead to an increase in the number of fraudulent claims either against insurance companies or in the courts?

• What are the financial or commercial consequences of extending the duty?

The impact of *Anns* resulted in the expansion of negligence as the policy reasons only acted to limit liability once a duty had been found to exist as opposed to limiting the existence of a duty – see *Junior Books Ltd v Veitchi Co Ltd* (1983). However, there was gradual criticism of and retraction from the approach taken by Lord Wilberforce, see *Peabody Donation Fund v Sir Lindsay Parkinson & Co Ltd* (1984) in which the court stressed that the proximity test had to be satisfied before a duty of care could be found to exist and *Leigh & Sillivan Ltd v Aliakmon Shipping Co Ltd* (1986) (known as *The Aliakmon*) in which Lord Brandon stated that when Lord Wilberforce laid down the two phased test in *Anns* he was:

'... dealing with the approach to the questions of existence and scope of duty of care in a novel type of factual situation which was not analogous to any factual situation in which the existence of such a duty had already been held to exist. He was not suggesting that the same approach should be adopted to the existence of a duty of care in a factual situation in which the existence of such a duty had repeatedly been held not to exist.'

This further limitation was developed in *Yuen Kun-yeu v Attorney-General of Hong Kong* (1987) in which Lord Keith stated that Lord Wilberforce's approach 'had been elevated to a degree of importance greater than it merits and greater perhaps than its author intended'. Finally, the decision in *Anns* was overruled by *Murphy v Brentwood District Council* (1990).

The present position, following this rapid retraction from *Anns*, appears to be that in establishing the existence of a duty of care in negligence, the plaintiff must show that the defendant foresaw that damage would occur to the plaintiff ie there was sufficient proximity in time, space and relationship between the plaintiff and the defendant (see *Bourhill v Young* (1943)). In practical terms, in many personal injury cases foreseeability of damage will determine proximity. The courts will then, where appropriate, consider whether it is just and reasonable to impose a duty and whether there are any policy reasons for denying or limiting the existence of a duty eg floodgates argument. The courts will not necessarily consider these in all cases.

In *Hill v Chief Constable of West Yorkshire* (1990) Hill's daughter was the last victim of the Yorkshire Ripper. She alleged that the police had failed to take reasonable care in apprehending the murderer as they had interviewed him but not arrested him prior to her daughter's unlawful killing. The House of Lords had to determine whether she was owed a duty of care by the police. Whilst confirming the need to establish foresight and proximity, the court went on to state that there were policy reasons for not allowing the existence of a duty in this case; the reason being that any other result may lead to police discretion being limited and 'exercised in a defensive frame of mind'. This may in turn distract the police from their most important function, 'the suppression of crime'.

11.2.2   Nervous shock

Nervous shock is a form of personal injury which may give rise to an action for damages. If damages are to be recoverable, nervous shock must take the form of a recognised mental illness; mental suffering such as grief is not recoverable. No physical injury need be suffered. The basis of liability for nervous shock depends on whether this type of injury was reasonably foreseeable and whether there was sufficient proximity between the plaintiff and the defendant.

In *Bourhill v Young* (1943) the plaintiff heard a motor accident as she alighted from a tram. A little while later she saw some blood on the road. She was pregnant and she alleged that as a result of seeing the 'aftermath' of the accident she suffered nervous shock leading to a miscarriage. It was held that the plaintiff did not fall within the class of person to whom it could be reasonably foreseen that harm might occur.

Indeed, it was made clear in this case that one could expect passers-by to have the necessary phlegm and fortitude not to suffer nervous shock as a result of seeing the aftermath of an accident. As a result the abnormally sensitive plaintiff will not recover for nervous shock unless the person with the normal phlegm and fortitude would have sustained shock in those circumstances (*Jaensch v Coffrey* (1854)).

As far as the courts are concerned persons claiming for nervous shock fall into distinct categories.

- The claimant experiences shock and illness after fearing for his or her own safety.

  In *Dulieu v White* (1901) a pregnant woman was serving in a public house when the defendant's employee negligently drove the van into the front of the building. The plaintiff was not physically injured but suffered severe shock leading to illness. It was held that she was allowed to recover damages as the shock and illness arose out of fear of immediate personal injury to herself.

- Where the claimant fears for the personal injury of a close relative.

  In *Hambrook v Stokes Bros* (1925) a lorry began to roll down a hill, out of control. A mother had just left her children when she saw the lorry go out of control. She could not see her children but heard the crash. She was told that a child with glasses had been hurt and one of her children wore glasses. She suffered shock which was so severe it eventually led to her death. It was held that her estate could recover damages even though her illness was caused by fear for her children, not for herself. The defendant should have foreseen that his negligence might put someone in such fear of bodily injury ie that they would suffer nervous shock and that this could be extended to cover fear for one's children.

  In *McLoughlin v O'Brian* (1982) a mother was told in her home that her family had been injured in a road accident two miles away. She suffered psychiatric illness caused by the shock of hearing this news and later seeing her family in hospital before they had received any treatment and were in a particular bloody state; one child had been killed. It was held that she should recover damages as the shock was a foreseeable consequence of the defendant's negligence. The courts felt that the proximity of the claimant to the accident was relevant. However 'proximity' here meant closeness in time and space. Furthermore, the shock must be caused by the sight or hearing of the event or its immediate aftermath.

The essential elements for establishing duty in similar cases arises out of Lord Wilberforce's dictum in *Mcloughlin*, which is that, in addition to foresight, the plaintiff must show that there was a close relationship between him or her and the person suffering injury; secondly, that there was sufficient proximity between the plaintiff and the accident in terms of time and space; finally, it was concluded that being told about the accident by a third party was outside the scope of the duty. The application of Lord Wilberforce's dictum was seen in *Alcock & Others v Chief Constable of the South Yorkshire Police* (1991). This case arose out of the accident at Hillsborough stadium in Sheffield involving Liverpool supporters who were crushed as a result of a surge of supporters being allowed into the ground by the police. The nervous shock claim was made by those friends and relatives who witnessed the scenes on television or heard them described on the radio or were at the ground. The House of Lords repeated the requirements for establishing duty of care in cases of nervous shock. There should be:

- A close and loving relationship with the victim if reasonable foresight is to be established.

- Proximity in time and space to the accident or its aftermath.

- Nervous shock resulting from seeing or hearing the accident or its immediate aftermath.

  It is still open to debate whether viewing simultaneous television is equivalent to seeing the accident. It is generally considered not to be, because the broadcasting guidelines prevent the showing of suffering by recognisable individuals. Furthermore, any such transmission may be regarded as a novus actus interveniens.

- Where the claimant suffers nervous shock through seeing injury to others, even though he is in no danger himself.

In *Dooley v Cammell Laird & Co* (1951) a faulty rope was being used on a crane to secure a load which was being loaded into the hold of a ship. The rope broke causing the load to fall into the hold where people were working. The crane driver suffered shock arising out of a fear for the safety of his fellow employees. It was held that the crane driver would recover damages as it was foreseeable that he was likely to be affected if the rope broke.

In *Chadwick v British Railways Board* (1967) Chadwick took part in the rescue operations after a train crash. He suffered a severe mental condition as a result of the horrific scenes. He had a previous history of mental illness. It was held that BTC were liable. It was reasonably foreseeable that in the event of an accident someone other than the defendant's employees would intervene and suffer injury. Injury by shock to a rescuer was reasonably foreseeable even if he suffered no physical injury.

It is certainly possible for an extension to the law in this area. For example, in *Attia v British Gas* (1987), the plaintiff was able to recover damages for nervous shock resulting from the sight of her house being burned down as a result of the defendant's negligence.

There are two categories of economic loss which may form the basis of a claim in negligence. Firstly, there is economic loss arising out of physical injury or damage to property and, secondly, there is what is known as 'pure' economic loss which is the sole loss sustained, unconnected with physical damage. Following recent developments only the former is now recoverable and the law has reverted to the decision in the following case for defining the extent of liability for economic loss.

11.2.3   Economic loss

In *Sparten Steel & Alloys Ltd v Martin & Co* (1973) the plaintiffs manufactured steel alloys 24 hours a day. This required continuous power. The defendant's employees damaged a power cable which resulted in a lack of power for 14 hours. There was a danger of damage to the furnace so this had to be shut down and the products in the process of manufacture removed, thereby reducing their value. The plaintiffs also suffered loss of profits. It was held that the defendants were liable for physical damage to the products and the loss of profit arising out of this. There was, however, no liability for economic loss unconnected with the physical damage.

The rule that economic loss was only recoverable where it was directly the consequence of physical damage was challenged in *Junior Books Ltd v Veitchi Ltd* (1982) in which a claim for pure economic loss was allowed on the basis of there being sufficiently close proximity between the plaintiffs and the sub-contractor who had carried out the work for the main contractor. However, following this case there was a gradual retraction from recovery for pure economic loss – see *Muirhead v Industrial Tank Specialities Ltd* (1986), where it was held that there was insufficient proximity between the purchaser of goods and the manufacturer of the goods with respect to a claim for economic loss. This was reinforced in the cases of *Simaan General Contracting Co v Pilkington Glass Ltd* (1988) and *Greater Nottingham Co-operative Society Ltd v Cementation Piling & Foundations Ltd* (1988), where the courts refused to find sufficient proximity in tripartite business relationships, although the decision in *Junior Books* appears to stand at least for the moment.

The expansion of the law in this area was seen to result from Lord Wilberforce's two stage test in *Anns v London Borough of Merton*. As the gradual withdrawal from that decision grew apace, it was inevitable that a final blow would be dealt to this test. Firstly in *D & F Estates Ltd v Church Commissioners for England* (1988) where it was held that a builder was not liable in negligence to the owner for defects in quality, only for personal injury or damage to other property thereby bringing back the distinction between actions in tort and contract. Additionally, it was held that pure economic loss could only be recovered in an action for negligent misstatement or where the circumstances fell within *Junior Books*; secondly, in *Murphy v Brentwood District Council* (1990) in which the decision in *Anns* was overruled; it being made clear that liability for pure economic loss could only be sustained in an action for negligent misstatement based on *Hedley Byrne*.

| 11.2.4 | Negligent misstatements |

The importance of the neighbour or proximity test can be seen in the extension of the duty of care to cover negligent misstatements which result in economic loss. Indeed as we have seen, this is the only heading under which pure economic loss can be claimed. This expansion of the duty arose out of the case of *Hedley Byrne & Co v Heller & Partners* (1964). Prior to this case there was only liability for negligent misstatements causing physical damage; intentionally dishonest or fraudulent statements or where there was a fiduciary or contractual relationship between the parties (*Derry v Peek* (1889)).

In *Hedley Byrne & Co v Heller & Partners* (1964) Hedley Byrne asked their bank to make enquiries into the financial position of one of their clients. The bank made enquiries of

Heller's bank, who gave a favourable reply about the client's financial position, adding the words 'without responsibility'. Hedley Byrne relied on this advice and lost a lot of money when their clients went into liquidation. However, they lost their action against the bank because of the exclusion clause which at that time was held to be valid. The importance of the case is the dictum on negligent misstatements. It was held that a duty of care exists where:

> '... one party seeking information and advice was trusting the other to exercise such a degree of care as the circumstances required, where it was reasonable for him to do that, and where the other party gave the information or advice when he knew or ought to have known the enquirer was relying on him.'

Liability for negligent misstatements is based on the existence of a special relationship ie the defendant must hold himself out in some way as having specialised knowledge, knowing that any information he gives will be relied upon by the plaintiff. Obviously lawyers, accountants, bankers, surveyors etc come within this 'special relationship'. Although as the law has developed some attempts to limit liability can be found in the case law. For example, in *Mutual Life & Citizens Assurance Co v Evatt* (1971) it was held that the defendant should be in the business of giving such advice, although the minority in this case required the plaintiff to make it clear to the defendant that he was seeking advice which he may then rely on. There is in general no liability for information given on a purely social occasion, but advice from friends on other occasions may result in liability (*Chaudhry v Prabhaker* (1988)). Silence or inaction can rarely amount to misstatement unless there was a duty on the defendant to disclose or take action. The courts have recognised that it is possible for there to be a voluntary assumption of responsibility by the defendant and reliance by the plaintiff on that assumption (*La Banque Financière de la Cité v Westgate Insurance Co Ltd* (1990)). Any attempt at excluding liability may be subject to the Unfair Contact Terms Act 1977 and would then have to satisfy the test of reasonableness laid down in s 2(2).

In considering whether a duty of care is owed by the defendant to the plaintiff, it is necessary to consider the particular position of the professional person who, through the nature of his or her job, will be giving advice or carrying out acts which may leave them open to an action in negligence.

11.3 Professional negligence

Whilst there may be a contractual relationship between an accountant and his client on which the client can sue, the

11.3.1 Accountants and auditors

contentious legal area arises in respect of other people who may rely on reports made or advice given in a non-contractual capacity. Indeed, in many situations the potential plaintiff may be unknown to the accountant. Whether there is liability appears to depend upon the purpose for which reports are made or accounts prepared.

In *JEB Fasteners v Marks Bloom & Co* (1983) the defendants who were accountants negligently overstated the value of stock in preparing accounts for their client. At the time of preparation the accountants were aware that their client was in financial difficulties and actively seeking financial assistance. After seeing the accounts, the plaintiff decided to take over the company. They then discovered the true financial position and sued the accountants for negligent misstatement. It was held that a duty of care was owed by the accountants as it was foreseeable that someone contemplating a takeover might rely on the accuracy of the accounts, but that they were not liable as their negligence had not caused the loss to the plaintiff. The evidence revealed that when they took over the company they were not interested in the value of the stock but in acquiring the expertise of the directors, so although they relied on the accounts the accounts were not the cause of the loss as they would have taken over the company in any respect.

The case of *Caparo Industries plc v Dickman* (1990) served to limit the potential liability of auditors in auditing company accounts. Accounts were audited in accordance with the Companies Act 1985. The respondents who already owned shares in the company, decided to purchases more shares and takeover the company after seeing the accounts. They then incurred a loss which they blamed on the negligently audited accounts which were inaccurate. It was held that when the accounts were prepared, a duty of care was owed to members of the company ie the shareholders, but only so far as to allow them to exercise proper control over the company. This duty did not extend to members as individuals and potential purchasers of shares. The onus was clearly on the appellants in these circumstances to make their own independent enquiries as it was unreasonable to rely on the auditors.

However, where express representations are made about the accounts and the financial state of the company by directors or financial advisers of that company with the intention that the person interested in the takeover will rely on them, a duty of care is owed (*Morgan Crucible Co plc v Hill Samuel Bank Ltd* (1991)).

11.3.2   Lawyers

Solicitors are usually in a contractual relationship with their client; however, there may be circumstances outside this relationship where they are liable in tort for negligent misstatements. The leading case is *Ross v Caunters* (1980). The defendant solicitors prepared a will under which the plaintiff was a beneficiary. The solicitors sent the will to the person instructing them but failed to warn him that it should not be witnessed by the spouse of a beneficiary. When the will was returned to them they failed to notice that one of the witnesses was the plaintiff's spouse. As a result the plaintiff lost her benefit under the will. It was held that a solicitor may be liable in negligence to persons who are not his clients either on the basis of the principle in *Hedley Byrne* or *Donoghue v Stevenson* which was specifically applied in this case; the plaintiff being someone so closely and directly affected by the solicitors acts that it was reasonably foreseeable that they were likely to be injured by any act or omission.

Some doubt has been cast upon the decision in *Ross v Caunters* but at least for the moment it remains good law. Barristers are in the position of not being in a contractual relationship with the 'client' ie the person they are representing, nor are they liable in tort for the way in which they conduct a case in court. There are policy reasons for this as the duty to the court is higher than the duty to the client and must be put first (*Rondel v Worsley* (1969)). In *Saif Ali v Sidney Mitchell* (1980) it was confirmed that a barrister was not liable for conduct of the case in court nor was he liable for pre-trial work connected with the conduct of the case in court. However, he would be liable in tort for negligent opinions ie written advice where there was no error on the part of the solicitor briefing him.

11.3.3 Surveyors

A duty of care is owed by surveyors, builders, architects etc to the client with whom they are generally in a contractual relationship. However, there may be liability in tort as a result of *Hedley Byrne*, although this hinges on the question of reasonable reliance by the third party and whether the defendant ought to have foreseen such reliance.

In *Yianni v Edwin Evans & Sons* (1982) surveyors acting for the building society valued a house at £15,000 and as a result the plaintiffs were able to secure a mortgage of £12,000. The house was in fact suffering from severe structural damage and repairs were estimated at £18,000. The basis of the plaintiff's claim was not only was the surveyor negligent but he ought reasonably to have contemplated that the statement would be passed on by the building society to the plaintiff and that they would rely on it, which they did. It was held that a duty of care was owed by the defendants. An important factor was that the price of the house indicated that the plaintiff was of modest means and would not be expected to obtain an independent valuation and who would in all probability rely on the defendant's survey which was communicated to them by the building society. The court was also confident that the defendants knew that the building society would pass the survey to the purchasers and that they would rely on it.

The decision in *Yianni* was approved in *Smith v Eric Bush* and *Harris v Wyre Forest District Council* (1989). The facts of the former case are very similar to Yianni in that the plaintiff was sent a copy of the surveyor's report by the building society. This report stated that no essential repairs were necessary and although it contained a recommendation on obtaining independent advice, the plaintiff chose to rely on the report. In fact, the property had defective chimneys. In Harris, the plaintiffs did not see the surveyor's report as it was stated on the mortgage application that the valuation was confidential and that no responsibility would be accepted for the valuation. However, the plaintiff paid the valuation fee and accepted the 95% mortgage on offer. When they attempted to sell the house three years later, structural defects were revealed and the property was deemed to be uninhabitable and unsaleable. It was held, in both cases, that there was sufficient proximity between the surveyor and the purchaser and that it was foreseeable that the plaintiff was likely to suffer damage as a result of the negligent advice. It was felt that, in general, surveyors knew that 90% of purchasers relied on their valuation for the building society; it was therefore just and reasonable for a duty to be imposed. The limitation on this decision is that it does not extend protection to subsequent purchasers, nor where the property is of a 'high' value (although this will need to be determined on the facts of each case). The attempt to exclude liability in this case was seen as an attempt to exclude the existence of a duty of care which it was felt was not within the spirit of the Unfair Contract Terms Act 1977 and could not be permitted.

The decision in *Murphy v Brentwood District Council* has seriously limited the potential liability of builders, architects, and quantity surveyors in respect of claims arising out of defective buildings. Where the defect is discovered prior to any injury to person or health or damage to property, other than the defective premises itself, this is to be regarded as pure economic loss not physical damage to property and is not therefore recoverable in negligence.

11.4 Breach of duty of care

Once the plaintiff has established that the defendant owes him a duty of care, the plaintiff must establish that the defendant is in breach of this duty. The test for establishing breach of duty was laid down in *Blyth v Birmingham Waterworks Co* (1856). A breach of duty occurs if the defendant:

> '... fails to do something which a reasonable man guided upon those considerations which ordinarily regulate the conduct of human affairs would do, or does something which a prudent and reasonable man would not do.'

The test is an objective test, judged through the eyes of the reasonable man. The fact that the defendant has acted less skillfully than the reasonable man would expect will usually result in breach being established. This is the case even where the defendant is inexperienced in his particular trade or activity. One cannot condone the incompetence of such defendants. For example, a learner driver must drive in the manner of a driver of skill, experience and care (*Nettleship v Weston* (1971)). However, the degree or standard of care to be exercised by such a person will vary as there are factors such as the age of the plaintiff which can increase the standard of care to be exercised by the defendant. The test is therefore flexible. The following factors are relevant.

In deciding whether the defendant has failed to act as the reasonable man would act, the degree of care must be balanced against the degree of risk involved if the defendant fails in his duty. It follows, therefore, that the greater the risk of injury or the more likely it is to occur, the more the defendant will have to do to fulfil his duty.

11.4.1   The likelihood of injury

In *Bolton v Stone* (1951) a cricket ground was surrounded by a 17 foot wall and the pitch was situated some way from the road. A batsman hit the ball exceptionally hard driving it over the wall where it struck the plaintiff who was standing on the highway. It was held that the plaintiff could not succeed in his action as the likelihood of such injury occurring was small, as was the risk involved. The slight risk was outweighed by the height of the wall and the fact that a ball had only been hit out of the ground six times in 30 years.

11.4.2   Egg-shell skull rule

The degree of care to be exercised by the defendant may be increased if the plaintiff is very young, old or less able-bodied in some way. The rule is that 'you must take your victim as you find him'. This is illustrated in *Haley v London Electricity Board* (1965), in which the defendants, in order to carry out repairs, had made a hole in the pavement. Haley, who was blind, often walked along this stretch of pavement. He was normally able to avoid obstacles by using his white stick. The precautions taken by the Electricity Board would have prevented a sighted person from injuring himself, but not a blind person. As a result Haley fell, striking his head on the pavement, and became deaf as a consequence. It was held that the Electricity Board were in breach of their duty of care to pedestrians. They had failed to ensure that the excavation was safe for all pedestrians, not just sighted persons. It was clearly not reasonably safe for blind persons, yet it was foreseeable that they may use this pavement.

There are other cases which you might wish to refer to in this field eg *Gough v Thorne* (1966) concerning young children; *Daly v Liverpool Corporation* (1939) – old people; *Paris v Stepney BC* (1951) – disability.

11.4.3   Cost and practicability

Another factor in deciding whether the defendant is in breach of his duty to the plaintiff, is the cost and practicability of overcoming the risk. The foreseeable risk has to be balanced against the measures necessary to eliminate it. If the cost of these measures far outweighs the risk, the defendant will probably not be in breach of duty for failing to carry out these measures. This is illustrated by the case of *Latimer v AEC Ltd* (1952). A factory belonging to AEC became flooded after an abnormally heavy rainstorm. The rain mixed with oily deposits on the floor making the floor very slippery. Sawdust was spread on the floor but there was insufficient to cover the whole area – most of the floor was covered. Latimer, an employee, slipped on a part of the floor to which sawdust had not been applied. It was held that AEC Ltd was not in breach of their duty to the plaintiff. It had taken all reasonable precautions and had eliminated the risk as far as it practicably could without going so far as to close the factory. There was no evidence to suggest that the reasonably prudent employer would have closed down the factory and as far as the court was concerned the cost of doing that far out weighed the risk to the employees.

Compare this case with *Haley v London Electricity Board* where the provision of two foot barriers around excavations in the pavement was practicable and would have eliminated the risk to blind people.

11.4.4   Social utility

The degree of risk has to be balanced against the social utility and importance of the defendant's activity. If the activity is of particular importance to the community, then in the circumstances the taking of greater risks may be justified.

In *Watt v Hertfordshire CC* (1954) the plaintiff, a fireman, was called out to rescue a woman trapped beneath a lorry. The lifting jack had to be carried on an ordinary lorry as a suitable vehicle was unavailable. The jack slipped injuring the plaintiff. It was held that the employer was not in breach of duty. The importance of the activity and the fact that it was an emergency was found to justify the risk involved.

If the defendant can show that what he has done is common practice, then this is evidence that a proper standard of care has been exercised. However, if the common practice is in itself negligent then his actions in conforming to such a practice will be actionable (see *Paris v Stepney BC*).

11.4.5   Common practice

The standard of care to be exercised by people professing to have a particular skill is not be judged on the basis of the reasonable man. The actions of a skilled person must be judged by what the ordinary skilled man in that job or profession would have done eg the reasonable doctor, plumber, engineer etc. Such a person is judged on the standard of knowledge possessed by the profession at the time the accident occurred. Obviously there is an onus on the skilled person to keep himself abreast of changes and improvements in technology .

11.4.6   Skilled persons

In *Roe v Minister of Health* (1954) a patient was paralysed after being given a spinal injection. This occurred because the fluid being injected had become contaminated with the storage liquid which had seeped through minute cracks in the phials. It was held that there was no breach of duty since the doctor who administered the injection had no way of detecting the contamination at that time.

Furthermore, the common practice of the profession may, if this is followed, prevent liability. This can be seen in *Bolam v Friern Hospital Management Committee* (1957). Bolam broke his pelvis whilst undergoing electro-convulsive therapy treatment at the defendant's hospital. He alleged that the doctor had not warned him of the risks, nor had he been given relaxant drugs prior to treatment and no one had held him down during treatment. It was held that the doctor was not in breach of duty (and there was therefore no vicarious liability) because this form of treatment was accepted at that time by a certain body of the medical profession.

The burden of proof in establishing breach of duty normally rests on the plaintiff. In certain circumstances the inference of negligence may be drawn from the facts. If this can be done the plaintiff is relieved of the burden which moves to the defendant to rebut the presumption of negligence. This is known as *res ipsa loquitur* ie the thing speaks for itself. It can only be used where the only explanation for what happened is the negligence of the defendant, yet the plaintiff has insufficient evidence to establish the defendant's negligence in

11.4.7   *Res ipsa loquitur*

the normal way. There are three criteria for the maxim to apply:

- Sole management or control

  It must be shown that the damage was caused by something under the sole management or control of the defendant, or by someone for whom he is responsible or whom he has a right to control (*Gee v Metropolitan Railway* (1873)).

- The occurrence cannot have happened without negligence

  This depends on the facts of each case. If there are other possible explanations as to how the incident occurred, *res ipsa loquitur* will fail. In *Mahon v. Osborne* (1939) a patient died after a swab was left in her body after an operation. No one could explain how this had happened, therefore *res ipsa loquitur* applied.

- Cause of the occurrence is unknown

  If the defendant can put forward a satisfactory explanation of how the accident occurred which shows no negligence on his part then the maxim is inapplicable. In *Pearson v NW Gas Board* (1968) the plaintiff's husband was killed and her house destroyed when a gas main fractured. She pleaded *res ipsa loquitur*. However, the Gas Board put forward the explanation that the gas main could have fractured due to earth movement after a heavy frost. This explanation was plausible and as it showed no negligence on their part, they were not liable.

  If the defendant can rebut the presumption of negligence by giving a satisfactory explanation, it is open to the plaintiff to establish negligence in the normal way. In practice he is unlikely to succeed as if he had sufficient evidence in the first place he would not have pleaded *res ipsa loquitur*.

11.5   Resultant damage

The plaintiff must show that he has suffered some injury, not necessarily physical. Furthermore, he must show that this injury was caused by the defendant's negligence. This is known as 'causation in fact'. The 'but for' test is used to establish whether the defendant's negligence was the cause of the injury to the plaintiff.

11.5.1   The 'but for' test

In order to satisfy the test the plaintiff must show that 'but for' the defendant's actions the damage would not have occurred. If the damage would have occurred irrespective of a breach of duty on the part of the defendant, then the breach is not the cause.

In *Cutler v Vauxhall Motors Ltd* (1971) the plaintiff suffered a grazed ankle while at work due to the defendant's negligence.

The graze became ulcerated because of existing varicose veins and the plaintiff had to undergo an immediate operation for the removal of the veins. It was held that the plaintiff could not recover damages for the operation because the evidence was that he would have to undergo the operation within five years irrespective of the accident at work.

If the same result would have occurred regardless of the breach, then the courts are unlikely to find that the breach caused the injury (see *Barnett v Chelsea & Kensington Hospital Management Committee* (1969). Recent case law has not been sympathetic to the plaintiff where there have been a number of potential causes of the injury. The onus is on the plaintiff to show that the defendant's breach was a material contributory cause of their injury (*Wilsher v Essex Area Health Authority* (1988) and *Hotson v East Berkshire Area Health Authority* (1987). There can also be problems where there are two or more independent tortfeasors, in establishing how far each one is responsible for the damage caused.

In *Baker v Willoughby* (1970) the plaintiff injured his leg through the defendant's negligence, leaving him partially disabled. Subsequently, the plaintiff was shot in the same leg by another person and as a result the leg had to be amputated. It was likely that leg would have had to have been amputated as a result of the shooting anyway. It was held that the first defendant was liable for the plaintiff's disability (not the amputation) for the rest of his life. Irrespective of the amputation it would have been a continuing disability and this was reflected in the responsibility imposed on the defendant. The liability for the existing disability did not cease when the second incident took place.

The 'but for' test can be used to establish causation on the facts. However, once this has been established it does not mean that the defendant will be liable for all of the damage to the plaintiff. There must be causation in law. This can be seen through the maxim *novus actus interveniens* or a new intervening act.

Where there is a break in the chain of causation the defendant will not be liable for damage caused after the break. The issue is whether the whole sequence of events is the probable consequence of the defendant's actions and whether it is reasonably foreseeable that these events may happen. This break in the chain is caused by an intervening act and the law recognises that such acts fall into three categories.	11.5.2 *Novus actus interveniens*
A natural event does not automatically break the chain of causation. If the defendant's breach has placed the plaintiff in	11.5.3 A natural event

the position where the natural event can add to that damage, the chain will not be broken unless the natural event was totally unforeseen.

In *Carslogie Steamship Co Ltd v Royal Norwegian Government* (1952) a ship owned by Carslogie had been damaged in a collision caused by the defendant's negligence. The ship was sent for repair and on this voyage suffered extra damage caused by the severe weather conditions. This resulted in the repairs taking 40 days longer than anticipated. It was held that the bad weather acted as a new intervening act for which the defendant was not liable. The effect of the new act in this case prevented the plaintiff from recovering compensation for the time it would have taken to repair the vessel in respect of the collision damage as the ship would have been out of use due to the damage caused by the weather.

11.5.4   Act of a third party

Where the act of a third party following the breach of the defendant causes further damage to the plaintiff, such act may be deemed to be a novus; the defendant would not then be liable for damage occurring after the third party's act.

In *Lamb v Camden London BC* (1981) due to the defendant's negligence a water main was damaged causing the plaintiff's house to be damaged and the house vacated until it had been repaired. While the house was empty, squatters moved in and caused further damage to the property. It was held that the defendant was not liable for the squatter's damage. Although it was a reasonably foreseeable risk it was not a likely event. Furthermore, it was not the duty of the Council to keep the squatters out.

The third party's act need not be negligent in itself to break the chain of causation, although the courts take the view that a negligent act is more likely to break the chain than one that is not negligent (*Knightley v Johns* (1982)).

11.5.5   Act of the plaintiff himself

In *McKew v Holland, Hannen and Cubbitts (Scotland) Ltd* (1969) the plaintiff was injured at work. As a result his leg, on occasions, gave way without warning. He was coming downstairs when his leg gave way, so he jumped, rather than fall head first, and badly injured his ankle. It was held that the defendants were not liable for this additional injury. The plaintiff had not acted reasonably in attempting to negotiate the stairs without assistance and his actions amounted to a *novus actus interveniens*.

Where it is the act of the plaintiff which breaks the chain it is not a question of foresight but of unreasonable conduct.

It must be understood that even where causation is established, the defendant will not necessarily be liable for all of the damage resulting from the breach. This was not always the case and the way in which the law has developed must be considered.

In *Re Polemis & Furness, Withy & Co* (1921) the plaintiff's ship was destroyed by fire when one of the employees of the company to whom the ship had been chartered negligently knocked a plank into the hold. The hold was full of petrol vapour. The fall of the plank caused a spark as it struck the side and this ignited the vapour. It was held that the defendants were liable for the loss of the ship, even though the presence of petrol vapour and the causing of the spark were unforeseen. The fire was the direct result of the breach of duty and the defendant was liable for the full extent of the damage even where the manner in which it took place was unforeseen.

The case of *Re Polemis* is no longer regarded as the current test for remoteness of damage, even though it has not been distinguished or overruled. The test currently used arose out of *The Wagon Mound No 1* (1961). The defendants negligently allowed furnace oil to spill from a ship into Sidney harbour. The oil spread and came to lie beneath a wharf owned by the plaintiffs. The plaintiffs had been carrying out welding operations and on seeing the oil they stopped welding in order to ascertain whether it was safe. They were assured that the oil would not catch fire and so resumed welding. Cotton waste which had fallen into the oil caught fire. This in turn ignited the oil and this fire spread to the plaintiff's wharf. It was held that the defendants were in breach of duty. However, they were only liable for the damage caused to the wharf and slipway through the fouling of the oil. They were not liable for the damage caused by fire because damage by fire was at that time unforeseeable. This particular oil had a high ignition point and it could not be foreseen that it would ignite on water. The court refused to apply the rule in *Re Polemis*.

The test of reasonable foresight arising out of the *Wagon Mound* clearly takes into account such things as scientific knowledge at the time of the negligent act. The question to be asked in determining the extent of liability is 'is the damage of such a kind as the reasonable man should have foreseen?' This does not mean that the defendant should have foreseen precisely the sequence or nature of the events. Lord Denning in *Stewart v West African Air Terminals*(1964) said:

'It is not necessary that the precise concatenation of circumstances should be envisaged. If the consequence was one which was within the general range which any

11.5.6   Remoteness of damage

reasonable person might foresee (and was not of an entirely different kind which no one would anticipate), then it is within the rule that a person who has been guilty of negligence is liable for the consequences.'

This is illustrated in the case of *Hughes v Lord Advocate* (1963) where employees of the Post Office who were working down a manhole, left it without a cover but with a tent over it and lamps around it. A child picked up a lamp and went into the tent. He tripped over the lamp knocking it into the hole. An explosion occurred in which the child was burned. The risk of the child being burned by the lamp was foreseeable. However, the vapourisation of the paraffin in the lamp and its ignition were not foreseeable. It was held that the defendants were liable for the injury to the plaintiff. It was foreseeable that the child might be burned and it was immaterial that neither the extent of his injury or the precise chain of events leading to it was foreseeable.

The test of remoteness is not easy to apply. The cases themselves highlight the uncertainty of the courts. It is a flexible test which can be subject to policy issues – see *Doughty v Turner Manufacturing Co Ltd* (1964); *Tremain v Pike* (1969) and *Robinson v Post Office* (1974).

11.6   Defences

The extent of the liability of the defendant may be reduced or limited by one of the defences commonly pleaded in negligence actions.

11.6.1   Contributory negligence

Where the plaintiff is found in some way to have contributed through his own fault to his injury, the amount awarded as damages will be reduced accordingly (Law Reform (Contributory Negligence) Act 1945). The onus is on the defendant to show that the plaintiff was at fault and that this contributed to his injury.

The court, if satisfied that the plaintiff is at fault, will reduce the amount of damages by an amount which is just and reasonable, depending on the plaintiff's share of the blame. For example, damages may be reduced by anything from 10% to 75%. However, a 100% reduction has been made (see *Jayes v IMI (Kynoch) Ltd* (1985).

11.6.2   *Volenti non fit injuria*

Volenti or consent as it applies to negligent acts, is a defence to future conduct of the defendant which involves the risk of a tort being committed. Volenti may arise from the express agreement of the plaintiff and defendant or it may be implied from the plaintiff's conduct.

In *ICI v Shatwell* (1965) the plaintiff and his brother ignored the safety precautions issued by their employer and breached the regulations in testing detonators. As a result, the plaintiff was injured in an explosion. The action against the employer was based on vicarious liability and breach of statutory duty on the part of the plaintiff's brother. It was held that the defence of *volenti* would succeed. The plaintiff not only consented to each act of negligence and breach of statute on the part of his brother, but also participated in it quite willingly.

It must be stressed that this particular case highlights extreme circumstances where *volenti* is likely to succeed. However, if the defence is to succeed it must be shown that the plaintiff was fully informed of the risks when he gave his consent.

In *Dann v Hamilton* (1939) a girl accepted a lift in the car of a driver whom she knew to be drunk. She could have used alternative transport. She was injured as a result of his negligent driving. It was held that although she knew of the risk, this was insufficient to support the defence of *volenti*. It was necessary to show that she had consented to the risk, which could not be established. She therefore succeeded in her action against the driver.

Following this case, it is unlikely that this defence will succeed where the implied consent is given before the negligent act occurs. In practice the courts do not look favourably on this defence in respect of negligent actions and therefore it is not usually pleaded.

Finally, there is a limitation period for commencing an action in tort. The Limitation Act 1980 states that generally an action must be brought within six years from the date on which it occurred. If the action is for personal injury, the period is three years from the date on which it occurred, or the date of knowledge of the injury, whichever is later.

Negligence

The tort of negligence imposes a duty to take reasonable care to prevent harm or loss occurring from one's actions.

The elements of the tort which must be established by the plaintiff are:

- duty of care;
- breach of duty;
- resultant damage.

Duty of care

The test for establishing duty is the 'neighbour' test as expounded by Lord Atkin in *Donoghue v Stevenson* (1932).

This is further influenced by:

- *Peabody Donation Fund v Sir Lindsay Parkinson & Co Ltd* (1984);
- *Leigh & Sillivan Ltd v Aliakmon Shipping Co Ltd* (1986);
- *Yuen Kun-yeu v A-G Hong Kong* (1987);
- *Hill v Chief Constable of West Yorkshire* (1990);
- *Murphy v Brentwood District Council* (1990).

The current test therefore requires consideration of the following:

- foresight;
- proximity;
- 'just and reasonable'.

Nervous shock

This is a form of injury which can be defined as a recognised mental condition; it is not dependent upon physical injury. However, foresight and proximity must be established.

- *Bourhill v Young* (1943);
- *Dulieu v White* (1901) – the plaintiff may recover where he or she fears for his/her own safety;
- *Hambrook v Stokes Bros* (1925) – in which the plaintiff feared for the safety of a close relative;
- *McLoughlin v O'Brian* (1982);

- *Alcock & Others v Chief Constable of South Yorkshire* (1991);
- *Dooley v Cammell Laird & Co* (1951);
- *Chadwick v British Railways Board* (1967).

Economic loss

Liability for economic loss arising out of physical injury or damage to property may be compensated in negligence; however, liability for pure economic loss cannot, in general, be compensated:

- *Sparten Steel & Alloys Ltd v Martin & Co* (1973);
- *Junior Books v Veitchi Ltd* (1982);
- *Muirhead v Industrial Tank Specialities Ltd* (1986);
- *Simaan General Contracting Co v Pilkington Glass Ltd* (1988);
- *Greater Nottingham Co-operative Society Ltd v Cementation Piling & Foundations Ltd* (1988);
- *D&F Estates Ltd v Church Commissioners for England* (1988).

Pure economic loss arising from negligent misstatements is the exception to the general rule and such loss can therefore be compensated:

- *Hedley Byrne & Co v Heller & Partners* (1964);
- *Mutual Life & Citizens Assurance Co v Evatt* (1971);
- *Chaudhry v Prabhaker* (1988);
- *La Banque Financière de la Cité v Westgate Insurance Co Ltd* (1990).

Many professions have been deemed to owe a duty of care to persons other than their clients and may therefore be liable for economic loss arising from their negligent statements:

- *JEB Fasteners v Marks Bloom & Co* (1983);
- *Caparo Industries plc v Dickman* (1990);
- *Ross v Caunters* (1980);
- *Rondel v Worsley* (1969);
- *Saif Ali v Sidney Mitchell* (1980);
- *Yianni v Edwin Evans & Sons* (1982);
- *Smith v Eric Bush; Harris v Wyre Forest District Council* (1989);
- *Murphy v Brentwood District Council.*

Breach of duty

The test for establishing breach of duty is whether the defendant has acted as a 'reasonable man' in all the circumstances of the case. The courts will take into account the:

- likelihood of harm occurring (*Bolton v Stone* (1951));

- egg-shell skull rule (*Haley v London Electricity Board* (1965); *Paris v Stepney BC* (1951));

- cost and practicability of taking precautions (*Latimer v AEC* (1952));

- social utility of the act (*Watt v Hertfordshire CC* (1954));

- common practice (*Roe v Minister of Health* (1954));

In certain circumstances the plaintiff may rely on the maxim *res ipsa loquitur* in order to establish breach. However, the following must be shown:

- sole management or control on the part of the defendant;

- the occurrence could not have happened without negligence;

- the cause of the occurrence is unknown.

The plaintiff must show that the breach of duty on the part of the defendant was the cause of his loss. The test for establishing causation in fact is the 'but for' test:

Resultant damage

- *Cutler v Vauxhall Motors Ltd* (1971);

- *Barnett v Chelsea & Kensington Hospital Management Committee* (1969);

- *Wilsher v Essex Area Health Authority* (1987);

- *Hotson v East Berkshire Area Health Authority* (1987);

- *Baker v Willoughby* (1970).

The chain of causation may be broken by an intervening act which may be one of the following:

- a natural event (*Carslogie Steamship Co Ltd v Royal Norwegian Government* (1952));

- an act of a third party (*Lamb v Camden London Borough Council* (1981));

- an act of the plaintiff (*McKew v Holland, Hannen & Cubbitts (Scotland) Ltd* (1969)).

The extent of the defendant's liability may be limited by the rules for determining remoteness of damage:

- *Re Polemis & Furness, Withy & Co* (1921);

- *The Wagon Mound (No 1)* (1961);

- *Hughes v Lord Advocate* (1963);

- *Robinson v Post Office* (1974);

Defences   Damages may be reduced by the plaintiff contributory negligence (Law Reform (Contributory Negligence) Act 1945).

The defence of *volenti* or consent may operate as a complete defence (*ICI v Shatwell* (1965); *Dann v Hamilton* (1939)).

Chapter 12

Employers' Liability

The tort of employers' liability arises out of the duty on an employer to take reasonable care for the safety of his employees whilst they are at work. If, as a result of an accident at work, an employee is injured, he may be able to establish that the employer is in breach of the personal duty owed to him. However, should an action for employer's liability be unavailable, the injured employee may have the same rights as any other individual injured by another employee which is to pursue an action for vicarious liability (see below).

It was not until the late 19th century that employees were able to proceed with such claims. The courts originally took the view that the doctrine of 'common employment' precluded an action against the employer where the employee had been injured by the actions of a fellow employee (*Priestley v Fowler* (1837)); the rationale for this being that the employee had impliedly agreed to accept any risks incidental to his contract of employment. There was also concern expressed for the possible financial burden placed on employers having to pay compensation for industrial accidents if such actions were allowed to proceed. In addition, the defences of *volenti* and contributory negligence removed any chance of success in such claims as volenti in particular was freely available to the employer. Gradually, the doctrine of common employment was removed and limitations placed on the use of volenti as a defence (*Smith v Baker & Sons* (1891)); as a result the tort of employers' liability was allowed to develop.

Employers' liability is a negligence based tort, in that it is a specialised form of negligence arising out of a duty imposed by the employer/employee relationship. It is therefore necessary to refer to the basic elements of that tort. It gives the employee the right to sue the employer when he is injured at work for negligent acts by the employer arising out of the course of his employment. In order to ensure that the employer can pay any award of damages the Employer's Liability (Compulsory Insurance) Act 1969 imposes a duty on the employer to take out the necessary insurance cover.

12.1 Duty of care

The employer's duty of care is owed to each individual employee and, as it is a personal duty, it cannot be delegated by the employer to anyone else. This was made quite clear in

Wilsons & Clyde Coal Co v English (1938) where the day to day responsibility for the mine was delegated to a mine manager as required by statute. However, the court concluded that the ultimate responsibility for health and safety remained with the employer; see also *McDermid v Nash Dredging & Reclamation Ltd* (1987) and *Morris v Breaveglen Ltd T/A Anzac Construction Co* (1993) which reaffirms this. The duty is only owed whilst the employee is acting within the course of his employment ie is doing something reasonably incidental to his main job.

In *Davidson v Handley-Page Ltd* (1945) the plaintiff was washing his tea-cup in the sink at his place of work when he slipped and hurt his leg whilst standing on a duck-board. The duck-board had become slippery because water was constantly splashed upon it. It was held that the employer was in breach of his duty because the employee was carrying out a task which was reasonably incidental to his job; tea breaks being an accepted part of working life.

As a general rule employees are not acting within the course of their employment whilst travelling to and from work. The exception to this was recognised in *Smith v Stages & Darlington Insulation Co Ltd* (1989) which offers some protection to peripatetic workers or any employee who may have to work away from his main base. Where employees are paid their normal wage for this travelling time, they will be within the course of their employment.

As the duty is of a personal nature the standard of care will vary with the individual needs of each employee. It follows, therefore, that special regard must be had for the old, young, inexperienced and less able-bodied. The general nature of the duty can be expressed as follows:

The employer must take reasonable care in the way he conducts his operations so as not to subject his employees to unnecessary risks (see *Smith v Baker & Son* (1891)).

12.2   Scope of the employer's duty

This was defined in *Wilsons & Clyde Coal Co v English* (1938). Following this case, the employer's duty has been determined as extending to the provision of:

• competent fellow employees;

• safe plant and appliances;

• safe place of work;

• safe system of work.

However, it has been recognised that there is an overlap between the duties owed at common law and the duties implied into the contract of employment, a breach of which would allow the employee to pursue either cause of action. An example of this can be seen in *Johnstone v Bloomsbury Health Authority* (1991) where it was concluded that requiring junior hospital doctors to work excessive hours may be a breach of the employer's implied duty, although the implied contractual duty, to take reasonable care for the safety of employees, would have to be read subject to the express terms in the contract of employment.

The remit of the employer's duty is open to expansion through the case law. In *McFarlane v EE Caledonia* (1993), a claim was made that an employer owed a duty to prevent psychiatric injury. The Court of Appeal concluded that as the plaintiff was not directly involved in the accident and did not fall within the recognised categories of plaintiffs who can recover as outlined in *Alcock v Chief Constable of South Yorkshire* (1991), the employer cannot be liable.

| | 12.2.1 | Competent fellow employees |

The employer must ensure that all his staff are competent to do the job which they have been employed to do. He must therefore make sure that they have the necessary experience and qualifications, and where necessary, must be prepared to train them accordingly. If an employees is injured as a result of the incompetence of a fellow employee, then the employer may be liable. The word 'incompetence' covers a range of ineptitude; many of the cases arising out of practical jokes. In this situation, whether the employer is liable will depend on the depth of his knowledge about the incompetent employee. If, for example, the employer has been put on warning or given notice that the employee is capable of committing an incompetent act, such as a practical joke, he will be liable.

In *O'Reilly v National Rail & Tramway Appliances Ltd* (1966) O'Reilly was employed with three others to break up scrap from railways. His colleagues persuaded him to hit, with his sledge-hammer, a shell case embedded between the railway sleepers. When he did this the shell exploded. It was held that the employer was not in breach of his duty because he had no previous knowledge that these workmen played practical jokes or were capable of encouraging such an act. He had not therefore failed to employ competent fellow employees.

The previous conduct of the 'incompetent employee' is therefore extremely relevant. Where the employer has been given notice, he should take suitable action to ensure that such conduct does not result in something more serious; failure to take action will leave the employer open to a claim in the event of an accident arising out of the employee's incompetence.

Depending on the nature of the previous conduct, dismissal of the incompetent employee may be justified.

In *Hudson v Ridge Manufacturing Co Ltd* (1957) Hudson was on his way to the sick room when a fellow employee tripped him up and broke his wrist. This employee was known as a practical joker and had been warned by his employer to stop fooling about. It was held that the employer was in breach of his duty because he was aware of his employee's tendency to fool around. He should have done more to curb this employee even if this meant dismissal.

Interestingly, the employer will have primary liability in these circumstances for a deliberate and blatant act as well as the negligent act. However, an isolated incident will not incur liability (*Smith v Crossley Bros Ltd* (1951)). A claim based on vicarious liability may be open to an injured employee where he is unable to show that the employer had breached this particular duty, for example, through lack of prior knowledge (see *Harrison v Michelin Tyre Co Ltd* (1985)).

12.2.2 Safe plant and appliances

The employer must not only provide his employees with the necessary plant and equipment to the do job safely, but must also ensure that such plant and equipment is safe ie properly maintained. For example, guards must be provided on dangerous machinery to protect the employee from injury and these guards must be inspected regularly to ensure that they are securely in position and are not damaged in any way.

In *Bradford v Robinson Rentals Ltd* (1967) Bradford was employed as a driver. He was required to drive over 400 miles in extremely cold weather in a van with a broken window and a heater which did not work. He suffered severe frost bite. It was held that the van was not safe and therefore the employer had failed in his duty to provide safe plant and equipment. Although the conditions were extreme, it was foreseeable that the employee would suffer some 'injury' if sent out on a long journey in a van in that condition. A further illustration of this duty can be seen in *Taylor v Rover Car Co Ltd* (1966). Taylor was using a hammer and chisel when a piece of metal flew off the chisel and blinded him in one eye. This batch of chisels was in a defective state when supplied by the manufacturers. It was held that Taylor's employer was liable because a similar incident had occurred four weeks previously without any one being injured. This meant that the employer should have known of the likelihood of such an accident occurring. To avoid this, the chisels should have been taken out of use and returned to the manufacturer.

If the previous incident in Taylor's case had not occurred, Taylor's only remedy at that time would have been against the manufacturer. However, the Employer's Liability (Defective Equipment) Act 1969 provides that where an employee is injured at work as a consequence of defective equipment supplied by his employer and the defect is the fault of a third party eg the manufacturer, the employer will be deemed to be negligent and therefore responsible for the injury. This statute removes the need to establish foresight on the part of the employer in cases like Taylor's.

In the earlier case of *Davie v New Merton Board Mills Ltd* (1959) the issue of whether an employer could be liable for a manufacturer's negligence where an employee was injured by a fragmented tool was considered. The conclusion was that the employer could not be responsible for a manufacturer's negligence. Obviously, the Employer's Liability (Defective Equipment) Act reverses this decision. This Act is potentially wide in scope. 'Equipment' has been held to include a defective ship (*Coltman v Bibby Tankers Ltd* (1988)) and a flagstone (*Knowles v Liverpool City Council* (1993)).

The employer must ensure that his employees are not exposed to any dangers arising out of the place where the employee is expected to work. This covers any place under the control of the employer including access and egress and may extend to the premises of a third party, although, in the latter case, the employer may not reasonably be expected to go to the same lengths as he would on his own premises (*Wilson v Tyneside Window Cleaning Co* (1958)).

In *Smith v Vange Scaffolding & Engineering Co Ltd* (1970) Smith was employed on a building site by Vange. There were other contractors on site. As Smith returned to the changing hut at the end of the working day, he tripped over the cable of a welding machine which had been left there by a contractor. Vange were aware of the obstructions on site which made access to and from the place of work difficult and dangerous, but they had not complained to the other contractors. It was held that the employer had failed in his duty to his employee, because being aware of the situation he should have made the necessary complaints to the main contractor. It was foreseeable that such an accident might occur and reasonable precautions should have been taken.

The remit of this duty extends to consideration of the nature of the place and the potential risks involved, the work to be carried out, the experience of the employee and the degree of control or supervision which the employer can reasonably exercise. There may be situations where a safe place of work overlaps with the employer's duty to provide a safe system of work. Finally, the duty may apply where the

12.2.3   Safe place of work

employer sends employees overseas to work. However, whether there has been a breach of duty will depend on whether the employer acted reasonably in the circumstances of that particular case (*Cook v Square D Ltd* (1992)).

12.2.4   Safe system of work

The duty of the employer to provide a safe system of work extends to a consideration of the following by the employer: the physical layout of the job, safety notices, special procedures, protective clothing, training and supervision.

In order to fulfil this duty the employer must take into account all *foreseeable* eventualities including the actions of his employees. Any system, to be safe, must reduce the risks to the employee to a minimum; it is accepted that not all risks can be eliminated. Furthermore, the employer must do more than introduce a safe system of work, he must ensure that it is observed by his employees. The case law highlights the breadth of this duty.

For example, it can extend to preventing staff being exposed to risk of violence if this is a foreseeable risk (*Charlton v Forrest Printing Ink Co Ltd* (1980)). This aspect of the duty will also cover claims for compensation for work-related upper-limb disorder (WRULD/RSI) (*Bettany v Royal Doulton (UK) Ltd* (1993)).

The contentious issue surrounds instruction and supervision. Is it sufficient to order an employee to take safety precautions or should they be supervised as well if the duty is to be satisfied? The answer depends on the degree of risk and the experience of the employee concerned, including how far the employee has been warned of the risks (*Pape v Cumbria County Council* (1992)) .

In *Woods v Durable Suites Ltd* (1953) Woods worked in the veneer department at Durable Suites. He was an extremely experienced employee. As there was a risk of dermatitis from the synthetic glues, his employer posted up a notice specifying the precautions to be taken. Woods had also been instructed personally by the manager in the protective measures but had not observed them fully. As a result he contracted dermatitis. It was held that the employer was not liable for failing to provide a safe system of work because he had taken all reasonable care in posting up notices and providing barrier cream etc. He was under no obligation, given the age and experience of Woods to provide someone to watch over him to make sure he followed the precautions.

Constant supervision is, on the whole, not necessary where the employees have the necessary experience and have been trained or instructed accordingly. However, the degree of supervision is commensurate to the severity of the risk.

In *Bux v Slough Metals Ltd* (1974) Bux's job involved the removal of molten metal from a furnace and the pouring of this metal into a die-casting machine. Goggles were supplied and Bux was made aware of the risks. He refused to wear the safety goggles because they misted up and he complained to the supervisor who informed him that no other goggles were available. He was injured when molten metal splashed into his eye. It was held that the employer was liable because where the work was of a particularly hazardous nature, he must do more than merely provide safety equipment. He should constantly urge his employees to use or wear it.

The courts in considering this duty will need to determine whether the system is safe and whether it has been properly implemented. The employer needs to do both if he is to avoid liability.

Once duty is established, the remaining essentials are judged on the same basis as any action in negligence. The burden is on the employee to show that the employer is in breach of his duty. The employee must prove fault on the part of the employer ie has the employer failed to act as a reasonable employer, alternatively can *res ipsa loquitur* be established? If the employer has taken all reasonable precautions considering all of the circumstances of the case, then he will not be liable (see *Latimer v AEC Ltd* (1953)).

The standard of care will vary with respect to the individual needs of each employee. The employer must have special regard for the old, young, inexperienced and employees with special disabilities ie the standard of care will be increased.

In *Paris v Stepney District Council* (1951) Paris worked for the council in one of their garages. One of his jobs, which he did frequently, was to chip out rust from under buses and other vehicles owned by the council. At that time it was not customary to provide safety goggles for such work. Paris was already blind in one eye. One day as he was chipping out rust a fragment of rust entered his good eye and he was made totally blind. It was held that the employer had failed to exercise the necessary standard of care. It was foreseeable that there was an increased risk of greater injury to this particular employee because of the nature of his existing disability. He should therefore have been provided with safety goggles which at the very least would have reduced the risk.

This case illustrates the basic rule that 'you must take your victim as you find him' – otherwise known as the 'egg-shell skull rule'. In applying this rule, whether there has been a

12.3   Breach of duty

breach will be a question of fact in each case (see *James v Hepworth & Grandage Ltd* (1968)). The standard of care is increased in potentially high risk occupations where an employee may be illiterate or may not comprehend English. This can be seen in *Hawkins v Ian Ross (Castings) Ltd* (1970). The employer employed a large number of Asians as labourers. Hawkins was carrying a ladle of molten metal with the assistance of one such labourer. When he shouted to him to stop, the labourer did not understand and carried on walking. Hawkins overbalanced and was injured by the molten metal spilling over his leg. It was held that the employer had failed in his duty because where he chooses to employ labourers or indeed any staff who may not have a good understanding of the English language, the standard of care is increased. Furthermore, this increase is not confined to the particular employee but is extended to their workmates as there is a foreseeable increase in the risk to them of having to work with people who do not understand instructions.

12.4 Causation and resultant damage

Having established duty and breach, the employee must show that he has suffered injury as a result of the employer's breach of duty. 'Injury' is not confined to physical injury but includes damage to personal property, loss of earnings etc. The test for establishing liability is the one used in negligence ie the 'but for' test. The question which has to be answered by the court is therefore: 'but for' the employer's breach of duty would the employee have been injured? If the answer is no, causation is established.

In *McWilliams v Arrol Ltd* (1962) a steel erector employed by Arrol fell from scaffolding and was killed. The employer had provided safety harnesses in the past, but since they had not been worn they had been removed to another site. It was held that although the employer was in breach of his duty, he was not liable because it could not be proved that McWilliams would have worn the harness even if it had been available. The 'but for' test was not satisfied.

Even after causation has been established the employer is not necessarily liable for all the damage to his employee. He will only be liable for foreseeable damage. This does not mean that the precise nature or extent of the injury has to be foreseen, only that some harm will result from the breach of duty. However, there is legal limit to the extent of liability imposed by the *Wagon Mound (No 1)* (1961) (above). Applying this rule, the employer will only be liable for the foreseeable consequences of his breach ie not the unexpected. In *Doughty v Turner Manufacturing* (1964) a lid made of asbestos and cement covering a bath of sulphuric acid was knocked accidentally into the acid. A chemical reaction took place between the cover and the acid. In the eruption which followed Doughty was severely burned. It was held that the employer was not liable because the only harm which could be foreseen from the incident was splashing. A chemical reaction of this type resulting in an eruption was at the time unknown and therefore unforeseeable. This is regarded as a rather harsh decision since it demands a degree of foresight as to the way in which the injury occurred. The decision is doubtful in the light of such cases as *Hughes v Lord Advocate* (1963) and *Smith v Leech, Brain & Co* (1962) in which Smith's lip was splashed with molten metal. At the time, unknown to anyone, his lip contained cancerous tissue which became malignant as a result of the burn. He subsequently died of cancer. It was held that the employer was liable for his death from cancer because the risk of being splashed with molten metal was foreseeable. Smith's death was therefore merely an extension of the foreseeable injury which was a burn. This latter case is a much more sympathetic interpretation of the rule in the *Wagon Mound*.

The principal remedy available for employers' liability is compensation for personal injury; the object being to put the plaintiff in the position he would have been in if the accident had never occurred. The limitation period for bringing such an action is three years from the date on which the cause of action arose or the date of knowledge, whichever is the later (Limitation Act 1980).

There are no defences which are unique to this particular tort. In general, the main ones pleaded are contributory negligence and volenti; the former may result in a reduction in the amount of damages payable, the latter is rarely accepted by the courts in actions founded in employers' liability.

12.4.1   Remedies and defences

As a general rule vicarious liability only arises out of the employer/employee relationship, although it can be found in the principal/agent relationship and as an exceptional case in the employer/independent contractor relationship. It is dependent upon this type of special relationship being established.

12.5   Vicarious liability

Vicarious liability is not a tort; it is a concept which is used to impose strict liability on a person who does not have primary liability ie is not at fault. Literally, it means that one person is liable for the torts of another. The employer is therefore liable for the torts of his employee. This liability only arises while the

12.5.1   Meaning of vicarious liability

employee is acting within the course of his employment. The concept has found favour with the courts and plaintiffs alike, because, realistically, the employer is likely to have the money to pay for any claim for damages, whereas the main tortfeasor, the employee, will not. This does not mean that the employee will escape liability. The employer can insist that he is joined in any action or, if the employer is found to be vicariously liable, he may insist in an indemnity from his employee. The effect of this is that the employee will have to pay towards the damages imposed on the employer (see the Civil Liability (Contribution) Act 1978) which provides for this.

It must not be forgotten that this tort depends on the primary liability of the employee being established ie the employee must have committed a tort. Once this is done the plaintiff has the option to sue the employer, the employee or both.

| 12.5.2 | Employer/employee relationship |

The plaintiff must establish that there is in existence an employer/employee relationship (or in less common situations a principal/agent relationship) ie a contract of service as opposed to a contract for services. In the majority of cases this may not be an issue, but just because the word 'employee' is used in the contract, it does not automatically follow that it is a contract of service (or employment). There are tests for establishing this relationship which are considered in depth in the chapter on employment law and to which reference should be made.

| 12.5.3 | Scope of vicarious liability |

Once it is established that there is in existence a contract of service and that the employee has committed a tort ie has primary liability, the consideration of whether the employer should be vicariously liable can take place. This stage is important because the employer will only be liable if the employee is 'acting within the course of his employment' when he commits the tort. It is therefore essential to consider what is meant by this in law. If the employee is outside the scope of his employment, the injured person has no choice but to sue the employee who may not be in a financial position to compensate him.

| 12.5.4 | Course of employment |

The interpretation given by the courts is wide as in the past they have favoured making the employer liable, if it is at all possible to do so. The onus is on the plaintiff to show that the employee is a servant and that his tortious act was committed whilst he was going about his employer's business. Once this is established the onus moves to the employer who must show that the tortious act was one for which he was not responsible. As a general rule, to be within the course of employment, one of the following must be established:

- The act must be incidental to the job the employee was employed to do;

- The act should have been authorised by the employer, either expressly or impliedly;

- The authorised act has been carried out in a wrongful, negligent or unauthorised manner.

These can best be illustrated through the case law which shows how far the courts are prepared to go in holding an employer vicariously liable. The following cases relate to situations where the employee was found to be 'within the course of his employment'.

In *Century Insurance Co Ltd v Northern Ireland Road Transport Board* (1942) Davison was employed as a tanker driver for the NIRTB. He was delivering petrol at a garage. Whilst the underground storage tank was being filled with petrol, Davison lit a cigarette and threw away the lighted match. The petrol vapour ignited resulting in an explosion. The employer's insurance company claimed that the driver's actions regarding the cigarette were outside the course of his employment as being wholly unauthorised; thereby avoiding liability on the part of the employer and payment of compensation by the insurance company. It was held that the employer was vicariously liable for the negligent act of the employee. The lighting of the cigarette was an act of convenience on the part of the employee and although it was not necessarily for the employer's benefit it did not prevent him from being made liable. It was the time and place at which the employee struck the match which was negligent. The employee was seen to be carrying out the job he was employed to do in a negligent manner.

From this case it can been seen that such acts as taking a tea-break, having a cigarette, going to the washroom etc are all acts which are incidental to the main job, although it is still necessary to consider all the facts of the case at the time of the tortious act; of course, the question as to whether, in the present climate of no smoking policies, the smoking of a cigarette would be seen as incidental to one's employment is debatable. The next case is regarded as the leading authority with respect to actions which are specifically prohibited by the employer.

In *Rose v Plenty* (1976) Plenty was employed as a milkman by the Co-operative dairy. A notice had been posted up in the depot which prohibited all milkmen from using young children to deliver milk and from giving lifts to them on the milk float. Plenty ignored this notice and engaged the assistance of Rose, a boy of 13 years. Rose was injured whilst riding on the milk float through the negligent driving of Plenty. It was held that, applying the decision in *Limpus v London General Omnibus Co* (1862), since the prohibited act was being done for the purpose of the employer's business and not for the employee's own benefit or purpose, Plenty was within the course of his employment and therefore the employer was vicariously liable.

Obviously, where the employee carries out a prohibited act all the circumstances will have to be considered to see if he remains within the course of his employment. However, the key to establishing vicarious liability in such cases is to ask the question: 'Who is the intended beneficiary of the prohibited action?' In *Rose v Plenty*, Lord Denning applied his own earlier judgment in *Young v Edward Box & Co Ltd* (1951) in which he said:

> 'In every case where it is sought to make the master liable for the conduct of his servant the first question is to see whether the servant was liable. If the answer is yes, the second question is to see whether the employer must shoulder the servant's liability.'

This approach gives little weight to the issue of the 'course of employment' by adopting the view that, generally, it is the employer who will have the money to pay the compensation because of his insurance cover and, therefore, if it is at all possible to do so, he should be made responsible for his employee's tortious acts. It should not be forgotten that the concept of vicarious liability may also enable an employee who has been injured by a fellow employee to recover compensation, even though a claim for employer's liability would fail. In *Harrison v Michelin Tyre Co Ltd* (1985)) Harrison was injured when a fellow employee, Smith, deliberately tipped up the duck-board on which he was standing at his machine. The employer contended that Smith, who caused the injury, was on a 'frolic of his own' when he caused the injury. However, the court held that although it was an unauthorised act, Smith was going about his job when he committed the act, which was so closely connected with his employment, he remained within the course of his employment, thereby resulting in the employer being vicariously liable. Some doubt about the decision in *Harrison* was expressed in *Aldred v Nacanco* (1987). Vicarious liability extends to acts which may be crimes as well as torts eg assault, fraud. Where force or violence is used by the employee, the courts will look closely at the circumstances surrounding its use and question whether it was necessary or excessive. Early case law illustrates that the use of force may result in the employer being vicariously liable (*Poland v Parr & Sons* (1927));

although as the social climate has changed so has the attitude of the courts (*Keppel Bus Co Ltd v Sa'ad bin Ahmad* (1974)). Whether the employee has an implied authority to use force in a given situation, such as protecting his employer's property and why and how that force is used are key issues.

The following cases consider the position where the employee is put in a position of trust and abuses that position so that a crime or tort is committed.

In *Morris v Martin & Sons Ltd* (1966) Morris's mink stole was sent by her furrier to Martin's to be cleaned. Whilst there, an employee of Martin who had been entrusted with the cleaning of the fur, stole it (tort of conversion). It was held that the employer was liable for the act of conversion of their employee. Martin's were bailees for reward of the fur and were therefore under a duty to take reasonable care of it. It was then entrusted to an employee to do an act which was within the course of his employment ie clean it. What the employee did in stealing the fur was merely an abuse of his job.

A critical element in this case was the fact that Martins' had become bailees of the fur and would therefore probably have been liable for anything happening to it. There is a further limitation on the application of the rule in *Morris v Martin & Sons*; it can only serve to make the employer vicariously liable where the goods come into the employee's possession as part of his job. If, for example, an employee not involved in the cleaning of the fur had stolen it, the employer would not have been vicariously liable. The courts have reinforced the limit on the application of the decision in Morris's case by requiring a nexus between the criminal act and the circumstances of the employment. In *Heasmans v Clarity Cleaning Co Ltd* (1987) an employee of a firm contracted to clean offices, whose job involved the cleaning of telephones, dishonestly made use of the telephones to make private calls. It was held that the telephone calls were outside the purpose for which the man was employed. For an employer to be liable for the criminal acts of his employees, there must be some nexus between the criminal act of the employee and the circumstances of his employment. In this case, the requirement to dust the telephones merely provided the employee with an opportunity to commit the crime – access to the premises was an insufficient nexus. How far the question of nexus is becoming an issue in all cases of vicarious liability can be seen in *Irving v Post Office* (1987) and *Aldred v Nacanco* (1987). Where an employee is involved in a fraud, the fact that the employer has placed the employee in a position to perpetrate the fraud may result in the employer being vicariously liable.

In *Lloyd v Grace, Smith & Co* (1912) Lloyd went to the defendant solicitors to discuss some properties she had for investment purposes. She saw their managing clerk who persuaded her to sell the properties and to sign some documents which, unknown to her, transferred the properties to him. He then disposed of them for his own benefit. It was held that the solicitors were liable for the fraudulent act of their employee, even though they did not benefit from the fraud. They had placed him in a position of responsibility which enabled him to carry out the fraud. Also, as far as the general public was concerned he was in a position of trust and appeared to have the authority for his actions.

The facts of Lloyd's case are rather special and the decision is based on the special relationship between solicitor and client which is one of trust. The court did not regard 'benefit to the employer' as an issue. In reality there can be no set formula for deciding whether an employer should be vicariously liable. The fact that in many of the cases it appears that justice was seen to be done, probably justifies Lord Denning's stance in *Young v Edward Box & Co Ltd.*

12.6   Outside the course of employment

In considering those cases in which the employee has been held to be outside the course of employment, a significant issue has been the deviation of the employee from the job he was employed to do. Once again there is no set criteria for judging this issue; it remains a question of fact in each case, based on the nature of the job and the actions of the employee. The standard is laid down in *Hilton v Thomas Burton (Rhodes) Ltd* (1961). Four workmen were allowed to use their employer's van as they were working on a demolition site in the country. At lunchtime they decided to go to a cafe some seven miles away. Before reaching the cafe they changed their minds and set off to return to the site. On the return journey, one of them was killed through the negligent driving of the van driver. It was held that the employer was not vicariously liable. By travelling such a distance to take a break, they were no longer doing something incidental to their main employment; nor were they doing anything for the purpose of their employer's business. As far as the court was concerned they were 'on a frolic of their own'.

Following this case it is pertinent to ask how far the employee has deviated from his course of employment. This is a question of degree which depends on the facts of each case. There are cases dealing with prohibited acts which have reached the decision that the employee is outside the course of his employment. It should be noted that many of these decisions

were made before *Rose v Plenty* (1965) which is seen as the
watershed for such cases (see *Twine v Bean's Express Ltd* (1946).
However, the problem of tortious acts which are also crimes
has not been totally resolved, although it is possible to
distinguish the case law on its facts.

In *Warren v Henlys Ltd* (1948) a petrol pump attendant
employed by Henlys used verbal abuse when wrongly
accusing Warren, a customer, of trying to drive away without
paying for petrol. Warren called the police and told the
attendant that he would be reported to his employer. This so
enraged the attendant that he physically assaulted Warren. It
was held that the employer was not liable. The act of violence
was not connected in any way to the discharge of the pump
attendant's duties. When he assaulted Warren, he was not
doing what he was employed to do but was acting in an
unauthorised manner. The act was done in relation to a
personal matter affecting his personal interests, not in respect
of the protection of his employer's property as in *Poland v Parr*.

Finally, both the Sex Discrimination Act 1975 and the Race
Relations Act 1976 recognise a statutory form of vicarious
liability which results in the employer being liable for acts of
discrimination carried out by his employees. Whether the
employer is so liable will depend on whether the employee is
acting within the course of his employment when he commits
the act. In *Irving v Post Office* (1987) a postman took the
opportunity whilst sorting mail to write racist remarks on post
addressed to his neighbour. It was held that the employer
would not be liable for such actions since the employee had
gone beyond what he was employed to do as the only
authorised act in these circumstances would have been an
amendment to the address.

Both statutes recognise that an employer may escape being
vicariously liable if he can show that he took all reasonably
practicable steps to prevent or stop the act of discrimination.

12.6.1 Principal and agent

The rules relating to the vicarious liability of a principal for the
tortious acts of his agent operate in the same was as those for
the employer/employee. However the key to the principal's
liability will be based on whether the agent has exceeded his
authority. As can be seen in the chapter on Agency, an agent's
authority can be extremely wide in that it can be express,
implied, ostensible and usual. There is therefore more scope
for making the principal vicariously liable (see *Lloyd v Grace,
Smith & Co* (1912)).

12.6.2 Employer and independent contractor

As a general rule the employer is not liable for the torts of any
independent contractor he chooses to employ. However, he

may be made a joint tortfeasor with the independent contractor where he has:

- Ratified or authorised the tortious act.

- Contributed to the commission of the tort by the independent contractor, either by the way in which he directed the work or by interfering with the work.

- Been negligent in the selection of his independent contractor.

  In *Balfour v Barty-King* (1957) Barty-King's water-pipes were frozen. She asked two men at a nearby building site to help unfreeze them. They did this by using a blow-lamp rather than a heated brick, on the lagged pipes in her loft. The lagging caught fire and the fire spread to the adjoining premises. It was held that Barty-King was jointly liable for the negligence of the contractor. She had chosen them, invited them onto her premises and then left them to do the job. She should have exercised more care, not only in her selection, but also in overseeing their work.

- A non-delegable duty eg under the Factory Act 1961 and related statutes (see *Wilsons & Clyde Coal v English* (1938)).

- Asked the independent contractor to carry out work which is particularly hazardous, or is situated on the highway.

  In *Salsbury v Woodland* (1970) the independent contractor was contracted to fell a tree in his client's garden close to the highway. He was an experienced tree-feller but was negligent in felling the tree. Telephone lines were brought down and the plaintiff, whilst attempting to move the wires from the highway, was struck by a car. It was held that the person employing the independent contractor was not liable. The work was not being carried out on the highway and near to the highway is not the same thing. Furthermore, this work would only be regarded as extra-hazardous if it had been carried out on the highway. The independent contractor must bear sole responsibility.

  The criteria for judging whether work is particularly hazardous involves looking at where the work is to be carried out, whether members of the public are at risk and what the dangers are (see *Honeywell & Stein Ltd v Larkin Bros Ltd* (1934)).

Employer's Liability

Introduction

An employer is under a duty to take reasonable care in respect of the health and safety of his employees. This duty is personal in that it is owed to each individual employee and cannot be delegated.

> *Wilsons & Clyde Coal Co v English* (1938)
>
> *McDermid v Nash Dredging & Reclamation Ltd* (1987)

The duty is owed whilst the employee is acting within the course of his employment.

> *Davidson v Handley-Page Ltd* (1945)
>
> *Smith v Stages & Darlington Insulation Co Ltd* (1989)

The scope of the duty is four-fold:

- To provide competent fellow employees

  O'Reilly v National Rail & Tramway Appliances Ltd (1966)

  Hudson v Ridge Manufacturing Co Ltd (1957)

  Harrison v Michelin Tyre Co Ltd (1985)

- To provide safe plant and appliances

  Bradford v Robinson Rentals Ltd (1967)

  Taylor v Rover Car Co Ltd (1966)

  Employer's Liability (Defective Equipment) Act 1969

  Coltman v Bibby Tankers Ltd (1988)

  Knowles v Liverpool City Council (1993)

- To provide a safe place of work

  Smith v Vange Scaffolding & Engineering Co Ltd (1970)

- To provide a safe system of work

  Charlton v Forrest Printing Ink Co Ltd (1980)

  Bettany v Royal Doulton (UK) Ltd (1993)

  Woods v Durable Suites Ltd (1953)

  Bux v Slough Metals Ltd (1974)

Breach of duty

As this tort is negligence based the injured employee must establish that the defendant failed to act like a reasonable employer. The courts will consider the same factors as discussed in the chapter on negligence.

Latimer v AEC Ltd (1953)

Paris v Stepney Borough Council (1951)

James v Hepworth & Grandage Ltd (1968)

Hawkins v Ian Ross (Castings) Ltd (1970)

Causation

The plaintiff must show that 'but for' the defendant's breach of duty his injury would not have occurred and that harm was foreseeable.

McWilliams v Arrol Ltd (1962)

Doughty v Turner Manufacturing (1964)

Smith v Leech, Brain & Co (1962)

Vicarious liability

An employer is, in general, liable for torts committed by his employees whilst they are acting within the course of their employment. Whilst the employee has primary liability for the tort and can be sued personally, if the plaintiff pursues an action against the employer, the employee may be joined in the action or his employer may, where a claim is unsuccessfully defended, seek an indemnity from his employee.

- There must be in existence an employer/employee relationship

  The test for determining this can be found in the chapter on employment law.

- The employee must be acting within the course of his employment

  This may be doing something incidental to his or her job or carrying out an authorised act in a wrongful, negligent or unauthorised manner:

- Cases which illustrate 'within the course of employment'

  Century Insurance Co Ltd v Northern Ireland Road Transport Board (1942)

  Rose v Plenty (1976)

  Young v Edward Box & Co Ltd (1951)

  Harrison v Michelin Tyre Co Ltd (1985)

  Poland v Parr & Sons (1927)

  Morris v Martin & Sons Ltd (1966)

  Lloyd v Grace Smith & Co (1912)

- Cases which illustrate 'outside the course of employment'

  Hilton v Thomas Burton (Rhodes) Ltd (1961)

  Warren v Henlys Ltd (1948)

Aldred v Nacanco Ltd (1987)

Heasmans v Clarity Cleaning Co Ltd (1987)

Irving v Post Office (1987)

The concept of vicarious liability arises where there is in existence a 'special relationship'. It can therefore also arise between principal and agent and in limited circumstances between employer and independent contractor.

Balfour v Barty-King (1957)

Salsbury v Woodland (1970)

Honeywell & Stein Ltd v Larkin Bros Ltd (1934)

Chapter 13

Agency

The general assumption is that individuals engaging in business activity carry on that business by themselves on their own behalf, but it is not uncommon for such individuals to engage others to represent them and negotiate business deals on their behalf. Indeed, the role of the middleman is a commonplace one in business and commerce. The legal relationship between such a representative, or middleman, and the business person making use of them is governed by the law of agency.

An agent is a person who is empowered to represent another legal party, called the principal, and brings the principal into a legal relationship with a third party. It should be emphasised that the contract entered into is between the principal and the third party. In the normal course of events the agent has no personal rights or liabilities in relation to the contract. This outcome represents an accepted exception to the usual operation of the doctrine of privity in contract law (see para 6.6).

Since the agent is not actually entering into contractual relations with the third party there is no requirement that the agent has contractual capacity although, based on the same reasoning, it is essential that the principal has full contractual capacity. Thus, it is possible for a principal to use a minor as an agent although the minor might not have contractual capacity to enter into the contract on their own behalf.

There are numerous examples of agency relationships. For example, as their names imply, estate agents and travel agents are expressly appointed to facilitate particular transactions. Additionally, employees may act as agents of their employers in certain circumstances; or friends may act as agents for one another.

Some forms of agency merit particular consideration:

- A *general agent*, as the title indicates, has the power to act for a principal generally in relation to a particular area of business, whereas a *special agent* only has the authority to act in one particular transaction.

- A *del credere* agent is one who, in return for an additional commission by way of payment, guarantees to the principal that in the event of a third party's failure to pay for goods received the agent will make good the loss.

- A *commission agent* is a hybrid form which lies mid-way between a full principal/agent relationship and the relationship of an independent trader and client. In essence the agent stands between the principal and the third party and establishes no contract between those two parties. The effect is that although the commission agent owes the duties of an agent to his principle he contracts with the third party as a principal in his own right. The effectiveness of this procedure is undermined by the normal operation of the agency law relating to an undisclosed principal (see below para 13.6.2).

- The position of a *mercantile agent/factor* is defined in the Factors Act (1889) as an agent:

  '... having in the customary course of his business as such agent authority either to sell goods, or to consign goods for the purpose of sale, or to buy goods, or to raise money on the security of goods.'

- A *power of attorney* arises where an agency is specifically created by way of a deed.

13.3   Creation of agency

No one can act as an agent without the consent of the principal, although consent need not be expressly stated.

In *White v Lucas* (1887) a firm of estate agents claimed to act on behalf of the owner of a particular property although that person had denied them permission to act on his behalf. When the owner sold the property to a third party introduced through the estate agents they claimed their commission. It was held that the estate agents had no entitlement to commission as the property owner had not agreed to their acting as his agent.

The principal/agent relationship can be created in a number of ways. It may arise as the outcome of a distinct contract, which may be made either orally or in writing, or it may be established purely gratuitously where some person simply agrees to act for another. The relationship may also arise from the action of the parties.

It is usual to consider the creation of the principal/agency relationship under four distinct categories.

13.3.1   Express appointment

This is the most common manner in which a principal/agent relationship comes into existence. In this situation the agent is specifically appointed by the principal to carry out a particular task or to undertake some general function. In most situations the appointment of the agent will itself involve the establishment of a contractual relationship between the principal and the agent but need not necessarily depend upon a contract between those parties.

For the most part, there are no formal requirements for the appointment of an agent, although where the agent is to be given the power to execute deeds in the principal's name they must themselves be appointed by way of a deed (ie they are given power of attorney).

An agency is created by ratification when a person who has no authority purports to contract with a third party on behalf of a principal. Ratification is the express acceptance of the contract by the principal. Where the principal elects to ratify the contract it gives retrospective validity to the action of the purported agent. There are, however, certain conditions which have to be fully complied with before the principal can effectively adopt the contract.

13.3.2   Ratification

- The principal must have been in existence at the time when the agent entered into the contract

  Thus, for example, in *Kelner v Baxter* (1866) where the promoters attempted to enter into a contract on behalf of the, as yet unformed, company it was held that the company could not ratify the contract after it was created and that the promoters, as agents, were personally liable on the contract. (This is now given statutory effect under s 36(C) of the Companies Act 1985.)

- The principal must have had legal capacity to enter into the contract when it was made

  When the capacity of companies to enter into a business transaction was limited by the operation of the doctrine of *ultra vires* (see para 15.5.1 below) it was clearly established that they could not ratify any such *ultra vires* contracts. Similarly, it is not possible for minors to ratify a contract even though it was made in their name.

- An undisclosed principal cannot ratify a contract

  The agent must have declared that he was acting for the principal. If the agent appeared to be acting on his own account then the principal cannot later adopt the contact (see *Keighley, Maxsted & Co v Durant* (1901)).

- The principal must adopt the whole of the contract

  It is not open to the principal to pick and choose which parts of the contract to adopt but they must accept all of its terms.

- Ratification must take place within a reasonable time

  It is not possible to state with certainty what will be considered as a reasonable time in any particular case. Where, however, the third party with whom the agent contracted becomes aware that the agent had acted without authority, he can set a time limit within which the principal must indicate their adoption of the contract for it to be effective.

13.3.3   Implication

This form of agency arises from the relationship that exists between the principal and the agent and from which it is assumed that the principal has given authority to the other person to act as his agent. Thus, it is implied from the particular position held by individuals that they have the authority to enter into contractual relations on behalf of their principal. Thus, whether an employee has the actual authority to contract on behalf of his employer depends on the position held by the employee; and, for example, it was decided in *Panorama Developments v Fidelis Furnishing Fabrics Ltd* (1971) that a company secretary had the implied authority to make contracts in the company's name relating to the day to day running of the company.

Problems most often occur in relation to the implied *extent* of a person's authority rather than their actual appointment (but see *Hely-Hutchinson v Brayhead Ltd* as an example of the latter).

13.3.4   Necessity

Agency by necessity occurs under circumstances where, although there is no agreement between the parties, an emergency requires that an agent take particular action in order to protect the interests of the principal. The usual situation which gives rise to agency by necessity occurs where the agent is in possession of the principal's property and due to some unforeseen emergency the agent has to take action to safeguard that property.

- In order for agency by necessity to arise there needs to be a genuine emergency.

  In *Great Northern Railway Co v Swaffield* (1874) the railway company transported the defendant's horse and when no one arrived to collect it at its destination it was placed in a livery stable. It was held that the company was entitled to recover the cost of stabling as necessity had forced them to act as they had done as the defendant's agents.

- There must also be no practical way of obtaining further instructions from the principal.

  In *Springer v Great Western Railway Co* (1921) a consignment of tomatoes arrived at port after a delayed journey due to storms. A railway strike would have caused further delay in getting the tomatoes to their destination so the railway company decided to sell the tomatoes locally. It was held that the railway company was responsible to the plaintiff for the difference between the price achieved and the market price in London. The defence of agency of necessity was not available as the railway company could have contacted the plaintiff to seek his further instructions.

- The person seeking to establish the agency by necessity must have acted *bona fide* in the interests of the principal

  See *Sachs v Miklos* (1948).

This form of agency is also known as agency by holding out and arises where the principal has led other parties to believe that a person has the authority to represent him. (The authority possessed by the agent is referred to as apparent authority. See below.) In such circumstances, even though no principal/agency relationship actually exists in fact, the principal is prevented (estopped) from denying the existence of the agency relationship and is bound by the action of his purported agent as regards any third party who acted in the belief of its existence.

13.3.5   Estoppel

- To rely on agency by estoppel the principal must have made a representation as to the authority of the agent

  In *Freeman & Lockyer v Buckhurst Park Properties Ltd* (1964) a property company had four directors but one director effectively controlled the company and made contracts as if he were the managing director even though he had never actually been appointed to that position and therefore, as an individual, had no authority to bind the company. The other directors, however, were aware of this activity and acquiesced in it. When the company was sued in relation to one of the contracts entered into by the unauthorised director it was held that it was liable as the board which had the actual authority to bind the company had held out the individual director as having the necessary authority to enter such contracts. It was therefore a case of agency by estoppel.

- As with estoppel generally, the party seeking to use it must have relied on the representation

  In *Overbrooke Estates Ltd v Glencombe Properties Ltd* (1974) a notice which expressly denied the authority of an auctioneer to make such statements as actually turned out to be false was successfully relied on as a defence by the auctioneer's employers.

13.4   The authority of an agent

In order to bind a principal any contract entered into must be within the limits of the authority extended to the agent. The authority of an agent can be either actual or apparent.

13.4.1   Actual authority

Actual authority can arise in either of two ways:

* Express actual authority

  This is explicitly granted by the principal to the agent. The agent is instructed as to what particular tasks he has to perform and is informed of the precise powers he is given to fulfil those tasks.

* Implied actual authority

  This refers to the way in which the scope of express authority may be increased. Third parties are entitled to assume that agents holding a particular position have all the powers that are usually provided to such an agent. Without actual knowledge they may safely assume that the agent has usual authority. (This has been referred to above in relation to implied agency.)

  In *Watteau v Fenwick* (1893) the new owners of a hotel continued to employ the previous owner as its manager. They expressly forbade him to buy certain articles including cigars. The manager, however, bought cigars from a third party who later sued the owners for payment as the manager's principal. It was held that the purchase of cigars was within the usual authority of a manager of such an establishment and that for a limitation on such usual authority to be effective it must be communicated to any third party.

13.4.2   Apparent authority

Apparent authority is an aspect of agency by estoppel considered above. It can arise in two distinct ways:

* Where a person makes a representation to third parties that a particular person has the authority to act as their agent without actually appointing the agent.

  In such a case the person making the representation is bound by the actions of the apparent agent (see *Freeman & Lockyer v Buckhurst Park Properties Ltd* (1964)). The principal is also liable for the actions of the agent where he knows that the agent claims to be his agent and he does nothing to correct that impression.

* Where a principal has previously represented to a third party that an agent has the authority to act on their behalf.

  Even if the principal has subsequently revoked the agent's authority they may still be liable for the actions of the former agent unless they have informed third parties who had previously dealt with the agent about the new situation (see *Willis Faber & Co Ltd v Joyce* (1911)).

If an agent contracts with a third party on behalf of a principal, the agent impliedly guarantees that the principal exists and has contractual capacity. The agent also implies that he has the authority to make contracts on behalf of that principal. If any of these implied warranties prove to be untrue then the third party may sue the agent *in quasi-contract* for breach of warrant of authority. Such an action may arise even though the agent was genuinely unaware of any lack of authority.

In *Yonge v Toynbee* (1910) a firm of solicitors was instructed to institute proceedings against a third party. Without their knowledge their client was certified insane and although this automatically ended the agency relationship they continued with the proceedings. The third party successfully recovered damages for breach of warrant of authority since the solicitors were no longer acting for their former client.

13.4.3   Warrant of authority

The following considers the reciprocal rights and duties which principal and agent owe each other.

13.5   The relationship of principal and agent

The agent owes a number of duties, both express and implied, to the principal. These duties are as follows:

13.5.1   The duties of agent to principal

- To perform the agreed undertaking according to the instructions of the principal

  A failure to carry out instructions will leave the agent open to an action for breach of contract. This, of course, does not apply in the case of gratuitous agencies where there is no obligation whatsoever on the agent to perform the agreed task. See *Turpin v Bilton* (1843) where an agent was held liable for the loss sustained by his failure to insure his principal's ship prior to its sinking.

- To exercise due care and skill

  An agent will owe a duty to act with reasonable care and skill, regardless of whether the agency relationship is contractual or gratuitous. The level of skill to be exercised, however, should be that appropriate to the agent's professional capacity and this may introduce a distinction in the levels expected of different agents. For example a solicitor would be expected to show the level of care and skill that would not be expected of a competent member of that profession whereas a layperson acting in a gratuitous capacity would only be expected to perform with such degree of care and skill as a reasonable person would exercise in the conduct of their own affairs (see *Keppel v*

Wheeler (1927) where the defendant estate agents were held liable for failing to secure the maximum possible price for a property).

• To carry out instructions personally

Unless expressly or impliedly authorised to delegate the work, an agent owes a duty to the principal to act personally in the completion of the task. The right to delegate may be agreed expressly by the principal or it may be implied from customary practice or arise as a matter of necessity. In any such case the agent remains liable to the principal for the proper performance of the agreed contract.

• To account

There is an implied duty that the agent keep proper accounts of all transactions entered into on behalf of the principal. The agent is required to account for all money and other property received on the principal's behalf and should keep his own property separate from that of the principal.

In addition to these contractual duties there are general equitable duties which flow from the fact that the agency relationship is a *fiduciary* one; ie it is one based on trust. These general fiduciary duties are:

• Not to permit a conflict of interest to arise

An agent must not allow the possibility of his personal interest conflicting with the interests of his principal without disclosing that possibility to the principal. Upon full disclosure it is up to the principal to decide whether or not to proceed with the particular transaction. If there is a breach of this duty the principal may set aside the contract so affected and claim any profit which might have been made by the agent.

In *McPherson v Watt* (1877) a solicitor used his brother as a nominee to purchase property which he was engaged to sell. It was held that since the solicitor had allowed a conflict of interest to arise the sale could be set aside. It was immaterial that a fair price was offered for the property.

The corollary to the above case is that the agent must not sell his own property to the principal without fully disclosing the fact (see *Harrods v Lemon* (1931)). This leads into the next duty which is:

• Not to make a secret profit or misuse confidential information

An agent who uses his position as an agent to secure financial advantage for himself, without full disclosure to his principal, is in breach of his fiduciary duty. Upon disclosure the principal may authorise the agent's profit but full disclosure is a necessary precondition (see *Hippisley v Knee Bros* (1905) for a clear-cut case). An example of the strictness with which this principle is enforced may be seen in the case of *Boardman v Phipps* (1967) in which agents were held to account for profits made from information which they had gained from their position as agents, even though their action also benefitted the company they were acting for.

- Not to take a bribe

  This duty may be seen as merely a particular aspect of the general duty not to make a secret profit but it goes so much to the root of the agency relationship that it is usually treated as a distinct heading in its own right. Again for a clear-cut case see *Mahesan v Malaysian Government Officers Co-operative Housing Society* (1978) where the plaintiff received a bribe to permit a third party to profit at his principal's expense.

  Where it is found that an agent has taken a bribe the following civil remedies are open to the principal:

- to repudiate the contract with the third party;

- to dismiss the agent without notice;

- to refuse to pay any monies owed to the agent or to recover such monies already paid;

- to claim the amount of the bribe;

- to claim damages in the tort of deceit for any loss sustained as a result of the payment of the bribe.

  The payment of the bribe may also have constituted a breach of criminal law.

It is a simple matter of fact that the law does not generally provide agents with as many rights in relation to the number of duties it imposes on them. The agent, however, does benefit from the clear establishment of three general rights. These rights are:

13.5.2   The rights of an agent

- To claim remuneration for services performed

  It is usual in agency agreements for the amount of payment to be stated, either in the form of wages, or commission or indeed both. Where a commercial agreement is silent on the matter of payment the court will imply a term into the agreement requiring the payment of a reasonable remuneration. Such a term will not be implied in contradiction of the express terms of the agreement. See *Re Richmond Gate Property Co Ltd* (1965) where it was held that no remuneration could be claimed where an agreement stated that payment would be determined by the directors of the company but they had not actually decided on any payment.

- To claim indemnity against the principal for all expenses legitimately incurred in the performance of services

  Both contractual and non-contractual agents are entitled to recover money spent in the course of performing their agreed task. In the case of the former the remedy is based on an implied contractual term and in the case of a gratuitous agent it is based on the remedy of restitution. Money can, of course, only be claimed where the agent has been acting within his actual authority.

- To exercise a lien over property owned by the principal

  This is a right to retain the principal's goods, where they have lawfully come into the agent's possession, and hold them against any debts outstanding to him as a result of the agency agreement. The nature of the lien is usually a *particular* one relating to specific goods which are subject to the agreement and not a *general* one which entitles the agent to retain any of the principal's goods even where no money is owed in relation to those specific goods. The general lien is only recognised on the basis of an express term in the contract or as a result of judicially recognised custom, as in banking.

13.6 Relations with third parties

In the words of Wright J in *Montgomerie v United Kingdom Mutual Steamship Association* (1891), once an agent creates a contract between the principal and a third party, '*prima facie* at common law the only person who can sue is the principal and the only person who can be sued is the principal'. In other words, the agent has no further responsibility. This general rule is, however, subject to the following particular exceptions which in turn tend to depend upon whether the agent has actually disclosed the existence of the principal or not.

13.6.1 Where the principal's existence is disclosed

Although the actual identity of principal need not be mentioned, where the agent indicates that he is acting as an agent, the general rule is as stated above; only the principal and the third party have rights and obligations under the contract.

Exceptionally, however, the agent may be held liable as a party to the contract. This can occur:

- At third party insistence

  Where the agent has expressly accepted liability with the principal in order to induce the third party to enter the contract.

- By implication

  Where the agent has signed the contractual agreement in his own name without clearly stating that he is merely acting as a representative of his principal he will most likely be liable on it.

- In relation to bills of exchange

  As in the previous situation, where an agent signs a bill of exchange without sufficiently indicating that they are merely acting as the agent of a named principal they will become personally liable on it.

- In relation to the execution a deed

  Where the agent signs the deed, other than under a power of attorney, he will be personally liable on it.

Even in the case of an undisclosed principal, where the agent has authority but has failed to disclose that he is acting for a principal, the general rule is still that a contract exists between the principal and the third party which can be enforced by either of them. The following, however, are some modifications to this general rule:

13.6.2   Where the principal's existence is not disclosed

- The third party is entitled to enforce the contract against the agent and in turn the agent can enforce the contract against the third party. In both cases the principal can intervene to enforce or defend the action on his own behalf.

- As stated previously an undisclosed principal cannot ratify any contract made outside of the agent's actual authority.

- Where the third party had a special reason to contract with the agent the principal may be excluded from the contract. This will certainly apply in relation to personal contracts such as contracts of employment and, possibly, on the authority of *Greer v Downs Supply Co* (1927), where the third party has a right to set off debts against the agent.

- Authority exists in *Said v Butt* (1920) where a theatre critic employed someone to get him a ticket for a performance he would not have been allowed into, for claiming that an undisclosed principal will not be permitted to enforce a contract where particular reasons exist as to why the third party would not wish to deal with him. This decision appears to run contrary to normal commercial practice and is of doubtful merit.

It is certain, however, that where the agent actually misrepresents the identity of the principal, knowing that the third party would not otherwise enter into the contract, the principal will not be permitted to enforce the contract (see *Archer v Stone* (1898)).

| 13.6.3 | Payment by means of an agent |

Payment by means of an agent can take two forms:

- Payment by the third party to the agent to pass on to the principal

  In this situation, if the principal is undisclosed, then the third party has discharged liability on the contract and is not responsible if the agent absconds with the money. However, if the principal is disclosed then any payment to the agent only discharges the third party's responsibility if it can be shown that the agent had authority, either express or implied, to receive money.

- Payment by the principal to the agent to pass on to the third party

  In this situation the general rule is that if the agent does not pay the third party, the principal remains liable. This remains the case in the situation of an undisclosed principal (see *Irvine & Co v Watson & Sons* (1880)).

| 13.6.4 | Breach of warrant of authority |

As has been stated above (para 13.4.3) where an agent purports to act for a principal without actually having the necessary authority, the agent is said to have breached his warrant of authority. In such circumstances the third party may take action against the purported agent.

| 13.6.5 | Liability in tort |

An agent is liable to be sued in tort for any damages thus caused. However, the agent's right to indemnity extends to tortious acts done in the performance of his actual authority. In addition, the principal may have action taken against him directly, on the basis of *vicarious liability* (see para 12.5).

13.7 Termination of agency

The principal/agent relationship can come to end in two distinct ways; either by the acts of the parties themselves either jointly or unilaterally, or as an effect of the operation of law.

| 13.7.1 | Termination by the parties |

There are a number of ways in which the parties can bring an agency agreement to an end.

- By mutual agreement

  Where the agency agreement is a continuing one the parties may simply agree to bring the agency relationship to an end on such terms as they wish. Where the agency was established for a particular purpose then it will automatically come to an end when that purpose has been achieved. Equally, where the agency was only intended to last for a definite period of time then the end of that period will bring the agency to an end.

- By the unilateral action of one of the parties

Because of the essentially consensual nature of the principal/agency relationship it is possible for either of the parties to bring it to an end simply by giving notice of termination of the agreement. Although the agency relationship will be ended by such unilateral action, in situations where the principal has formed a contractual relationship with the agent such unilateral termination may leave the principal open to an action for damages in breach of contract.

- Irrevocable agreements

In some circumstances it is not possible to revoke an agency agreement. This situation arises where the agent has 'authority coupled with an interest'. Such an irrevocable agency might arise where a principal owes money to the agent and the payment of the debt was the reason for the formation of the agency relationship. For example, where in order to raise the money to pay off his debt the principal appoints his creditor as his agent to sell some particular piece of property, the principal may not be at liberty to bring the agency to an end until the sale has taken place and the debt paid off.

This refers to the fact that an agency relationship will be brought to an end by:

13.7.2   Termination by operation of law

- Frustration

Contracts of agency are subject to discharge by frustration in the same way as ordinary contracts are (see para 9.4 for the general operation of the doctrine of frustration).

- The death of either party

Death of the agent clearly brings the agreement to an end as does the death of the principal. The latter situation may, however, give rise to problems where the agent is unaware of the death and continues to act in the capacity of agent. In such circumstances the agent will be in breach of his warrant of authority and will be personally liable to third parties.

- Insanity of either party

  As in the previous situation the insanity of either party will bring the agency to an end but agents similarly will have to be careful so as not to breach their warrant of authority by continuing to act after the insanity of the principal (see *Yonge v Toynbee* (1910) para 13.4.3 above).

- Bankruptcy

  The bankruptcy of the principal generally will end the agency agreement, but the bankruptcy of the agent will only bring it to an end where it renders him unfit to continue to act as an agent.

Agency

An agent is a person who is empowered to represent another legal party, called the principal, and brings the principal into a legal relationship with a third party.

Agency agreements may be either contractual or gratuitous.

Definition

Agency requires the consent of the principal but such consent may be implied from circumstances.

Agency may arise expressly, by ratification, by implication, by necessity, or by estoppel.

Creation of agency

Actual authority may be divided into express actual authority and implied actual authority.

Apparent authority is based on estoppel and operates in such a way as to make the principal responsible for his action or inaction as regards someone who he knows purports to be his agent. Particular problems arise in relation to ex-employees and ex-agents generally.

Nature of agent's authority

If an agent contracts with a third party on behalf of a principal, the agent impliedly guarantees that the principal exists and has contractual capacity and that he has that person's authority to act as his agent. If this is not the case the agent is personally liable to third parties for breach of warrant of authority.

Warrant of authority

The duties of agent to principal are:

The duties of agent to principal

- to perform the undertaking according to instructions;
- to exercise due care and skill;
- to carry out instructions personally;
- to account;
- not to permit a conflict of interest to arise;
- not to make a secret profit or misuse confidential information;
- not to take a bribe.

The rights of an agent	The rights of an agent are:

- to claim remuneration for services performed;
- to claim indemnity for all expenses legitimately incurred in the performance of services;
- to exercise a lien over property owned by the principal.

Relations with third parties

Where the agent indicates that he is acting as an agent, the general rule is that only the principal and the third party have rights and obligations under the contract.

Exceptions can occur:

- at the insistence of the third party;
- by implication;
- in relation to bills of exchange;
- in relation to deeds.

Where the principal's existence is not disclosed:

- the agent can enforce the contract against the third party;
- the principal can enforce the contract against the third party;
- the third party can choose to enforce the contract against the agent or the principal;
- an undisclosed principal cannot ratify any contract made outside of the agent's actual authority.

Where the third party had a special reason to contract with the agent the principal may be excluded from the contract.

Where the agent misrepresents the identity of the principal the third party may not be bound by the contract.

Payment by means of an agent

If the agent does not pay the third party, the principal remains liable.

If the agent absconds with money paid by the third party then, if the principal is undisclosed, he sustains the loss. If, however, the principal is disclosed, the agent must have had authority to accept money or else the third party is liable.

Termination of agency

Agreements may end:

- by mutual agreement;
- by the unilateral action of one of the parties;
- through frustration;
- due to the death, insanity or bankruptcy of either of the parties.

Chapter 14

Partnership Law

The partnership is a fundamental form of business/commercial organisation. Historically, the partnership predated the registered limited company as a means for uniting the capital of separate individuals and it was of the utmost importance in financing the Industrial Revolution in the UK in the 18th and 19th centuries.

As an economic form the partnership is still important. However, since the last quarter of the 19th century, as unlimited partnerships have transformed themselves into private limited companies, partnership law has given way to the control of company law as a form of legal regulation. This shift goes some of the way to explaining why partnership case authorities tend to be so old. It could be argued that nowadays the important partnership cases take place in the Companies Court. The continued relevance of partnership law should not be underestimated, however, since it remains the essential form of organisation within the sphere of such professional activity as the law, accountancy and medicine, where there is either no wish, or need, for limited liability.

The legal regulation of partnerships is mainly to be found in the Partnership Act 1890 (PA). This Act recognised the existing business and commercial practice and at least some of the previous decisions of common law and equity as they affected partnerships.

In line with the consensual nature of partnership undertakings the Act did not seek to set out to achieve a complete codification of the law but merely to establish a basic framework whilst leaving open the possibility for partners to establish their own terms. The limited nature of the Partnership Act means that reference has to be made to cases decided by the courts both before and after the Act in order to understand the full scope of partnership law (s 46 expressly maintains all the rules of the common law and equity except where they are inconsistent with the provisions of the Act).

A key attribute of the partnership is the fact that its members are liable to the full extent of their personal wealth for the debts of the business. The Limited Partnership Act 1907, however, allows for the formation of limited partnerships. For members of a partnership to gain the benefit

14.1 Introduction

14.2 The Partnership Acts

of limited liability under this legislation the following rules apply:

- Limited partners are not liable for partnership debts beyond the extent of their capital contribution, but in the ordinary course of events they are not permitted to remove their capital.

- One or more of the partners must retain full, ie unlimited, liability for the debts of the partnership.

- A partner with limited liability is not permitted to take part in the management of the business enterprise and cannot usually bind the partnership in any transaction (contravention of this rule will result in the loss of limited liability).

- The partnership must be registered with the Companies Registry.

14.3   Definition of partnership

Section 1 of the PA states that 'partnership is the relation which subsists between persons carrying on a business in common with a view to profit'.

In relation to this definition it should be noted that:

- The section expressly excludes companies registered under the Companies legislation.

- The nature of the relationship is a contractual one

  Partners enter into the agreement on the terms that they themselves have negotiated and acceded to. As a consequence they are contractually bound by those terms, as long as they do not conflict with the express provisions of the PA, and they may be enforced by the law in the same way as other contractual terms.

- It is a requirement that a business be carried on

  The term business includes any trade, occupation, or profession. The mere fact that individuals jointly own property does not necessarily mean that they are partners if the property is not being used by them to pursue some collective business activity. See also *Britton v Commissioners of Customs & Excise* (1986), where it was held that the fact that a wife received a share of the profits of her husband's business did not make her a partner in the business since this was a purely domestic arrangement.

- Partnerships may be created for the purposes of a single venture

  It is usually the case that partnerships continue over an extended period of time but this is not necessarily the case.

- The business must be carried on with a view to profit

An immediate result of this provision is that neither charitable nor mutual benefit schemes are to be considered as partnerships.

It used to be the case that the mere receipt of a share of profit was enough to make a person a partner and responsible for partnership debts (see *Waugh v Carver* (1793)). Nowadays, although the receipt of a share of profits may be prima facie evidence of a partnership relationship, it is not conclusive.

Section 2(2) of the PA expressly states that the sharing of 'gross returns' does not in itself indicate the existence of a partnership agreement, since such an arrangement may simply represent a form of payment for the individual concerned. Thus, by way of example, the authors of this book will receive a percentage of the total sales value of the book. That, however, does not make them partners of the publishers, so, if publication of the book results in massive losses for the publishers, third parties cannot look to the authors for any money owed.

Even receiving a share of 'net profits' does not necessarily indicate a partnership. For example, a person would not be treated as a partner where they received payment of a debt by instalments made from business profits; or where they received wages in the form of a share of profit; or received interest on a loan to a business the rate of which varied in relation to the level of the business's profits. (See also *Britton v Commissioners of Customs & Excise* (1986) mentioned above.)

It is sometimes thought necessary to distinguish between different types of partners but in reality such a division is of most use in pointing out particular dangers inherent in a failure to adopt an active, if only a supervisory, role in a partnership enterprise. Thus a *general partner* is the typical member of a partnership. The term is actually used in the Limited Partnership Act to distinguish that usual type from the unusual limited partner. The general partner is one who is actively engaged in the day to day running of the business enterprise whereas the *limited partner* is actually precluded from participating in the management of the enterprise.

Section 24(5) of the PA provides that *every* partner is entitled to take part in the management of the partnership business. The partnership agreement may place limitations on the *actual authority* of any such person but, unless an outsider is aware of the limitation, the partnership is responsible for any business transaction entered into by a partner within his *usual authority*. (For further consideration of these types of authority see below.)

14.3.1   Types of partners

A *dormant* or *sleeping partner* is a person who merely invests money in a partnership enterprise but, apart from receiving a return on capital invested, takes no active part in the day to day running of the business. The limited partner in a limited partnership may be seen as a dormant partner. The term is used more generally, however, to refer to people who simply put money into partnership enterprises without taking an active part in the business and yet do not comply with the formalities required for establishing a limited partnership. The essential point that has to be emphasised in this regard is that, in so doing, such people place themselves at great risk. The law will consider them as general partners in the enterprise and will hold them personally and fully liable for the debts of the partnership to the extent of their ability to pay. By remaining outside the day to day operation of the business such people merely surrender their personal unlimited liability into the control of the active parties in the partnership.

14.4 The legal status of a partnership

A partnership is an organisation established by individuals to pursue some business activity. Although the law is permissive in relation to the establishment of such enterprises, there are particular ways in which the law impinges on and controls, not just the operation of partnerships, but their very formation and existence.

14.4.1 Legal personality

The definition of a partnership expressly states that it is 'a relationship between persons'. The corollary of this is that the partnership has no existence outside of, or apart from, that relationship. In other words, the partnership has no separate legal personality apart from its members as does a joint-stock company.

Although Scottish law does grant corporate personality to the partnership without the benefit of limited liability, in English law a partnership is no more than a group of individuals collectively involved in a business activity. Section 4 of the PA, however, does recognise an element of unity within the partnership organisation to the extent that it permits the partnership to be known collectively as a 'firm' and permits the business to be carried out under the firm's name. In addition, the procedural Rules of the Supreme Court, Ord 81, provides that legal action may be taken by, and against, the partners in the firm's name, although any award against the partnership may be executed against any of the individual partners.

A partnership is illegal if it is formed to carry out an illegal purpose or to carry out a legal purpose in an illegal manner. In such circumstances the courts will not recognise any partnership rights between the persons involved but will permit innocent third parties, who have no knowledge of any illegality, to recover against them.

Partnerships are generally not lawful if they consist of more than 20 persons as provided by s 716 of the Companies Act 1985. However, certain professional partnerships, such as solicitors, accountants and surveyors etc, are exempt from this maximum limit.

14.4.2 Illegal partnerships

There are two distinct aspects relating to capacity:

14.4.3 Capacity

• Capacity of individuals to join a partnership

The general common law rules relating to capacity to enter into contracts apply in the particular case of the membership of a partnership. Thus, any partnership agreement entered into by a minor is voidable during that person's minority and for a reasonable time after they have reached the age of majority. If the former minor does not repudiate the partnership agreement within a reasonable time of reaching the age of majority then they will be liable for any debts as a *de facto* partner. Third parties cannot recover against partners who are minors but they can recover against any other adult partners.

Mental incapacity does not necessarily prevent someone from entering into a partnership, but subsequent mental incapacity of a partner may be grounds for the dissolution of a partnership.

• Capacity of the partnership

A particular consequence of the fact that the partnership is, at least in the perception of the law, no more than a relationship between individuals is that there are no specific rules controlling the contractual capacity of partnerships, other than those general rules which constrain individuals' capacity to enter into contracts.

Section 5 of the PA provides that each partner is the agent of the firm and the other partners for *the purpose of the business of the partnership* but as that purpose is determined by the members, and as is not fixed by law, it can be changed by the unanimous agreement of those members. (See the alteration of the partnership agreement below para 14.5.2.)

There are no specific legal requirements governing the formation of a partnership. Partnerships arise from the agreement of the parties involved and are governed by the

14.5 Formation of a partnership

general principles of contract law. An agreement to enter into a partnership, therefore, may be made by deed, or in writing, or by word of mouth. Such agreement may even be implied from the conduct of the parties.

14.5.1   The partnership agreement

It is usual for the terms of the partnership to be set out in written form. The document produced is known as the articles of partnership. The parties involved, no doubt after some negotiation, decide what they wish to be specifically included in the articles. Any gaps in the articles will be filled in by reference to the PA or the existing common law and equitable rules relating to partnerships but it is necessary for the future partners to provide for any unusual or specialised terms to be included in the articles.

The detailed provisions in articles of partnership usually refer to such matters as: the nature of the business to be transacted, the name of the firm, the capital contributions to be made by the individual partners, the drawing up of the business accounts, the method of determining and sharing profits, and the dissolution of the partnership. It is also usual for there to be a provision for disputes between partners to be referred to arbitration for solution.

The partnership agreement is an internal document and although it has effect between the partners it does not necessarily affect the rights of third parties. Thus, where the agreement seeks to place limitations on the usual authority of a partner, it is effective with regard to the internal relations of the partners but does not have any effect as regards an outsider who deals with the partner without knowledge of the limitation.

In *Mercantile Credit v Garrod* (1962) two people, Parkin and Garrod, were partners in a garage business mainly concerned with letting garages and repairing cars. The partnership agreement expressly excluded the sale of cars. After Parkin had sold a car, to which he had no title, to the plaintiffs they claimed back the money they had paid from Garrod.

It was held that since selling cars was within the usual scope of a garage business it was within the usual authority of a partner in such a business. Parkin, therefore, had acted within his implied authority and the partnership was responsible for his actions. The plaintiffs had no knowledge of the limitation contained within the articles and could not be subject to it.

14.5.2   Alteration of partnership agreement

Just as the consensual nature of the partnership relationship allows the parties to make the agreement in such terms as they wish so are they equally free to alter those terms at a later date.

Section 19 of the PA, however, enacts the common law rule that any decision to alter the terms of partnership articles must be made unanimously. Consent does not have to be expressed but may be inferred from the conduct of the partners.

In *Pilling v Pilling* (1887) the articles of partnership entered into between a father and his two sons stated that the business was to be financed by the father's capital and that such capital was to remain his personal property and not be treated as the partnership property. The articles also stated that the father should receive interest on his capital. In practice, however, the sons as well as the father received interest on the partnership capital. It was held that the capital originally provided by the father was partnership property and that the conduct of the parties in treating it as such had amounted to a valid alteration of the written agreement.

Partnerships may use the words '& Company' or its alternative form '& Co' in their name eg a firm of solicitors may call itself Brown, Smith & Co. This merely indicates that names of all the partners are not included in the firm's name. As has been seen above, it in no way indicates that the partnership has any existence apart from its constituent members or that those members have the benefit of limited liability. Even in the case of limited partnerships someone must accept full liability for partnership debts. Section 34 of the Companies Act consequently makes it a criminal offence for a partnership to use the word limited or the abbreviation Ltd in its name.	14.5.3 The firm's name

A partnership may trade under the names of the individual partners or it may trade under a collective name. Any name must comply with both the Business Names Act 1985 and the common law provisions relating to the tort of 'passing off'.

Section 4 of the Business Names Act requires that, where a partnership does not trade under the names of all of its members, the names of individuals must be displayed on the business premises and on the firm's business documents. Where the partnership is a large one with more than 20 members the individual names do not have to be listed on business documents but a list of all partners must be available for inspection at the firm's principal place of business. Any failure to comply with this requirement may result in the person in breach not being able to enforce a claim against another party who was disadvantaged by the breach.	14.5.4 Business Names Act 1985

There is no longer any requirement that business names be registered as such but the Act requires the approval of the Secretary of State for Trade and Industry before certain names can be used. Such names may imply that the business is related in some way to the Crown, the government, local authorities or other official bodies.

14.5.5	Passing off

The Business Names Act does not prevent one business from using the same, or a very similar, name as another business. However, the tort of 'passing off' prevents one person from using any name which is likely to divert business their way by suggesting that the business is actually that of some other person, or is connected in any way with that other business. It thus enables people to protect the goodwill they have built up in relation to their business activity. See *Ewing v Buttercup Margarine Company Ltd* (1917) where the plaintiff successfully prevented the use by the defendants of a name that suggested a link with his existing dairy company. For a more up to date and less serious case, see *Stringfellow v McCain Foods GB Ltd* (1984) in which the owner of the famous Stringfellow's nightclub failed to prevent a manufacturer of long thin oven-chips from calling their product by the same name.

14.5.6	Arbitration clauses

The consensual nature of the relationship on which any partnership is based has been repeatedly emphasised. It should always be remembered, however, that even the best of friends can fall out and when they are engaged in a joint business venture any such conflict may be disastrous for the business. In an attempt to forestall such an eventuality, and to avoid the cost, delay and publicity involved in court procedure it is standard practice for partnership articles to contain a clause referring disputes to arbitration for solution.

The actual procedure of arbitration has been considered in Chapter 4 but it should be recognised that arbitration, although relatively cheaper than the court system is not cheap in absolute terms. Nor can it deal with situations where the partners have reached the stage where their continued conflict prevents the effective operation of the business. In such circumstance it is probably wiser if the partnership is wound up on just and equitable grounds under s 35 of the PA. (See below and *Re Yenidje Tobacco Co Ltd* (1916) as an example where the partnership principle was extended to a quasi-partnership company.)

14.6	**The relation of partners to one another**

The partnership agreement is contractual in nature, the partnership also involves a principal/agency relationship, but is complicated by the fact that partners are, at one and the same time, both agents of the firm and their fellow partners, and principals as regards those other partners. Partners are equally subject to the equitable rights and duties that derive from their being in a fiduciary position in relation to another. Thus, the legal nature of the partnership involves a complicated mixture of elements of contract, agency and equity.

The fiduciary nature of the partnership relationship imports the usual duties that derive from such a relationship, which can be summed up under the general heading of a duty to act in good faith. In addition to these general fiduciary duties ss 28-30 of the PA lay down specific duties as follows:

14.6.1   Duties of partners

• The duty of disclosure

   Section 28 provides that partners must render true accounts and full information in relation to all things affecting the partnership to the other partners or their legal representatives.

   In *Law v Law* (1905) one partner accepted an offer from the other to buy his share of the firm. He only later discovered that certain partnership assets had not been disclosed to him and sought to have the contract set aside. The court decided that as the purchasing partner had breached the duty of disclosure, the agreement could have been set aside. In actual fact the parties had come to an arrangement so it was not necessary for such an order to be granted.

• The duty to account

   Section 29 provides that partners must account to the firm for any benefit obtained, without consent, from any transaction concerning; the partnership; its property, including information derived from membership of the partnership; its name; or its business connection. As with fiduciary duties generally such profit is only open to challenge where it is undisclosed. Full disclosure is necessary and sufficient to justify the making of an individual profit from a partnership position.

   In *Bentley v Craven* (1953) Craven was in partnership with the plaintiff in a sugar refinery business. He bought sugar on his own account and later sold it to the partnership at a profit, without declaring his interest to the other partners. It was held that the partnership was entitled to recover the profit from the defendant.

• The duty not to compete

   Section 30 provides that where a partner competes with the partnership business, without the consent of the other partners, then that person shall be liable to account to the partnership for any profits made in the course of that business. Once again it is essential to note that full disclosure is necessary to validate any such profits made in competition with the partnership. (See *Trimble v Goldberg* (1906) for a case where the court declined to recognise competition in relation to a partnership; but the likely severity of the court's approach can be surmised from the company law case of *Industrial Development Consultants v Cooley*(1972).)

14.6.2   Rights of partners

Subject to express provision to the contrary in the partnership agreement s 24 of the PA sets out the rights of partners. Amongst the most important of these are the rights:

- To share equally in the capital and profits of the business

  Even where the partnership agreement is silent on the matter s 24 does not mean that someone who has contributed all, or the greater part, of the capital of a firm must share it equally with the other partners. In such circumstances it would most likely be decided that the facts of the case provided evidence of such contrary intention as to rebut the statement in the Act. What the section does mean is that even in the same circumstances the partners will share profits equally, although it is not unusual to find clauses in agreements which recognise differences in capital input by providing for profits to be shared on an *unequal* basis. The same effect can be achieved by permitting interest to be paid on capital before profits are determined and it should also be noted that where partners advance additional capital to the firm they are entitled to interest at 5%.

  The corollary of this right is the duty to contribute equally to any losses of capital even where no capital was originally brought into the business. For example, if A & B enter into a partnership with A providing all of the capital £10,000 but sharing the profits equally. If upon winding up the business has accrued a loss of £2,000 then both parties are required to contribute to the loss. In effect B will have to contribute £1,000 and A will only receive a return of £9,000

- To be indemnified by the firm for any liabilities incurred or payments made in the course of the firm's business

  This may be seen as merely an express declaration of the usual right of an agent to indemnity. The right of an agent to act outside their authority in the case of necessity is also expressly set out in s 24.

- To take part in the management of the business

  The unlimited nature of the ordinary partnership means that involvement in such a business brings with it the risk of one's personal wealth. It is essential under such circumstances, therefore that partners are able to protect their interests by taking an active part in the operation of the business in order to assess and control the level of their risk. It is for this reason that the right to take part in the management of the business is stated expressly. In the case of *quasi-partnership* companies the courts will imply such a right.

A partner is generally not entitled to receive any salary for acting in the partnership business but it is not unusual for the agreement to provide for the payment of a salary to particular partners before the determination of net profit.

- To have access to the firm's books

This right follows from, and is based on, the same reasoning as the previous provision. The books are normally kept at the firm's principal place of business.

- To prevent the admission of a new partner or prevent any change in the nature of the partnership business

Any differences relating to the partnership business can be decided by the majority but unanimity is required to change the nature of the business. Again this reflects the need for individual partners to accept risk voluntarily. They have only accepted existing business risks and cannot be forced to alter or increase that risk.

Similarly, as principals, they have agreed to give their authority to bind them and make them liable for partnership debts to particular individuals. They cannot be forced to extend that authority against their wishes.

In addition to the above rights, s 25 provides that no majority can expel another partner, unless such power is contained in the partnership agreement. Even where such a power is included it must be exercised in good faith. See *Blisset v Daniel* (1853) where the majority attempted to expel a partner in order to acquire his share of the business cheaply; and *Green v Howell* (1910) where a partner was properly expelled for 'a flagrant breach of his duties'. For more recent cases see *Kerr v Morris* (1987) and *Walters v Bingham* (1988).

Property may be owned collectively by all of the partners and thus amount to partnership property. Alternatively, it is possible for property to be used by the partnership as a whole yet remain the personal property of only one of the partners.

Section 20 of the PA states that partnership property consist of all property brought into the partnership stock or

14.6.3   Partnership property

acquired on account for the purposes of the firm. Section 21 further states that any property bought with money belonging to the firm is deemed to have been bought on account of the firm.

Whether any particular item of property belongs to the firm or not is always a matter of fact to be determined in relation to the particular circumstances of any case. If there is no express agreement that property is to be brought into the firm as partnership property; the court will only imply such a term to the extent required to make the partnership agreement effective.

In *Miles v Clarke* (1953) Clarke had carried on a photography business for sometime before taking Miles into partnership. The partnership agreement merely provided that the profits should be divided equally. When the partners fell out a dispute arose as to who owned the assets used by the partnership. It was held that only the consumable stock-in-trade could be considered as partnership property. The leases of the business premises and other plant and equipment remained the personal property of the partner who introduced them into the business.

It is important to distinguish between partnership property and personal property for the following reasons:

- Partnership property must be used exclusively for partnership purposes (s 20)

  This may been seen as a statement of the general duty not to make a personal profit from a fiduciary position without full disclosure. Thus, partners are not supposed to use partnership property for their own personal benefit or gain and if they were to do so they would be liable to account to the partnership for any profit made.

  It also makes it clear that partners do not own the firm's assets directly. All they have, under s 30, is the *partnership lien* over those assets which entitles them on dissolution to participate in any surplus after their realised value has been used to pay off partnership debts.

- Any increase in the value of partnership property belongs to the partnership

  As a consequence the increased value when realised will be divided amongst all of the partners.

- Any increase in the value of personal property belongs to the person who owns the property

  Consequently, the increased value will not have to be shared with the other partners.

- On the dissolution of the firm, partnership property is used to pay debts before personal property

  This is clearly stated in s 39 which has been considered above in relation to the nature of the 'partnership lien'.

- Partnership and personal property are treated differently in the satisfaction of claims made by partnership creditors as opposed to personal creditors

  Under s 23, a writ of execution can only be issued against partnership property in respect of a judgment against the partnership. A personal creditor of a partner may not, therefore, take action against partnership property. They can, however, apply for a charging order against that partner's share in the partnership which would entitle them to receive the partner's share of profits, or assets on dissolution, to the extent of the debt and interest. The other partners may redeem the charge at any time by paying off the debt, in which case the charge becomes vested in them.

- On the death of a partner any interest in partnership land will pass as personalty, whereas land owned personally will pass as realty

  In effect, this means that the interest may pass to different people depending on whether the party has made an appropriate will or not.

  In relation specifically to land s 22 enacts the equitable doctrine of *conversion* by providing that any such partnership property is to be treated as personal property.

Unless the partnership agreement states otherwise, partners are at liberty to mortgage or assign absolutely their shares in partnerships to outsiders. The assignee is, however, only entitled to the share of profits due to the partner assigning the shares, or on dissolution, to the appropriate share of partnership assets. Section 31 makes it clear that any such assignee does not become a partner and has no right whatsoever to get involved in the management of the business. In *Garwood v Paynter* (1903) Garwood charged his shares to a trust, of which his wife was one of the beneficiaries. When the other partners began to pay themselves salaries, Mrs Garwood objected on the grounds that such payment reduced the net profit of the firm and hence indirectly the income to the trust. It was held that the payment of salaries was an internal management matter and therefore the trustees, who were assignees, by virtue of s 31 could not interfere in the absence of fraud.

The assignee does not take over responsibility for partnership debts. These remain the liability of the assignor.

14.6.4   Assignment of a share in a partnership

Where, however, the assignment is absolute, the assignee must indemnify the assignor in respect of future liabilities arising from the business.

14.7   The relation of partners to outsiders

Of equal importance to the internal relationships of the partnership is the relationship of the members of the partnership to outsiders who deal with the partnership and, in particular, the extent to which the partnership, and hence the partners, are liable for the actions of the individual partners.

14.7.1   The authority of partners to bind the firm

As stated in s 5 of the PA, every partner is an agent of the firm and of the other partners. Each partner, therefore, has the power to bind co-partners and make them liable on business transactions. The partnership agreement may, however, expressly seek to limit the powers of particular members. The effect of such limitations depends on the circumstances of each case. They do not apply where the other partners have effectively countermanded the restriction. This can occur in two ways:

• if the other partners give their *prior* approval for a partner to exceed his actual authority then the partner in question has express actual authority and the firm is bound by his action;

• if the other partners give their approval *after* the event then they have ratified the transaction and the partnership is again liable.

The firm may also be liable, even where the other partners have not expressly approved the action in excess of authority, as long as the partner has acted within his implied powers ie within the usual scope of a partner in the particular business concerned (see *Mercantile Credit v Garrod* above para 14.5.1). If, however, the outsider had actual knowledge of the partner's lack of authority then the partnership is not bound by the transaction.

Every partner, other than a limited partner, is presumed to have the implied authority to enter into the following transactions:

• to sell the firm's goods;

• to buy goods of a kind normally required by the firm;

• to engage employees;

• to employ a solicitor to act for the firm in defence of an action or in pursuit of a debt.

The above implied powers apply equally to trading and non-trading partnerships. Partners in trading firms, those which essentially buy and sell goods, have the following additional implied powers:

- to accept, draw, issue, or endorse bills of exchange or other negotiable instruments on behalf of the firm;

- to borrow money on the credit of the firm;

- to pledge the firm's goods as security for borrowed money.

Every partner is responsible for the full amount of the firm's liability. Outsiders have the choice of taking action against the firm collectively, or against the individual partners. Where damages are recovered from one partner only, the other partners are under a duty to contribute equally to the amount paid.

- Liability on debts and contracts

  Under s 9 of the PA the liability of partners as regards debts or contracts is joint. The effect of joint liability used to be that, although the partners were collectively responsible, a person who took action against one of the partners could take no further action against the other partners, even if they had not recovered all that was owing to them.

  That situation was remedied by the Civil Liability (Contributions Act (1978) which effectively provided that a judgement against one partner does bar a subsequent action against the other partners.

- Liability for torts

  Under s 10 of the PA the liability of partners with regard to torts or other wrongs committed in the ordinary course of the partnership business is joint and several. In such a situation there is no bar on taking successive actions against partners in order to recover all that is due.

  It should be emphasised that, in order for the partnership to responsible, the wrong sued on must have been committed in the ordinary course of partnership business or with the express approval of all the partners. If a tort is committed outside this scope then the partner responsible is personally liable.

  In *Hamlyn v Houston & Co* (1815) one of the partners in Houston & Co bribed a clerk employed by the plaintiff in order to get information about their rival's business. Hamlyn sued the defendant partnership to recover the loss he claimed to have suffered as a consequence. It was held that the defendant firm were liable for the wrongful act of the individual partner as he had acted within the usual

14.7.2   The nature of partners' liability

scope of his authority, although he had used illegal methods in doing so.

But see *Arbuckle v Taylor* (1815) where the partnership was not liable because the individual partner had gone beyond the general scope of the partnership business.

14.7.3   The liability of incoming and outgoing partners

A person who is admitted into an existing firm is not liable to creditors of the firm for anything done before they became a partner (see s 17). The new partner can, however, assume such responsibility by way of the device known as *novation*. This is the process whereby a retiring partner is discharged from existing liability and the new constituted partnership takes the liability on themselves. Novation is essentially a tripartite contract involving the retiring partner, the new firm, and the existing creditors. As creditors effectively give up rights against the retiring partner, their approval is required. Such approval may be express or it may be implied from the course of dealing between the creditor and the firm.

In *Thompson v Percival* (1834) Charles and James Percival had been in partnership until Charles retired. The plaintiff creditors, on applying for payment, were informed that James alone would be responsible for payment as Charles had retired. As a consequence, they drew a bill for payment against James alone. It was held subsequently that they no longer had a right of action against Charles since their action showed that they had accepted his discharge from his liability.

Creditors do not have to accept a novation. A creditor may still hold the retired partner responsible for any debts due at the time of retirement. The newly constituted firm may, however, agree to indemnify the retiring partner against any such claims.

Apart from novation, a retired partner remains liable for any debts or obligations incurred by the partnership prior to retirement. The date of any contract determines responsibility: if the person was a partner when the contract was entered into then they are responsible, even if the goods under the contract are delivered after they have left the firm. The estate of a deceased person is only liable for those debts or obligations arising before death.

Where someone deals with a partnership after a change in membership they are entitled to treat all the apparent members of the old firm as still being members until they receive notice of any change in the membership. In order to avoid liability for future contracts a retiring partner must take the following action:

• ensure that individual notice is given to existing customers of the partnership; and

- advertise the retirement in the *London Gazette*. This serves as general notice to people who were not customers of the firm prior to the partner's retirement, but knew that that person had been a partner in the business. Such an advert is effective whether or not it comes to the attention of third parties.

A retired partner owes no responsibility to someone who had neither dealings with the partnership nor previous knowledge of his membership.

In *Tower Cabinet Co Ltd v Ingram* (1949) Ingram and Christmas had been partners in a firm known as Merry's. After it was dissolved by mutual agreement, Christmas carried on trading under the firm's name. Notice was given to those dealing with the firm that Ingram was no longer connected with the business, but no notice was placed in the London Gazette. New notepaper was printed without Ingram's name. However, the plaintiffs, who had no previous dealings with the partnership, received an order on old notepaper on which Ingram's name was included. When Tower Cabinet sought to enforce a judgment against Ingram, it was held that he was not liable since he had not represented himself as being a partner, nor had the plaintiffs been aware of his membership prior to dissolution.

Failure to give notice of retirement is one way in which liability arises on the basis of estoppel or 'holding out'. Alternatively, anyone who represents themselves, or knowingly permits themselves to be represented, as a partner is liable to any person who gives the partnership credit on the basis of that representation. Although they may become liable for partnership debts they are not, however, partners in any other sense. (In *Tower Cabinet Co Ltd v Ingram* the defendant was not affected by partnership by estoppel since he was never actually aware that he had been represented as being a partner.)

14.7.4 Partnership by estoppel

There are a number of possible reasons for bringing a partnership to an end. It may have been established for a particular purpose and that purpose has been achieved, or one of the partners might wish to retire from the business, or the good relationship between the members, which is essential to the operation of a partnership, may have broken down. In all such cases the existing partnership is dissolved although in the second case a new partnership may be established to take over the old business.

14.8 Dissolution and winding up of the partnership

As has been repeatedly emphasised the partnership is based on agreement. It is created by agreement and it may be

14.8.1 Grounds for dissolution

brought to an end in the same way. However, subject to any provision to the contrary in the partnership agreement, the Partnership Act provides for the dissolution of a partnership on the following grounds:

- The expiry of a fixed term or the completion of a specified enterprise (s 32(a) and (b))

  If the partnership continues after the preset limit it is known as a *partnership at will* and it can be ended at any time thereafter at the wish of any of the partners.

- The giving of notice (s 32(c))

  If the partnership is of indefinite duration then it can be brought to an end by any one of the partners giving notice of an intention to dissolve the partnership.

- The death or bankruptcy of any partner (s 33(1))

  Although the occurrence of either of these events will bring the partnership to an end it is usual for partnership agreements to provide for the continuation of the business under the control of the remaining/solvent partners. The dead partner's interest will be valued and paid to his personal representative, and the bankrupt's interest will be paid to his trustee in bankruptcy.

- Where a partner's share becomes subject to a charge under s 23 (s 33(2))

  Under such circumstances dissolution is not automatic but it is open to the other partners to dissolve the partnership.

- Illegality (s 34)

  The occurrence of events making the continuation of the partnership illegal will bring it to an end. An obvious case would be where the continuation of the partnership would result in trading with the enemy (see *R v Kupfer* (1915)). The principle applied equally, however, in a more recent and perhaps more relevant case, *Hudgell, Yeates & Co v Watson* (1978). Practising solicitors are legally required to have a practice certificate. However, one of the members of a three person partnership forgot to renew his practice certificate and thus was not legally entitled to act as a solicitor. It was held that the failure to renew the practice certificate brought the partnership to an end; although a new partnership continued between the other two members of the old partnership.

  In addition to the provisions listed above, the court may, mainly by virtue of s 35 of the PA, order the dissolution of the partnership under the following circumstances:

- Where a partner becomes a patient under the Mental Health Act 1983

  The procedure is no longer taken under s 35 of the PA, but where the person is no longer able to manage their affairs because of mental incapacity the Court of Protection may dissolve a partnership at the request of the person's receiver or the other partners.

- Where a partner suffers some other permanent incapacity

  This provision is analogous to the previous one. It should be noted that it is for the other partners to apply for dissolution and that the incapacity alleged as the basis of dissolution must be permanent. It is not unusual for partnerships to include specific clauses in their agreement in order to permit dissolution on the basis of extended absence from the business (see *Peyton v Mindham* (1971) where a clause in a partnership covering medical practice provided for termination after nine months continuous absence or a total of 300 days in any period of 24 months).

- Where a partner engages in activity prejudicial to the business

  Such activity may be directly related to the business such as the misappropriation of funds. Alternatively, it may take place outside the business but operate to its detriment. Examples might be a criminal conviction for fraud.

- Where a partner persistently breaches the partnership agreement

  This provision also relates to conduct which makes it unreasonable for the other partners to carry on in business with the party at fault.

- Where the business can only be carried on at a loss

  This provision is a corollary of the very first section of the Partnership Act in which the pursuit of profit is part of the definition of the partnership form. If such profit cannot be achieved then the partners are entitled to avoid loss by bringing the partnership to an end.

- Where it is just and equitable to do so

  The courts have wide discretion in relation to the implementation of this power. A similar provision operates within company legislation and the two provisions come together in the cases involving *quasi-partnerships*. On occasion courts have wound up companies on the grounds that they would have been wound up had the business assumed the legal form of a partnership. For examples of this approach see *Re Yenidje Tobacco Co Ltd* (1916) and *Ebrahimi v Westbourne Galleries Ltd* (1973).

After dissolution the authority of each partner to bind the firm continues so far as is necessary to wind up the firm's affairs and complete transactions that have begun but are unfinished at the time of dissolution (s 38). Partners cannot, however, enter into new contracts.

14.8.2   Winding up

Since the introduction of the Insolvency Act 1986 partnerships as such are not subject to bankruptcy although the individual partners may be open to such procedure. Partnerships may be wound up as 'unregistered companies' under Part V of the Insolvency Act where they are unable to pay their debts.

14.8.3   Treatment of assets on dissolution

On dissolution the value of the partnership property is realised and the proceeds are applied in the following order:

- in paying debts to outsiders;

- in paying to the partners any advance made to the firm beyond their capital contribution;

- in paying the capital contribution of the individual partners.

Any residue is divided between the partners in the same proportion as they shared in profits (s 44 of the PA).

If the assets are insufficient to meet debts, partners' advances and capital repayments, then the deficiency has to be made good out of any profits held back from previous years, or out of partners' capital, or by the partners individually in the proportion to which they were entitled to share in profits.

An example will clarify this procedure. Partners A, B and C contributed £5,000, £3,000 and £1,000 respectively. In addition, A made an advance to the firm of £1,000. On dissolution the assets realised £8,000, and the firm had outstanding debts amounting to £2,500. The procedure is as follows:

Firstly the creditors are paid what is due to them from the realised value of the assets. Thus £8,000 - £2,500 = £5,500.

Secondly A's advance of £1,000 is paid back, leaving £4,500.

Assuming that there was no agreement to the contrary profits and losses will be shared equally. The actual loss is determined as follows:

Original capital	£9,000
Minus money left	£4,500
	£4,500

This loss of £4,500 has to be shared equally in this case. Each partner has to provide £1,500 to make good the shortfall in capital. In the case of A and B this is a paper transaction as the payment due is simply subtracted from their original capital contribution. C, however, actually has to make a contribution of £500 from his personal wealth as his due payment exceeds his original capital. The outcome is as follows:

A's share of net assets is £5,000 less £1,500 =   £3,500

B's share of net assets is £3,000 less £1,500 =   £1,500

C's share of net assets is £1,000 less £1,500 =   -£500

A provision in the partnership agreement for profits to be shared in proportion to capital contribution ie in the ratio 5:3:1, would have the following effect:

A would contribute five ninths of the £4,500 loss, ie £2,500

B would contribute three ninths of the £4,500 loss, ie £1,500

C would contribute one ninth of the £4,500 loss, ie £ 500

Their shares in net assets would therefore be as follows:

A: (£5,000 - £2,500) = £2,500

B: (£3,000 - £1,500) = £1,500

C: (£1,000 - £500)   =   £500

Where a partner is bankrupt on the dissolution of a firm the partnership assets are still used to pay partnership debts. It is only after the payment of partnership debts that any surplus due to that partner is made available for the payment of the partner's personal debts.

14.8.4   Bankruptcy of partners

Where one partner is insolvent and there is a deficiency of partnership assets to repay the firm's creditors and any advances, the burden of making good the shortfall has to be borne by the solvent partners in the proportion to their share in profits. If, however, the shortfall only relates to capital then the situation is governed by the rule in *Garner v Murray* (1904). This rules means that in any such situation the solvent partners are not required to make good the capital deficiency due to the insolvency of their co-partner. As a consequence there will be a shortfall in the capital fund which has to be borne by the solvent partners in proportion to their capitals.

To return to the original example:

The net assets were £4,500 and the capital deficiency was £4,500. All three partners were to contribute £1,500. In effect C was the only one actually to pay out any money since A and B merely suffered an abatement in the capital returned to them. However, if it is now assumed that C is insolvent and can make no contribution the situation is as follows:

C loses his right of repayment so this reduces the capital fund required to pay back partners' contributions to £8,000.

As previously, A and B contribute their portion of the total loss taking the available capital fund up to £7,500 (ie £4,500 + (2 x £1,500)).

There still remains a shortfall of £500. This is borne by A and B in proportion to their capital contribution. Thus A suffers a loss of five eighths of £500; and B suffers a loss of three eighths of £500.

So from the capital fund of £7,500:

A receives £5,000 - (5/8 x £500) = £4,687.50 (in reality he simply receives £3,187.50).

B receives £3,000 - (3/8 x £500) = £2,812.50 (in reality he simply receives £1,312.50).

Summary of Chapter 14

Partnership Law

Section 1 of the PA states that 'partnership is the relation which subsists between persons carrying on a business in common with a view to profit.'

Simply receiving a payment from profits is not sufficient automatically to make a person a partner in a business concern.

Definition of partnership

A partnership has no separate legal personality apart from its members as does a joint-stock company.

Partnerships are generally limited to 20 members, however, certain professional partnerships are exempt from this maximum limit.

The legal status of a partnership

There are no specific legal requirements governing the formation of a partnership. Partnerships arise from the agreement of the parties involved and are governed by the general principles of contract law.

The partnership agreement is an internal document and although it has effect between the partners it does not necessarily affect the rights of third parties.

Formation of a partnership

In addition to these general fiduciary duties ss 28-30 of the PA lay down the specific duties of disclosure; to account; not to compete.

Duties of partners

Subject to express provision to the contrary in the partnership agreement s 24 of the PA sets out the rights of partners. Amongst the most important of these are the rights:

Rights of partners

- to share equally in the capital and profits of the business;
- to be indemnified by the firm for any liabilities incurred or payments made in the course of the firm's business;
- to take part in the management of the business;
- to have access to the firm's books;
- to prevent the admission of a new partner;
- to prevent any change in the nature of the partnership business.

Partnership property	It is important to distinguish between partnership property and personal property for the following reasons:

- partnership property must be used exclusively for partnership purposes;

- any increase in the value of partnership property belongs to the partnership;

- any increase in the value of personal property belongs to the person who owns the property;

- on the dissolution of the firm partnership property is used to pay debts before personal property;

- partnership and personal property are treated differently in the satisfaction of claims made by partnership creditors as opposed to personal creditors;

- on the death of a partner any interest in partnership land will pass as personalty, whereas land owned personally will pass as realty.

The authority of partners to bind the firm	Authority can be actual or implied on the basis of the usual authority possessed by a partner in the particular line of business carried out by the firm.
Partners' liability on debts	Every partner is responsible for the full amount of the firm's liability. Outsiders have the choice of taking action against the firm collectively, or against the individual partners. Where damages are recovered from one partner only, the other partners are under a duty to contribute equally to the amount paid.

Partners may be liable for debts, contracts and for torts. |
| **Partnership by estoppel** | Failure to give notice of retirement is one way in which liability arises on the basis of estoppel or 'holding out'. Alternatively, anyone who represents themselves, or knowingly permits themselves to be represented, as a partner is liable to any person who gives the partnership credit on the basis of that representation. |
| **Dissolution of the partnership** | Grounds for dissolution are: |

- the expiry of a fixed term or the completion of a specified enterprise;

- the giving of notice;

- the death or bankruptcy of any partner;

- where a partner's share becomes subject to a charge;

- illegality;
- where a partner becomes a patient under the Mental Health Act;
- where a partner suffers some other permanent incapacity;
- where a partner engages in activity prejudicial to the business;
- where a partner persistently breaches the partnership agreement;
- where the business can only be carried on at a loss;
- where it is just and equitable to do so.

Winding up

Since the introduction of the Insolvency Act 1986 partnerships as such are not subject to bankruptcy. Partnerships may be wound up as 'unregistered companies' under Part V of the Insolvency Act.

Treatment of assets on dissolution

On dissolution the value of the partnership property is applied in the following order:

- in paying debts to outsiders;
- in paying to the partners any advance made to the firm beyond their capital contribution;
- in paying the capital contribution of the individual partners.

Any residue is divided between the partners in the same proportion as they shared in profits.

- illegality;

- where a partner becomes a patient under the Mental Health Act;

- where a partner suffers some other permanent incapacity;

- where a partner engages in activity prejudicial to the business;

- where a partner persistently breaches the partnership agreement;

- where the business can only be carried on at a loss;

- where it is just and equitable to do so.

Since the introduction of the Insolvency Act 1986 partnerships as such are not subject to bankruptcy. Partnerships may be wound up as 'unregistered companies' under Part V of the Insolvency Act.

Winding up

On dissolution the value of the partnership property is applied in the following order:

Treatment of assets on dissolution

- in paying debts to outsiders;

- in paying to the partners any advance made to the firm beyond their capital contribution;

- in paying the capital contribution of the individual partners.

Any residue is divided between the partners in the same proportion as they shared in profits.

Chapter 15

Company Law

This chapter deals with the formation and regulation of a common alternative form of business association to the partnership, namely the registered company. The flexibility of the company form of organisation is shown by the fact that it is used by businesses of widely different sizes and needs; from the one-man business to the trans-national corporation.

15.1   Introduction

Companies differ from partnerships in that they are bodies corporate, or corporations.

15.2   Corporations and their legal characteristics

Corporations can be created in one of three ways:

15.2.1   Types of corporation

- By grant of royal charter

  Such corporations are governed mainly by the common law. Although the very earliest trading companies were created by royal charter in order to secure monopoly privileges, nowadays this method of incorporation tends to be restricted to professional, educational and charitable institutions and is not used in relation to business enterprises.

- By special Act of Parliament

  Such bodies are known as statutory corporations. Although this method of incorporation was common during the 19th century, particularly in relation to railway and public utility companies, it is not greatly used nowadays, and certainly not by ordinary trading companies.

- By registration under the Companies Acts

  Since 1844 companies have been permitted to acquire the status of a corporation simply by complying with the requirements for registration set out in general Acts of Parliament. This is the method by which the great majority of trading enterprises are incorporated. The current legislation is the Companies Act 1985, as subsequently amended.

Whereas English law treats a partnership as simply a group of individuals trading collectively, the effect of incorporation is that a company once formed has its own distinct legal personality, separate from its members.

15.2.2   The doctrine of separate personality

The doctrine of separate or corporate personality is an ancient one and an early application of it can be seen in *Salmon v the Hamborough Co* (1671). The usual case cited in relation to separate personality is *Salomon v Salomon & Co* (1897). Salomon had been in the boot and leather for some time. Together with other members of his family he formed a limited company and sold his previous business to it. Payment was in the form of cash, shares and debentures (the latter is loan stock which gives the holder priority over unsecured creditors if the company is wound up). When the company was eventually wound up it was argued that Salomon and the company were the same and, as he could not be his own creditor, his debentures should have no effect. Although previous courts had decided against *Salomon*, the House of Lords held that under the circumstances, in the absence of fraud, his debentures were valid. The company had been properly constituted and consequently it was, in law, a distinct legal person, completely separate from Salomon.

It is important to note that, contrary to what some, if not most text-books state, the *Salomon* case did not establish the doctrine of separate personality. It merely permitted its application to one-man companies.

15.2.3   The effects of incorporation

A number of consequences flow from the fact that corporations are treated as having legal personality in their own right.

- Limited liability

   No one is responsible for anyone else's debts unless they agree to accept such responsibility. Similarly, at common law, members of a corporation are not responsible for its debts without agreement. However, registered companies ie those formed under the Companies Acts, are not permitted unless the shareholders agree to accept liability for their company's debts. In return for this agreement the extent of their liability is set at a fixed amount. In the case of a company limited by shares the level of liability is the amount remaining unpaid on the nominal value of the shares held. In the case of a company limited by guarantee it is the amount that shareholders have agreed to pay on the event of the company being wound up.

- Perpetual succession

   As the corporation exists in its own right changes in its membership have no effect on its status or existence. Members may die, be declared bankrupt or insane, or transfer their shares without any effect on the company. As an abstract legal person the company cannot die, although its existence can be brought to an end through the winding up procedure (see para 15.10).

- Business property is owned by the company

  Any business assets are owned by the company itself and not the shareholders. This is normally a major advantage in that the company's assets are not subject to claims based on the ownership rights of its member. It can, however, cause unforeseen problems.

  In *Macaura v Northern Assurance* (1925) the plaintiff had owned a timber estate. He later formed a one-man company and transferred the estate to it. He continued to insure the estate in his own name. When the timber was lost in a fire it was held that Macaura could not claim on the insurance since he had no personal interest in the timber which belonged to the company.

  What the member owns is so many shares in the company and the precise nature of the share will be considered below (see para 15.6).

- The company has contractual capacity in its own right and can sue and be sued in its own name

  The nature and extent of a company's contractual capacity will be considered in detail later (see para 15.5.1) but for the moment it should be noted that contracts are entered into in the company's name and it is liable on any such contracts. The extent of the company's liability, as opposed to the member's liability, is unlimited and all its assets may be used to pay off debts.

  The board of directors are the agents of the company. Members as such are not agents of the company; they have no right to be involved in the day to day operation of the business and they cannot bind the company in any way.

- The rule in *Foss v Harbottle*

  This states that where a company suffers an injury, it is for the company, acting through the majority of the members, to take the appropriate remedial action. Perhaps of more importance is the corollary of the rule which is that an individual cannot raise an action in response to a wrong suffered by the company.

There are a number of occasions, both statutory and at common law, when the doctrine of separate personality will not be followed. On these occasions it is said that the veil of incorporation, which separates the company from its

15.2.4   Lifting the veil of incorporation

members, is pierced, lifted or drawn aside. Such situations arise:

- Under the Companies legislation

  Section 24 of the Companies Act 1985 provides for personal liability of the member where a company carries on trading with fewer than two members; and s 229 requires consolidated accounts to be prepared by a group of related companies.

  Section 213 of the Insolvency Act 1986 provides for personal liability in relation to fraudulent trading and s 214 does the same in relation to wrongful trading.

- At common law

  As in most areas of law that are based on the application of policy decisions it is difficult to predict when the courts will ignore separate personality. What is certain is that the courts will not permit the corporate form to be used for a clearly fraudulent purpose or to evade a legal duty.

  In *Gilford Motor Co Ltd v Horne* (1933) an employee had covenanted not to solicit his former employer's customers. After he left their employment he formed a company to solicit those customers. It was held that the company was a sham and the court would not permit it to be used to avoid the prior contract.

  As would be expected the courts are prepared to ignore separate personality in times of war to defeat the activity of shareholders who might be enemy aliens. See *Daimler Co Ltd v Continental Tyre and Rubber Co (GB) Ltd* (1917).

  Where groups of companies have been set up for particular business ends the courts will not usually ignore the separate existence of the various companies unless they are being used for fraud. There is authority for treating separate companies as a single group as in *DHN Food Distributors Ltd v Borough of Tower Hamlets* (1976) but later authorities have cast extreme doubt on this decision (see *Woolfson v Strathclyde RC* (1978) and *National Dock Labour Board v Pinn & Wheeler* (1989)).

15.3	**Types of companies**	Although the distinction between public and private companies is probably the most important, there are a number of ways in which companies can be classified.
15.3.1	Limited and unlimited companies	One of the major advantages of forming a company is limited liability, but companies can be formed without limited liability. Such companies receive all the benefits that flow from incorporation except limited liability but in return they do not

have to submit their accounts and make them available for public inspection.

The great majority of companies, however, are limited liability companies. This means, as explained above, that the maximum liability of shareholders is fixed and cannot be increased without their agreement. There are two ways of establishing limited liability:

- By shares

  This is the most common procedure. It limits liability to the amount remaining unpaid on shares held. If the shareholder has paid the full nominal value of the shares to the company then that is the end of responsibility with regard to company debts .

- By guarantee

  This type of limited liability is usually restricted to non-trading enterprises such as charities and professional and educational bodies. It limits liability to an agreed amount which is only called on if the company cannot pay its debts on being wound up. In reality, the sum guaranteed is usually a nominal sum so no real risk is involved on the part of the guarantor.

The essential difference between these two forms is an economic one although different legal rules have been developed to apply to each of them.

15.3.2   Public and private companies

- Private companies

  Private companies tend to be small-scale enterprises owned and operated by a small number of individuals who are actively involved in the day to day running of the enterprise. Many such companies are sole traders or partnerships which have registered as companies in order to take advantage of limited liability. Outsiders do not invest in such companies and indeed they are precluded from offering their shares to the public at large. Their shares are not quoted on any share market and in practice tend not to be freely transferable. The legal validity of such private companies was clearly established in the Salomon case and since then the courts and legislation have developed specific rules governing their operation.

- Public limited companies

  Public companies, on the other hand, tend to be large, and to be controlled by directors and managers rather than owners. They are essentially a source of investment and have freely transferable shares which are quoted on the Stock Exchange.

As a consequence of the difference with regard to ownership and control many of the provisions of the Companies legislation, designed to protect the interests of shareholders in public companies are not applicable to private companies. In his leading text on company law, Professor John Farrar lists some 18 differences in the way in which the legislation operates as between public and private companies. The most important of these are as follows:

- Public companies must have at least two directors whereas private companies need only have one. This recognises the reality of the true one-man business. It is important to note that the Companies (Single Member Private Companies) Regulations 1992 provide for the formation of a limited company with only one member. These regulations are in line with the European Union's Twelfth Company Law Directive:

- The requirement to keep accounting records is shorter for private companies: three years as opposed to seven years for public companies;

- The controls over distribution of dividend payments is relaxed in relation to private companies.

- Private companies may purchase their own shares out of capital whereas public companies are strictly forbidden from doing so;

- Private companies can provide financial assistance for the purchase of their own shares where public companies cannot;

- There are fewer and looser controls over directors in private companies with regard to their financial relationships with their companies than there are in public companies;

- Anything that might be done by way of a resolution of a general meeting or a meeting of a class of members may instead be achieved by a resolution in writing signed by all the members of the company without the need to convene any such meeting;

- Private companies may pass an *elective resolution* dispensing with the need to appoint auditors annually, to lay accounts before an annual general meeting, or indeed to hold annual general meetings at all. An elective resolution also permits private companies to reduce the majority needed to call meetings at short notice from 95% to 90%.

It may also be suggested that in cases involving private limited companies, which the courts view as quasi-partnerships, other general company law principles are applied less rigorously or not at all. See for example *Ebrahimi v Westbourne Galleries Ltd* (1973) where the court seemed to play down the effect of separate personality in such instances. Consider also *Clemens v Clemens Bros Ltd* (1976) over which much ink has been spilled in trying to establish a general rule concerning the duties owed by majority to minority shareholders. The reality is that there was no general principle that could be applied: the case merely reflects the court's willingness to treat what they see as quasi-partnerships in an equitable manner. What is certain about the *Clemens* case is that it would find no application in public limited companies.

There is much to be said for the suggestion that private limited companies should be removed from the ambit of the general Companies legislation and be given their own particular legislation. It is apparent that they are not the same as public companies and cannot be expected to submit to the same regulatory regime as applies to the latter. In practice the law recognises this but only in a round-about way by treating them as exceptions to the general law relating to public companies. The argument, however, is that they are not exceptions; they are completely different, and this difference should be clearly recognised by treating them as a legal form *sui generis*.

This description of companies relates to the way in which large business enterprises tend to operate through a linked structure of distinct companies. Each of these companies exists as a separate corporate entity in its own right but the group are required to be treated as a single entity in relation to the group accounting provisions under s 229 of the Companies Act.

The Companies Act 1989 changed the definition of holding and subsidiary companies in s 736 of the 1985 Companies Act. The new section states that one company, S, is a subsidiary of another company, H, its holding company, in any of the following circumstances:

- Where H holds a majority of voting rights in S.

- Where H is a member of S and has a right to appoint or remove a majority of its board of directors.

- Where H is a member of S and controls a majority of the voting rights in it.

- Where S is a subsidiary of a company which is in turn a subsidiary of H.

15.3.3   Parent and subsidiary companies

Section 258 defines the relationship of parent and subsidiary companies in a similar way but introduces the idea of the parent exercising a dominant influence over the subsidiary company.

15.3.4   Small, medium and large companies

Companies can be categorised in relation to their size. Small and medium sized companies are subjected to relaxation in relation to the submission of accounts under s 246. Which category a company fits into depends on its turnover, balance sheet valuation and number of employees.

A small company must satisfy two of the following requirements:

Turnover	not more than £2 million
Balance sheet	not more than £975,000
Employees	not more than 50

A medium sized company must satisfy two of the following requirements:

Turnover	not more than £8 million
Balance sheet	not more than £3.9 million
Employees	not more than 250

15.4   Formation of companies

The Companies Act establishes a strict procedure with which companies have to comply before they can operate legally. The procedure, which in the case of public companies involves two stages, is as follows:

15.4.1   Registration

A registered company is incorporated when particular documents are delivered to the registrar of companies (s 10). On registration of these documents the registrar issues a certificate on incorporation (s 13). The documents required under s 10 are:

• A memorandum of association;

• Articles of association (unless Table A articles are to apply: see below);

• A statement detailing the first directors and secretary of the company with their written consent and the address of the company's registered office.

In addition, a statutory declaration that the necessary requirements of the Companies Act have been complied with must be submitted under s 12.

15.4.2   Commencement of business

A private company may start its business and use its borrowing powers as soon as the certificate of registration is issued. A public company, however, cannot start business or borrow money until it has obtained an additional certificate from the registrar under s 117. In relation to public companies there is a requirement that they have a minimum allotted share capital, at present £50,000 (s 11), and the second certificate confirms that the company has met that requirement.

The constitution of a company is established by two documents; the memorandum of association, and the articles of association. If there is any conflict between the two documents, the contents of the memorandum prevail over anything to the contrary contained in the articles; although provisions in the articles may be used to clarify particular uncertainties in the memorandum.

15.5   The constitution of the company

As will be seen, there is a large measure of freedom as to what is actually included in such documents but this latitude is extended within a clearly established framework of statutory and common law rules. Model memorandums and articles of association are set out in the Companies (Tables A to F) Regulations 1985, although companies may alter the models to suit their particular circumstances and requirements.

The memorandum of association mainly governs the company's external affairs. It represents the company to the outside world, stating its capital structure, its powers and its objects. The document submitted to the registrar of companies must be signed by at least two subscribers from amongst the company's first shareholders. Every memorandum must contain the following clauses:

15.5.1   The memorandum of association

• The name clause

Except in relation to specifically exempted companies such as those involved in charitable work, companies are required to indicate that they are operating on the basis of limited liability. Thus, private companies are required to end their names either with the word 'limited' or the abbreviation 'ltd'; and public companies must end their names with the words 'public limited company' or the abbreviation 'plc'. Welsh companies may use the Welsh language equivalents (ss 25 and 27). Equally, it amounts to a criminal offence to use the words 'public limited company' or 'limited' in an improper manner (ss 33 and 34).

A further aspect of this requirement for publicity is that companies display their names outside their business premises, on business documents and on their seal. In addition to committing a criminal offence, any person who fails to use a company's full name on any document will be personally liable for any default. See Penrose v Martyr (1858) where a company secretary was held personally liable when he failed to indicate that the company against which he had drawn a bill of exchange was in fact a limited company.

A company's name must not be the same as any already registered, nor should it constitute a criminal offence, be offensive, or suggest unauthorised connection with the government or any local authority (s 26). A 'passing off' action may be taken against a company as previously considered in relation to partnership law (see para 14.5.5).

The name of a company can be changed by a special resolution of the company (s 28).

- The registered office clause

This is the company's legal address. It is the place where legal documents such as writs or summonses can be served on the company. It is also the place where particular documents and registers, such as the register of members, are required to be kept available for inspection. The memorandum does not state the actual address of the registered office, but only the country within which the company is registered, whether Scotland or England and Wales. The precise location of the registered office, however, has to be stated on all business correspondence (s 351). It is not necessary that the registered office be the company's main place of business and indeed it is not unusual for a company's registered office to be the address of its accountant or lawyer.

- The objects clause

Companies registered under the various Companies Acts are not corporations in the same way as common law corporations are. It was established in *Ashbury Railway Carriage and Iron Co Ltd v Riche* (1875) that such companies were established only to pursue particular purposes. Those purposes were stated in the objects clause of the company's memorandum of association and any attempt to contract outside of that limited authority was said to be *ultra vires* and, as a consequence, void.

It was felt for a long time that the operation of the *ultra vires* doctrine operated unfairly on outsiders and various attempts were made to reduce the scope of its application. Since the introduction of the Companies Act 1989 it is fortunately no longer necessary to enter into a detailed consideration of the history and operation of the doctrine of *ultra vires*. After the 1989 Act, *ultra vires* has been effectively reduced to an internal matter and does not affect outsiders; and even as a means of limiting the actions of directors it has been considerably weakened (see ss 35, 35A and 35B).

Whereas in the past companies used to register extended objects clauses to provide for unforeseen eventualities, now under the new legislation they can simply register as 'a general commercial company' which will empower them to 'carry on any trade or business whatsoever' and 'to do all such things as are incidental or conducive to the carrying on of any trade or business' (s 3A).

Companies can alter their objects clause by passing a special resolution, by virtue of s 4, although such procedure is subject to a right of appeal to the courts within 21 days by the holders of 15% of the issued capital of the company. However, given the effect of the 1989 Act this element of control will only have indirect effect on the external relations of the company to the extent that members may bring proceedings to prevent directors from acting beyond the stated objects of the company (s 35(2)).

- The limited liability clause

  This clause simply states that the liability of the members is limited. It must be included even where the company has permission not to use the word 'limited' in its name.

- The authorised share capital clause

  This states the maximum amount of share capital that a company is authorised to issue. The capital has to be divided into shares of a fixed monetary amount as no-fixed-value shares are not permissible in UK law.

- The association clause

  This states that the subscribers to the memorandum wish to form a company and agree to take the number of shares placed opposite their names.

  It should also be recalled that the memorandum of public companies must contain a clause stating that they are public companies.

The articles primarily regulate the internal working of the company. They govern the rights and relations of the members to the company and *vice versa*, and the relations of the members between themselves. As provided in s 14 of the Companies Act, the articles are to be treated as an enforceable contract; although it has to be stated that it is a peculiar

15.5.2   The articles of association

contract, in that its terms can be altered by the majority of the members without the consent of each member.

The articles deal with such matters as the allotment and transfer of shares, the rights attaching to particular shares, the rules relating to the holding of meetings, and the powers of directors.

A company is at liberty to draw up its own articles but regulations made under the Companies Act provide a set of model articles known as *Table A*. Companies do not have to submit their own articles and if they do not, then Table A applies automatically. The provisions contained in Table A also apply to the extent that they have not been expressly excluded by the company's particular articles. Usually, companies adopt Table A with appropriate modifications fitting to their own situation.

Articles can be altered by the passing of a special resolution. Any such alteration has to be made 'bona fide in the interest of the company as a whole', but the exact meaning of this phrase is not altogether clear. It is evident that it involves a subjective element in that those deciding the alteration must actually believe they are acting in the interest of the company. There is additionally, however, an objective element. In *Greenhalgh v Arderne Cinemas Ltd* (1951) it was stated that any alteration had to be in the interest of the 'individual hypothetical member'; thus, the alteration that took a pre-emptive right from a particular member was held to be to the advantage of such a hypothetical member, although it severely reduced the rights of a real member. Such distinction between concrete and hypothetical benefits is a matter of fine distinction although it can be justified. In any case persons suffering from substantive injustice are now at liberty to make an application under s 459 for an order to remedy any unfairly prejudicial conduct (see para 15.9.2).

The following two cases may demonstrate the difference between the legitimate use and the abuse of the provision for altering articles: each of them relates to circumstances where existing shareholders' rights were removed.

In *Brown v British Abrasive Wheel Co* (1919) an alteration to the articles of the company was proposed to give the majority shareholders the right to buy shares of the minority. It was held under the circumstances of the case that the alteration was invalid since it would benefit the majority shareholders rather than the company as a whole.

In *Sidebottom v Kershaw Leese & Co* (1920) the alteration to the articles gave the directors the power to require any shareholder who entered into competition with the company to transfer their shares to nominees of the directors at a fair price. It was held that under these circumstances the alteration permitting the expropriation of members' interests was valid since it would benefit the company as a whole.

There are many different definitions of capital. The way in which a company raises such money as it needs takes the form of either share capital or loan capital.

15.6   Capital

A share has been defined as 'the interest of the shareholder in the company measured by a sum of money, for the purposes of liability in the first place and of interest in the second, but also consisting of a series of mutual covenants entered into by all the shareholders' (Borland's Trustees v Steel (1901)).

15.6.1   Share capital

On the basis of this definition it may be taken that:

- The nominal value of the share normally fixes the amount which the shareholder is required to contribute to the assets of the company;

- The share represents a proportionate interest in the business. This right is, however, no more than the contingent rights to receive a dividend payment and attend and vote at general meetings of the company. As has been seen above, in considering separate personality, the concrete capital assets of the business are the property of the company and there is no direct link between the shareholder and those assets. Shareholders merely have the right to participate in the profit generated by concrete assets while the company continues to operate and only has a claim against the assets when the company is wound up.

   Section 182 of the Companies Act 1985 provides that shares are personal property and are transferable in the manner provided for in the company's articles of association. Although the articles of private limited companies tend to restrict the transfer of shares within a close group of people, it is an essential aspect of shares in public limited companies that the investment they represent is open to immediate realisation and to that end they are made freely transferable subject to following the appropriate procedure.

The word 'capital' is used in a number of different ways in relation to shares:

15.6.2   Types of share capital

- Nominal or authorised capital

   This is the figure stated in the company's memorandum of association. It sets the maximum number of shares that the company can issue together with the value of each share. There is no requirement that companies issue shares to the full extent of their authorised capital.

- Issued or allotted capital

  This represents the nominal value of the shares actually issued by the company. It is more important than authorised capital as a true measure of the substance of the company. If a company is willing to pay the registration fee it can register with an authorised capital of £1 million yet only actually issue two £1 shares. Public companies must have a minimum issued capital of £50,00 (s 11 Companies Act 1985).

- Paid-up capital

  This is the proportion of the nominal value of the issued capital actually paid by the shareholder. It may be the full nominal value, in which case it fulfils the shareholder's responsibility to outsiders; or it can be a mere part payment, in which case the company has an outstanding claim against the shareholder. Shares in public companies must be paid up to the extent of at least a quarter of their nominal value (s 101 Companies Act 1985).

- Called and uncalled capital

  Where a company has issued shares as not fully paid up it can at a later time 'make a call' on those shares. This means that the shareholders are required to provide more capital, up to the amount remaining unpaid on the nominal value of their shares. Called capital should equal paid-up capital: uncalled capital is the amount remaining unpaid on issued capital.

- Reserve capital

  This arises where a company passes a resolution that it will not 'make a call' on any unpaid capital. The unpaid capital then becomes a reserve, only to be called upon if the company cannot pay its debts from existing assets in the event of its liquidation.

15.6.3   Types of shares

Companies can issue shares of different value, and with different rights attached to them. Such classes of shares can be distinguished and categorised as follows:

- Ordinary shares

  These shares are sometimes referred to as 'equity' in the company. Of all the types of shares they carry the greatest risk but in recompense receive the greatest return. The *nominal value* of shares is fixed but the *exchange value* of the shares in the stock market fluctuates in relation to the performance of the company and the perception of those dealing in the stock exchange. It is perhaps a matter of regret that the typical shareholder, and that includes the institutional investor, relates more to the performance of their shares in the market than to the actual performance of their company in productive terms.

• Preference shares

These shares involve less of a risk than ordinary shares. They may have priority over ordinary shares in two respects; dividends and repayment. They carry a fixed rate of dividend which has to be paid before any payment can be made to ordinary shareholders. Such rights are cumulative unless otherwise provided. This means that a failure to pay a dividend in any one year has to be made good in subsequent years.

As regards repayment of capital, preference shares do not have priority unless, as is usually the case, this is specifically provided for. Also, without specific provision preference shares have the same rights as ordinary shares; but it is usual for their voting rights to be restricted. Preference shareholders are entitled to vote at class meetings convened to consider any alteration to their particular rights, but apart from that they are usually restricted to voting in general meetings when their dividends are in arrears.

• Deferred shares

This type of share postpones the rights of its holder to dividends until after the ordinary shareholders have received a fixed return. In effect, the ordinary shares are treated as preference shares and the deferred shares as ordinary shares. It is no longer a common form of organisation.

• Redeemable shares

These are shares issued on the understanding that they may be bought back by the company (s 159). Redemption may be at the option of either the company or the shareholder, depending on the terms of issue. Companies, in any case, now have the right, subject to conditions, to purchase their own shares, and, therefore, are no longer restricted to buying redeemable shares (s 162).

Companies usually acquire the capital they need to engage in their particular business through the issue of shares. It is, however, also common practice for companies to borrow

15.6.4   Loan capital

additional money to finance their operation. Such borrowing does not give the lender any interest *in* the company but represents a claim *against* the company. The relationship between company and the provider of loan-capital is the ordinary relationship of debtor/creditor, although specific mechanisms exist to facilitate the borrowing of companies and secure the interests of their creditors.

15.6.5   Debentures

A debenture is a document which acknowledges the fact that a company has borrowed money. The use of the term debenture, however, is extended to cover the loan itself: A debenture may be issued to a single creditor. Alternatively, it may signify the company's indebtedness to a large number of people, in which case each of the creditors has a proportionate claim against the total 'debenture stock'. With regard to repayment, debts rank in order of creation, so earlier debentures have to be paid before those created later. It is usual, however, for debentures to be issued in a series. In such circumstances a *pari passu* clause is introduced into the document expressing the debt. This has the effect that all of the loans made within the series rank equally with regard to repayment.

Debentures may be issued as redeemable, or irredeemable under s 193 Companies Act 1985. In addition, they may carry the right to convert into ordinary shares at some later time. Debentures may be transferred from the current holder to another party subject to the proper procedure under s 183 Companies Act 1985.

Debentures differ from shares in the following respects:

- Debenture holders are *creditors* of the company; they are not members as shareholders are;

- As creditors they receive *interest* on their loans; they do not receive dividends as shareholders do;

- They are entitled to receive interest whether the company is profitable or not, even if the payment is *made out of the company's capital*; shareholders' dividends must not be paid out of capital;

- Debentures may be *issued at a discount* ie at less than their nominal value; whereas shares must not be issued at a discount and the company must receive the equivalent to the shares' nominal value.

15.6.6   Company charges

Debentures which have no security are referred to as 'unsecured loan stock', although it is usual for debentures to provide security for the amount loaned. Security means that in the event of the company being wound up the creditor with a secured debt will have priority as regards repayment over any unsecured creditor.

There are two types of security for company loans:

- Fixed charge

  In this case a specific asset of the company is made subject to a charge in order to secure a debt. The company cannot thereafter dispose of the property without the consent of the debenture holders. If the company fails to honour its commitments, then the debenture holders can sell the asset to recover the money owed. The asset most commonly subject to fixed charges is land, although any other long-term capital asset may also be charged, as may such intangible assets as book debts. It would not be appropriate to place a fixed charge against stock in trade as the company would be prevented from freely dealing with it without the prior approval of the debenture holders. This would obviously frustrate the business purpose of the enterprise.

- Floating charge

  This category of charge does not attach to any specific property of the company until it crystallises through the company committing some act or default. On the occurrence of such an event, the floating charge becomes a fixed equitable charge over the assets detailed, the value of which may be realised in order to pay the debt owed to the floating charge holder.

  The floating charge is most commonly made in relation to the 'undertaking and assets' of a company. In such a situation the security is provided by all the property owned by the company, some of which may be continuously changing, such as stock in trade. The use of the floating charge permits the company to deal with its property without the need to seek the approval of the debenture holders.

All charges, including both fixed and floating, have to be registered with the Companies Registry within 21 days of their creation. If they are not registered then the charge is *void*, ie ineffective, against any other creditor, or the liquidator of the company; but it is still valid against the company. Effectively, this means that the charge holder loses priority as against other creditors.

In addition to registration at the Companies Registry, companies are required to maintain a register of all charges on their property. Although a failure to comply with this

15.6.7   Registration of charges

requirement constitutes an offence it does not invalidate the charge.

15.6.8 Priority of charges

In relation to properly registered charges of the same type, charges take priority according to their date of creation. However, with regard to charges of different types, a fixed charge takes priority over a floating charge even though it was created after it.

Generally, there is nothing to prevent the creation of a fixed charge after the issuing of a floating charge, and, as a legal charge against specific property, that fixed charge will still take priority over the earlier floating charge. It is possible, however, for the debenture creating the original floating charge to include a provision preventing the creation of a later fixed charge taking priority over that floating charge.

15.7 Directors

Shareholders in public limited companies typically remain external to the actual operation of the enterprise in which they have invested. They also tend to assess the performance of their investment in relation to the level of dividend payment and the related short-term movement of share prices on the stock exchange rather than in relation to any long-term business strategy. These factors have led to the emergence of what is known as *the separation of ownership and control*. As suggested, this idea refers to the fact that those who provide a company's capital are not actually concerned in determining how that capital is used within the specific business enterprise. In effect, the day to day operation of the business enterprise is left in the hands of a small number of company directors whilst the large majority of shareholders remain powerless to participate in the actual business from which they derive their dividend payments.

In theory the shareholders exercise ultimate control over the directors through the mechanism of the general meeting. The separation of ownership and control, however, has resulted in the concentration of power in the hands of the directors and has given rise to the possibility that directors might operate as a self-perpetuating oligarchy who seek to run the company in their own interests rather than in the interests of the majority of shareholders. In the light of the lack of fit between theory and practice, statute law has intervened to place a number of specific controls on the way in which directors act.

15.7.1 The position of directors

It is a feature of the companies legislation that it tends to define terms in a tautological way, using the term to be defined as part of the definition. Thus s 741 of the Companies

Act defines the term director to include 'any person occupying the position of director, by whatever name called'. The point of this definition is that it emphasises the fact that it is the function the person performs rather than the title given to them that determines whether they are directors or not. Section 741 also introduces the concept of the 'shadow director'. This is a person who, although not actually appointed to the board, instructs the directors of a company as to how to act. The point is that such a person is subject to all the controls and liabilities that the ordinary directors are subject to.

The actual position of a director may be described in a number of ways.

- They are *officers* of the company (s 744);

- The board of directors is the *agent* of the company and under Table A Article 84 the board may appoint one or more managing directors. They are therefore able to bind the company without incurring personal liability. It should be noted that directors are not the agents of the shareholders (see below in relation to the powers of directors);

- Directors are in a *fiduciary* relationship with their company. This means that they are in a position similar to trustees. The importance of this lies in the nature of the duties it imposes on directors (see below);

- Directors are *not employees* of their companies *per se*. They may, however, be employed by the company in which case they will usually have a distinct service contract detailing their duties and remuneration. Apart from service contracts, the articles usually provide for the remuneration of directors in the exercise of their general duties.

The first directors are usually named in the articles or memorandum. Subsequent directors are appointed under the procedure stated in the articles. The usual procedure is for the company in general meeting to elect the directors by an ordinary resolution.

Casual vacancies are usually filled by the board of directors co-opting someone to act as director. That person then serves until the next Annual General Meeting when they must stand for election in the usual manner.

15.7.2 Appointment of directors

There are a number of ways in which a person may be obliged to give up their position as a director:

15.7.3 Removal of directors

- Rotation

  Table A provides that one third of the directors shall retire at each AGM, being those with longest service. They are, however, open to re-election and in practice are usually re-elected.

- Retirement

  Directors of public companies are required to retire at the first AGM after they have reached the age of 70. They may of course retire at any time before then.

- Removal

  A director can be removed at any time by the passing of an ordinary resolution of the company (s 303). The company must be given special notice (28 days) of the intention to propose such a resolution.

  The power to remove a director under s 303 cannot be removed or restricted by any provision in the company's documents or any external contract. It is possible, however, for the effect of the section to be avoided in private companies by the use of weighted voting rights.

  In *Bushell v Faith* (1969) the articles of association of a company, which had three equal shareholders each of whom was a director, provided that on a vote to remove a director that person's shares would carry three votes as against its usual one. The effect of this was that a s 303 resolution could never be passed. The House of Lords held that such a procedure was legitimate, although it has to be recognised that it is unlikely that such a decision would be extended to public limited companies.

  As regards private/quasi-partnership companies it has been held, in *Re Bird Precision Bellows Ltd* that exclusion from the right to participate in management provides a ground for an action for a court order to remedy unfairly prejudicial conduct under s 459 Companies Act (see further below).

- Disqualification

  The articles of association usually provide for the disqualification of directors on the occurrence of certain circumstances: bankruptcy, mental illness, or prolonged absence from board meetings.

  In addition, individuals can be disqualified from acting as directors up to a maximum period of 15 years under the Company Directors Disqualification Act 1986. This Act was introduced in an attempt to prevent the misuse of the company form. One of its specific aims was the control of what are described as 'phoenix companies'. These are companies which trade until they get into financial trouble and accrue extensive debts. Upon this eventuality the company ceases trading only for the person behind the company to set up another company to carry on essentially the same business, but with no liability to the creditors of the former company. Such behaviour is reprehensible and clearly an abuse of limited liability. The Company Directors Disqualification Act seeks to remedy this practice by preventing certain individuals from acting as a company director.

Grounds for disqualification include:

Persistent breach of the companies legislation;

Committing offences in relation to companies;

Fraudulent trading;

General unfitness.

Article 70 of Table A provides that the directors of a company may exercise all the powers of the company. It is important to note that this power is given to the board *as a whole* and not to individual directors, although Article 72 does allow for the delegation of the board's powers to one or more directors.

> **15.7.4 Power of directors as a board**

Article 70 gives the board of directors general power but the articles may seek to restrict the authority of the board within limits expressly stated in the company's constitutional documents. The effectiveness of such restrictions has been greatly reduced by the operation of s 35 of the 1985 Act as amended by the 1989 Act. As a consequence of s 35, as it now is, not only can the power of a company not be challenged on the grounds of lack of capacity but neither can the actions of its directors be challenged on the basis of any limitation contained in the company's documents. This provision is subject to the requirement that any third party must act in good faith, although such good faith is presumed subject to proof to the contrary.

There are three ways in which the power of the board of directors may be extended to individual directors. These ways are however simply particular applications of the general law of agency considered previously in Chapter 13 of this book.

> **15.7.5 The power of individual directors**

• Express actual authority

This category is unproblematic in that it arises from the express conferral by the board of a particular authority onto an individual director. For example, it is possible for the board to specifically authorise an individual director to negotiate and bind the company to a particular transaction.

- Implied actual authority

  In this situation the person's authority flows from their position. Article 84 provides for the board of directors to appoint a managing director. The board of directors may confer any of their powers on the managing director as they see fit. The mere fact of appointment, however, will mean that the person so appointed will have the *implied authority* to bind the company in the same way as the board, whose delegate they are. Outsiders, therefore, can safely assume that a person appointed as managing director has all the powers usually exercised by a person acting as a managing director.

  Implied actual authority to bind a company may also arise as a consequence of the appointment of an individual to a position other than that of managing director.

  In *Hely-Hutchinson v Brayhead Ltd* (1968) although the chairman and chief-executive of a company acted as its *de facto* managing director he had never been formally appointed to that position. Nevertheless, he purported to bind the company to a particular transaction. When the other party to the agreement sought to enforce it, the company claimed that the chairman had no authority to bind it. It was held that although the director derived no authority from his position as chairman of the board he did acquire such authority from his position as chief executive and thus the company was bound by the contract he had entered into on its behalf.

- Apparent or ostensible authority/agency by estoppel

  This arises where an individual director has neither express or implied authority. Nonetheless, the director is held out by the other members of the board of directors as having the authority to bind the company. If a third party acts on such a representation then the company will be estopped from denying its truth.

  Problems tend to arise where someone acts as a managing director without having been properly appointed to that position. In such a situation, although the individual concerned may not have the *actual authority* to bind the company, they may still have *apparent authority* and the company may be estopped from denying their power to bind it to particular transactions.

  In *Freeman & Lockyer v Buckhurst Park Properties (Mangal) Ltd* (1964) although a particular director had never been appointed as managing director, he acted as such with the clear knowledge of the other directors and entered into a contract with the plaintiffs on behalf of the company. When the plaintiffs sought to recover fees due to them under that contract it was held that the company was liable: a properly appointed managing director would have been able to enter into such a contract and the third party was entitled to rely on the representation of the other directors that the person in question had been properly appointed to that position.

At common law, the duties owed by directors to their company and the shareholders, employees and creditors of that company were at worst non-existent or at best notoriously lax. Statute has, by necessity, been forced to intervene to increase such duties in order to provide a measure of protection for those concerned.

15.7.6   Directors' duties

As fiduciaries, directors owe the following duties to their company (it is imperative to note that the duty is owed to the company as a distinct legal person and not the shareholders of the company so the rule in *Foss v Harbottle* applies, see above para 15.2.3):

- The duty to act bona fide in the interests of the company

  In effect this means that directors are under an obligation to act in what they genuinely believe to be the interest of the company.

- The duty not to act for any collateral purpose

  This may be seen as a corollary of the preceding duty in that directors cannot be said to acting *bona fide* if they use their powers for some ulterior or collateral purpose. For example, directors should not issue shares to particular individuals in order merely to facilitate, or indeed prevent, a prospective take-over bid (see *Howard Smith v Ampol Petroleum* (1974) & *Hogg v Cramphorn* (1967). The breach of such a fiduciary duty is, however, subject to *post hoc* ratification (see *Bamford v Bamford* (1970)).

- The duty not to permit a conflict of interest and duty to arise

  This equitable rule is strictly applied by the courts and the effect of its operations may be seen in *Regal (Hastings) v Gulliver* (1942) where the directors of a company owning one cinema provided money for the creation of a subsidiary company to purchase two other cinemas. After the parent and subsidiary companies had been sold at a later date, the directors were required to repay the profit they had made on the sale of their shares in the subsidiary company on the grounds that they had only been in the situation to make that profit because of their positions as directors of the parent company. (The profits made went back to the parent company which was by then in the hands of the person who had paid the money to the directors in the first place.)

15.7.7   Company secretary

Section 744 Companies Act includes the company secretary amongst the officers of a company. Every company must have a company secretary and although there are no specific qualifications required to perform such a role in a private company, s 286 of the Companies Act requires that the directors of public company must ensure that the company secretary has the requisite knowledge and experience to discharge their functions. Section 286(2) sets out a list of professional bodies, membership of which enables a person to act as a company secretary.

Although old authorities, such as *Houghton & Co v Northard Lowe & Wills* (1928) suggest that company secretaries have extremely limited authority to bind their company, later cases have recognised the reality of the contemporary situation and have extended to company secretaries potentially extensive powers to bind their companies. As an example consider *Panorama Developments Ltd v Fidelis Furnishing Fabrics Ltd* (1971). In this case the Court of Appeal held that a company secretary was entitled:

> '... to sign contracts connected with the administrative side of a company's affairs, such as employing staff and ordering cars and so forth. All such matters now come within the ostensible authority of a company's secretary.'

15.7.8   Company auditor

Section 384 CA requires all companies to appoint an auditor whose duty it is under s 235 CA to report to the company's members whether or not the company's accounts have been properly prepared and to consider whether the directors' report is consistent with those accounts.

In the case of a newly registered company the first auditors are appointed by the directors until the first general meeting at which they may be reappointed by the members of the company. Thereafter, auditors are appointed annually at general meetings at which accounts are laid (s 385). It should be recalled that private companies may, by means of an elective resolution, dispense with the requirement to appoint auditors annually. In such circumstances the existing auditor is deemed to be reappointed for each succeeding year (s 386). The Secretary of State has the power to appoint an auditor where the company has not appointed one (s 387).

Section 389 provides that a person can only be appointed as an auditor where they are members of a recognised supervisory body such as the Institute of Certified Accountants or the Chartered Association of Certified Accountants. A person cannot be appointed where they are officers or employees of the company in question.

An auditor may be removed by an ordinary resolution of the company. Where auditors resign they are required to submit a statement setting out any circumstances that should be brought to the attention of the members of the company. A resigning auditor can require the company to call an extraordinary general meeting to consider any such statement (s 392A).

The tortious liability of auditors is considered above in para 11.3.1.

15.8   Company meetings

In theory, the ultimate control over a company's business lies with the members in general meeting. In practice, however, the residual powers of the membership are restricted to their ultimate control over the company's memorandum and articles of association, although this control has been reduced by the introduction of the new s 35 of the 1985 Act, together with their control of the composition of the board of directors. The reality of such limited theoretical powers are further constrained by the practicalities involved with the operation of company meetings.

In line with this approach, some powers are specifically reserved to the members by statute, such as the right to petition for voluntary winding up; and Article 70 of Table A provides that the shareholders, by passing a special resolution, can instruct the directors to act in a particular way. In reality, the ideal-typical shareholder tends either not to be bothered to take an active part in the conduct of company meetings or to use their votes in a way directed by the board of directors.

One would obviously conclude that a meeting involved more than one person and indeed there is authority to that effect in *Sharp v Dawes* (1876) in which a meeting between a lone member and the company secretary was held not to be validly constituted. It is possible, however, for a meeting of only one person to take place in the following circumstances:

- In the case of a meeting of a particular class of shareholders and all the shares of that class are owned by the one member;

- By virtue of s 371 Companies Act 1985 the court may order the holding of a general meeting at which the quorum is to be one member. This eventuality might arise in a quasi-partnership where a recalcitrant member of a two-person company refused to attend any meetings thus preventing the continuation of the enterprise.

15.8.1   Types of meetings

There are three types of meeting:

- The annual general meeting

  By virtue of s 366 of Companies Act 1985, every company is required to hold an annual general meeting (AGM) every calendar year; subject to a maximum period of 15 months. This means that if a company holds its AGM on 1 January 1995, then it must hold its next AGM by 31 March 1996 at the latest.

  In line with the recognised distinction between public and private companies the Companies Act of 1989 introduced a provision in the form of a new s 366A, which permitted private companies, subject to approval by a unanimous vote, to dispense with the holding of an AGM.

  If a company fails to hold an AGM then any member may apply to the Secretary of State, under s 367, to call a meeting in default.

- The extraordinary general meeting

  An extraordinary general meeting (EGM) is any meeting other than an AGM. EGMs are usually called by the directors, although members holding 10% of the voting shares may requisition such a meeting.

- The class meeting

  This refers to the meeting of a particular class of shareholder ie those who hold a type of share providing particular rights, such as preference shares considered above (para 15.6.3).

  Under s 381A of the Companies Act 1985 it is no longer necessary for a private company to convene a general meeting where the members have unanimously signed a written resolution setting out a particular course of action.

15.8.2   Calling meetings

Meetings may be convened in a number of ways by various people:

- By the Directors of the company under Article 37 of Table A. Apart from this usual power, directors of public limited companies are required, under s 142 Companies Act 1985, to call meetings where there has been a serious loss of capital, defined as the assets falling to half or less than the nominal value of the called up share capital;

- By the members using the power to requisition a meeting under s 368 Companies Act 1985. To require the convening of a company meeting any shareholders must hold at least one-tenth of the share capital carrying voting rights. If the directors fail to convene a meeting as required within 21 days of the deposit of the requisition, although the actual date of the meeting may be within eight weeks of the date of requisition, then the requisitionists may themselves convene a meeting and recover any expenses from the company;

- By the auditor of a company under s 392A which provides for a resigning auditor to require the directors to convene a meeting in order to explain the reason for the auditor's resignation;

- The Secretary of State may under s 367, on the application of any member, call a meeting of a company where it has failed to hold an AGM as required under s 366;

- The court may order a meeting under s 371 where it is impracticable otherwise to call a meeting.

Proper and adequate notice must be sent to all those who are entitled to attend any meeting, although the precise nature of the notice is governed by the Articles of Association.

15.8.3 Notice of meetings

- Time

  This is set out in s 369 Companies Act 1985. The minimum period of notice is 21 clear days for an AGM and 14 clear days for all other meetings, except those called to consider a special resolution, which also require 21 clear days notice. Shorter notice is permissible: in the case of an AGM where all the members entitled to attend agree; in the case of any other meeting where holders of 95% of the nominal value of the voting shares agree. Private companies, by means of an elective resolution, may reduce this latter requirement to 90%.

- Content

  Adequate notice of the content of any resolution must be sent to members so that they can decide whether to attend the meeting or to appoint a proxy to vote in line with their instructions.

It is usually the prerogative of the directors to decide which motions will be put to the company in the general meeting. Members, however, may set the agenda where they have requisitioned an EGM under the procedure established in s 368 (see above). In relation to an AGM, s 376 provides a procedure

15.8.4 Agenda

whereby a minority of members, amounting to one-twentieth of the total voting rights or 100 members holding an average of £100 worth of shares, may have a motion considered. This mechanism is complicated and expensive and the practicalities of trying to use it, especially in large public companies, means that it is not often used.

The difficulties involved in ordinary members getting issues onto the agenda also extend to resolutions to remove directors. Although s 303 provides for the removal of directors on the passing of an ordinary resolution, it was held in *Pedley v Inland Waterways Association Ltd* (1977) that a disgruntled member could only get such a resolution onto the agenda if he satisfied the requirements of s 376.

15.8.5 Types of resolutions

There are essentially three types of resolution:

* An ordinary resolution

  This requires a simple majority of those voting. Members who do not attend or appoint a proxy, or who attend but do not vote, are disregarded.

  Notice in relation to an ordinary resolution depends on the type of meeting at which it is proposed, 21 days for an AGM and 14 days for an EGM, although in relation to an ordinary resolution to remove a director under s 303, the company must be given special notice of 28 days. It should be noted that in this latter case the notice is given to the company whereas usually it is the company that is required to give notice to the members.

* An extraordinary resolution

  This requires a majority of not less than three-quarters of those voting. An extra-ordinary resolution requires a minimum of 14 days notice, but if it is to be voted on at an AGM notice of 21 days will be required.

* A special resolution

  This requires a majority of not less than three-quarters but in all circumstances members must be given 21 days notice of its contents.

  In considering types of resolutions it should be recalled that private companies, by virtue of s 381A, can function on the basis of *written resolutions*. The effect of this is that anything that can be done by means of passing a resolution at a general meeting can be done by all of the members signing the resolution without the need to convene a meeting.

  It should also be recalled that private companies, by virtue of s 379A, can pass *elective resolutions* as a means of dispensing with particular requirements of the Companies Act. The formalities that can be avoided relate to:

- the duration of directors' authority to allot shares;

- the need to lay accounts and reports before general meetings;

- the majority required to sanction the holding of meetings at short notice;

- the need to appoint auditors on an annual basis.

The elective resolution itself requires 21 days' notice and must be passed unanimously, although it may be effected by means of the procedure relating to written resolutions considered previously.

This is the minimum number of persons whose presence is required for the transaction of business at any meeting. The precise details are set out in the Articles of Association, although s 370 and Table A Article 41 sets the minimum at two who must be continuously present at the meeting.

15.8.6   Quorum

A resolution is decided upon initially by a show of hands unless a poll is demanded. On a show of hands every member has one vote. In a poll it is usual for each share to carry a vote and thus for the outcome of the poll to reflect concentration of interest in the company (for exceptions to this see Bushell v Faith above para 15.7.3).

15.8.7   Votes

Table A Article 41 enables any two members or the chairman to call for a poll.

Section 372 Companies Act 1985 provides that any member of a company who is entitled to attend and vote at a meeting may appoint another person as their proxy, ie to act as their agent in exercising the member's voting right. Every notice of a meeting must state the member's right to appoint a proxy and although the articles may require notice of the appointment of a proxy to be given to the company they may not require more than 48 hours notice. Proxies need not be members of the company. They have no right to speak at meetings of public companies but may speak in private companies. They are not allowed to vote on a show of hands but only in regard to a poll vote.

15.8.8   Proxies

Although s 370 provides that any member may act as chair, Article 43 states that the chairman of the board of directors shall preside. The chairman conducts the meeting and must preserve order and ensure that it complies with the provisions of the companies legislation and the company's articles. He

15.8.9   Chairman

may adjourn it with the consent of, or where instructed to do so by, the meeting. The chairman has a casting vote in the case of equality. He is under a general duty at all times to act bona fide in the interests of the company as a whole and thus must use his vote appropriately.

15.8.10   Minutes

Section 382 requires that minutes of all general meetings and directors' meetings must be kept and are regarded as evidence of the proceedings when signed by the chairman.

15.9   Majority rule and minority protection

It has been seen how the day to day operation of a company's business is left in the hands of its directors and managers with shareholders having no direct input into business decisions. Even when the members convene in general meetings the individual shareholder is subject to the wishes of the majority as expressed in the passing of appropriate resolutions. In normal circumstances the minority has no grounds to complain even though the effect of majority rule may place them in a situation they do not agree with. Even where the minority shareholders suspect that some wrong has been done to the company it is not *normally* open to them to take action. This situation is encapsulated in what is known as the rule in *Foss v Harbottle* (1843) (see above para 15.2.3) in which case individual members were not permitted to institute proceedings against the directors of their company. It was held that if any wrong had been committed it had been committed against the company and that it was for the company acting through the majority to decide to institute proceedings.

Particular problems may arise where those in effective control of a company use their power in such a way as either to benefit themselves or cause a detriment to the minority shareholders. In the light of such a possibility the law has intervened to offer protection to minority shareholders. The source of the protection may be considered in three areas.

15.9.1   Common law

At common law it has long been established that those controlling the majority of shares are not to be allowed to use their position of control to perpetrate what is known as a *fraud on the minority*. In such circumstances the individual shareholder will be able to take legal action in order to remedy their situation.

In *Cook v Deeks* (1916) directors, who were also the majority shareholders of a company, negotiated a contract on its behalf. They then took the contract for themselves and used their majority voting power to pass a resolution declaring that the company had no interest in the contract. On an action by the minority shareholder in the company it was held that the majority could not use their votes to ratify what was a fraud on the minority. The contract belonged to the company in equity and the directors had to account to the company for the profits they made on it. Thus, the minority shareholder was not excluded from benefitting from the contract.

In circumstances where the minority shareholders disagree with the actions of the majority, but without that action amounting to fraud on the minority, one remedy is simply to leave the company. In a listed public limited company this procedure is easily achieved by selling the shares held but things are more difficult in the case of small private companies. In these quasi-partnership cases an alternative to bringing a derivative action in the name of the company is to petition to have the company wound up or to apply to the court for an order to remedy any unfairly prejudicial conduct.

15.9.2   Statutory protection

- Just and equitable winding up

  Section 122(g) of the Insolvency Act 1986 (hereafter IA) gives the court the power to wind up a company if it considers it just and equitable to do so. Such an order may be applied for where there is evidence of a lack of probity on the part of some of the members. It may also be used in small private companies to provide a remedy where there is either deadlock on the board, or a member is removed from the board altogether or refused a part in the management of the business.

  In *Re Yenidje Tobacco Co Ltd* (1916) the company only had two shareholders who also acted as its directors. After quarrelling, the two directors refused to communicate with one another except through the company secretary. It was held that the company was essentially a partnership and that as a partnership would have been wound up in this eventuality, the company should be wound up as well.

  In *Re Westbourne Galleries* also known as *Ebrahimi v Westbourne Galleries* (1973) a business which two parties had carried on previously as a partnership was transformed into a private limited company. After a time, one of the two original partners was removed from the board of directors of the company. It was held that the removal from the board, and the consequential loss of the right to participate in the management of the business, was ground for winding up the company.

- Unfairly prejudicial conduct

  Use of the procedure under s 122 of the IA is likely to have extremely serious consequences for the business. Indeed, the fact that the company has to be wound up will probably result in losses for all of the parties concerned. It is much better if some less mutually destructive process can be used to resolve disputes between members of private companies.

Under s 459 of the Companies Act 1985, any member may petition the court for an order on the grounds that the affairs of the company are being conducted in a way that is unfairly prejudicial to the interests of some of the members. Section 461 gives the court general discretion as to the precise nature and content of any order it makes to remedy the situation. The following case demonstrates the operation and scope of the procedure.

In *Re London School of Electronics* (1986) the petitioner held 25% of the shares in the company LSE. The remaining 75% were held by another company, CTC. Two directors of LSE, who were also directors and the principal shareholders in CTC, diverted students from LSE to CTC. The petitioner claimed that such action deprived him of his share in the potential profit to be derived from those students. It was held that the action was unfairly prejudicial and the court instructed CTC to purchase the petitioners shares in LSE at a value which was to be calculated as if the students had never been transferred.

Section 459 procedure has also been used in cases where a member has been excluded from exercising a legitimate expectation to participate in the management of a company' business (see *Re Bird Precision Bellows Ltd* (1984)).

And in *Re Sam Weller & Sons Ltd* (1990) the court decided that the failure to pay dividends may amount to unfairly prejudicial conduct.

Section 459 is an extremely active area of company law and has probably replaced s 122 of the IA as the most appropriate mechanism for alleviating the distress suffered by minority shareholders; it is essential, however, to note that the cases considered above all involved *economic partnerships* which had merely assumed the *company legal form* as a matter of internal and external convenience. The same outcomes would not be forthcoming in relation to public limited companies. The statutory protections still apply in the case of public companies but it is extremely unlikely that they would be used as freely or as widely as they are in quasi-partnership cases.

15.9.3   Investigations

In order for minority shareholders to complain they must know what is going on in their company. It is part of their situation as minority shareholders, however, that they do not have access to all the information that is available to the directors of the company. As a possible means of remedying this lack of information and thus as a means of supporting minority protection the Department of Trade and Industry has been given extremely wide powers to conduct investigations into the general affairs of companies, their membership, and dealings in their securities. Such powers are framed extremely widely and the courts have accepted the need for such wide powers; but this theoretical power is much limited in practice by a reluctance on the part of government to finance their use and by those given the powers to use them adequately.

Bearing in mind the foregoing caveats, the Secretary of State has the power under s 431 Companies Act 1985 to appoint inspectors to investigate the affairs of a company on application by the following:

• The company itself after passing an ordinary resolution;

• Members holding 10% of the company's issued share capital;

• 200 or more members.

Under s 432 the Secretary of State may order such an investigation where:

• The company's affairs have been conducted with intent to defraud creditors, or for an unlawful or fraudulent purpose;

• The company's affairs have been conducted in a manner unfairly prejudicial to some part of the members;

• The promoters or managers have been found guilty of fraud;

• The shareholders have not been supplied with proper information.

In addition, under s 442, the Secretary of State has the power to appoint inspectors to investigate the ownership and control of companies. Investigations may also be instigated into directors' share dealings under s 446 Companies Act, and into insider dealing under s 177 Financial Services Act 1986.

Once appointed, the investigators have very wide powers under s 433 to examine the affairs of related companies; and under s 434 to require the officers of the company to attend for interview and to produce documents as required.

Consequent upon an investigation the Secretary of State may take any of the following actions:

- Petition to have the company wound up under s 124 of the IA 1986;

- Petition for an order under s 459;

- Bring a civil action in the name of the company against any party;

- Apply to the courts to have any director disqualified from acting as a director in future under s 8 Company Directors Disqualification Act 1986.

Given the extent of the powers given to the Secretary of State and the investigators appointed by him, it is a little ironic, if not symptomatic of the failures in the system of company investigations, that some of the most famous cases of the early 1970s ie *Re Pergamon Press Ltd* (1971) and *Maxwell v Dept of Trade and Industry* (1974) involved the late, and generally unlamented, publishing mogul Robert Maxwell. Maxwell's death in the 1990s revealed the corruption and criminal illegality on which his business empire had been based and had been sustained. The blameworthy part of the Maxwell saga was, however, that his corrupt behaviour was an open secret that should have been investigated before it reached its inevitable disastrous conclusion.

15.10 Winding up and administration orders

Winding up and administrative orders are alternative mechanisms for dealing with companies whose business activity is in a state of potentially terminal decline.

15.10.1 Winding up

Winding up, or liquidation, is the process whereby the life of the company is terminated. It is the formal and strictly regulated procedure whereby the business is brought to an end and the company's assets are realised and distributed to its creditors and members. The procedure is governed by the IA 1986 and may be divided into three distinct categories.

- Compulsory winding up

  This is a winding up ordered by the court under s 122 of the Insolvency Act 1986. Although there are seven distinct grounds for such a winding up, one of which, depending upon just and equitable grounds, has already been considered, the most common reason for winding up of company is its inability to pay its debts. Section 123 provides that if a company with a debt exceeding £750 fails to pay it within three weeks of receiving a written demand then it is deemed unable to pay its debts.

- A members' voluntary winding up

  This takes place when the directors of a company are of the

opinion that the company is solvent ie capable of paying off its creditors. The directors are required to make a statutory declaration to that effect and the actual liquidation process is initiated by a special resolution of the company.

- A creditors' voluntary winding up

  This occurs when the directors of the company do not believe that it will be able to pay off its debts and thus do not make the necessary declaration required for a members' voluntary winding up. The creditors may form a committee of inspection which oversees the actions of the liquidator. Again, the liquidation is initiated by a special resolution of the company.

Administration is a relatively new procedure having been introduced in line with the recommendations of the Cork Report of 1982. The aim of the administration order is to save the business as a going concern by taking control of the company out of the hands of its directors and placing it in the hands of an administrator. Alternatively, the procedure is aimed at maximising the realised value of the business assets.

15.10.2   Administration orders

The rules are set out in the Insolvency Act 1986. Section 8 of that Act provides that where the court is satisfied that the company is, or is likely to become, unable to pay its debts it may issue an administrative order to achieve one or more of the following purposes:

- The survival of the whole or part of the business as a going concern;

- The approval of a voluntary arrangement under Part 1 of the 1986 IA by which the creditors reach an agreement between themselves and the company as to the satisfaction of their debts;

- The sanctioning of a compromise or arrangement under s 425 of the Companies Act 1985;

- A more advantageous realisation of the assets of the company than would be effected on the winding up of the company.

Once an administration order has been issued it is no longer possible to commence winding up proceedings against the company or enforce charges, retention of title clauses or even hire purchase agreements against the company. This major advantage is in no small way undermined by the fact that an administration order cannot be made after a company has entered the liquidation process. Since companies are required to inform any person who is entitled to appoint a receiver of the fact that the company is applying for an administration order it is open to any secured creditor to enforce their rights and to forestall the administration procedure. This would cause the secured creditor no harm, since their debt would more than likely be covered by the security, but it could well lead to the end of the company as a going concern.

15.11   Insider dealing

One of the most important attributes of a share is the right to participate in the profit generated by a company, although for the purposes of company law, the value of a share is fixed at its nominal value.

However, the exchange-value of the share, ie the amount of money that can be realised by selling the share, which essentially reflects the value of the share as a source of income, changes in line with the profitability of the company. This fluctuation in the exchange-value of shares in listed public limited companies is readily apparent in the constantly changing value of shares on the stock exchange. It is, of course, the fact that share prices fluctuate in this way that provides the possibility of individuals making large profits, or losses, in speculating in shares. It also, however, provides other people with the opportunity to take advantage of their close relationship with particular companies in order to make profits from illegal share dealing. Such illegal trading in shares is known as insider dealing and is now governed by Part V of the Criminal Justice Act 1993 which repeals and replaces The Company Securities (Insider Dealings) Act 1985.

Section 52 of the Criminal Justice Act states that an individual who has information as an insider is guilty of insider dealing if they deal in securities that are price-affected securities in relation to the information. They are also guilty of an offence if they encourage others to deal in securities that are linked with this information.

Section 56 makes it clear that securities are 'price affected' in relation to inside information if the information, made public, would be likely to have a significant effect on the price of those securities.

Section 57 defines an insider as a person who knows that they have inside information and knows that they have the information from an inside source. This section also states that 'inside source' refers to information acquired through being a director, employee or shareholder of an issuer of securities, or having access to information by virtue of their employment. Additionally, and importantly, it also treats as insiders those who acquire their information from those primary insiders previously mentioned.

There are a number of defences to a charge of insider dealing. For example, s 53 makes it clear that no person can be so charged if they did not expect the dealing to result in any profit or the avoidance of any loss.

On summary conviction an individual found guilty of insider dealing is liable to a fine not exceeding the statutory maximum and/or a maximum of six months imprisonment. On indictment the penalty is an unlimited fine and/or a maximum of seven years imprisonment.

Company Law

Separate personality is where the company exists as a legal person in its own right, completely distinct form the members who own shares in it.

The effects of incorporation

Limited Liability refers to the fact that the potential liability of shareholders is fixed at a maximum level equal to the nominal value of the shares held.

Perpetual succession refers to the fact the company continues to exist irrespective of any change in its membership. The company only ceases to exist when it is formally wound up.

The company owns the business property in its own right – shareholders own shares; they do not own the assets of the business they have invested in.

The company has contractual capacity in its own right and can sue and be sued in its own name – members, as such, are not able to bind the company.

The courts will, on occasion, ignore separate personality. Examples can be given in relation to statutory provision, and the use of the company form as a mechanism for perpetrating fraud. It is difficult, however, to provide a general rule to predict when the courts will take this approach, other than to a see it as depending on judicial views as to public policy.

Lifting the veil of incorporation

This is an essential distinction which causes/explains the need for different legal provisions to be applied to the two forms. The essential difference is to be found in the fact that the private company is really an economic partnership seeking the protection of limited liability.

Public and private companies

The memorandum of association governs the company's external affairs. It represents the company to the outside world, stating its capital structure, its powers and its objects.

The company's documents

The articles of association regulate the internal working of the company.

A share has been defined as 'the interest of the shareholder in the company measured by a sum of money, for the purposes of liability in the first place and of interest in the second, but

Share capital

also consisting of a series of mutual covenants entered into by all the shareholders' (*Borland's Trustees v Steel* (1901)).

The main ways of categorising shares is in terms of: nominal or authorised capital; issued or allotted capital; paid up and unpaid capital; called and uncalled capital.

Types of shares

Shares can be divided into: ordinary, preference, deferred and redeemable shares, each of which carries particular and distinct rights.

Loan capital

The term debenture refers to the document which acknowledges the fact that a company has borrowed money and also refers to the actual debt.

In the case of a *fixed charge* a specific asset of the company is made subject to a charge in order to secure a debt.

A *floating charge* does not attach to any specific property of the company until it *crystallises* through the company committing some act or default.

All charges, both fixed and floating, have to be registered with the Companies Registry within 21 days of their creation.

In relation to properly registered charges of the same type, they take priority according to their date of creation. As regards charges of different types, a fixed charge takes priority over a floating charge even though it was created after it.

Directors

The board of directors is the agent of the company and may exercise all the powers of the company. Individual directors may be described as being in a *fiduciary relationship* with their companies.

A director can be removed at any time by the passing of an ordinary resolution of the company (s 303).

Individuals can be disqualified from acting as directors up to a maximum period of 15 years under the Company Directors Disqualification Act 1986.

As fiduciaries directors owe the following duties to their company: to act *bona fide* in the interest of the company; not to act for a collateral purpose; or to permit a conflict of interest to arise.

Meetings

In theory, the ultimate control over a company's business lies with the members in general meeting. In practice, however, the residual powers of the membership are extremely limited.

There are three types of meeting: the annual general meeting; the extraordinary general meeting; and the class meeting.

Proper and adequate notice must be sent to all those who are entitled to attend any meeting, although the precise nature of the notice is governed by the Articles of Association.

There are three types of resolution: the ordinary resolution; the extraordinary resolution; and the special resolution.

Voting is by a show of hands or according to the shareholding on a poll. Proxies may exercise voting rights if properly appointed.

Majority rule and minority protection

The majority usually dictate the action of a company and the minority is usually bound by the decisions of the majority. Problems may arise where those in effective control of a company use their power in such a way as to benefit themselves or to cause a detriment to the minority shareholders.

Three remedies are available to minority shareholders:

- The minority may seek court action to prevent the majority from committing *a fraud on the minority*;

- An order to have the company wound up on *just and equitable grounds* may be applied for where there is evidence of a lack of probity on the part of some of the members. It may also be used in small private companies to provide a remedy where there is either deadlock on the board, or a member is removed from the board altogether or refused a part in the management of the business;

- Under s 459 of the Companies Act 1985, any member may petition the Court for an order on the grounds that the affairs of the company are being conducted in a way that is *unfairly prejudicial* to the interests of some of the members.

In addition to the above remedies, the Secretary of State has the power under s 431 Companies Act 1985 to appoint inspectors to investigate the affairs of a company.

Winding up

Liquidation, is the process whereby the life of the company is brought to an end.

There are three possible procedures: compulsory winding up; a members' voluntary winding up; and a creditors' voluntary winding up.

Administration

This is a relatively new procedure aimed at saving the business as a going concern by taking control of the company out of the hands of its directors and placing it in the hands of an of an administrator. Alternatively, the procedure is aimed at maximising the realised value of the business assets.

Once an administration order has been issued it is no longer possible to commence winding up proceedings against the company or enforce charges, retention of title clauses or even hire purchase agreements against the company.

Insider dealing

This is now governed by Part V of the Criminal Justice Act 1993 which repeals and replaces The Company Securities (Insider Dealings) Act 1985. The legislation is aimed at dealing with those who trade in shares on the basis of inside information which is not available to others. It is a criminal offence for an individual who has information as an insider to deal in price-affected securities in relation to the information. It is also an offence if they encourage others to deal in securities that are linked with the information.

Chapter 16

Individual Employment Rights (1)

The law relating to individual employment rights has undergone numerous changes over the past two decades either in the form of statutory regulation or through the interpretation of the law by the industrial tribunals or courts. In recent times, the policy has been one of deregulation which has led to some abuse of individual employment rights by employers, clearly illustrated by the reduction in state support for collective bargaining and trade union rights. However, the impact of European Community law has halted the deregulation progress in some areas, in particular, discrimination and maternity rights; a further halt may be called if the Social Chapter is fully implemented. Although the UK government has strongly resisted the expansion of EC legislation into the area of social policy.

It must be borne in mind, when considering individual employment rights, that the legislation has been drafted to protect full-time rather than part-time employees. As a result, thousands of workers do not qualify for employment protection on the basis that they are either self-employed or work part-time, even though the trend in working patterns shows that there has been an increase in these groups of workers eg a recent Labour Force survey shows that about 5 million people now work less than 30 hours per week, with married women accounting for 75% of all part-time workers. These changes have come about because of changes in the labour market with a reduction in full-time employment in the manufacturing industries and a growth in employment in the service sector which has traditionally employed a greater proportion of part-time workers.

The relationship between the employee and the employer is governed by the contract of employment which forms the basis of the employee's employment rights. It is therefore important to comprehend the meaning of this term. Employees are employed under a contract of employment or contract of service whereas self-employed persons ie independent contractors are employed under a contract for services. There are tests which enable the courts to distinguish between the two types of contract particularly where there are disputes. The following example assists in distinguishing between employees and independent contractors.	**16.1 Contract of employment**

If you employ a plumber to install your washing machine you do not become an employer as he is an independent contractor, although he may be employed by a firm of plumbers. If you were to employ a nanny as a general rule she would become your employee and you would therefore be responsible for deductions from her salary eg tax, national insurance etc.

The distinction between a contract of service and a contract for services must be appreciated because where a person is employed under the former, he is afforded a certain amount of statutory and common law protection, whereas a person employed under the latter is not, although limited exceptions can be found in the Equal Pay Act 1970, the Sex Discrimination Act 1975 and the Race Relations Act 1976.

16.1.1   Employee v Independent Contractor

Although for the majority of people at work there is no problem in deciding whether they are employees or independent contractors, there may be occasions where the distinction is not clear cut. Over the years the courts have devised tests for establishing employee status. These tests will be considered in chronological order since, although the early tests are still of relevance, the multiple test and the mutuality of obligations test are now at the forefront should the question of employment status arise.

16.1.2   Control test

In applying the control test the question to be asked is, does the person who is to be regarded as the employer control the employee or servant? Control extends to not just what the employee does but how he does it. If the answer is in the affirmative, there is an employer/employee relationship. The reasoning behind this question was that an independent contractor may be told what to do, but probably had a discretion on how to do his work. However, in the modern workplace this question has become a little unreal and therefore this test has fallen into decline as the sole test applied by the courts, although it is still a vital element in the multiple test.

In *Walker v Crystal Palace Football Club* (1910) Walker was employed as a professional footballer with the defendant club. It became necessary to decide whether he was employed under a contract of service or a contract for services. It was held that he was employed under a contract of service or employment because he was subject to the control of his master in the form of training, discipline and method of play.

One of the problems in applying the control test was that, if interpreted strictly, it resulted in skilled and professional people being categorised as independent contractors, which at a time when there were limited employment rights was not a problem for them, but proved to be a problem for persons injured as a result of their negligence at work who would be unable to rely on the principle of vicarious liability to claim against the employer. As a result the courts saw fit to develop another test which would reflect this development in the workplace by recognising that skilled and professional people could also be employees.

This test was developed to counter the deficiencies of the control test. In applying the integration test, the question to be asked is how far is the servant/employee integrated into the employer's business? If it can be shown that the employee is fully integrated into the employer's business, then there is in existence a contract of employment. It is clear that an independent contractor does not become part of the employer's business. The use of this test was confirmed in *Stevenson, Jordan, and Harrison Ltd v MacDonald and Evans* (1952) in which Lord Denning expressed the following view:

16.1.3   Integration test

> 'One feature which seems to run through the instances is that, under a contract of service, a man is employed as part of the business and his work is done as an integral part of the business;whereas, under a contract for services, his work, although done for the business, is not integrated into it but is only accessory to it.'

In *Whittaker v Minister of Pensions & National Insurance* (1967) Whittaker was employed as a trapeze artist in a circus. She claimed industrial injuries benefit as a result of an accident sustained at work. Initially this was refused on the basis that she was not an employee of the circus. She was, however, able to show that for at least half of her working day she was expected to undertake general duties other than trapeze work, such as acting as usherette and working in the ticket office. It was held that her general duties showed that she was an integral part of the business of running a circus and was therefore employed under a contract of employment.

Although this test developed due to the impracticalities of the control test, it never gained popularity with the courts. It was successfully used in cases such as *Cassidy v Ministry of Health* (1951) to establish that highly skilled workers, such as doctors and engineers can be employed under a contract of employment and may even have a type of duel employment where, in some circumstances, they are to be regarded as employees and in other self-employed. The control test was clearly inapplicable to these situations. The need to develop a test which would suit all circumstances became of paramount importance . Employers were able to avoid various aspects of the statutory provisions by categorising employees as self-employed when in reality this was not necessarily the case, but at that time there was no test to cover these situations eg an employer could avoid tax and national insurance provisions as well as liability for accidents caused by these persons whilst going about their jobs. As a result the following test was developed.

16.1.4   Multiple test

The multiple test is by definition much wider than both the control test and the integration test. It requires numerous factors to be taken into account in deciding whether a person is employed under a contract of service or a contract for services. It arose out of the case of *Ready Mixed Concrete (South East) Ltd v Minister of Pensions & National Insurance* (1968). RMC previously employed a number of lorry drivers under a contract of employment. The company then decided to dismiss the drivers as employees. However, it allowed them to purchase their vehicles, which had to be painted in RMC's colours. The contract between the drivers and the company stated that the drivers were independent contractors. This was disputed by the Minister who believed the drivers were employees and therefore RMC were liable for national insurance contributions. There were number of stipulations under the contract. The drivers had to wear the company's uniform and the company could require repairs to be carried out to the vehicles at the drivers' expense. The vehicle could only be used for carrying RMC's product for a fixed period and the drivers were told where and when to deliver their loads, although if a driver was ill he could use a substitute driver to do the deliveries for him. It was held by MacKenna J that a contract of service exists if three conditions are fulfilled:

'1.   The servant agrees that, in consideration of a wage or other remuneration, he will provide his own work and skill in the performance of some service for his master.

2.   He agrees, expressly or impliedly, that in the performance of that service he will be subject to the other's control in a sufficient degree to make that other master.

3.   The other provisions of the contract are consistent with its being a contract of service.'

In this case it was decided that the drivers were independent contractors as there were factors which were inconsistent with the existence of a contract of employment eg the ability to provide a replacement driver if the need arose.

This test has proved to be most adaptable in that it only requires evaluation of the factors which are inconsistent with the existence of a contract of employment. It is important to appreciate that there is no exhaustive list of inconsistent factors. The courts will ask questions such as who pays the wages? Who pays income tax and national insurance? Is the person employed entitled to holiday pay?

It will treat as irrelevant the fact that there is a contract in which someone is termed 'independent contractor' when the other factors point to him being an employee. This is illustrated in *Market Investigations Ltd v Minister of Social Security* (1969) in which Market Investigations employed Mrs Irving as an interviewer on an occasional basis. If she was selected from the pool of interviewers maintained by the firm, she was not obliged to accept the work. However, if she accepted, she was given precise instructions of the methods to be used in carrying out the market research and the time in which the work had to be completed. She could, however, choose the hours she wanted to work and do other work at the same time as long as she met Market Investigations deadlines. It was held that she was an employee of the company every time she decided to undertake work for them. It was felt that the question to be asked is 'is the person who has engaged himself to perform these services performing them as a person in business on his own account?' If the answer is yes, then there is a contract for services, while if the answer is no, there is a contract of service.

Obviously, as in the *RMC* case, there are other factors which may have to be taken into account, although the courts are reluctant to state what other factors should be considered, except an element of control. It is important that the multiple test is flexible so that it can adapt with changes in the labour environment. Unfortunately, these tests have tended to result in the atypical worker being categorised as self-employed. This is particularly true of casual or seasonal workers, even though in practical terms they may see themselves tied to a particular firm and therefore have an obligation to that business. There have, however, been some developments in this area which provide possible redress for such workers. The test which has developed is known as the mutuality of obligations test. This arose out of the case of *O'Kelly v Trusthouse Forte plc* (1983). O'Kelly and his fellow appellants were worked on a casual basis as wine waiters at the Grosvenor House Hotel. They were regarded as regular casuals in that they were given preference in the work rota over other casual staff. They had no other employment. They sought to be classified as employees so that they could pursue an action for unfair dismissal. They argued that if they were to be classified as employees then each independent period of work for THF could be added together and the qualifying period of employment under the Employment Protection (Consolidation) Act 1978 would be met. It was held that the regular casuals in this case were self-employed as there was no mutuality of obligation on the part of either party in that THF were not obliged to offer work nor were O'Kelly and his colleagues obliged to accept it when it was offered. The preferential rota system was not a contractual promise. The court made it clear that an important factor in determining whether there is a contact of service in this type of situation is the custom and practice of the particular 'industry'. The case of *Wickens v Champion Employment* (1984) supports the decision in O'Kelly. However, a more liberal approach was taken in *Nethermore (St Neots) v Gardiner & Taverna* (1984) in which home workers making clothes on a piecework basis were accorded employee status on the basis that a mutuality of obligation arose out of an irreducible minimum obligation to work for that company 'by the regular giving and taking of work over periods of a year or more'.

| 16.1.5 | Loaning or hiring out of employees |

One area of contention involves the loaning or hiring out of an employee; the issue being whose employee is he? This is particularly important in respect of who should be vicariously liable for the employee's torts. As can be seen in *Mersey Docks & Harbour Board v Coggins & Griffiths (Liverpool) Ltd* (1947), there is a rebuttable presumption that when an employee is loaned out he remains the employee of the first/original employer. In Mersey Docks, a crane and its driver were hired out to C & G to assist in the loading of a ship. C & G paid the driver's wages. Whilst the crane driver was doing this work, he negligently injured an employee of the stevedores, C & G. The issue to be decided by the courts was whether the Harbour Board or Coggins and Griffiths were vicariously liable for the crane driver's negligence. It was held that the Harbour Board remained the employer of the crane driver. He was under their ultimate control as to the work he should do, even though he was under the temporary direction of the stevedores ie the original employer retained the right to hire, dismiss and decide on his work, even though day-to-day control passed to the stevedores.

The courts are reluctant to find that there has been a transfer of employment where employees are loaned or hired out, unless there is consent on the part of the employee or there is an agreement which clearly states the position in the event of liability accruing. There may, however, be exceptional circumstances where the courts may declare that *pro hac vice* (for that one occasion), a loaned or hired employee has become the employee of the 'second' employer as in *Sime v Sutcliffe Catering* (1990).

In general terms there are no formalities involved in the formation of a contract of employment. The contract itself may be oral or in writing, with the exception of apprenticeship deeds and articles for merchant seamen which, obviously, by their nature have to be in writing. It follows, therefore, that within reason the parties ie the employer and employee to the contract can decide on whatever terms they wish. This, however, raises the issue of the respective bargaining position of the parties as the employer will always be in the strongest position. In industries which have traditionally had strong trade union representation, a collective agreement may form the basis of the employment terms, where it is expressly agreed that such agreements should be incorporated into the contract. The contract may also be subject to implied terms which will be considered subsequently.

16.2   Formation of the contract of employment

Although the contract of employment itself need not be in writing the employee must be given written particulars of the main terms. This is required by s 1 EPCA. These written particulars must be supplied within two months of the date on which employment commenced. The particulars must contain the following:

16.2.1   Written statement of terms

- The names of the parties and the date on which the employment commenced; if there is a change of employer resulting in continuity of employment, the date on which continuity commences must be specified.

- The rate of pay or the method of calculating it.

- The intervals at which wages are to be paid eg weekly, monthly.

- Terms and conditions relating to hours of work.

- Terms and conditions relating to holidays and holiday pay.

- The length of notice which the employee must give and is entitled to receive on termination of his employment.

- Job title and description.
  The Trade Union Reform and Employment Rights Act 1993 (TURERA) has made the following changes so that the statement must also include the following:

- Where the employment is non-permanent, the period for which it is expected to continue;

- Either the place of work or where the employee is required or permitted to work at various places, an indication of that fact, plus the address of the employer.

- Any collective agreement which directly affects the terms and conditions of employment including, where the employer is not a party, the persons by whom they were made.

- Where an employee is required to work outside the UK for more than a month, the period of such work, the currency of remuneration, any additional remuneration or benefit by reason of the requirement to work outside the UK and 'any terms and conditions relating to his return to the UK'.

These form the basis of the written particulars and the employer must provide this information in one document (EPCA s2(2)(b)). In addition, the employer must specify the following:

- Any disciplinary rules which apply to the employee or reference to the document containing them.

- The person to whom he can apply if he is dissatisfied with any disciplinary decision relating to him.

- The grievance procedure, including the person to whom he can apply if he has a grievance relating to his employment.

- The document containing rights to sick pay and pension schemes.

At the very least, the employee must have reasonable access to this information. Any agreed changes must be communicated to the employee in writing within one month of the change. It is permissible for the employer to refer the employee to additional terms contained in a document, such as a collective agreement, as long as it is reasonably accessible. The written statement whilst not being a contract, is *prima facie* evidence of what is agreed between the employee and his employer. If the employer fails to provide a statement or if there is a disagreement with respect to its contents or if a change has not been properly notified, the employee may apply to an industrial tribunal in order for it to determine which particulars ought to be included in the statement. In such cases applications must be brought within three months of termination of the contract of employment.

The following employees qualify for a statement of written particulars under s 1: all those who have worked for more than one month, but excluding those employed under a contract which normally involves employment for less than eight hours weekly.

The express terms are those agreed upon by the employer and employee on entering into the contract of employment. They may be oral or in writing and will cover such things as the point on the salary scale at which the employee will commence employment. However, oral terms may be open to dispute and it is in the interests of both parties to have such terms in writing eg a restraint of trade clause is unlikely to be enforceable unless it is in writing. Disputes about 'oral' terms may result in the employee pursuing an action for clarification before an industrial tribunal. A breach of an express term of the contract may result in the dismissal of the employee and if it is a breach by the employer may enable the employee to resign and bring an action for constructive dismissal. A collective agreement made between the employer or his association and a trade union may be expressly incorporated into the contract of employment. Such agreements usually provide a comprehensive set of terms and conditions for particular types of employees. In such cases the trade union usually has equal bargaining power to the employer. Where they are expressly incorporated under s 1 EPCA 1978 they will bind the employer and the employee.

16.2.2   Express terms

Implied terms may arise out of the custom and practice of a particular industry eg deductions from wages for bad workmanship were accepted as a term of contracts in the cotton industry. The courts may be the final arbiter as to whether an implied term is incorporated into the contract. Collective agreements may become implied terms of the contract, even if there is no reference to the agreement in the written particulars. However, such incorporation will depend on knowledge by the employee and some form of acceptance by his local union representatives.

16.2.3   Implied terms

Implied terms generally have to be read subject to any express terms which may be to the contrary. Although where the implied term is necessary to give efficacy to the contract, the implied term will take precedence over the express term. This is illustrated in *Johnstone v Bloomsbury Health Authority* (1991).

A hospital doctor was obliged to work a stipulated number of hours under his contract, plus additional hours if required. As a result the doctor found himself working, on average, over 80 hours per week and as a result he became ill. It was held that the express term regarding the additional hours had to be read subject to the implied term of care and safety. The implied term in this case was necessary to 'give efficacy to the contract'.

In addition, a number of standard implied terms have developed in respect of the employer/employee relationship. These take the form of duties imposed on the respective parties. A breach by the employee may result in disciplinary action or even dismissal; a breach by the employer may result in legal proceedings before a tribunal.

16.3   Duties imposed on the employer

Duties imposed on the employer are to provide work; to pay wages; indemnify the employee; hold in mutual respect and to provide for the care and safety of the employee.

16.3.1   To provide work

An employer will not be in breach of the implied duty to provide work as long as he continues to pay his employees even though there may be no work available. Although in certain situations the employer may be liable for failing to provide work, for example, if a reduction in the employee's earnings occurs (this is most likely to affect those employees on piece-work or commission – see *Devonald v Rosser & Son* (1906)). Furthermore, if the employee needs to work in order to maintain particular skills then to deny him this right may also be a breach of this duty.

In *Collier v Sunday Referee Publishing Co Ltd* (1940) Collier was employed as a sub-editor with the defendant's newspaper. The defendant sold the newspaper and continued to pay the plaintiff although he was not provided with any work. Collier claimed the company was under a duty to supply work. It was held that there was a breach of the duty to provide work in this case as the plaintiff had been appointed to a particular job which had been destroyed on the sale of the newspaper. However Asquith J stated:

'It is true that a contract of employment does not necessarily, or perhaps normally, oblige the master to provide the servant with work. Provided I pay my cook her wages regularly she cannot complain if I choose to eat all my meals out.'

Interestingly, the courts took this duty one step further in *Langston v Amalgamated Union of Engineering Workers* (1974) in which Langston refused to join the trade union. As a result of union pressure his employers were forced to suspend him from work on full pay. It was said (*obiter*) that where a person employs a skilled employee who needs practice to maintain or develop those skills, there may be an obligation to provide a reasonable amount of work.

16.3.2   To pay wages

As a general rule the employer must pay his employees their wages even if there is no work available. In relation to piece-workers this means that they should be given the opportunity to earn their pay. However, it is possible for the employer to exclude or vary this implied term by providing that there will be no pay where there is no work available.

Where the employee in the course of his employment necessarily incurs expenses on behalf of his employer, he is entitled to be reimbursed by him. This extends to such things as postage, parking fees, damage to property etc.

16.3.3   To indemnify the employee

The employer is under a duty to treat his employees with respect. The basis of the employment relationship is mutuality of respect, trust and confidence. In deciding whether there has been a breach of this term the actions of the employer are of great importance.

16.3.4   Mutual respect

In *Donovan v Invicta Airways Ltd* (1970) Donovan, an airline pilot, was subjected to abusive conduct by his employer on a number of occasions. As a result Donovan resigned. It was held that in this particular case the incidents were not substantial enough to treat the contract as broken.

It is clear that there is now a duty under which all of the parties to the contract of employment must treat each other with due consideration and courtesy. In *Isle of Wight Tourist Board v Coombes* (1976) a director was heard to describe his personal secretary as 'an intolerable bitch on a Monday morning'. This was held to be a breach of the duty of mutual respect and was conduct which entitled her to resign.

This duty is based on the law of negligence and is dealt with in detail in the chapter on employer's liability. Suffice it to say the common law requires the employer to take reasonable care for the safety of his employees and this duty extends to the provision of competent fellow employees, safe plant and equipment, safe place of work and safe system of work.

16.3.5   To provide for the care and safety of the employee

There are a number of duties imposed on the employee, many of which are tied to the idea of trust and confidence underpinned by the concept that the employee owes a degree of loyalty to his employer.

16.4   Duties imposed on the employee

If an order given by the employer is reasonable and lawful, it must be obeyed. Indeed failure to obey may give the employer the right to dismiss the employee. Whether an order is lawful and reasonable is a question of fact in each case depending upon the nature of the job.

16.4.1   To obey lawful and reasonable orders

In *Pepper v Webb* (1969) an employer instructed his gardener to carry out certain planting work in the garden. The gardener swore at his employer and indicated that he was not prepared to obey the instructions. It was held that the employee was in breach of his implied duty as the orders were not only lawful but reasonable in the circumstances.

Any dismissal for failing to follow an illegal order ie to commit a criminal offence, is unlawful and the employee will either be able to pursue an action for unfair or wrongful dismissal (see *Morrish v Henlys (Folkestone) Ltd* (1973) where a refusal to falsify the accounts did not amount to a breach of contract on the part of the employee). Further protection is provided by TURERA 1993 in respect of dismissals in connection with health and safety if an employee has refused to work where there is a serious and imminent danger; such dismissals are automatically unfair.

16.4.2   To act faithfully

This duty is fundamental to the relationship of the employer and employee. The employee's first loyalty must be to his employer. The duty encompasses such things as confidentiality, not competing with the employer etc.

In *Faccenda Chicken Ltd v Fowler* (1986) Fowler was employed as a sales manager by Faccenda Chicken. He resigned with a number of other employees and set up in competition with his previous employer selling chickens. Although there was no restraint of trade clauses in the contract, the plaintiff alleged that the duty of confidentiality had been broken as information such as lists of customers had been copied and used by the defendant. It was held that as the scope of the duty to act faithfully varied according to the nature of the contract of employment, it was necessary to consider all the circumstances of the case, in particular the nature of the employment and the information obtained and used ie was it the type of information which was a trade secret and therefore highly confidential? It was held that the employer's claim would be rejected as the information was not so confidential that it could be covered by an implied prohibition on its use.

This case limits the protection afforded to the employer with respect to confidential information, since the only information which will be protected is that which could be legitimately protected by a restraint of trade clause and does not appear to cover information 'recalled' by the employee as opposed to that copied or memorised.

Working for another employer while still in the employ of the original employer may also be a breach of the duty to act faithfully. Generally, this will only amount to a breach where the second employer is in competition with the first employer or where the nature of the contract is one of exclusivity or there is a conflict of interest. In all other circumstances the courts will not seek to curb an employee's legitimate spare time activities . If, for example, an employee was a car mechanic by day and worked in a public house at night, there would be no breach (see *Nova Plastics Ltd v Froggatt* (1982)) in which it was held that even where an employee worked for a competitor in his spare time, there had to be some evidence of potential harm).

In *Hivac Ltd v Park Royal Scientific Instruments Ltd* (1946) employees of the plaintiff company were found to be working in their spare time for a company which was in direct competition with their employer. The employees concerned were doing the same job at both establishments. It was held that the employees were under a duty not to work for a competitor of their employer where this work would conflict with their duty of fidelity and may inflict harm on their employer's business.

The employer may prevent his employees either working for rival firms or setting up a business in competition with him after they have left their employment by including in the contract of employment an express term which restricts the employees future employment in some way. Such clauses are known as covenants in restraint of trade. Many professional people such as solicitors, accountants etc will have this type of clause in their contracts. Restraint of trade clauses are only valid if they are reasonable in all the circumstances of the case ie the protection afforded the employer must not be excessive. Furthermore, the interests of the public must be considered, this being particularly relevant with respect to trade secrets, inventions etc. Such clauses will also be subject to rules of construction and severance which may result in part of a clause being struck out.

In *Home Counties Dairies Ltd v Skilton* (1970) Skilton was a milkman. His contract of employment contained a clause which provided that for a period of one year after the termination of his contract with Home Counties Dairies he would not sell milk or dairy produce to any person who had been a customer of the dairy for the last six months of his contract and whom he had served. Soon after leaving his employment he set up his own milk round in the same area as he had worked for the dairy company. It was held that the former employer should be awarded an injunction to prevent Skilton from working this area. The clause in his contract was valid as the time limit was reasonable in order to protect the interests of the dairy.

Under the heading of fidelity the employee must not disclose confidential information which he has acquired in the course of his employment. The duty extends to trade secrets, financial state of the company, new designs etc.

In *Cranleigh Precision Engineering Co Ltd v Bryant* (1965) Bryant was the managing director of a firm which designed swimming pools. He left the company and started his own business using information which he had gained from his previous employment. It was held that Bryant was in breach of the implied term in his contract of employment as he could only have gained this information from his previous employment. He had made improper use of information gained in confidence to the detriment of his former employer.

16.4.3   To use skill and care

The employee is under a duty to use reasonable skill and care in the performance of the job. If he does so and incurs loss or damage the employer will indemnify him. However, should the employee be grossly incompetent, the employer may have grounds to dismiss him. The duty extends to taking proper care of the employer's property (see *Superlux v Plaistead* (1958)).

In *Lister v Romford Ice and Cold Storage Co Ltd* (1957) Lister, a lorry driver employed by the Romford Ice company, negligently reversed his lorry, seriously injuring a fellow employee. The company claimed an indemnity from Lister on the grounds that he had broken the implied term of skill and care in his contract of employment. It was held that the employer was entitled to an indemnity because the employee had failed to use reasonable skill and care as required by the implied terms. Lister was therefore liable for the damages awarded to his fellow employee.

See also *Janata Bank v Ahmed* (1981) in which a bank manager who failed to check adequately customers' credit worthiness before giving them loans and arranging credit, was held to be personally responsible for failing to use sufficient skill and care.

16.4.4   Not to take bribes or make a secret profit

Whilst this duty is part and parcel of the general duty of fidelity it extends to accounting for any monies or gifts received which may compromise an employee. A breach of this duty by an employee is an abuse of position and may result in a fair dismissal. This is illustrated in *Sinclair v Neighbour* (1967) in which a clerk in a betting-shop took £15 from the till without the permission of his employer whom he knew would refuse. The clerk intended to replace it the next day. However, in the interim the employer discovered what the clerk had done and dismissed him. It was held that the clerk had not acted honestly in attempting to deceive his employer and therefore the employer was entitled to dismiss him.

In *Reading v Attorney-General* (1951) Reading, who was a sergeant in the British Army based in Egypt, used his position to accompany lorries containing illicit spirits, so that they would not be stopped by the police. Over a period of time Reading received £20,000 for his 'services'. When his role was finally discovered, he was arrested and the army authorities confiscated his money. When he was released from prison he brought an action for the return of the money. It was held that Reading was in breach of the implied duty not to take bribes or make secret profits. He had misused his position of trust and had therefore to account for those 'profits' to his employer. He was not entitled to have any of the money returned to him.

In *British Syphon Co Ltd v Homewood* (1956) Homewood was employed as chief technician by the plaintiff company in the design and development department. During his employment he designed a new type of soda syphon. He did not disclose his invention to his employers. He then left his employment and applied for letters patent in respect of his invention. It was held that the invention and the profits from it belonged to his employer. The invention was clearly related to his employer's business and they were therefore entitled to the benefits from it.

The common law position regarding employees' inventions has been qualified by ss 39-41 Patents Act 1977 and s 11 Copyright, Designs and Patents Act 1988. In such cases the invention or design will only belong to the employer if:

- It is made in the course of normal duties or duties specifically assigned and the invention could reasonably be expected to derive from that work.

- It is made in the normal course of duties and, at the time of the invention, there is a special obligation to further the employer's business interests.

16.5   Equal pay

The legal requirement for ensuring equality between men and women's terms of employment can be found in the Equal Pay Act 1970 (EPA 1970) and Article 119 and Directive 75/117 of the Treaty of Rome. Although these legislative provisions protect men and women alike, the evidence suggests that a women's average earnings are only 70-75% of a man's average earnings and therefore in practical terms most cases for equal pay are brought by women. This is further compounded by the segregation of women into jobs perceived as 'women's jobs' which are traditionally in the service sector and in the lower pay bracket. Job segregation is seen as a major obstacle to equality in employment.

16.5.1   Equality clause

The EPA 1970 incorporates an equality clause into all contracts of employment (s 1(1)). As a result of this clause any term in the contract of employment which is less favourable to the woman (or man) compared with a similar clause in a man's contract (or vice versa), will be deemed to be no less favourable and if the contract of the woman does not contain a beneficial term which is to be found in the man's contract, her contract will be deemed to contain such a clause.

The EPA 1970 is not restricted to claims for pay but applies to any terms in the applicant's contract which are less favourable than the comparator's. In theory the equality clause should operate automatically without recourse to the industrial tribunal system, although in reality many complainant's have had to resort to the tribunals.

16.5.2   Claiming equality

To bring a claim under the EPA 1970, the applicant must show that he or she is employed under a contract of service or under a contract for services where there is a requirement for them personally to do the work (s 1(6)). This provides the opportunity for a greater number of people to be afforded some equality protection (see *Mirror Group Newspapers Ltd v Gunning* (1986)).

The applicant must be in the same employment as her comparator ie she should be employed by the same employer at the same establishment or by the same employer or an associated employer at an establishment where common terms and conditions are observed (s 1(6)). This section recognises the need for as wide a choice as possible in selecting a comparator within the acceptable confines of the legislation ie it would be totally unreasonable to allow comparison between unrelated employers or industries. The term 'common terms and conditions' was considered in *Leverton v Clwyd CC* (1989). Ms Leverton the applicant was a nursery nurse employed by Clwyd County Council. She selected as her comparators in her equal value claim, male clerical staff employed by Clwyd County Council but at a different establishment. This comparison would only be valid, therefore, if she and her comparators were subject to 'common terms and conditions'. It was held that s 1(6) required a comparison between the terms and conditions observed at the establishment at which the woman was employed and the establishment at which the men were employed, applicable either generally or to a particular class of employee to which both the woman and the men belonged. In this particular case they were both employed under the same collective agreement which was applied generally. It was irrelevant that there were some differences between the actual terms of their contracts, s 1(6) was therefore satisfied (see also *British Coal Corporation v Smith* (1994)).

The applicant must select a comparator of the opposite sex. The choice of comparator is a decision for the applicant (see *Ainsworth v Glass Tubes Ltd* (1977)) and he or she may apply for an order of discovery in order to select the most appropriate comparator (see *Leverton v Clwyd CC* (above)). However, more importantly the comparator must be or have been in existence. Whilst, therefore, comparison with a predecessor of the opposite sex is allowed as decided by the ECJ in *Macarthys v Smith* (1980), comparison with the hypothetical comparator is not permitted. This in effect prevents any claim from applicants in segregated industries where there is no one of the opposite sex falling within s 1(6).

16.5.3   Comparator

Equality can only be claimed on one of the following grounds:

- like work;

- work rated equivalent;

- work of equal value.

16.6   Grounds of claim

'Like work' is defined by s 1(4) as either the same work or work of a broadly similar nature where the differences (if any) between the applicant's job and the comparator's job are not of practical importance in relation to the terms and conditions of employment. The application of s 1(4) can be seen in:

16.6.1   Like work (s 1(2)(a))

Capper Pass Ltd v Lawton (1977) where Mrs Lawton was a cook employed in the director's dining room where she provided lunched for up to 20 directors each day. She claimed equal pay on the basis of 'like work' with two male assistant chefs in the works canteen who provided some 350 meals per day. It was held that a two-stage test should be applied:

- Is the work the same or, if not, is it of a broadly similar nature? The EAT suggested that a broad approach should be adopted to this question without a minute examination of the differences between the jobs;

- If the work is broadly similar, are the differences of practical importance? In applying this test, it was concluded that Mrs Lawton was employed on 'like work' as her work and that of her comparator fell within s 1(4).

Additionally, there may be other factors which have a bearing on whether s 1(4) is satisfied. Additional responsibility may justify a difference in pay (see *Eaton Ltd v Nuttall* (1977); whereas, in general, the time at which work is done should be ignored (*Dugdale v Kraft Foods Ltd* (1977)) unless it brings with it additional responsibilities (*Thomas v NCB* (1987)). Payment of a different basic rate for night shift workers may well contravene the equality provisions although shift premiums payable for unsociable hours may circumvent the Act (*Calder & Cizakowsky v Rowntree Macintosh Confectionery Ltd* (1993)). Finally, the tribunal is concerned with what the applicant and the comparator actually do in practice, not necessarily what their job descriptions are under their contracts – see *Shields v Coomes (Holdings) Ltd* (1978) where a woman employed in a betting shop claimed equal pay with a male employee who appeared to be doing the same job as a counterhand. She was paid 62p per hour while he received £1.06p. The employer claimed that the difference in pay resulted from the fact that the man was also required to deal with trouble-makers. The reality was that he had never been called upon to cope with a disturbance and had never received any training in the event of this happening. The applicant was therefore found to be on 'like work'.

16.6.2   Work rated equivalent (s 1(2)(b))

An applicant may bring an equality claim if her job has been rated as equivalent with that of her male comparator by virtue of a job evaluation scheme. This section can only be used where there is in existence a complete and valid scheme, the validity of which has been accepted by the parties who agreed to its being carried out (*Arnold v Beecham Group Ltd* (1982)). Such schemes must comply with s 1(5) Equal Pay Act 1970. The interpretation of this, resulting from the case of *Bromley v H & J Quick Ltd* (1988), is that all valid schemes as well as being non-discriminatory must be analytical and not involve the subjective views of management as to the grading of an employee. Comparisons must therefore be made of the various demands upon the employees under the headings laid down in s 1(5) ie effort, skill, decision etc. As a result some job evaluations will not satisfy the decision in *Bromley* or s 1(5) and can therefore be challenged. Some guidance on analytical schemes is offered in *Eaton v Nuttall* (1977) and the ACAS Job Evaluation booklet.

16.6.3   Equal value (s 1(2)(c))

This head of claim originated from a case brought by the European Commission against the UK government for failing to comply with Article 119 and Directive 75/117 in that there was no provision in UK law for claims of equality where jobs were of equal value. This was highlighted by the fact that there was no right on the part of the employee to compel an employer to carry out a job evaluation scheme under s 1(2)(b) (see *EC Commission v UK* (1982)). As a result the UK was forced to amend the EPA 1970 by inserting a provision on equal value. This had the effect of making the equality law available to a greater number of claimants.

It was thought from the wording of the Act, that this head of claim could only be used if there was no 'like work' or 'work rated equivalent' claim available. However, a potential loop-hole was spotted by at least one employer which involved the use of the token man employed on 'like work' to prevent an equal value claim proceeding. In *Pickstone v Freemans plc* (1988) where the employer attempted to block an equal value claim in this way, the House of Lords concluded that the presence of a man doing like work to the applicant did not prevent the applicant bringing an equal value claim using another male comparator. In making this decision consideration was had of EC law, with the conclusion that any other construction would:

> '... leave a gap in the equal work provision, enabling an employer to evade it by employing one token man on the same work as a group of potential women claimants who were deliberately paid less than a group of men employed on work of equal value with that of the woman. This would mean that the UK had failed yet again to fully implement its obligations under EC law.'

The procedure in equal value claims is complex. The applicant makes an application to an industrial tribunal. Initially, the claim is sent to ACAS with a view to settling the claim. If this does not occur, the claim is then the subject of a preliminary hearing where it is decided whether there are reasonable grounds for determining that the work is of equal value. The purpose of this hearing is to weed out hopeless cases ie where the jobs have been deemed unequal under a valid job evaluation scheme s 2(A)(1)(a). (There are proposals to remove this stage so that the issue can be referred directly to the independent expert.) The onus is on the applicant to prove that her job is of equal value to that of the comparator. The employer may introduce the genuine material factor defence at this stage but if he does so, he will not be allowed to plead it after the independent expert has reported back to the tribunal. If the tribunal is satisfied that there are reasonable grounds on which the claim may proceed the claim is then referred to an independent expert appointed from the ACAS panel. The expert carries out a thorough investigation of the jobs for comparison and reports in writing to the tribunal. Interestingly, the tribunal is not obliged to accept the report (*Tennants Textile Colours Ltd v Todd* (1989)).

16.6.4   Equal value procedure

One of the problems for the tribunal has been what amounts to work of equal value. At industrial tribunal level there has been some inconsistency, for example, in *Wells v F Smales & Son (Fish Merchants)* (1985) the tribunal adopted a broad brush approach in concluding that female fish packers were engaged in work of equal value to that of a male labourer even though

16.6.5   What amounts to equal value?

some of the women's work was assessed at only 75% of the value of the men's work. The tribunal concluded that the differences were not material. In *Brown & Royle v Cearn & Brown Ltd* (1985), however, the independent expert concluded that the applicant's work was worth 95% of her comparator's work, yet the tribunal declined to conclude that this was work of equal value as it was not 'precisely equal value'. In *Pickstone v Freemans* (1993) the industrial tribunal concluded that equal value does not have to be 100% value. Equal value also includes higher value (see *Murphy v Bord Telecom Eireann* (1988)).

16.6.6   Genuine material
          factor defence (s 1(3))

The Equal Pay Act provides a defence in equal pay cases if the employer can show that the variation between the women's contract and the men's contract is genuinely due to a material difference or factor which is not a difference in sex. In the case of 'like work' or 'work rated equivalent' claims, that factor must be a material difference whereas in 'equal value' claims it *may* be such a difference. The distinction has been, in reality, removed by the decision in *Rainey v Greater Glasgow Health Board* (1987) which went on to apply the criteria in *Bilka Kaufhaus GmbH v von Hartz* (1986) for establishing this defence. This requires the employer to show objectively justified grounds for the different treatment. There must be a real need on the part of the undertaking for the difference; it is not sufficient merely to show that the reason for the difference was not discriminatory. This criteria has been successfully used to uphold 'market forces' as a defence as in *Rainey v Greater Glasgow Health Board* (1987), but can no longer be used to justify inequalities arising out of collective bargaining agreements (see *Enderby v Frenchay Health Authority* (1993)).

The following are examples of genuine material factors. The location at which the applicant and her comparator work may justify the difference in terms eg work in London as compared with the provinces (see *Navy, Army and Air Force Institutes v Varley* (1976); 'red-circling' this occurs where the terms of an employee or group of employees are legitimately preserved eg where the job may have been down graded but existing staff have their terms protected. This is a legitimate defence as long as the red-circling is genuine and only applies to an existing person or pool of employees (*Snoxell v Vauxhall Motors Ltd* (1977)); as is economic necessity (see *Benveniste v University of Southampton* (1989)) although once the economic situation improves the employer is bound to redress the disparity in terms.

Article 119 provides that Member States shall maintain the application of the principle that men and women should receive equal pay for equal work. 'Pay' means the ordinary basic or minimum wage or salary and includes any payment in cash or kind which the worker receives in respect of his employment. This is not as wide as the EPA 1970 which extends equality to all terms of the contract, although in reality most claims are based on pay.

Article 119 is directly applicable and enforceable by an individual (see *Kowalski v Freie und Hansestadt Hamburg* (1990). It is supplemented by Directive 75/117, the equal pay directive. Generally, such directives are not enforceable by an individual as it is left to the Member State to comply with it using whatever form or method they choose. However, the equal pay directive is an exception to this as firstly it gives meaning and clarity to Article 119 and as a result is applied through Article 119; secondly, it fulfils the test in *Van Duyn v Home Office* (1975) which held that a directive could be enforced by an individual if it was 'sufficiently clear, precise, admitted of no exceptions and therefore of its nature needed no intervention by the national authorities'.

The directive states that:

'... the principle of equal pay for men and women outlined in Article 119 ... means, for the same work or for work to which equal value has been attributed, the elimination of all discrimination on grounds of sex with regard to all aspects and conditions of remuneration.'

The impact of the Article and its directive can be seen from the following cases in which a wide interpretation of the word 'pay' was made. In *Barber v Guardian Royal Exchange Assurance Group* (1990) occupational pension schemes were deemed to amount to pay and therefore the disparity between men and women's benefits under such schemes must be equalised; the decision in *Barber* also included *ex gratia* payments and redundancy payments; sick pay (*Rinner Kuhn v FWW Spezial Gebaudereingung GmbH* (1989)); transparency in incremental pay schemes (*Handels-Og Kontorfunktionaerernes Forbund i Danmark v Dansk Arbjdsgiverforening (acting for Danfoss)* (1989)).

16.7   EC law

The applicant must make her claim either whilst still in employment or within six months of leaving that employment. Although this limit has been thrown into doubt by the decision in *British Railways Board v Paul* (1988) which stated that the limit only applied to claims referred to an industrial tribunal by the Secretary of State (see *Etherson v Strathclyde Regional Council* (1992) for a counter view). EC law fails to impose a

16.8   Remedies

time limit for claims. However, the case law suggests that any claim based on EC law should be subject to the limits set for tribunal claims generally under domestic legislation (*Emmott v Minister for Social Welfare* (1991)).

If the applicant succeeds in her claim she may recover arrears of pay for a period of up to two years prior to the date on which proceedings began.

16.9 Sex and race discrimination

The law on sex and race discrimination is to be found in the Sex Discrimination Act 1975 (SDA) and the Race Relations Act 1976 (RRA) respectively. The RRA 1976 is modelled on the SDA 1975, although there are some differences which will be highlighted. However, for the most part, the statutes are the same and to that extent the applicability of the case law is interchangeable. The aim of the legislation is to eliminate discrimination and promote equality of opportunity. It is, however, arguable that legislation can be effective in doing this unless it is supported by the political will to succeed which at the very least means effective penalties must be provided. It also raises the question whether the Acts address the causes of discrimination, in particular, stereotyping resulting in job segregation which is not unlawful under the SDA 1975 and whilst it is unlawful under the RRA 1976, control is not particularly effective. Stereotyping may result in women and ethnic minorities being directed into the less skilled and therefore poorly paid jobs where there is little chance of career development. Some protection is afforded women but not racial groups by EC law.

16.9.1 EC law

The Equal Treatment Directive (76/207) provides that every Member State must introduce measures to enable individuals to pursue claims for equal treatment. An individual may pursue a claim against the State as an employer eg *Foster v British Gas plc* (1991) and *Doughty v Rolls Royce plc* (1992) which confirmed that an individual was allowed to rely on Article 5 of the directive against a body which is :

'... subject to the authority or control of the State or which has been made responsible, pursuant to a measure adopted by the State, for providing a public service under the control of the State and has for that purpose special powers beyond those which result from the normal rules applicable in relations between individuals.'

The directive enshrines the principle of equal treatment on grounds of sex and marital status. The directive applies to access to jobs and vocational guidance and training, collective agreements and working conditions including dismissal. The directive has been used by the European Commission to challenge the UK's failure to comply with it (*Commission of The European Communities v United Kingdom* (1984)); the subsequent legislation (SDA 1986) made sex discrimination in collective agreements unlawful. The most significant change made by *the 1986 Act arose from the decision in Marshall v Southampton & South-West Hampshire Area Health Authority* (1986).

The Area Health Authority had a policy which resulted in the dismissal of women because they had attained the State pension age which is a different age for men and women. As a result Ms Marshall was forced to leave her employment; she then decided to challenge this policy. It as held by the ECJ that the term 'dismissal' in Article 5 must be given a wide meaning; that being so the compulsory dismissal of workers pursuant to a policy concerning retirement, related to conditions governing dismissal which were then subject to Article 5. Where that policy then resulted in different retirement ages for men and women there had been a contravention of the Article.

The legislation covers anyone who seeks employment under a contract of employment or who is employed under a contract of employment. Protection from discrimination is also extended to discrimination by trade unions and employers' associations, employment agencies and qualifying bodies such as the Association of Chartered Accountants and the Law Society and partnerships.

16.9.2   Who is protected?

Discrimination is unlawful if it is based upon sex/gender or racial grounds or the marital status of the complainant. It is therefore unlawful to discriminate against a woman or man because of their gender or because they are married; however, it is not unlawful to discriminate against someone because they are single (s 3(1) SDA 1975). Similarly, it is unlawful to discriminate against someone on 'racial grounds'. This is defined as any of the following: colour, race, nationality or ethnic or national origins (s 3(1) RRA 1976). Ethnic origins have been given a wider interpretation than racial origins and as a result have brought more groups within the scope of the Act, although there is still a problem for those groups who can be equated with a religion rather than a race and, as a result, may not be protected by the legislation.

16.9.3   Types of unlawful discrimination

The test for establishing 'ethnic origin' can be found in *Mandla v Dowell Lee* (1983) in which it was decided that Sikhs constituted an ethnic group. It was stated by Lord Fraser that in order for a group to constitute an 'ethnic group' it must be regarded as a distinct community by virtue of certain characteristics, some of which are essential:

'... a long shared history; a cultural tradition of its own; a common geographical area or descent from a number of common ancestors; a common language; a common literature; a common religion different from that of neighbouring groups or from the general community surrounding it; being a minority or being an oppressed or dominant group within a larger community ...'

The test has been applied with some success to bring 'gypsies' within the RRA 1976 (see *CRE v Dutton* (1989)) but not rastafarians (*Dawkins v Department of the Environment* (1993)) as the latter were deemed to be no more than a religious sect and in any event there was no 'long shared history'. However, being a Jew may fall within the Act although whether an action will succeed depends upon the reason for the discrimination ie if a Jew is discriminated against because of his religion he will not be protected (see *Seide v Gillette Industries* (1980) and *Simon v Brimham Associates* (1987) each case must be considered on its merits).

Finally, both the SDA 1975 (s 5(3)) and the RRA 1976 (s 3(4)) require a 'like with like' comparison to be made so that the 'relevant circumstances between the comparators are the same or not materially different' (*Bain v Bowles* (1991)).

The types of discrimination which are recognised by the Acts are as follows.

16.10 Direct discrimination

This is aimed at both overt and covert acts against the individual and is not confined to hostile or intentional acts of discrimination. Direct discrimination occurs where a person is treated less favourably on grounds of their sex, race or marital status. In order to establish this type of discrimination comparison must be made with a person of the opposite sex or another race, however an hypothetical person can be used for this comparison. Although this head of claim has been difficult to establish in the past, in recent years the following test has been formulated which has helped the complainant and reinforces the fact that intention and motive, no matter how good, are not relevant. The test is as follows:

• Has there been an act of discrimination?

  If the answer is in the affirmative:

• But for the sex or race of the complainant, would he or she have been treated differently ie less favourably?

If the answer to this is in the affirmative, an act of direct discrimination has taken place (see *R v Birmingham City Council ex p EOC* (1989), followed in *James v Eastleigh Borough Council* (1990)). In the latter case, free swimming was provided for children under the age of three years and persons who had attained the state retirement age. Mr and Mrs James were both aged 61 and were both retired. When they went to the swimming baths owned by Eastleigh Borough Council Mrs James was able to take advantage of free swimming whilst her husband had to pay. Mr James alleged an act of direct discrimination which breached s 29 SDA which related to discrimination in the provision of goods facilities and services. Initially, in the Court of Appeal it was held that there was no act of discrimination as it was necessary to look at the reason for adopting the discriminatory policy which in this a case was to help the needy and therefore the discrimination was not on grounds of gender. However, on appeal to the House of Lords, it was decided to apply the 'but for' test and ask the question 'but for the complainant's sex would he have received the same treatment'; the answer was in the affirmative and as a result Eastleigh Borough Council had to alter their policy.

Further assistance in establishing direct discrimination can be found in the case of *Noone v North West Thames Regional Health Authority* (1988) which concluded that once the complainant has shown that there is a *prima facie* case of discrimination, even though actual evidence may be lacking, discrimination will be inferred unless the employer can show good reason for his actions which are not connected to the sex or race of the complainant.

There is no separate provision relating to harassment at work. Any complaint must be made under the heading of direct discrimination. The recognition of this as a serious head of claim is fairly recent. The definition of sexual harassment is wide and encompasses any conduct meted out in a particular way because of the complainant's gender or race ie it is not confined to conduct of a purely physical nature, even though many of the cases involve this type of conduct.

16.10.1 Sexual and racial harassment

In *Strathclyde Regional District Council v Porcelli* (1986) Mrs Porcelli was a laboratory assistant at a school under the control of Strathclyde Regional District Council. She was subjected to a variety of treatment from two male laboratory assistants who were intent on driving her from her job. This conduct involved brushing against her and making suggestive remarks as well as putting heavy equipment on the top shelves of the store. She made her claim and asked to be transferred. It was held that she had been discriminated against as the type of treatment was related to her sex and a man in a similar position would not have been treated the same way. The employer was found to be vicariously liable for the actions of the male laboratory assistants by virtue of s 41 SDA 1975.

The courts have gone further in holding that harassment need not be a course of conduct but can manifest itself in a single act of a serious nature. In *Bracebridge Engineering v Darby* (1990) it was held that employees committing such acts may be within the course of their employment resulting in the employer being vicariously liable for such acts. Racial harassment is akin to sexual harassment and to that extent racial insults may also be a form of racial harassment. However, in establishing either type of discrimination, the complainant must show that the treatment is to their detriment within s 6 SDA 1975 and s 4 RRA 1976 (see *De Souza v Automobile Association* (1986)).

The EC has intervened on the question of sexual harassment by firstly adopting a resolution relating to sexual harassment at work (Resolution No 6015/90 and secondly agreeing to a recommendation and Code of Practice on the protection and dignity of women and men at work. As a result, although the recommendation is not directly enforceable, the ECJ has ruled that the national courts must take such measures into account in applying National and Community law (*Grimaldi v Fonds des Maladies Professionelles* (1990)).

16.10.2   Discrimination and pregnancy

Discrimination related to pregnancy or maternity is part and parcel of direct discrimination. As a result a pregnant woman can at least in theory challenge unfavourable treatment because of her pregnancy as an act of direct discrimination. At one time it was thought that such treatment was not protected by the SDA 1975 on the basis that there could be no male comparator (see *Turley v Allders Department Stores Ltd* (1980)). However, some redress has been provided by cases such as *Hayes v Malleable Working Men's Club* (1985) and *Webb v EMO Cargo Ltd* (1993) although both these cases require comparison of the treatment of the pregnant woman with that of the sick man or at the very least a male employer who would be absent for an equivalent period. However the ECJ, in considering *Webb's* case ((1994)), has ruled that this comparison is no longer acceptable and that dismissal on account of pregnancy constitutes direct discrimination (see also *Dekker v Stichting Vormingscentrum voor Jong Volvassen (VJW Centrum) Plus* (1991)). Unfortunately, the 'sick man' syndrome still has a role to play in ECJ pronouncements as it has been held that the dismissal of a woman on grounds of absence due to an illness which arose from pregnancy was not necessarily discriminated against on grounds of sex. In this case it was thought to be quite legitimate to compare the treatment of the woman with how a sick man would have been treated, although it was decided that protection for the pregnant woman extended to the end of the maternity leave period (*Handels og Kontorfunktionaerernes Forbund i Danmark (acting for Hertz v Dansk Arbejdsgiverforening* (1991)).

These issues may have less significance as a result of TURERA 1993 which provides protection from dismissal for all pregnant employees and in connection with childbirth.

Indirect discrimination is aimed at conduct which on the face of it does not treat people differently ie it is race and gender neutral. However, it is the impact of this treatment which amounts to discrimination. It can therefore be subtle in nature and may be difficult to prove. The essentials are that:

16.11   Indirect discrimination

- a requirement or condition is applied equally to both sexes and all racial groups;

- a considerably smaller proportion of the complainant's sex or race can comply with it compared to the opposite sex or persons not of that racial group;

- the requirement or condition operates to the detriment of the complainant because he or she cannot comply with it;

- the requirement or condition can be justified irrespective of the gender or race of the complainant.

The burden of proof is initially on the complainant. Once a *prima facie* case has been made out, the burden moves to the employer to show that the requirement or condition is justified. Again the intention of the employer is irrelevant in establishing indirect discrimination, although it becomes important to the tribunal in deciding whether compensation should be awarded as both statutes provide that no compensation is payable for unintentional, indirect discrimination.

In isolating a requirement or condition the complainant must show that it operates as an absolute bar in that it amounts to 'a must' without which an applicant could not proceed. This is highlighted by *Perera v Civil Service Commission* (1983). Perera was a barrister from Sri Lanka who applied for the post with the defendants. The selection criteria which was applied to all candidates included age, practical experience in the UK, spoken and written English etc. Perera argued that these were requirements or conditions. It was held that they were not 'musts' without which an applicant could not succeed. The only relevant condition was that the applicant should be a barrister or solicitor and Perera fulfilled this condition.

This interpretation allows the employer to apply a wide range of criteria in making selections for employment or promotion and as long as they do not constitute a 'must', how he applies them will not be called into question under the Acts. Past cases show that age limits may be discriminatory as in *Price v Civil Service Commission* (1977), as may requirements to work full-time (*Holmes v Home Office* (1984) and *Briggs v North Eastern Education & Library Board* (1990)).

In determining what amounts to a 'considerably smaller proportion' the complainant must show, usually by the use of statistical evidence, that there is an adverse impact on his or her particular race or sex. Many complainants fail by selecting the wrong 'pool' for comparison.

In *Pearse v City of Bradford Metropolitan Council* (1988) Ms Pearse a part-time lecturer at Ilkley College was unable to apply for a full-time post at the college because the only persons eligible to apply were full-time employees of the local authority. She alleged that this amounted to indirect discrimination and submitted statistics which showed that only 21.8% of the female academic staff employed at the college were employed on a full-time basis compared with 46.6% of the male academic staff who could comply with the requirement/condition regarding full-time employment. It was held that Ms Pearse should fail in her claim because she had selected the incorrect pool for comparison; the correct pool would have been those with the appropriate qualifications for the post, without reference to the requirement/condition in question, rather than those eligible. As Ms Pearse's statistics related to the latter her claim failed.

Whether the complainant has selected the correct pool for comparison is a question of fact to be decided by the tribunal (see *Kidd v DRG (UK) Ltd* (1985)). In deciding this the tribunal will not allow the complainant to limit the pool so that it is best suited to her case (see *Jones v University of Manchester* (1993)).

The term 'can comply' has also been open to interpretation by the tribunals. It has been determined that the words mean 'can in practice' rather than 'can as a theoretical possibility' (*Price v Civil Service Commission* (1977) and *Mandla v Dowell Lee* (1983)).

Has the condition or requirement operated to the detriment of the complainant?

The complainant must show that she or he has suffered a detriment ie that she or he has been disadvantaged by the requirement or condition; in effect the complainant must have *locus standii*. The following have been held to amount to 'a disadvantage': requiring a woman to work part-time (*Home Office v Holmes*); transfer to a less interesting job (*Kirby v MSC* (1980)); conduct amounting to sexual harassment *(Wileman v Minilec Engineering Ltd* (1988)).

Once the complainant has established the above requisites, the onus of proof moves to the employer to show that the requirement or condition is justified irrespective of the gender, race or marital status of the complainant. The criteria for establishing justification has been clarified by the Court of Appeal in *Hampson v Department of Science* (1989) in which it was made clear that the test requires a balance to be struck between the discriminatory effect of the requirement or condition and the needs of the employer. The employer must show a real need on the part of the undertaking to operate such a practice (this must be objective; this will then be balanced against the discriminatory impact of the practice). If there is a less discriminatory alternative the employer must take it.

16.11.1   Justification

The RRA 1976 s 2 and the SDA 1975 s 4 both recognise victimisation as a separate form of discrimination. Victimisation occurs where the complainant is treated less favourably by reason that she or he has: brought proceedings against the discriminator or another person under the RRA, SDA or EPA; given evidence or information in connection with proceedings brought by any person against the discriminator or another person under the RRA, SDA or EPA; alleged that the discriminator or any other person has committed an act which would amount to a contravention of the RRA, SDA or EPA; or done anything under or reference to the SDA, RRA or EPA in relation to the discriminator or another. The complainant must show a clear connection between the action of the discriminator and his or her own conduct (presuming it falls within the above); if there is no more than a casual connection then the tribunal will be reluctant to find that victimisation has taken place.

16.11.2   Victimisation

In *Aziz v Trinity Street Taxis Ltd* (1988) Aziz, a taxi driver was a member of a co-operative, Trinity Street Taxis. He suspected acts of racial discrimination had taken place and he decided to tape conversations of members of the co-operative in order to acquire evidence. His actions were discovered and he was expelled from the co-operative. It was held that the expulsion did not amount to victimisation as, although his actions were within the provisions as being 'by reference to' the discrimination legislation, the evidence revealed that the members of the co-operative would have voted for the expulsion of any member who made secret recordings whatever their purpose, as it revealed a gross breach of trust between the members.

16.11.3   Segregation

The RRA s 1(2) makes unlawful the provision of separate facilities for members of different races even though they are equal in quality. The purpose of this is to prevent any form of apartheid. However, the interpretation of this section by the tribunal shows that there is no onus to prevent voluntary segregation of racial groups (see *PEL Ltd v Modgill* (1980)). The SDA 1975 does not contain a similar provision.

16.11.4   Scope of protection

Once the complainant has identified and established the grounds of discrimination, he or she must then show how they relate to s 6 SDA 1975 or s 4 RRA 1976 in so far as the discrimination is only unlawful if it occurs in the selection process; and in respect of the terms on which persons are employed; or within employment in respect of opportunities for training, promotion or other benefits; and finally in respect of the dismissal of employees or subjecting them to any other detriment (see *Saunders v Richmond LBC* (1977)).

16.11.5   Genuine occupational qualifications

Both the SDA 1975 s 7 and the RRA 1976 s 5 permit discrimination by an employer if it falls within the specified genuine occupational qualifications which include the following:

- The nature of the job demands a man or woman because of their physiology, excluding strength and stamina.

- Authenticity.

- Decency or privacy eg a female nurse in a girls boarding school (see *Etam plc v Rowan* (1989)).

- A post which requires the employee to live in, where there are no separate sleeping and sanitary facilities and it is unreasonable to expect the employer to provide them.

- A post in a private home which (for the SDA exemption only involves social or physical contact with the person living in the home).

- The holder of the post supplies individuals or persons of a particular race with personal services promoting their welfare, education etc (see *Lambeth LBC v CRE* (1990) and *Tottenham Green Under-Fives Centre v Marshall (No 2)* (1991)).

- A post which involves working abroad in a country whose laws and customs are such that the job can only be done by a man.

- The job is one of two which are held by a married couple.

In addition, there are exemptions for acts done to safeguard national security and there is special protection for women during pregnancy and childbirth. However, the Employment Act 1989 allows an employer to treat woman differently on grounds of health and safety where there is a statutory requirement in existence prior to the SDA which is for the protection of women in relation to pregnancy, maternity or other risks which are specially associated with women.

An applicant must bring a claim to the industrial tribunal within three months of the date on which the act complained of was committed. A complaint brought after this limit will only be heard by the tribunal if it was 'just and equitable' to do so. Where the act of discrimination is a continuing one the time limit runs from the date on which it was last committed.

16.12   Bringing a claim

A successful complainant may receive an award of compensation which may include a sum for actual losses such as expenses and wages, injury to feelings and future losses. However, no compensation will be awarded for indirect discrimination unless it is intentional. An amount of not less than £500 should be awarded for injury to feelings which should always form part of the award (*Sharifi v Strathclyde Regional Council* (1992)). The upper limit for compensation was £11,000. This was challenged in *Marshall v Southampton & South-West Hampshire Area Health Authority (No 2)* (1993) where it was held by the ECJ that the limit on compensation contravened EC law and should therefore be removed; in addition it was in order to award interest on compensation. Following *City of Bradford v Arora* (1991) an industrial tribunal may award aggravated damages, but following *Deane v London Borough of Ealing* (1993) can no longer award exemplary damages. The compensation limit of £11,000 for race discrimination claims was removed in July 1994.

16.12.1   Remedies

The industrial tribunal also has the power to:

- Make a declaration with respect to the rights of the complainant under the respective legislation; such a declaration is not enforceable and at the most can only be persuasive as far as the employer is concerned.

- Make a recommendation for the employer to take specific action eg order the employer to cease discrimination with respect to an individual complainant; however, this does not extend to a general order to cease a discriminatory practice, nor, failing the decision in *Noone v North West Thames Regional Health Authority (No 2)* (1988), does it extend to positive discrimination such as recommending that the applicant who has been the victim of discriminatory selection be awarded to the next available post.

16.13 Equal Opportunities Commission and the Commission for Racial Equality

The EOC and CRE have the following duties which are broadly similar:

- To work towards the elimination of discrimination.
- To promote equality of opportunity between men and women and racial groups and to promote good race relations.
- To keep under review the working of the equal opportunities legislation and propose amendments as necessary.

The Commissions are also granted various powers:

- To assist applicants in bringing complaints of discrimination.
- To undertake or assist research and education activities.
- To issue codes of practice.
- To conduct formal investigations for any purpose connected with the carrying out of their duties; following such investigations the Commission may issue a non-discrimination notice.

Individual Employment Rights (1)

An employee is employed under a contract of employment (or contract of service) whereas an independent contractor is employed under a contract for services. The distinction is important because many employment rights only accrue in an employer/employee relationship.

Contract of employment

The tests which have developed for establishing the employer/employee relationship are:

- Control test.

- Integration test.

- Multiple test (*Ready Mixed Concrete Ltd v Minister of Pensions & National Insurance* (1968); *Market Investigations Ltd v Minister of Social Security* (1969)).

- Mutuality of obligations test (*O'Kelly v Trusthouse Forte plc* (1983)).

- Loaning or hiring out of a servant (*Mersey Docks & Harbour Board v Coggins & Griffiths Ltd* (1947)).

Although there are no formalities involved in the formation of the contract of employment, every employee is entitled to a statement of written particulars (s 1 EPCA) within two months of the commencement of his employment.

Written statement of terms

Express terms are agreed between the employer and employee. Implied terms must be read subject to any express terms in the contract.

Express terms

Implied terms arise out of custom and practice or through the courts (*Johnstone v Bloomsbury Health Authority* (1991)).

Implied terms

The duties imposed on the employer are:

- to provide work (*Collier v Sunday Referee Publishing Co Ltd* (1940));

- to provide wages;

- to indemnify his employees;

- to have mutual respect (*Donovan v Invicta Airways Ltd* (1970));

- to provide for the safety of his employees.

The duties imposed on the employee are:

- to obey lawful and reasonable orders (*Pepper v Webb* (1969));

- to act with loyalty (*Faccenda Chicken Ltd v Fowler* (1986); *Hivac Ltd v Park Royal Scientific Instruments Ltd* (1946); *Home Counties Dairies v Skilton* (1970); *Cranleigh Precision Engineering Co Ltd v Bryant* (1965));

- to act with skill and care (*Lister v Romford Ice & Cold Storage Co Ltd* (1957));

- not to take bribes and secret profits (*Reading v AG* (1951); *British Syphon Co Ltd v Homewood* (1956)).

Equal pay

The Equal Pay Act 1970 incorporates an equality clause into every contract of employment which has the effect of equalising unfavourable terms between men and women's contracts and vice versa. Should a claim for equal pay be pursued, the applicant must select a comparator of the opposite sex and show:

- the same employer or associated employer;

- the same establishment or an establishment where common terms and conditions are observed (*Leverton v Clwyd CC* (1989)).

There are three heads of claim:

- like work – defined in s 1(4) (*Capper Pass Ltd v Lawton* (1977); *Shields v Coomes (Holdings) Ltd* (1978));

- work rated equivalent – defined in s 1(5);

- work of equal value (*Pickstone v Freemans plc* (1988)).

Genuine material factor defence

The employer must objectively justify any differing terms between the contracts of his male and female employees by showing a real need on the part of the undertaking for the difference in the light of the objective need (*Rainey v Greater Glasgow Health Board* (1987)).

EC law

EC law can be found in Article 119 and Directive 75/117 which lay down the principle of equal pay for equal work, including work of equal value. Although EC law is confined to pay, this has been given a wide interpretation by the ECJ (*Barber v Guardian Royal Exchange Assurance Group* (1990)).

Sex and race discrimination

Sex and race discrimination are governed by the Sex Discrimination Act 1975 and the Race Relations Act 1976.

Under these Acts discrimination on the grounds of sex, marital status (not single) and race are unlawful in the fields of employment, housing, education, and the provision of goods, facilities and services etc.

To bring a complaint under the RRA 1976, the complainant must establish 'racial grounds' or membership of a racial group s 3(1) (*Mandla v Dowell Lee* (1983)).

The test for establishing direct discrimination is the 'but for' test (*James v Eastleigh Borough Council* (1990)); or there may be an inference of discrimination (*Noone v North West Thames Regional Health Authority* (1988));

Direct discrimination

Harassment is a form of direct discrimination (*Strathclyde Regional District Council v Porcelli* (1986)) as is discrimination on grounds of pregnancy or connected with pregnancy (*Webb v EMO Cargo Ltd* (1994)).

- Requirement (*Perera v Civil Service Commission* (1983)).

Indirect discrimination

- Pool (*Pearse v City of Bradford Metropolitan Council* (1988)).

- Detriment (*Home Office v Holmes*).

- Justification (*Hampson v Department of Science* (1989)).

Victimisation occurs where the complainant is treated less favourably because he or she has brought proceedings etc, under the RRA or SDA or EOA (*Aziz v Trinity Street Taxis Ltd* (1988)).

Victimisation

Segregation occurs where racial groups are intentionally segregated in some way (*PEL Ltd v Modgill* (1980)).

Segregation

The employer has the opportunity to defend the act of discrimination on the basis that the sex or race of the employee is a genuine occupational qualification (SDA 1975 and RRA 1976).

Genuine occupational qualifications

Remedies are in the form of compensation which is now unlimited for sex discrimination and race discrimination.

Remedies

Sex discrimination is also covered by Article 119 and Directive 76/207 (the equal treatment directive). This can be directly enforced against the State as an employer or an emanation of the State (*Marshall v Southampton & South-West Hampshire Area Health Authority* (1986)).

EC law

Chapter 17

Individual Employment Rights (2)

The contract of employment may be terminated at common law in various ways, some of which do not amount to a dismissal eg death, mutual agreement, expiry of a fixed term contract (although this may amount to a statutory dismissal) and frustration. Frustration occurs where there is an unforeseen event which either makes it impossible for the contract to be performed at all, or at least renders its performance as something radically different from what the parties envisaged when they made the contract; the event must have occurred without the fault of either contracting party eg imprisonment or sickness. Termination by dismissal occurs where there is dismissal by notice, dismissal for fundamental breach or wrongful dismissal.

17.1   Termination

If the employer wishes to terminate his employee's employment, he must give the minimum period of notice stated required by the contract of employment or if there is nothing in the contract, the amount of notice required by s 49 EPCA 1978. Section 49 states that where an employee has been continuously employed between one month and two years he shall be given one week's notice; if he is employed for more than two years he is entitled to one week's notice for each year of employment subject to a maximum of 12 weeks.

17.2   Notice

Either party may waive their right to notice or terminate without notice in response to a serious breach of the contract by the other. The employer may give wages or salary in lieu of notice and s 49 does not prevent the employee from accepting such payment. To avoid legal action by the employee, the employer must have a legitimate reason in the eyes of the law to terminate the contract of employment. Where the employee wishes to terminate his contract of employment, he must give the minimum period of notice as stipulated in his contract. If there is nothing stated he must give a minimum of one weeks notice (s 49(2) EPCA 1978).

An employer may summarily dismiss his employee (ie without notice) for conduct which is judged to be sufficiently serious. In these circumstances the employee will lose his right to contractual and statutory notice. Conduct such as theft, violence etc will warrant such action on the part of the employer (see *Wilson v Racher* (1974). If the summary dismissal

17.2.1   Summary dismissal for fundamental breach

is not justified the employee may bring an action at common law for wrongful dismissal.

17.2.2   Wrongful dismissal

An action for wrongful dismissal at common law may be brought by an employee who does not qualify for unfair dismissal protection provided by the EPCA; or by an employee who has been dismissed unjustifiably without notice or has not been given the required period of notice. Following the Industrial Tribunals Extension of Jurisdiction (England and Wales) Order 1994, an action for breach of the employment contract may be commenced in the IT, subject to an award limit of £25,000. Compensation in the form of wages and damages can, in general, only be awarded for the notice period and will be subject to the calculation of damages in contract. How far other contractual remedies such as specific performance and injunctions are available is open to debate. Injunctions restraining a dismissal have been issued where the rules of natural justice have not been followed in circumstances where the employee is in public employment.

In *Irani v South West Hampshire Health Authority* (1985) the plaintiff was an ophthalmologist who was employed part-time in an out-patient eye clinic. He was dismissed with six weeks notice because of irreconcilable differences with the consultant in charge of the clinic. No criticism at all was made of his competence or conduct. In dismissing him the employers were in breach of the disciplinary procedure established by the Whitley Council and incorporated into his contract of employment. He sought an injunction to prevent the employers from dismissing him without first following the appropriate disciplinary procedure. The employers argued that this would be contrary to the general rule that injunctions cannot be issued to keep a contract of employment alive. The plaintiff successfully obtained his injunction on the basis that the case fell within the exception to the general rule in that trust and confidence remained between the employer and the employee; the breakdown in confidence between the consultant and Mr Irani did not affect Irani's relationship with the employer; secondly, damages was not an adequate remedy in this case since Mr Irani would become virtually unemployable throughout the National Health Service.

There have been further important decisions in this area eg *Ridge v Baldwin* (1964) in which a chief constable was dismissed without a proper opportunity to be heard in his own defence. He obtained a declaration that the decision to dismiss him was a nullity as it was in breach of the rules of natural justice. See also *Powell v LB Brent* (1987) in which an interlocutory injunction for specific performance was obtained.

It had previously been thought that an order for specific performance could not be awarded in respect of a contract of employment because the requisite mutual trust and confidence has generally been destroyed.

Employees who qualify for protection under the EPCA 1978 have the right not to be unfairly dismissed ie the employer must show that the reason for the dismissal was reasonable. The EPCA 1978 provides greater protection and a wider range of remedies for the unfairly dismissed employee and in this respect is a much needed provision in the light of the inadequacies of the common law. However, as the law has developed so has its complexity with the statistics revealing the low success rate of complaints eg in 1990/1 6,066 cases were actually heard by ITs – 3,536 were dismissed and 2,530 were upheld; of these only 63 ended in an order for reinstatement and re-engagement; the median award was £1,773.

17.2.3   Unfair dismissal

Protection from unfair dismissal under the EPCA 1978 is only available to employees ie those employed under a contract of service. There are further limits on those who pass this initial qualification.

The basic rule is that an employee must have worked at least 16 hours per week and have two years continuous employment in order to qualify. There is a presumption that continuity exists. The onus is therefore on the employer to show that it does not. After five years continuous employment provided the employee works eight hours per week he will be regarded as continuously employed and will therefore qualify.

17.3   Who qualifies under the EPCA?

The following people are specifically excluded from the unfair dismissal provisions of the EPCA:

- Share fishermen.

- Any employee who has reached the normal retirement age (this is recognised as 65 for men and women under the SDA 1986; or if relevant the contractual retirement age.

- Persons ordinarily employed outside Great Britain.

- Workers on fixed-term contracts who have waived in writing their right to claim if the contract is not renewed;

- Police and armed forces

- Where there is in existence a dismissal procedure agreement between the employer and an independent trade union which has been approved by the Secretary of State.

- Employees who at the time of their dismissal are taking industrial action or are locked out and there has been no selective dismissal or re-engagement of those taking part. Unofficial strikers may be selectively dismissed or re-engaged (Trade Union Labour Relations (Consolidation) Act (TULR(C)A) 1992 ss 237-238).

- Where the settlement of a claim for dismissal has been agreed with the involvement of ACAS and the employee has agreed to withdraw his/her complaint.

17.3.1   Claims

An applicant must bring a claim within three months of the effective date of termination. The IT may extend this limit if it considers that it was not reasonably practicable for the applicant to present it in time. The date of termination is therefore of importance in deciding whether a claim is made in time as well as the length of service etc.

17.3.2   Effective date of termination

The same rules apply for unfair dismissal and redundancy, although with respect to redundancy it is known as 'the relevant date'.

- Where the contract of employment is terminated by notice, whether by the employer or employee, the date of termination is the date on which the notice expires. If an employee is dismissed with notice, but is given a payment in lieu of notice, the effective date of termination is the date when the notice expires- *Adams v GKN Sankey* (1980).

- Where the contract of employment is terminated without notice, the date of termination is the date on which the termination takes effect ie the actual date of dismissal, not the date on which the notice would expire (*Robert Cort & Sons v Charman* (1981)). The exception to this rule is provided by s 55(5) EPCA, where the effective date is extended, either where summary dismissal has occurred despite the employee being entitled to the statutory minimum notice or where the actual notice given was less than that required by statute. In both cases the effective date is the expiration of the statutory notice period.

- Where the employer is employed under a contract for a fixed term, the date of termination is the date on which the term expires.

  One important issue has been what the effective date of termination is where the employee invokes the internal appeals procedure. It appears that if the appeal is subsequently rejected, the effective date is the date of the original dismissal (*J Sainsbury Ltd v Savage* (1981), unless the contract provides for the contrary (*West Midlands Co-operative Society v Tipton* (1986)).

The onus is on the employee to show that he has been dismissed within the meaning of the Act (s 55 EPCA). There are three ways in which dismissal can take place.

The employer may terminate the contract with or without notice. Such a dismissal may be made orally or in writing; however, if made orally the words used should be unambiguous (see *Futty v Brekkes Ltd* (1974)). Where the words are ambiguous the effect of the statement is determined by an objective test ie would the reasonable employer or employee have understood the words to be tantamount to a dismissal. One of the problems for the courts has been deciding whether there has been a dismissal within the meaning of the Act.

A termination which is mutually agreed between the employer and employee is not a dismissal. However, the courts have with some reluctance upheld this practice as it may work to the advantage of the employer in avoiding employment rights and thereby lead to an abuse of a dominant position. The courts will look closely to see whether there is genuine mutual agreement; this will be a question of fact in each case.

In *Igbo v Johnson Matthey Chemicals Ltd* (1986) the applicant requested extended leave to visit her husband and children in Nigeria. This was granted by her employers on the condition that she signed a document which stated that she had agreed to return to work on the 28 September 1986 and if she failed to do so her contract of employment would automatically terminate on that date. She signed the document. She failed to return on the due date because she was ill and as a result her contract was terminated. It was held by the Court of Appeal that the contract had not been terminated by mutual agreement but by dismissal. The document amounted to a means of avoiding employment rights and was therefore void by virtue of s 140(1).

It should be noted that where the employee is under notice of termination and he gives the employer a counter notice indicating an intention to leave before the expiry of the employer's notice, he is still deemed to have been dismissed for the purposes of the EPCA. Any counter notice must be in writing with respect to a claim for redundancy but not unfair dismissal.

Where the employee 'invites' a termination of his contract either by his inaction or conduct, this may amount to dismissal.

In *Martin v Yeoman Aggregates Ltd* (1983) Martin refused to get a spare part for the director's car. The director angrily told

17.4   Dismissal

17.4.1   Express termination of the contract of employment by the employer

the employee to get out. Five minutes later the director took back what he had said and instead suspended Martin without pay until he could act more rationally. Martin insisted that he had been dismissed. It was held that it was vital to industrial relations that both the employer and employee should have the opportunity to withdraw their words. It was up to a tribunal to decide whether the withdrawal had come too late to be effective.

Certainly immediate retraction is effective. However, a subsequent retraction will only be effective with the consent of the other party.

Where the employer invites the employee to resign this may amount to a dismissal. In *Robertson v Securicor Transport Ltd* (1972) Robertson had broken one of the works rules by signing for a load which had not actually been received. When his employer discovered what he had done they gave him the option of resignation or dismissal. He chose resignation. It was held that resignation in these circumstances amounted to dismissal by the employer because in effect there was no alternative action open to the employee. He would have been dismissed if he had not opted to resign on the invitation of his employer.

17.4.2	Expiration of a fixed term contract

As we have seen in certain situations a fixed term contract may be excluded from the protection afforded by the EPCA ie where the employee agrees before the term expires to forgo any claim for unfair dismissal. However, if a fixed term contract is not renewed and it is not within the excluded category, the failure to renew amounts to a dismissal (whether it is a fair dismissal is another issue). The courts have found it necessary to distinguish between a fixed term contract and a contract which terminates on the completion of a particular job or task – the latter being outside the EPCA provisions. Contracts terminable on the happening or non-happening of a particular event even if it is a future event, have been found to be a 'task' contract – see *Brown v Knowsley Borough Council* (1986).

The EPCA s 2 further requires that if the agreement amounts to a fixed term contract, the duration of the contract must be certain ie there must be a date on which the contract expires. It follows, therefore, that a contract to do a specific job which does not refer to a completion date cannot be a fixed term contract since the duration of the contract is uncertain.

Furthermore, at one time it was thought that a fixed term contract must run for the whole of the term and must not be capable of termination before the term expired eg by a clause giving either party the right to terminate (see *BBC v Ioannou*

(1975)). However, in *Dixon v BBC* (1979) it was held that a fixed term contract could exist even though it could be terminated by either party before it had run its full term.

Constructive dismissal is an important concept since the law recognises that an employee may be entitled to protection where he is put in a position in which he is forced to resign. Constructive dismissal arises where the employee is forced to terminate his contract with or without notice due to the conduct of his employer. The main problem for the courts is in deciding whether the employer's conduct warrants the action taken by the employee. It is now firmly decided that in order to permit the employee to constructively dismiss himself, the employer's actions must amount to a breach of contract and must therefore be more than merely unreasonable conduct.

17.4.3   Constructive dismissal

In *Western Excavating Ltd v Sharp* (1978) Sharp took time off from work without permission. When his employer discovered this he was dismissed. He appealed to an internal disciplinary board which substituted a penalty of five days suspension without pay. He agreed to accept this decision but asked his employer for an advance on his holiday pay as he was short of money; this was refused. He then asked for a loan of £40 which was also refused. As a result he decided to resign since this would at least mean that he would receive his holiday pay. At the same time he claimed unfair dismissal on the basis that he was forced to resign because of his employers' unreasonable conduct. Initially the tribunal found in Sharp's favour ie the employer's conduct was so unreasonable Sharp could not be expected to continue working there. However, the case eventually went to the Court of Appeal where it was decided that before a valid constructive dismissal can take place the employers' conduct must amount to a breach of contract which is such that it entitles the employee to resign. In this particular case there was no breach by the employer and therefore there was no constructive dismissal.

It would appear that if the breach by the employer is to allow the employee to resign it must be a breach of some significance and must go to the root of the contract eg a unilateral change in the employees' terms (express or implied and conditions of employment (see *British Aircraft Corporation v Austin* (1978)). If the employee does not resign in the event of a breach by his employer he will be deemed to have accepted the breach and waived his rights. However, the law recognises that he need not resign immediately but may, for example, wait until he has found another job (see *Cox Toner (International) Ltd v Crook* (1981)).

It is also recognised that a series of minor incidents can have a cumulative effect which results in a fundamental breach amounting to repudiation of the contract by the employer (*Woods v WM Car Services (Peterborough)* (1982) – the so-called 'last straw doctrine').

In *Simmonds v Dowty Seals Ltd* (1978) Simmonds was employed to work on the night shift. His employer attempted to force him to work on the day shift by threatening to take industrial action if he refused to be transferred from the night shift. He resigned. It was held that he was entitled to resign and could treat himself as constructively dismissed because the employers' conduct amounted to an attempt to unilaterally change an express term of his contract ie that he was employed to work nights.

The employee may also be able to claim where he is forced to resign when the employer is in breach of an implied term in the contract of employment. Although it must be stressed that the employee must not only be able to show the existence of the implied term but also what is required by the implied term ie its scope (see *Gardner Ltd v Beresford* (1978)).

It is also possible for the conduct of an immediate superior to amount to a fundamental breach on the part of the employer as long as the test for establishing vicarious liability is satisfied (*Hilton International Hotels Ltd (UK) Ltd v Protopapa* (1990)).

As a result of the decision in *Western Excavating Ltd v Sharp* it is clear that unreasonable conduct alone which makes life difficult for the employee so that he is put in a position where he is forced to resign will not automatically be deemed to be a constructive dismissal unless it can be found to be a breach of the express or implied terms on the part of the employer. The employee may have to depend on the generosity of the courts in establishing a breach of an implied term.

In the case of *Pepper & Hope v Daish* (1980), in December 1978, Pepper, who was employed by the defendants, negotiated for himself an hourly wage rate. In January 1979 his employers increased the hourly rate of all workers by 5% with the exception of Pepper. The employer would not increase Pepper's hourly rate accordingly and as a result Pepper resigned. He claimed constructive dismissal. It was held that Pepper would succeed in his claim. The tribunal was prepared to imply a term into his contract that he would be given any wage increases received by the hourly rate workers. Such a term had therefore been broken by his employer forcing him to resign. Whether the courts will always be as generous in their interpretation is open to debate.

An employee who is dismissed within the meaning of the Act is entitled to a written statement of the reasons for his dismissal (s 53 EPCA). He or she must, however, have been continuously employed for two years (s 15 Employment Act 1989). The employee must request the statement and it must be supplied within 14 days of this request. Failure to do so or to provide particulars which are inadequate or untrue will allow the employee to make a complaint to an IT. If the tribunal finds in favour of the employee it may declare the real reason for the dismissal and award the employee two weeks' pay. It has been held that a 'conscientiously formed belief that there was no dismissal was a reasonable ground for refusing to provide a written statement' (*Brown v Stuart Scott & Co* (1981)). The written statement is admissible in proceedings and any inconsistency between the contents of the statement and the reason actually put forward could seriously undermine the employer's case.

17.4.4   Reasons for the dismissal

Once the employee has established that he has been dismissed, be it by his employer or constructively, the onus moves to the employer to show that he acted reasonably in dismissing the employee and therefore the dismissal was fair (EPA 1980 s 3). The test of reasonableness requires consideration of what a reasonable employer would have done in the circumstances ie does it fall within 'the band of reasonable responses to the employee's conduct within which one employer might take one view, another quite reasonably another' (*Iceland Frozen Foods v Jones* (1982)). Whether the test is satisfied is a question of fact in each case. However, the IT will have regard to the substantive merits eg length of service, previous disciplinary record and any other mitigating circumstances with a view to maintaining consistency of treatment and procedural fairness ie whether the employer has adhered to the ACAS Code of Practice: Disciplinary Practices and Procedures in Employment which involves the provision of formal warnings, internal hearings, appeals procedures etc. The Code may be used as evidence to show that the employer has not acted reasonably.

17.5   Fair dismissals

In *Polkey v AE Dayton Services Ltd* (1987) Polkey was employed as a van driver. His employer in order to avoid more financial losses decided to make three van drivers redundant. There was no prior consultation; Polkey was merely handed a letter informing him that he was being made redundant. Polkey claimed that this amounted to unfair dismissal as the failure to consult showed that the employer had not acted reasonably in treating redundancy as a sufficient reason for dismissing him. It was held that in deciding whether the employer had acted reasonably the tribunal should have regard to the facts at the time of the dismissal and should not base their judgment on facts brought to light after the dismissal, such as whether the failure to consult would have made any difference to the dismissal or whether the employee had in practice suffered an injustice.

The importance of the decision in this case cannot be understated. As a result of this decision, procedural fairness is of paramount importance when considering the issue of unfair dismissal.

The grounds on which a dismissal is capable of being fair are laid down in s 57 of the EPCA. We shall consider each ground in turn.

17.5.1	Capability or qualifications

Capability is defined in s 57(4) as 'assessed by reference to skill, aptitude, health or any other physical or mental quality.' Whereas qualifications means 'any degree, diploma, or other academic, technical or professional qualification relevant to the position which the employee held.' In *Blackman v Post Office* (1974) Blackman was a telegraph officer. He was required to pass an aptitude test. He was allowed the maximum number of attempts which was three and he still failed. He was then dismissed. It was held that as the taking of an aptitude test was a qualification requirement of that job his dismissal was fair.

Before dismissing an employee for incompetence the employer should have regard to the ACAS code which offers some guidance on improving poor performance and certainly no dismissal should take place without formal warnings providing the employee with an opportunity to redress his position, unless the potential consequences of the incompetence are so serious that warnings are inappropriate (*Taylor v Alidair* (1978)).

The employer must not only be able to show that, for example, the employee was incompetent or inadequately qualified but that in the circumstances it was reasonable to dismiss him ie what would the reasonable employer have done? The court will have regard to all the surrounding circumstances such as training, supervision, what alternatives were available eg could the employee have been redeployed in another job etc. He may also have to show that he gave his employee a chance to improve his standing. If the employer is to be deemed to have acted reasonably he must be able to show that dismissal was the last resort.

In *Davison v Kent Meters Ltd* (1975) Davison worked on an assembly line. She was dismissed as a result of assembling 500 components incorrectly. She alleged that she had merely followed the instructions of the chargehand. The chargehand maintained that he had not given her any instructions. It was held that the dismissal was unfair. Davison should have received supervision and training in the assembly of the components. It was clear from the evidence that she had not; therefore her employer had not acted reasonably in dismissing her.

Persistent absenteeism may be treated as misconduct and should be treated under the disciplinary procedure. However, a long term absence, such as long term sickness should be treated as incapability. Whether the employer's action to dismiss for long term sickness absence is reasonable will depend on the particular circumstances of each case eg the nature of the illness, the length of the absence, the need to replace the absent employee etc. The employer will be expected to make a reasonable effort to inform himself of the true medical position of the employee. Although the consent of the employee is needed before access to medical records can be gained.

In deciding whether a dismissal for misconduct is to be regarded as fair, attention must be paid to the nature of the offence and the disciplinary procedure. For example, gross or serious misconduct may justify instant dismissal, whereas a trivial act may only warrant a warning in line with the disciplinary procedure. The word 'misconduct' is not defined in the EPCA, but it is established that it covers assault, refusal to obey instructions, persistent lateness, moonlighting, drunkenness, dishonesty, failing to implement safety procedures etc. Whether the commission of a criminal offence outside employment justifies a dismissal will depend upon its relevance to the actual job carried out by the employee.

17.5.2   Conduct

Before any dismissal for misconduct takes place, the employer must have established a genuine and reasonable belief in the guilt of the employee. This may involve carrying out a reasonable investigation. A false accusation without reasonable foundation may result in the employee resigning and claiming constructive dismissal (*Robinson v Crompton Parkinson Ltd* (1978)).

Remember that reference must also be made to what the reasonable employer would have done ie the test is an objective one.

In *Taylor v Parsons Peebles Ltd* (1981) a works' rule prohibited fighting. It was also the policy of the company to dismiss anyone caught fighting. The applicant had been employed by the company for 20 years without complaint. He was caught fighting and was dismissed. It was held that the dismissal was unfair. Regard must be had to the previous 20 years of employment without incident. The tribunal decided that the reasonable employer would not have applied the sanction of instant dismissal as rigidly because of the mitigating circumstances.

Where the employer is unable to identify the 'real culprit', the dismissal of all those involved may be fair, even where it is probable that not all were guilty of the act, provided three conditions are satisfied:

- The act of misconduct warrants dismissal;

- The IT is satisfied that the act was committed by at least one of the group being dismissed and all were capable of committing the act;

- The IT is satisfied that the employer has carried out a proper investigation to attempt to identify the persons responsible (see *Whitbread & Co v Thomas* (1988)).

In *Parr v Whitbread plc* (1990) Parr was employed as a branch manager at an off-licence owned by the respondents. He and three other employees were dismissed after it was discovered that £4,000 had been stolen from the shop in circumstances which suggested that it was an inside job. Each of the four had an equal opportunity to commit the theft and the employers found it impossible to ascertain which of them was actually guilty. It was held that applying the test in the *Thomas* case that the dismissals were fair.

17.5.3   Redundancy

Redundancy is *prima facie* a fair reason for dismissal. However, the employer must show that the reason for the dismissal was due to redundancy (s 57(2) EPCA). He must therefore be able to establish 'redundancy' within the meaning of the EPCA. A dismissal for reason of redundancy will be unfair if the employer had not acted as the reasonable employer would have acted in the circumstances. The following matters should be considered before the redundancies are put into effect:

- To give as much warning as possible;

- To consult with the trade union (see TULR[C]A ss 188-98);

- To adopt an objective rather than a subjective criteria for selection;

- To select in accordance with the criteria;

- To consider the possibility of redeployment rather than dismissal.

(See *Williams v Compair Maxam Ltd* (1982)).

In *Allwood v William Hill Ltd* (1974) William Hill Ltd decided to close down 12 betting shops. Without any warning they made all the managers redundant. They offered no alternative employment. The managers, as employees, complained that this amounted to unfair dismissal. It was held that in the circumstances this amounted to unfair dismissal. The employer should have considered possible alternatives such as transfer to other betting shops. Furthermore, the way in which the redundancies had taken place was not the way a reasonable employer would have acted.

It is important to realise that just because there is a redundancy situation within the meaning of the Act it does not automatically follow that any dismissal due to redundancy will be fair.

An important issue is whether the criteria used for selection of those employees who are to be made redundant is fair eg first in, first out (FIFO) or last in, first out (LIFO) or part-time staff first which may also amount to discrimination. Contravention of customary practices may be evidence that the dismissal is unfair.

In *Hammond-Scott v Elizabeth Arden Ltd* (1976) the applicant was selected for redundancy because she was close to retirement age. She had been employed by the defendants for many years but this was not taken into account when she was selected for redundancy. It was held that her selection for redundancy amounted to unfair dismissal because the employer had not acted reasonably in the circumstances. In view of her age, length of service and the fact that she was close to retirement age it would have had little financial effect on the company if they had continued to employ her until she retired.

In the following situation selection for redundancy will automatically be deemed to be unfair: where employees in similar positions are not made redundant and the reason a particular employee was selected for redundancy was because he was a member or non-member of a trade union or participated in trade union activities (s 153 TULR[C]A – this is no longer subject to any qualifying period of service).

If the dismissal is because the continued employment of the employee would result in a contravention of a statute or subordinate legislation either on the part of the employer or employee, the dismissal will be *prima facie* fair. For example, if the employee has been banned from driving yet his job requires him to hold a current driving licence; if he continues to fulfil his job specification he would be in breach of the Road

17.5.4   Statutory restrictions (s 57(2)(d))

Traffic Acts (*Fearn v Tayford Motor Company Ltd* (1975)); or if the employer in continuing to employ someone, was found to be contravening the Food and Drugs Acts.

As with all cases of dismissal the employer must act as the reasonable employer and must therefore consider any possible alternatives if the dismissal is to be regarded as fair (*Sandhu v Dept of Education & Science London Borough of Hillingdon* (1978)).

17.5.5	Some other substantial reason

Where the employer is unable to show that the reason for the dismissal was one of those referred to above, he may show 'some other substantial reason' (s 57(1)(b) EPCA). There is no exhaustive list of what is recognised in law as 'some other substantial reason'. The employer must not only show that his actions were reasonable, but also that the reason was 'substantial'. The following have been held to be valid reasons for dismissal although you must appreciate that it is a question of fact in each case:

- Conflict of personalities, primarily the fault of the employee; see *Treganowan v Robert Knee & Co* (1975). Dismissal should be a last resort after attempts to improve relations have taken place.

- Failure to disclose material facts in obtaining employment eg mental illness (see *O'Brien v Prudential Assurance Co Ltd* (1979)).

- Commercial reasons eg pressure from important customers to dismiss the employee (*Grootcon [UK] Ltd v Keld* (1984)).

- Failure to accept changes in the terms of employment; see *Storey v Allied Brewery* (1977). Any change must be justified by the employer as being necessary.

- Non-renewal of a fixed term contract; the employer must show a genuine need for temporary contracts and that the employee knew of the temporary nature of the contract from the outset (*North Yorkshire County Council v Fay* (1985)).

- A dismissal which satisfies Regulation 8(2) Transfer of Undertakings (Protection of Employment) Regulations 1981 in so far as the dismissal is for an 'economic, technical or organisational reason entailing changes in the workforce and the employer is able to show that his actions were reasonable'. Where the employer can satisfy Regulation 8 the employee may be able to claim redundancy (*Gorictree Ltd v Jenkinson* (1984)). Any other dismissal in connection with the transfer of the business is automatically unfair (*Litster v Forth Dry Dock & Engineering Co Ltd* (1989)).

The following are situations where dismissal is automatically unfair:

Where the employee is dismissed because of his actual or proposed membership of an independent trade union, or because he is not a member of a trade union or refuses to become a member, the dismissal is automatically unfair. This is also the case where the employee has taken part or proposes to take part in any trade union activities. The employee need not have the required qualifying period of employment in order to bring an action for unfair dismissal under this section.

The Trade Union Reform and Employment Rights Act 1993 s 24 provides that an employee is automatically unfairly dismissed where the principal reason for the dismissal is pregnancy or a reason connected with her pregnancy; or following her maternity leave period, dismissal for childbirth or a reason connected with child birth; this amends s 60 EPCA 1978.

Dismissals during strike or lock out are governed by TULR(C)A 1992 s 238. Generally dismissal of the participants during a strike, lock-out or other industrial action is not unfair as long as all those participating are dismissed and none re-engaged within three months of the dismissal. However, if only some of the participants are dismissed or have not been offered re-engagement within the three month period, an unfair dismissal claim may be brought. This exception is subject to the action being regarded as official by trade unions (s 20 TULR(C)A).

Where an employer dismisses an employee because of industrial pressure brought to bear by other employees the dismissal may be unfair. Section 63 provides that industrial pressure such as the threat of a strike if the applicant continues to be employed by the employer should be ignored by the tribunal which must consider the dismissal on the basis of whether the employer had acted reasonably.

Where pressure is put on an employer to dismiss the applicant by a trade union, because the applicant was not a member of a trade union, the trade union may be joined by the employer or applicant as party to the proceedings. The tribunal may then make an award against the trade union if it finds that the dismissal was unfair.

TURERA 1993 provides that an employee has the right not to be dismissed for:

17.6 Special situations

17.6.1 Trade union membership or activities (TULR(C)A 1992 s 152(1))

17.6.2 Pregnancy or childbirth

17.6.3 Industrial action

17.6.4 Industrial pressure

- Carrying out or proposing to carry out any health and safety activities for which he is designated by the employer;

- Bringing to his employer's attention, by reasonable means and in the absence of a safety representative or committee who could do so on his behalf, a reasonable health and safety concern (see *Harris v Select Timber Frame Ltd* (1994));

- In the event of danger which he could reasonably believe to be serious and imminent and which he could not reasonably be expected to avert, leaving or proposing to leave the workplace or any dangerous part of it, or (while the danger persisted) refusing to return;

- In circumstances of danger which he *reasonably* believes to be serious and imminent, taking or proposing to take appropriate steps to protect himself or other persons from danger.

17.7   Remedies

Where the dismissal is found to be unfair the tribunal has the power to make an order for reinstatement, re-engagement or compensation (of various types).

17.7.1   Reinstatement

In the case of reinstatement, the tribunal must ask the applicant if he wishes such an order to be made. The effect of an order for reinstatement is that the employer must treat the employee as if he had not been dismissed ie his employment is on the same or improved terms and conditions.

17.7.2   Re-engagement

If the applicant so wishes, the tribunal may make an order for re-engagement. The effect of this is that the applicant should be re-engaged by the employer or an associated employer in employment which is comparable to his previous employment or amounts to other suitable employment. The tribunal will specify the terms on which the applicant should be re-engaged and this may make provision for arrears of pay. The making of orders for reinstatement and re-engagement is at the discretion of the tribunal who will consider whether it is just and equitable to make such an order considering the conduct of the employee and whether it is practicable to do so.

Failure to comply fully with the terms of an order for reinstatement or re-engagement will result in an award of compensation being made by the IT, having regard to the loss sustained by the complainant, usually the basic award plus an additional award. The employer may raise 'impracticability' as a defence to such a claim.

17.7.3   Compensation

An award of compensation will be made where an order for reinstatement or re-engagement is not complied with or it is not practicable to make such an order. There are various types of compensation.

The calculation of the basic award is dependent upon the amount of continuous service in years which the applicant has attained.

Entitlement:	Years	Weeks pay for each year of employment
Age	18-21	½
	22-40	1
	41-65	1½

The maximum number of years which can be counted is 20 and the maximum amount of weekly pay is currently £205. The maximum basic award is at present £6,150. The basic award may be reduced by the tribunal on the grounds of contributory conduct on the part of the applicant. Where there is also an award of redundancy payments, the basic award will be reduced by the amount of redundancy payment as long as it is established that the dismissal was for reason of redundancy.

A 'weeks pay' relates to gross pay; if aged 64 the award is reduced by one-twelfth for each month after the complainant's 64th birthday. The basic award will be two weeks' pay where the reason for the dismissal was redundancy and the employee unreasonably refuses to accept a renewal of the contract or suitable alternative employment.

This is in addition to the basic award and is awarded at the discretion of the tribunal. The amount of the award is decided upon by the tribunal on the grounds of what is 'just and equitable in all the circumstances having regard to the loss sustained by the applicant in consequence of the dismissal'. At present the maximum amount of this award is £11,000. The amount of the award may be reduced by failure on the part of the employee to mitigate his loss, contributory conduct and any ex-gratia payment by the employer.

In making the award the tribunal will take into account loss of wages; expenses incurred in taking legal action against the employer; loss of future earnings; loss of pension rights and other benefits eg company car, the manner of the dismissal.

An additional award can be made where the employer fails to comply with an order for reinstatement or re-engagement and fails to show that it was not practicable to comply with such an order. The amount of this additional award will be between 13 and 26 weeks pay; if the dismissal is unfair because it is based on sex or race discrimination the additional award will be between 26 and 52 weeks pay.

17.7.7   Special award

Where the dismissal was found to be unfair on the grounds of trade union membership or non-membership and the applicant wanted reinstatement or re-engagement, but the tribunal were unable to make such an order or where it made an order and the employer failed to comply with it, a special award may be made (s 157 TULR(C)A 1992).

Such an award is subject to the following rules:

• If no order in respect of reinstatement or re-engagement is made, the special award is one weeks pay x 104, subject to a minimum of £13,400 and to a maximum of £26,800.

• If the employer fails to comply with an order for reinstatement or re-engagement and fails to show that it was not practicable to do so, the award is one weeks pay x 156, subject to a minimum of £20,100 and no maximum figure.

• Any special award may be reduced because of contributory conduct on the part of the employee s 155 TULR(C)A. However, the statute recognises that the following conduct should be ignored:

   (a) a breach by the employee of an undertaking to become a member of a trade union or to cease to be a member of a trade union or not to take part in the activities of a trade union;

   (b) a breach of an undertaking to make a payment in lieu of union membership or any objection to the employer making a deduction from his or her wages to cover payments in lieu.

17.8   Interim relief

Where an employee alleges dismissal for union/non-union membership or trade union activities, he or she can apply to the IT for an order for interim relief (s 161 TULR(C)A 1992).

Such an order will preserve the status quo until a full hearing of the case and as the effect therefore of reinstating or re-engaging the employee. In order to obtain an order for interim relief an application must be made to the IT within seven days immediately following the effective date of termination. This must be supported by a certificate signed by an authorised trade union official where the allegation relates to dismissal for trade union membership or taking part in trade union activities. Finally, it must appear to the IT that the complaint is likely to succeed at a full hearing.

Even where these conditions are satisfied the IT must then determine whether the employer is willing to reinstate or re-engage the employee. If the employer is not so willing, then the IT must make an order for the continuation of the employee's contract of employment until the full hearing, thus preserving continuity, pay and other employment rights.

Where the employer fails to comply with an interim relief order the IT must:

- Make an order for the continuation of the contract; and

- Order the employer to pay such compensation as the IT believes is just and equitable, having regard to the loss suffered by the employee.

Where an employer fails to observe the terms of a continuation order the IT shall:

- Determine the amount of any money owed to the employee;

- Order the employer to pay the employee such compensation as is considered just and equitable.

17.9 Redundancy

When an employee's services are no longer required by the business, either through the closing down of that business or perhaps the introduction of new technology, he will in general have been made redundant. Whether or not he is entitled to redundancy pay will depend upon whether the qualification rules and the key essentials are satisfied. The law in this area is weighted in favour of the employer who in order to avoid the higher compensation limits for unfair dismissal may well try to disguise an unfair dismissal situation as redundancy. The law relating to redundancy can be found in the Employment Protection (Consolidation) Act 1978 (EPCA) as amended. The purpose of the Act is to provide for the payment of compensation based on an employee's service and wages, to tide the employee over the period in which he is without a job. However, any entitlement to redundancy payments only exists where it is established that the employee's dismissal was by reason of redundancy within the meaning of the Act.

17.10 Qualifications

In assessing whether an employee qualifies for redundancy payment, the same rules apply as for unfair dismissal, so an employee must have been continuously employed by the same employer or an associated employer for a minimum of 16 hours per week for two years or, alternatively, eight hours per week for five years. The onus is on the employer to show that continuity has been broken or that there are weeks which do not count towards continuity and once again the same rules apply regarding continuity. Certain categories of employee are excluded from the provisions of the Act (as referred to earlier); some cases because existing arrangements between their employer and their trade union are better than the protection afforded by the Act.

17.11 Dismissal

The burden of proof in the initial stages of any claim for redundancy is on the employee to show that he was dismissed. There is then a presumption that the dismissal was for reason of redundancy and the burden moves to the employer to show that redundancy was not the reason for the dismissal.

Where an employee meets the basic qualification requirements he must show that he has been dismissed within the meaning of s 83 EPCA. Again the provisions which determine dismissal are the same as for unfair dismissal. An employee shall be treated as dismissed by his employer if, but only if:

- The contract of employment is terminated by the employer with or without notice; or

- It is a fixed term contract which has expired without being renewed; or

- The employee terminates the contract with or without notice in circumstances which are such that he is entitled to terminate it without notice by reason of the employer's conduct.

- The contract is terminated by the death of the employer, or the dissolution or liquidation of the firm (s 93).

It is clear, however, that the initiative to 'dismiss' the employee must come from the employer. An employee who resigns is not entitled to redundancy payment unless the constructive dismissal provision is satisfied (*Walley v Morgan* (1969)).

Whether a dismissal is within ss 83 or 93 is a question of fact in each case. For example, a variation in the terms of the employee's contract will amount to a dismissal if he does not agree to the new terms. If, however, the employee accepts the new terms there can be no dismissal and continuity is preserved.

In *Marriot v Oxford & District Co-operative Society Ltd* (1970) Marriot was employed as a foreman by the defendants. He was informed that from a certain date he would be employed on a lower grade and his rate of pay would be reduced accordingly. It was held that the variation in the terms of the existing contract amounted to termination by the employer which Marriot could treat as dismissal.

Clearly, there may be a term in the contract which allows the employer to vary the terms. If the employee in this situation does not like the new terms and chooses to leave his employment this will not amount to a dismissal for the purposes of the Act. One type of contentious term has proved to be the 'mobility clause' which many executive contracts contain. Where an employee refuses to comply with an express mobility clause requiring him to move, the refusal amounts to misconduct and therefore any dismissal cannot be treated as redundancy, but could leave the employer open to a claim of unfair dismissal. Furthermore, if the employee attempts to anticipate the employers actions and resigns, the resignation will not amount to a dismissal.

In *Morton Sundour Fabrics v Shaw* (1967) Shaw was employed as a foreman by Morton. He was informed that there may be some redundancies in the near future, but nothing specific was decided. In the light of what he had been told he decided to leave the firm in order to take another job. It was held that he had not been dismissed and therefore was not entitled to redundancy payments. His precipitous action could not be shown to relate to the subsequent redundancies made by his employer.

Obviously he would have succeeded had he waited until he had received his notice of redundancy. However, when he resigned there was no way of knowing exactly who would be made redundant (see *Doble v Firestone Tyre & Rubber Co Ltd* (1981)) which followed the decision in Morton.

In order for the employee to be entitled to redundancy payments he must have been dismissed 'for reason of redundancy'. There is a presumption that once the employee has shown that he has been dismissed, the reason for the dismissal was redundancy (s 91(2)). The onus is on the employer to show that the dismissal was for some reason other than redundancy.

17.12   Dismissals for reasons of redundancy

The EPCA provides a definition of 'redundancy' (s 81(2)):

[This is where] 'dismissal is attributable wholly or mainly to

(a) the fact that his employer has ceased, or intends to cease, to carry on the business for the purposes of which the employee was employed by him, or has ceased, or intends to cease, to carry on that business in the place where the employee was so employed; or

(b) the fact that the requirements of that business for employees to carry out work of a particular kind, or for employees to carry out work of a particular kind in the place where they were so employed have ceased or diminished or are expected to cease or diminish.'

In effect there are three situations in which the dismissal can be said to be for redundancy. These are as follows:

17.12.1 Cessation of the employer's business

This covers both temporary and permanent closures of the employer's business in respect of the type of work carried on at the premises and is on the whole straightforward. In *Gemmell v Darngavil Brickworks Ltd* (1967) the brickworks closed for a period of 13 weeks for substantial repairs to be carried out. Some of the employees were dismissed. It was held that the dismissal was for reason of redundancy even though part of the premises were still in use.

17.12.2 Closure or change in the place of work

Where the employer ceases to trade at a particular place as opposed to the cessation of the type of work, the dismissal of his employees will usually be for reason of redundancy. This is subject to any contract of employment which contains a 'clear and unambiguous mobility clause'. Such clauses will rarely be implied.

In *O'Brien v Associated Fire Alarms Ltd* (1969) O'Brien was employed by the defendants at their Liverpool branch. There was a shortage of work and he was asked to work in Barrow-in-Furness. He refused and was dismissed by his employer. He contended that the dismissal amounted to redundancy. It was held that as there was no clause in O'Brien's contract of employment which would have allowed his employer to move him to a different location, the dismissal was for reason of redundancy.

Where the employer only moves his place of work a short distance and/or remains within the same town or conurbation, any offer of work at the new place of employment to his existing employees may prevent any dismissal from being for reason of redundancy. Obviously it will depend on accessibility to the new premises as well as the terms on which the offer is made – remember the terms must not be worse than existing terms. It can therefore be within the employer's expectations that his employees will move to different premises without there being a redundancy situation if it is reasonable in all the circumstances of the case.

In *Managers (Holborn) Ltd v Hohne* (1977) the defendants occupied premises in Holborn in which Hohne was a manageress. They decided to move their business to Regent Street which was only a short distance away. Hohne refused to move there and claimed redundancy on the basis that there was no term in her contract which required her to move. It was held that the new premises were just as accessible as the old ones and therefore it was reasonable for her employer to expect her to move without there being any issue of redundancy. There was no evidence of any additional inconvenience to Hohne if she agreed to move to the new premises. She did not therefore succeed in her action.

Finally, this provision has been interpreted in such a way that it will only be satisfied if the place of work where the employee actually works and is expected to work ceases. If, therefore, there is a mobility clause, closure of the original place of work resulting in a move to the new place will not amount to redundancy (*UK Atomic Energy Authority v Claydon* (1974)).

As a general rule, where the employer is forced to dismiss employees because of a reduction in the work available such employees are surplus to the requirements of the business and any dismissal is for reason of redundancy. Furthermore, where there is a change in systems of work so that fewer employees are actually needed to do the job, this too can amount to redundancy. The courts are, from time to time, faced with the difficult task of deciding whether dismissal for failing to keep up with modern working practices is for reason of redundancy.

17.12.3   Diminishing requirements for employees

In *North Riding Garages v Butterwick* (1967) Butterwick had been employed at the same garage for 30 years and had risen to the position of workshop manager. The garage was taken over by the appellants and Butterwick was dismissed for inefficiency on the grounds that he was unable or unwilling to accept new methods of work which would involve him in some administrative work. It was held that the dismissal was not for reason of redundancy because the employee was still expected to do the same type of work subject to new working practices. As far as the court was concerned employees who remain in the same employment for many years are expected to adapt to new techniques and methods of work and even higher standards of efficiency. It is only when the new practices affect the nature of the work so that in effect there is no requirement to do that particular kind of work that a redundancy situation may arise.

In *Hindle v Percival Boats Ltd* (1969) Hindle was employed in the repair of wooden boats and had been so for many years. This type of work was in decline because of the increasing use of glass-fibre. He was dismissed because he was 'too good and too slow' and it was uneconomical to keep him. He was not replaced; his work was merely absorbed by existing staff. It was held that Hindle's dismissal was not for reason of redundancy. The court felt that the employer was merely shedding surplus labour and that this was not within the Act.

Clearly there are situations where 'shedding surplus labour' will amount to redundancy; each case must be considered on its merits.

In *Haden Ltd v Cowen* (1982) Cowen was employed as a regional supervisor. He was based in Southampton and had to cover a large part of southern England as part of his job. He suffered a mild heart attack. He was then promoted to divisional contracts surveyor by his employer as it was thought that this would make his life less stressful. One of the terms of his contract required him to undertake, at the discretion of the company, any duties which reasonably fell within the scope of his capabilities. The company was later forced to reduce the number of employees at staff level. Cowen was not prepared to accept demotion and was dismissed. He claimed both redundancy and unfair dismissal. It was held that Cowen was dismissed for reason of redundancy because there was no other work available within the terms of his contract ie as divisional contracts manager.

It is suggested that the true test of redundancy is to be found in this case and the issue to be considered is 'whether the business needs as much work of the kind which the employee could by his contract lawfully be required to do'. This is not a question of the day-to-day function of the employee but what he could be expected to do under his contract of employment; see (*Pink v White & Co Ltd* (1985)). It is also clear from the case law that the re-organisation of work does not amount to redundancy where the employees concerned are subject to a flexible job description rather than being confined to work of a particular kind eg '... and any work which may be required by the employer'. Although, a move from day shift to night shift work or vice versa may be 'work of a particular kind' (*Macfisheries Ltd v Findlay* (1985)).

17.12.4   **Lay-off and short time (ss 87-89 EPCA)**

Redundancy payment may be claimed where an employee has been laid off or kept on short time for either four or more consecutive weeks or for a series of six or more weeks (of which not more than three are consecutive) within a period of

13 weeks. The employee must give written notice to his employer no later than four weeks from the end of the periods referred to, of his intention to claim redundancy payment and should terminate his employment by giving at least one week's notice or the period stipulated in the contract of employment. Following this action by the employee, the employer may serve a counter-notice within seven days of the employee's notice contesting the claim and stating that there is a reasonable chance that, within four weeks of the counter-notice the employee will commence a period of 13 weeks consecutive employment. This then becomes a matter for the tribunal.

If the employer withdraws the counter-notice or fails to employ the employee for 13 consecutive weeks the employee is entitled to the redundancy payment.

Under the EPCA continuity is preserved in the following situations, so that past service will count in the new employment:

17.13   Change in ownership and transfer of undertakings

- Change of partners;

- Where trustees or personal representatives take over the running of the company when the employer dies;

- Transfer of employment to an associated employer;

- Transfer of an undertaking, trade or business from one person to another.

Where there is a change in the ownership of a business and existing employees either have their contract renewed or are re-engaged by the new employer, this does not amount to redundancy and continuity is preserved (s 94) eg where the business is sold as a going concern, rather than a transfer of the assets. However, if the employee has reasonable grounds for refusing the offer of renewal he may be treated as redundant (s 82(6)).

Section 94 is subject to the Transfer of Undertakings (Protection of Employment) Regulations 1981. The Regulations apply to the sale or other disposition of commercial and non-commercial undertakings (see s 33 TURERA 1993 which brought the UK in line with EC Directive 77/187 – the Acquired Rights Directive). The transfer must be of the whole or part of a business, not merely a transfer of assets (*Melon v Hector Powe Ltd* (1980)); nor do the Regulations apply to a change in ownership resulting from a transfer of shares. Where there is the transfer of a business which is within the Regulations, the contracts of employment of the employees are also transferred, as if they had been made by the transferee. This not only protects continuity but puts the 'new' employer in the same position as the original employer. As a result all existing rights etc attained by employees are preserved and become enforceable against the new business. Such 'transfers' are subject to the consent of the employee. If the employee objects, the transfer will in effect terminate the contract of employment, but this termination will not amount to a 'dismissal' (TURERA s 33(4)). If following a transfer, there is a subsequent dismissal the employee may claim unfair dismissal or if it is for 'an economic, technical or organisational reason', redundancy payment may be claimed.

The contentious issue concerning the position of employees who are dismissed prior to a transfer (enabling the employers to evade the Regulations potentially) has been resolved by *Litster & Others v Forth Dry Dock & Engineering Co Ltd* (1989) in which it was decided that where employees are dismissed in these circumstances, they must be treated as if they were still employed at the time of transfer. As a result the Regulations are to be applied to such employees. The transferee employer will be responsible for any unfair dismissals unless they can be shown to be for an 'economic, technical or organisational' reason entailing a change in the workforce.

17.13.1 Offer of alternative employment

The offer of alternative employment is covered by s 82 EPCA 1978. The general rule is that where the employer makes an offer of suitable alternative employment which is unreasonably refused by the employee, the employee will be unable to claim redundancy. This contract, which is either a renewal or a re-engagement, must take effect on the expiry of the old contract or within four weeks. Clearly, the main issue is what amounts to 'suitable'. Consideration must be had of the old terms and conditions compared with the new ones, ie the nature of the work, remuneration, hours, place, skills and experience including qualifications etc. Where the conditions of the new contract do not differ materially from the old contract regarding place, nature of the work pay etc. then the question of suitability does not arise. It is a question of fact in each case as to whether an offer can be deemed 'suitable' with the onus resting on the employer to establish suitability. However, the facts must be considered objectively.

In *Taylor v Kent CC* (1969) Taylor was made redundant from his post as headmaster of a school. He was offered a place in the pool of supply teachers from which temporary absences were filled in schools. There was no loss of salary or other rights other than status. Taylor refused the offer. It was held that his refusal was reasonable. The offer was not suitable because of the loss of status since he was being removed from a position as head of a school to an ordinary teacher.

A loss of fringe benefits has been held to be a reasonable refusal (*Sheppard v NCB* (1966)). However, the refusal of an offer of a job which may only last a short period could be deemed to be unreasonable (*Morganite Crucible v Street* (1972)). The issue for the IT is two-fold: firstly whether the job offered is suitable and then whether the employee has acted reasonably in refusing the offer (*Spencer & Griffin v Gloucestershire CC* (1985)).

In considering whether a refusal by the employee is reasonable, regard must be had for the personal circumstances of the employee, such as housing and domestic problems. It may be reasonable for an employee to refuse a job offer which involves a move to London when he lives in the Midlands because of the housing problems associated with a move to the Home Counties. However, a refusal based upon a personal whim will be unreasonable (see *Fuller v Stephanie Bowman (Sales) Ltd* (1977). In *Rawe v Power Gas Corporation* (1966) it was held to be reasonable to refuse a move from the south-east of England to Teeside because of marital difficulties. Finally, even where the IT finds that the offer was suitable, it does not automatically follow that a refusal by the employee is unreasonable (*Cambridge & District Co-operative Society Ltd v Ruse* (1993)).

Remember the onus is on the employer to show that the employee's rejection of the offer is unreasonable. Where the offer of alternative employment is accepted by the employee there is deemed to be continuity of employment between the former contract and the new contract.

The employee is entitled to a trial period of four weeks (or longer if agreed with the employer) if his contract is renewed on different terms and conditions. If the employee terminates his employment during the trial period for a reason connected with the new contract, he will be treated as having been dismissed on the date his previous contract was terminated. Whether he will be entitled to redundancy will depend on whether it was a suitable offer of alternative employment and whether his refusal to accept it was reasonable (see *Meek v Allen Rubber Co Ltd & Secretary of State for Employment* (1980)). If the employer dismisses the employee during the trial period for whatever reason, the dismissal is to be treated as redundancy.

An employee is entitled to a reasonable amount of time off to seek work or retrain once notice of redundancy has been

17.13.2   Trial period (s 84 EPCA)

received (s 31 EPCA). This right is confined to those employees who meet the qualifying periods. Failure to provide time off may result in the employee making a complaint to an IT who may award two-fifths of a week's pay.

17.14 Calculation of redundancy payment

The employee must inform his employer, in writing, of his intention to claim a redundancy payment from him. If the employer does not make the payment or there is a dispute over entitlement the matter is referred to an industrial tribunal. As a general rule the claim must be made within six months of the date of termination of the contract of employment. This period can be extended at the discretion of the industrial tribunal but cannot exceed 12 months.

17.14.1 Method of calculation

Method of calculation is the same for unfair dismissal considered above.

The maximum award at present is therefore £6,150 ie 20 x 1½ x £205.

There are factors which may affect the award of redundancy payment and result either in its reduction or loss. These are as follows:

- Misconduct by the employee during the period of notice
  Depending upon the severity of the misconduct the tribunal may decide that the employee is no longer entitled to his redundancy payment or that it should be reduced.

- Strike action
  If the employee is involved in a strike during his period of notice he will still be entitled to redundancy payment. However, if he receives his notice of dismissal while on strike he will not be entitled to claim redundancy payment.

17.14.2 Procedure for handling redundancies

Procedure for handling redundancies is governed by s 188 TULR(C)A (as amended by TURERA 1992) which imposes a duty on the employer to consult with 'authorised representatives' of recognised independent trade unions at the earliest opportunity. Such consultation must take place even if only one employee is being made redundant. Where consultation cannot take place at the earliest opportunity, the fall back rules are as follows:

- At least 90 days before the first dismissal takes effect, where he or she proposes to make 100 or more employees redundant at one establishment within a period of 90 days or less.

- At least 30 days before the first redundancy takes effect, where he or she proposes to make 10 or more employees redundant at one establishment within a 30 day period.

Consultation must include consideration of ways in which the redundancies can be avoided, a possible reduction in the numbers of employees being dismissed anything which might mitigate the effects of the redundancy ex gratia payment etc (TURERA). The employer must also disclose the following during the consultations:

- The reasons for the proposed redundancies;

- The number and description of the employees whom it is proposed to make redundant;

- The total number of employees of that description employed at that establishment.

- The method of selection eg last in, first out (LIFO), part-timers first etc;

- The method of carrying out the redundancies having regard to any procedure agreed with the trade union.

During these consultations the trade union may make any representations which it sees fit. The employer may not ignore these representations and must give his reasons if he chooses to reject them. Where there are special circumstances such as insolvency the employer need only do what is reasonably practicable to comply with the consultation requirements.

Where the employer fails to comply with the consultation procedure in circumstances where it was reasonably practicable to expect him to do so, the trade union can complain to the industrial tribunal. If the tribunal finds in favour of the trade union it must make a declaration to this effect and it may make a *protective award* to those employees who were affected. This award which is discretionary takes the form of remuneration for a protected period. The length of the protected period usually reflects the severity of the breach by the employer. However, the protected period:

17.14.3   Effect of non-compliance with the procedure

- Must not exceed 90 days where it was proposed to make 100 or more redundant within 90 days;

- Is 30 days where it was proposed to make 10 or more redundant;

- Is 28 days if the redundancies do not fall within (a) and (b).

All employees covered by the protective award are entitled to one week's pay for each week of the protected period.

By virtue of s 193 TULR(C)A an employer must notify the Secretary of State of his intentions where he proposes:

17.14.4   Notification of redundancies to the Secretary of State

- To make 100 or more employees redundant at one establishment within a 90 day period; the notification must take place within 90 days.

- Where he proposes to make 10 or more employees redundant within a 30 day period; the notification must take place within 30 days.

Failure to meet these requirements may result in prosecution. However, there is a 'special circumstances' defence where it is not reasonably practicable for the employer to comply with the law on notification.

Individual Employment Rights (2)

The contract of employment may be terminated by agreement, death, frustration or performance. As a general rule an employer must give notice if he wishes to terminate his employee's contract. The minimum periods of notice are laid down in s 49 EPCA 1978. An employee wishing to terminate his contract must give at least one week's notice.

Termination

Summary dismissal is dismissal without notice for a serious breach of the contract.

Summary dismissal

Wrongful dismissal is summary dismissal without just cause (*Irani v South West Hampshire Health Authority* (1985)).

Wrongful dismissal

Protection for unfair dismissal is provided by the EPCA 1978. All employees must satisfy the qualifying period of at least two years' continuous service and not belong to the excluded groups.

Unfair dismissal

Rules are the same for redundancy and unfair dismissal where:

Effective date of termination

- Termination is with notice and the effective date/relevant date is the date on which the notice expires.

- Termination is without notice and the effective date is the date on which termination takes effect.

The employee must show that he has been dismissed within the meaning of the EPCA.

Dismissal

This may amount to:

- Express termination by the employer
  Igbo v Johnson Matthey Chemicals Ltd (1986)
  Martin v Yeoman Aggregates Ltd (1983)
  Robertson v Securicor Transport Ltd (1972)

- Expiration of a fixed term contract which is not renewed

- Constructive dismissal where the employee is entitled to terminate his contract
  Western Excavating Ltd v Sharp (1978)

Simmonds v Dowty Seals Ltd (1978)

Pepper & Hope v Daish (1980)

- Written reasons for the dismissal

  Where the employee makes a written request for a statement of the reasons for his dismissal, the employer must supply this information within 14 days.

- Fair dismissals

  Once the employee has established dismissal the onus moves to the employer to show that he acted reasonably and that therefore the dismissal was fair (s 3 EPCA).

  The employer must show that his conduct was:

- The reasonable response

  Polkey v AE Dayton Services Ltd (1987)

- The capability or qualifications of the employee were inadequate

  Davison v Kent Motors Ltd (1975)

- The conduct of the employee merited dismissal

  Taylor v Parsons Peebles Ltd (1981)

  Parr v Whitbread plc (1990)

- There was a redundancy situation

  Allwood v William Hill Ltd (1974)

  Hammond-Scott v Elizabeth Arden Ltd (1976)

  Statutory restrictions

  Some other substantial reason

- Automatically unfair

  Trade union membership or activities

  Pregnancy and childbirth

  Industrial action

  Health and safety matters

- Remedies

  Reinstatement

  Re-engagement

  Basic award

  Compensatory award

  Additional award

  Special award

  Interim relief order

Redundancy occurs when an employee is dismissed because his services are no longer required or the business ceases. The employee may have a claim for redundancy payments. The employee must show:

- Qualification period of two years continuous employment and not within excluded classes.

- Dismissal by his employer

  The conduct of the employer may allow the employee to treat himself as dismissed (*Marriot v Oxford & District Co-operative Society Ltd* (1970)).

  An anticipation of redundancy may not amount to dismissal (*Morton Sundour Fabrics v Shaw* (1967)).

  Once dismissal has been established, there is a presumption that the reason for the dismissal was redundancy. There are three situations which are deemed to be 'for reason of redundancy'.

- Cessation of the employer's business

  This may occur where only part of the premises are closed (*Gemmell v Darngavil Brickworks Ltd* (1967)).

- Closure or change in the place of work

  Movement of employees may require a 'mobility clause' unless the move is only a short distance (*O'Brien v Associated Fire Alarms Ltd* (1969) and *Managers (Holborn) Ltd v Holne* (1977)).

- Diminishing requirements for employees

  Failure to keep up with new practices is not a redundancy situation (*North Riding Garages v Butterwick* (1967); *Hindle v Percival Boats Ltd* (1969)).

  Shedding surplus labour may amount to redundancy (*Haden v Cowen* (1982)).

Redundancy

Redundancy payment may be made where an employee has been laid off or kept on short time.

Lay-off and short time

Change in ownership occurs where there is a transfer of a whole or part of the business (*Melon v Hector Powe* (1980)).

The Transfer of Undertakings Regulations apply to employees dismissed prior to the transfer (*Litster & Others v Forth Dry Dock & Engineering Co Ltd* (1989)).

Change in ownership and transfer of undertakings

Taylor v Kent CC (1969) – an unsuitable offer may be refused.

Offer of alternative employment

Trial period

A trial period is four weeks.

Procedure for handling redundancies

The correct procedure for handling redundancies is to consult with representatives of a recognised independent trade union. Failure to consult may result in a protective award. Notification of redundancies should be given to the Secretary of State.

Chapter 18

Negotiable Instruments and Consumer Credit

A negotiable instrument is a document which represents the right to a sum of money and, by definition, the right to sue for that money can be negotiated to another person. It is negotiated by delivery of that document to another person, or in some cases, delivering the document and endorsing it with a signature. The person who may be held liable vis à vis the document, need not be notified that it has been transferred. The person who holds the document can sue the person who is obligated to pay. The following are the main characteristics of a negotiable instrument:

18.1   Introduction

- Title passes on delivery if it is payable to bearer and on delivery and endorsement if it is payable to order ie the payee is named or indicated with reasonable certainty.

- The current holder can sue in his own name.

- Notice of transfer need not be given.

- A bona fide holder for value takes the instrument free from any prior defect in the title.

There are three main types of negotiable instrument – bills of exchange, cheques and promissory notes; a cheque is merely a form of a bill of exchange drawn on a bank whilst promissory notes are a mere promise by one person to pay money to another eg a bank note. Whilst transactions using bills of exchange and cheques are regulated by the Bills of Exchange Act 1882 and the Cheques Act 1957 and 1992, the development of the law pre-dates this time. Bills of exchange have been in use since the 14th century, providing an essential form of credit for medieval merchants trading throughout Europe. The demand for a system which eradicated the need to carry vast amounts of money, but which at the same time provided the holder of the bill with a contractual right to be paid, became imperative. England was a little slower to recognise the legitimacy of the bill of exchange; bills of exchange were legalised in 1697; thus, the concept of negotiability was finally legitimised. Whilst there has been a natural decline in the use of bills of exchange as the banking system has developed, the legacy of negotiability remains the bed-rock of the system.

18.2   Bills of exchange

The bill of exchange is similar to the modern cheque, except that it is made out by the seller who is owed the money and not by the person who owes the money. For example:

£5,000   London 1 June 1994

Three months after the date pay John Smith £5,000 for value received.

To: Paul Jones

In this example the seller is John Smith and the buyer is Paul Jones. The advantage of this arrangement is that the seller can shop around for someone to buy the bill from him (known as discounting). This means that the seller gets his money and the buyer gets time to pay. The person who discounts the bill usually makes his profit by paying slightly less for the bill than the sum agreed on the bill. The buyer in turn will normally pay a little over the price for his goods so that the seller receives the correct money when the bill is discounted.

A bill of exchange is defined in s 3(1) Bills of Exchange Act 1882 as follows:

'A bill of exchange is an unconditional order in writing addressed by one person to another, signed by the person giving it, requiring the person to whom it is addressed to pay on demand, or at a fixed or determinable future time, a sum certain in money to, or to the order of, a specified person, or to bearer.'

This definition needs to be divided into its various components and examined in more detail.

18.2.1   An unconditional order in writing

This means that payment must not be dependent upon any conditions, such as 'when the goods arrive' or stipulate a particular fund as in *Fisher v Calvert* (1879) since such terms are held to be conditions. Although the latter must be distinguished from an unconditional order to pay which is then subject to an indication of a particular fund from which the drawee is to be reimbursed, as in *Guaranty Trust Co of New York v Hannay & Co* (1918) which was deemed to be an unconditional order satisfying the definition. To make the order subject to the signing of a receipt form is conditional (*Bavins v Great Northern Railway Co* (1910)). However, in contrast, where the words 'to be retained' were written on a cheque, this amounted to a condition between the drawer and the payee and did not affect the unconditional nature of the order to the bankers (*Roberts & Co v Marsh* (1915)).

Section 11 of the Act prevents any instrument payable on a contingency from being a bill and the happening of the event does not cure the defect (*Palmer v Pratt* (1824)). An event which can be deemed to be absolutely certain is not regarded as a contingency eg an instrument payable in the event of a person's death is valid (*Colehan v Cooke* (1742)).

The order must be in writing. This includes print but excludes metal (Coinage Act 1870); although the Act does not stipulate where the order should be written eg a man once wrote his cheque to the tax office on the back of his shirt and this was considered a legitimate negotiable instrument.

The drawee must be named or indicated on the bill with reasonable certainty. Section 6(2) prevents an instrument being a bill where there are two or more drawees either in the alternative or in succession. However, where the bill is addressed to two or more drawees it is valid. The drawer and drawee may not be the same person.	**18.2.2** Addressed by one person to another
The drawer must sign the bill. This does not mean personally as long as the authority of the drawer is indicated eg use of official stamp etc. It goes without saying that a forged signature or one made without authority does not satisfy s 3, although this is subject to s 55(2) which covers the situation where the drawer's signature may have been forged (see below).	**18.2.3** Signed by the person giving it
The bill must either be payable on presentation or on the date specified or the nearest working date. It is possible to specify the date by reference to a particular event as long as that event is certain to occur. The date must be certain so that the holder can present for payment and if necessary give notice of dishonour within the specified period. Where a date is omitted, the bill may be made valid by the insertion of a date by the holder.	**18.2.4** To pay on demand or at a fixed or determinable future time
A specific sum must be stated. It can be payable by instalments or with interest, but it must be a fixed price eg 'pay however much is owed' does not meet the definition. The bill can be payable in a foreign currency and the rate of exchange can be specified. Interestingly, an order to pay in ECUs would not satisfy the definition since this is not a foreign currency but a unit of account.	**18.2.5** Sum certain in money
The bill is incomplete without the name of the payee. The person in possession may insert the name of the payee (s 20).	**18.2.6** To the order of a specified person or bearer
There are various terms used to describe the parties to a bill of exchange; these are as follows:	**18.2.7** Parties to the bill

- Drawer

  The person who draws up the bill and gives the order to pay is the drawer.

- Payee

  The person who is to be paid on the bill is the payee; the drawer and the payee may be the same person.

- Drawee

  The person on whom the bill is drawn up is the drawee of the bill ie the person who in the first instance is liable for payment. The drawee becomes the *acceptor* once he or she has accepted it by writing 'accepted' and signing it.

- Holder

  Section 2 defines the holder as the 'payee or endorsee of a bill who is in possession of it, or the bearer thereof; a holder can seek payment on the bill and can transfer the bill, but cannot enforce it. There are, however, different categories of holder who have distinct rights with respect to the bill.

- Holder for value

  This is the holder of a bill for which value has at some time been paid. It would appear that this does not apply to the original payee (*MK International Development Co Ltd v Housing Bank* (1991)). He or she can enforce the bill against anyone who signed it prior to the giving of value, but is not protected if any defects in title have arisen eg if there has been a theft or fraud. What this means, in effect, is that a holder for value has exactly the same rights as the person who negotiated the bill to him. Value could have been given for the bill in the past, in contrast to the rules in contract where past consideration is not sufficient.

- Holder in due course

  Before a person can be said to be a holder in due course a number of conditions must be satisfied:

  (a) There must be a holder. This does not include the original payee of the bill who remains in possession as the original payee cannot be a holder in due course (*RE Jones Ltd v Waring & Gillow Ltd* (1926); a holder in due course is a person to whom the bill is negotiated. The drawer can become a holder in due course by virtue of s 29(3) of the Act and will then acquire rights against the acceptor (*Jade International Steel Stahl und Eisen GmbH & Co KG v Robert Nicholas (Steels) Ltd* (1978). To be a holder in due course he must have given value; it is insufficient that value be given at some time. However, the presumption is that every holder is deemed to be a holder in due course (s 30(2)) unless it is admitted or established that the acceptance or the issue or negotiation of the bill is affected by fraud, duress or illegality. In the latter circumstances, the holder must prove that subsequent to the fraud, illegality or duress, value was provided in good faith; this will then reinstate the presumption.

(b) The bill must be complete and regular on its face ie there must be a date, amount and no alteration on the face of the bill. In *Arab Bank Ltd v Ross* (1952), a bill drawn in favour of F & FN Co was endorsed F & FN. It was held that the bill was not complete and regular on the face of it.

(c) The bill must not be overdue. The time for payment must not have passed. If the bill is payable on demand, it will be deemed to be overdue if it appears to have been in circulation for an unreasonable length of time (s 36(3)).

(d) Without notice of previous dishonour. The holder in due course must take the bill in good faith and without warning or prior knowledge of any previous dishonour; negligence does not amount to notice.

(e) Without notice of defect in title. Section 29(2) provides that 'the title of a person who negotiates a bill is defective when he obtained the bill or the acceptance thereof, by fraud, duress or force and fear or other unlawful means, or an illegal consideration or when he negotiates it in breach of faith or under such circumstances as amount to fraud'. Notice includes actual notice as well as constructive notice – to put on enquiry (see *Manchester Trust v Furness* (1895)).

18.2.8   Negotiation

It has already been stated that negotiation can take place by delivery or by delivery and endorsement. Endorsements are usually found on the back of the bill and can consist of a signature only, in which case the bill becomes payable to the bearer or an instruction and a signature eg 'pay Peter' signed by Paul. A bearer bill is negotiated simply by delivery. It is either expressly made payable to the bearer on the front of the bill or endorsed by signature alone. Furthermore, where the bill is made payable to a non-existent payee, it becomes a bearer bill.

In *Clutton v Attenborough & Son* (1897) a clerk employed by Attenborough made out a cheque to George Brett which Mr Attenborough signed. George Brett did not exist. It was held that the cheque was payable to bearer.

This can also be seen in *Bank of England v Vagliano Bros* (1890) where a clerk forged bills payable to the name of a real person, but since there was no intention that he should be paid, the court regarded the payee as fictitious and declared the bills to be bearer bills. Where a bill is incomplete ie missing the date or amount, it is known as inchoate and the holder may complete it within the authority granted and within a reasonable time (s 20) (see *Griffiths v Dalton* (1946)).

One of the problems associated with negotiation is the forged or unauthorised endorsement which is likely in cases of fraud or theft. In the case of a bearer bill, the transferee will receive a defective title rather than none at all. A defective title gives the holder the right to sue anyone who endorsed the bill subsequent to the theft or fraud. If he can show that he is a holder in due course then the defect in title is cured. If the bill is not a bearer bill and an endorsement is forged then the holder cannot sue on the bill itself, but can sue the person who transferred it to him for breach of warranty of genuineness and, similarly, he can sue anyone who has endorsed the bill subsequent to the forgery .

In *Kreditbank Cassel v Schenkers Ltd* (1927) Schenkers had a business in London and a branch in Manchester. The manager of the Manchester branch drew up seven bills, purportedly on behalf of Schenkers and signed them as Manchester manager. The bills were dishonoured and Kreditbank sued Schenkers as drawers. It was held that the bills were forgeries and Schenkers were not liable to pay.

18.2.9   Endorsements

When a bill is negotiated it will be subject to any endorsements which the endorser has written on the bill and duly signed. If there are two or more endorsements on the bill, they are presumed to have been made in the order in which they appear on the bill.

Each endorsement amounts to the creation of a new drawer. There are four types of endorsement:

* Blank

  This is the simple signature of the payee on the back of the bill. As such an endorsement does not specify an endorsee and the bill becomes a bearer bill (s 34(1)).

* Special

  Where the payee writes the name of another payee on the back eg pay John Smith or order. If the bill is a bearer bill the insertion of a person's name above the signature cannot convert the bill to an order bill (see *Mile Associates (Australia) Pty Ltd v Bennington Pty Ltd* (1975).

* Conditional

  If a condition is added to the signature by the endorser, eg *sans recours*, the condition may be ignored by the payer and payment to the endorsee is valid whether the condition has been fulfilled or not (s 33).

- Restrictive

  This type of endorsement prevents further negotiation of the bill eg pay X only. The endorsee has the right to receive payment, but cannot transfer his rights.

  A bill can continue to be negotiated until payment is made or a restrictive endorsement is added (s 36). The endorser of a bill becomes liable on it and the holder may seek payment from the endorser if the acceptor fails to honour the bill subject to a restrictive endorsement such as *sans recours* (s 55(1)). Anyone transferring the bill after endorsement incurs the liabilities of an endorser, except the transferor of a bearer bill who incurs no liability.

In order to obtain payment on the bill the payee must be a holder for value or a holder in due course. If the bill is presented in good time which is usually within a few days of the stipulated date (three days grace after the due date is acceptable), then the drawer and endorsers are discharged from their responsibilities under the bill. If the bill is payable on demand, then it must be paid within a reasonable time after the bill is issued and that time is determined by the nature of the bill and the facts of the case (s 45(4)). Failure to present for payment at the proper time and place may release prior parties from their liabilities.

18.2.10   Presentment for payment

In *Yeoman Credit Ltd v Gregory* (1963) the plaintiff company held a bill payable on 9 December 1959. The bill had been accepted by EC Ltd and was payable at the NP Bank. It had been personally endorsed by way of guarantee by G who was managing director of EC Ltd. The plaintiffs were informed by a director of EC Ltd that there were no funds available at the NP Bank and that the bill should be presented to the M Bank. The plaintiffs acted upon this advice, without obtaining the consent of G or the other endorsers and presented the bill to the M Bank on 9 December 1959. The M Bank refused payment. The plaintiffs then presented the bill to the NP Bank on 10 December 1959 (again it was dishonoured). The plaintiffs then took action against G where it was held that G was discharged from liability as the bill had not been presented at the NP Bank on the correct day.

In addition, the bill must be presented at a reasonable hour, on a business day and, if the place is not specified, at the address of the drawee or acceptor. In the following circumstances presentment for payment may be dispensed with:

- Where on proof of reasonable diligence it cannot be effected;

- Where the drawee is a fictitious person;

- Where presentment has been waived either expressly or impliedly.

- In the case of an accommodation bill, where the drawee is not bound to accept or pay the bill and the drawer has no reason to believe the bill would be paid if presented and where the endorser has no reason to believe that the bill would be paid if presented.

18.2.11 Presentment for acceptance	Presentment of the bill for acceptance must be made by the holder to the acceptor or his agent. Presentment must be made at a reasonable hour on a business day, before the bill is overdue (s 41(1)(a)). Section 41(2) excuses the need for presentment where it has proved to be impossible despite the exercise of reasonable diligence.
18.2.12 Notice of dishonour	A bill is dishonoured for non-payment if it is not paid when presented for payment at the correct time, or remains unpaid after the due date where presentment for payment is excused. It is also dishonoured for non-acceptance in similar circumstances.

If the bill is dishonoured, a notice of dishonour must be given to anyone who the holder intends to make liable on the bill. Notice of dishonour need not take any particular form, written or verbal will suffice, provided that the people who might be sued are made aware that the bill is dishonoured. The return of the dishonoured bill is a sufficient notice of dishonour. The rules about notice, time and content can be found in ss 49 and 50 of the Act. The holder can formally note or 'protest' the bill by giving formal notice to a notary of the time of dishonour. A person may escape liability if he is not given notice within a reasonable time (s 48).

However, notice of dishonour may be dispensed with where it can be shown:

- After reasonable diligence has been exercised, the notice cannot be given or does not reach the person intended.

- That notice has been waived, either expressly or impliedly.

- As regards the drawer, that one of the following is satisfied: the drawer and drawee are the same person; the drawee is fictitious or does not have contractual capacity; the drawer is the person to whom the bill is presented for payment; the drawer has countermanded payment; the drawee as per agreement between himself and the drawer is under no obligation to accept or pay the bill.

- As regards the endorser, that one of the following is satisfied: at the time he endorsed the bill the endorser was aware that the drawee was a fictitious person or did not have contractual capacity; the bill is an accommodation bill; where the endorser is the person to whom the bill is presented for payment.

Damages are available in the event of dishonour and these can be not only for the amount of the bill, but also for the interest which should have accumulated from the point at which the bill reached maturity and the expenses associated with noting and protesting.

The protesting of a bill should normally be carried out by a notary. However, it is possible, if a notary is not available at the place of dishonour, for an independent person (householder and two witnesses) to certify that the bill was presented for payment and that payment was refused. The form of the protest should be as follows:

18.2.13 Protesting a bill

- It must be signed by the notary.
- Name the person at whose request the bill is protested.
- Specify the date and place of protest (normally where the bill is dishonoured) and the reason for the protest.
- State the nature of the demand and the answer given.
- Enclose a copy of the bill.

Acceptance for honour occurs where a person who has no liability on a bill accepts it, normally after the drawee/acceptor has failed to pay on the due date ss 65-68. Acceptance for honour may be for part rather than the whole value of the bill. However, in order for such acceptance to be valid the acceptance for honour must be written on the bill, indicating that it is acceptance for honour and be signed by the acceptor for honour. Unless otherwise stated, the acceptance is deemed to be for the honour of the drawer. Once the bill has been accepted for honour, the acceptor for honour becomes liable to the holder and all parties subsequent to the parties for whose honour he has accepted. This liability accrues from the time when it is presented to the drawer for payment, if it is not paid by the drawer and is protested for non-payment and the acceptor has notice of these facts.

18.2.14 Acceptance for honour

The only persons who can be liable on a bill are those who have signed it. The signature of a company or agent will

18.2.15 Liability of the parties

suffice (*Ringham v Hackett* (1980)), although the agent must indicate on the bill that he is signing on behalf of a principal if he wishes to avoid liability. Section 25 stipulates that a signature by procuration operates as notice that the agent has only a limited authority to sign and therefore the principal will only be liable where the agent is acting within his authority (*Reckitt v Barnett* (1929)).

R provided T with the power of attorney to draw cheques on his behalf. T bought a car from B and paid for it using a cheque signed 'R by T his attorney'. B knew the car was bought by T for his own use. It was held that B must refund the cheque to R since he was aware of the lack of authority.

18.2.16   Forged signatures

Section 24 provides that a forged or unauthorised signature on a bill is wholly inoperative and no person can acquire rights under it (*Kreditbank Cassel v Schenkers Ltd* (1927)). There are, however, a number of exceptions:

- The person against whom payment is sought may be estopped from setting up the forgery or lack of authority as a defence (s 24).

- Estoppel by representation express or implied, where a person acknowledges a forged acceptance or endorsement as his own (see *Bank of England v Vagliano Bros* (1891) (above) and *Greenwood v Martins Bank Ltd* (1933) (below)).

- Estoppel by negligence – where the acceptor is a bank, the customer owes a duty of care and failure to exercise this duty may operate in estoppel by negligence.

  In *London Joint Stock Bank Ltd v Macmillan & Arthur* (1918) the defendants authorised their clerk to complete cheques for them to sign. He filled in a cheque payable to a firm or to bearer showing the sum as £2 in figures only. One of the partners signed as drawer. The clerk then altered the figures to £120, filled in the words to match and cashed the cheque at the London Joint Stock Bank where his employers had their account. It was held (HL) that a duty of care is owed by the customer to his bank to avoid drawing a cheque in such a manner as would facilitate fraud or forgery.

  The extent of this duty was further considered in *Tai Hing Cotton Mill Ltd v Lui Chong Hing Bank Ltd* (1986).

- Statutory estoppel. Sections 54 and 55 estop an acceptor or endorser respectively from denying to a holder in due course, the existence of the drawer, the genuineness of his signature, his capacity and authority to draw the bill.

- The endorsee of a bill agrees to pay the bill should it be dishonoured by the acceptor. In effect, the act of endorsement acts as a guarantee that all the signatures prior to the endorsement are regular and valid. The holder in due course may proceed on the basis of estoppel against those who signed after the forgery.

  Where the payee is fictitious or non-existent the bill may be treated as a bearer bill. This can then be transferred by simple delivery and any signatures by way of endorsement are to be regarded as non-essential; the payee's forged signature can therefore be disregarded as in *Bank of England v Vagliano Bros* (1891). However, the transferor may be liable to his immediate transferee for value in the following circumstances: where the bill is a forgery or if the transferor knew the bill would not be paid or if the transferor had a defective title.

It is of importance to anyone who may be affected by the bill to know how and when the bill can be considered discharged, because at that point all obligations cease. There are a variety of ways in which this might happen and the most common of these are:

18.2.17   Discharge of a bill

- By payment in due course;

- When a bill is cancelled intentionally (s 63);

- When a bill is altered.

  Payment in due course is payment to the holder of the bill after the bill has reached maturity, without notice that the title is defective. When a bill is cancelled intentionally the bill is only discharged when the cancellation is apparent. If a bill has been altered in some material way, the bill is discharged except against the person who authorised the alteration and all subsequent endorsers (s 64).

Whilst a cheque is merely a bill of exchange drawn on a bank, it operates in a different way to a bill. This is in part due to banking practice which for most purposes treats a cheque as a money payment order eg allows the customer to draw money from his account. Cheques came into use when merchants were finding increasing difficulties in discounting bills of exchange. The banks could offer this service, provided they secured some protection for themselves against the possibilities of economic loss.

18.3   Cheques

A cheque is defined by s 73 of the Bills of Exchange Act 1882 as:

'... a bill of exchange drawn on a banker payable on demand'.

As it is a form of bill, the rules relating to bills of exchange apply. 'Banker' is defined as a body of persons who carry on the business of banking as their main business. A banker must:

- Take current accounts;

- Pay cheques drawn on itself;

- Collect cheques drawn on customers.

A body which fails to comply with the definition will not be recognised by the Bills of Exchange Act 1882 or the Cheques Act 1957 as a bank and will not therefore be entitled to statutory protection normally afforded paying and collecting banks. Building societies have acquired recognition of their 'banking' role by virtue of the Building Societies Act 1986 which extends the provisions of the Bills of Exchange Act and the Cheques Act to building societies.

18.3.1 The differences between cheques and other bills of exchange

A cheque is not 'accepted'. The drawee is always the banker and the bank is not liable to the holder of the cheque, only to the customer. In contrast, in the case of a bill of exchange, the drawee, who is always the 'acceptor', is liable to the holder of the bill.

A cheque is always drawn on a banker and payable on demand. A bill may be drawn on anyone and may be payable on demand or at a fixed or determinable future time.

A cheque can be crossed in several ways (see below); whereas bills of exchange cannot be crossed.

If a cheque is returned to a banker, no notice of dishonour is necessary in order to claim against the drawer. This is in contrast to a bill of exchange which would require such a notice.

A banker who pays out on a cheque with a forged or unauthorised endorsement in good faith and in the ordinary course of business is not liable to the holder or to his customer. If, however, the drawee of a bill of exchange pays a bill with a forged endorsement he is still liable to the true owner.

Delay in presentment of a cheque for payment does not discharge the drawer of a cheque unless he suffers actual loss from the delay. Such damage will only occur when the bank on which the cheque is drawn is unable to honour it.

In *Wheeler v Young* (1897) W received a cheque from Young in payment of his rent. The cheque was received on a Friday. On the Saturday Wheeler posted it to his bank. The bank received the cheque on the Monday and sent it on to its head office which received it on Tuesday. It was duly presented for payment to Young's bank for payment on the Wednesday. On that day Young's bank stopped payment. It was held that there had been an unreasonable delay on the part of Wheeler in presenting the cheque and, as a result, it had not been presented within a reasonable time. Young was discharged from liability.

A bill of exchange payable on demand, however, must be presented within a reasonable time or the drawer of the bill will be discharged from liability.

A cheque is generally crossed by drawing two parallel lines across it (s 76). If a banker on whom the cheque is drawn fails to pay other than in accordance with the crossing, he is liable to the true owner of the cheque for any loss (s 79). The types of crossings generally recognised are as follows:

18.3.2   Crossings

- A general crossing

  This is simply when parallel lines are drawn across a cheque or parallel lines with '& Co' or '& Company' written between them. Such a cheque can only be paid through a bank and not over the counter.

- A special crossing

  This is when the name of a particular bank is written between the parallel lines and then only that bank can accept payment.

- 'Not negotiable'

  This can be written between the lines, with or without the name of a bank. This phrase does not actually stop the cheque from being negotiated, but, because the person receiving the cheque has notice that it should not be negotiable, that person acquires no better title than the person who negotiated it to him (the transferor) (s 81). This means, in practice, that he accepts a risk since he accepts the cheque with any defects in title. It is therefore unlikely that anyone would accept a cheque with this crossing.

  In *Wilson & Meeson v Pickering* (1946) Wilson drew a cheque which was crossed 'not negotiable' and handed it to his clerk to fill in the amount and the name of the payee. The clerk acting outside her authority, inserted a sum and gave the cheque to Pickering as payment for her own debt. It was held that as the clerk had no title to the cheque Pickering could acquire no better title and as a result Wilson was not liable on the cheque.

- 'Account payee'

  When this is written across a cheque, it is a direction to the collecting bank that the proceeds are only to be credited to the account of the named payee. The cheque is still negotiable in theory (it would not be if the phrase read 'account payee only') but the bank will be liable to the owner if it credits an account of a person who holds the cheque without justification. In practice, this means that the bank would be unlikely to accept the cheque for anyone other than the named payee because of the risk involved. This type of crossing is least open to fraud.

  In *House Property Co v London County & Westminster Bank* (1915) a cheque which was crossed 'account payee' was made payable to FSH or bearer. The customer of the bank had possession but no right to the cheque. The bank collected payment and credited his account. It was held that the bank was liable in conversion to the true owner because it was negligent as the customer was neither FSH not the proper bearer.

  However, where the bank is merely collecting the cheque on behalf of another bank, there is no duty to ensure that the other bank credits the payee (*Importers Co Ltd v Westminster Bank* (1927)).

18.3.3   Relationship between banker and customer

The relationship between a banker and his customer is one of debtor and creditor. It is a relationship founded in contract. Although the word 'customer' is not defined by statute, at common law a customer is someone who has an account in his own name at a bank (*Ladbroke & Co v Todd* (1914)). A number of duties arise out of the banker/customer relationship. As well as the express terms and duties expressed in the banking agreement, there are also implied duties.

18.3.4   Duties of the customer

Duties of the customer are as follows:

- A customer owes a duty of care to his bank not to draw up cheques carelessly

  The purpose of this duty is to limit the opportunity for fraud or forgery (see *London Joint Stock Bank Ltd v Macmillan & Arthur* (1918) (above)). The Banking Act 1979 (s 47) confirms that the duty only applies to the customer, although the negligence of another party to the cheque may result in a reduction in damages on the basis of contributory negligence (*Lumsden & Co v London Trustee Savings Bank* (1971).)

  Whether the customer owes a duty to his bank to take reasonable care in the conduct of his business with regard to the drawing of cheques etc is still open to judicial debate. In *Tai Hing Cotton Mill Ltd v Liu Chong Hing Bank Ltd* (1986), if a company had checked its monthly statements it would have detected the dishonesty of a clerk who had been forging cheques over a period of six years. The plaintiff company brought an action against the bank for wrongfully debiting its account. The Privy Council held that there was no duty to check bank statements nor to have internal controls which would prevent such fraud. However, had the company acquired knowledge of the forgeries they would have been bound to inform the bank and would then have been estopped for failing to do so. Obviously it is open to the bank to insert a clear express term imposing such a duty on its customer.

- A customer is under a duty to inform the bank of forgeries

  If a customer fails in this duty, he may be estopped from denying the validity of the forged signature.

  In *Greenwood v Martins Bank Ltd* (1933) a wife had been forging her husband's signature. The husband was aware that this had been happening but failed to inform his bank. In the case in question she obtained £410 by virtue of the forged cheque at which point he decided to inform the bank. He brought an action against the bank for wrongly debiting his account. It was held that the husband could not claim the money from the bank as he had deprived the bank of the right of action against the forger by his silence. His lack of action amounted to an estoppel that the cheques were genuine.

Duties of the bank to its customers are as follows:

- To pay money to the order of the customer

  The bank must honour cheques or other orders drawn on the customer's account provided the account has sufficient funds or is within an agreed overdraft limit. If the banker fails to do this he may be liable in action by the customer for wrongful dishonour of the cheque amounting to breach of contract. If the customer is a private individual as opposed to a trader, he will only receive nominal damages in the absence of evidence of actual loss.

  In *Rae v Yorkshire Bank* (1988) the plaintiff was allowed an overdraft facility of up to £1,500 by his bank. The bank then dishonoured two cheques and refused to allow the plaintiff to cash a cheque, even though none of these transactions would have taken the plaintiff beyond his overdraft limit. The plaintiff claimed damages for humiliation and

18.3.5   Duties of the bank to its customers

inconvenience. It was held that since he was not a trader and could not show a specific loss, the plaintiff would only be able to recover nominal damages from the bank.

Furthermore, a cheque returned with the wording 'refer to drawer' may leave the bank open to a claim of defamation if they have failed to honour it when sufficient funds have been present in the account.

Where a customer issues an order countermanding payment, as the customer's agent the bank may be liable if it fails to obey the countermand, although this will only be the case where the bank has actual knowledge of an authenticated countermand.

In *Curtice v London City & Midland Bank Ltd* (1908) the customer sent a telegram countermanding payment of a cheque. This telegram was placed in the letter-box of the bank, but due to the fault of the bank was not removed from the box until after the cheque had been paid. It was held that there had not been an effective countermand and therefore the bank was not liable in contract, although of course an action in negligence may have succeeded.

There is now a clearly stated duty of care owed by the bank to its customer in the performance of its duties (*Barclays Bank plc v Quince Care Ltd* (1988)).

Where the customer uses a cheque guarantee card to support a cheque, this amounts to a contractual guarantee by the bank as agent for the customer that the cheque will not be dishonoured through lack of funds. The use of such cards results in the customer losing the right to countermand the cheque, unless the signature of the customer is forged (see *Re Charge Card Services Ltd* (1989)).

There are limits on the banker's duty with respect to the payment of cheques for his customer. These may arise under an insolvency order or a winding up order under the Insolvency Act 1986 when a bank may quite legitimately refuse to pay cheques on behalf his customer.

• To keep the affairs of his customer secret

To breach the duty of confidentiality may result in an action for breach of contract. In releasing confidential information, awards of damages may be substantial depending upon the nature of the breach and the impact on the customer, especially if he is a business client. There are, however, exceptional circumstances where the bank can legitimately release information without being in breach of duty:

(a) by law – statute may authorise, if not compel, the bank to release information about the customer's account eg inland revenue statutes; the bank is not necessarily obliged to inform his customer that the information has been released. (See *Barclays Bank v Taylor* (1989)).

(b) by public duty – the bank may be under a discretionary duty to release information in the public interest – eg where in times of war the customer is trading with the enemy.

(c) where it is in the interests of the bank to make a disclosure.

(d) by express or implied consent of the customer – disclosure of information to subsidiaries is usually based on implied consent of the customer; supplying financial references.

- There is a duty to keep customers correctly informed about their financial position. As part of the duty the bank must maintain the customers' account correctly. If the customer is misled by an inaccurate statement of his account and acts upon this irregularity, the bank will be unable to recover any money which has been wrongly credited. However, the action taken by the customer must amount to a material alteration of his position which is such as to be inequitable for him to repay the money and therefore create an estoppel against the bank (*United Overseas Bank v Jiwani* (1976)).

Some protection is afforded both the paying and collecting bank where they fail to act in accordance with their customers' instructions.

18.4   Protection of the banker

The ordinary principles of common law provide that if a paying bank pays a customer's cheque to a person not entitled to it, he will be liable to the owner in conversion and he cannot debit the customer's account. This may, in limited circumstances, be subject to the doctrine of estoppel as applied against the customer. Under statute the paying bank has four possible defences in this situation:

18.4.1   Paying bank

- Section 59 Bills of Exchange Act 1882 provides that the payment of a bill at the correct time, to the holder in good faith and without notice of any defect in the holder's title discharges the drawee. It therefore discharges the banker in these conditions when he has paid to the bearer of a 'pay bearer' cheque. It does not protect the banker in the case of an order cheque (made out to a specific payee), where there is a forged endorsement because such a person will not be a 'holder' of the cheque since he has no title to it.

- Section 60 of the Bills of Exchange Act 1882 protects the banker 'if when there is a forged endorsement the banker pays the cheque drawn on him, payable on demand to order, in good faith and in the ordinary course of business, he is deemed to have paid the cheque in due course' (ie it will be treated as if the cheque had been properly paid). In this case the drawer of the cheque is treated as having discharged his liability and as stated, the bank can debit the customer's account and is not liable in conversion. The protection afforded by s 60 is in recognition of the fact that a bank cannot be expected to check every endorsement.

  In *Charles v Blackwell* (1877) X drew a cheque in favour of Y's order. Z stole the cheque and forged Y's signature as an endorsement. X's bank paid Z in good faith and in the ordinary course of business. It was held that the bank could debit X's account.

  The limitation on s 60 is that it will only protect the bank where the endorsement is not irregular and the cheque has no material alterations, both of which would amount to notice to the bank who would not then be acting in good faith (see *Carpenter's Co v British Mutual Banking Co Ltd* (1938) and *Bank of England v Vagliano Bros* (1891).

- Section 1 Cheques Act 1957 provides that where a banker pays a cheque drawn on himself in good faith and in the ordinary course of business he is protected, despite there being an irregular endorsement or a missing endorsement. This section makes it clear that endorsement is not necessary when presenting a cheque for payment. The protection under s 1 is limited to payment to the original payee. It therefore follows that it is the endorsement of the original payee which is missing or irregular.

- Section 80 Bills of Exchange Act 1882 states that if a banker pays out on a cheque that has been crossed to another banker, then provided it acts in good faith and without negligence, he is protected from liability to the true owner in the event of payment being made to someone other than the true owner. Similarly, if the cheque has been crossed specially, then the banker is protected if he paid out to the bank specified on the crossing. Protection under s 80 only applies to crossed cheques and in the absence of proof of negligence.

18.4.2   Collecting bank

As a general rule a collecting bank would be liable in conversion where it collects payment of a valid cheque for anyone other than the true owner. However, some protection is afforded the collecting bank in the following circumstances:

- Section 2 Cheques Act 1957 enables the collecting bank to have the same rights to hold the cheque as a 'holder in due course' even without the cheque being endorsed to it. The collecting bank also has a lien on any cheque validly presented to it if the customer's balance is insufficient to meet the unpaid debt.

- Section 4 Cheques Act 1957 protects the bank from being sued in the tort of conversion. If the bank receives payment for the customer in good faith and without negligence, the bank does not incur any liability. The bank is only protected where it collects for a customer ie as agent or where it collects for itself as holder for value. In acting without negligence the customer must show that the bank failed to comply with the standards of reasonable banking practice (*Lloyd's Bank Ltd v EB Savory & Co* (1933), where the bank was found to have been negligent in failing to ascertain the name of the new customer's husband's employer. Whilst this may not amount to negligence today it serves to illustrate that what amounts to reasonable banking practice is subject to change. Current banking practice may be open to liability if it is inherently negligent ie mere common practice will not always defeat claims of negligence. However, it is suggested in *Marfani & Co Ltd v Midland Bank Ltd* (1968) that the onus is on the defendant to show that he acted without negligence and that the standard of care required of the bank is the ordinary practice of a careful banker; it follows, therefore, that there is no need to subject every account to a microscopic examination. This was supported by the decision in *Thackwell v Barclays Bank plc* (1986).

The collecting bank is also bound by law to fulfil certain duties. These are:

- To check references and enquire into identity and circumstances when an account is opened by a new customer (*Lumsden & Co v London Trustee Savings Bank* (1971)).

- To be alert to the obvious forms of misappropriation eg to check up on a cheque drawn in favour of the customer's employer. A failure of this duty, whilst giving rise potentially to liability, only occurs where the bank has been put on enquiry. In *Thackwell v Barclays Bank* (1986) S paid two cheques into an account, one after the other. One cheque was made payable to S and was endorsed with his own signature. The other cheque was drawn by J. The payee of the cheque was T. This cheque was forged by S who forged T's signature. The assistant manager witnessed the forgery of T's signature by S. He glanced separately at each endorsement on each cheque without noticing the fraud. It was held that the bank were liable for the negligent actions of their employee and could not establish the defence under s 4 as a reasonable bank would have been put on enquiry.

This duty is further illustrated in *Underwood Ltd v Bank of Liverpool & Martins Ltd* (1924). Underwood was the sole director and major shareholder of Underwood Ltd. His private bank was L Bank but the company's account was at another bank. Cheques drawn in favour of Underwood Ltd were paid into Underwood's personal account and payment was collected by L Bank. Underwood Ltd sued L Bank for conversion. It was held that L Bank were liable as they had been negligent in not enquiring whether Underwood Ltd had a separate account and if they had, why cheques were not paid into it.

18.5   Promissory notes

Section 83 Bills of Exchange Act 1882 defines a promissory note as:

- an unconditional promise in writing

- made by one person to another

- signed by the maker

- engaging to pay

- on demand

- or at a fixed or determinable future time

- a sum certain in money

- to or to the order of a specified person or to bearer.

A promissory note shares many of the characteristics of a bill of exchange, although since there is no acceptor the rules relating to acceptance and presentment for acceptance do not apply. To be valid it must be delivered to the payee or bearer. A person who endorses a promissory note has the same duties and liabilities as the endorser of a bill of exchange. A promissory note differs from a bill of exchange in that it is not drawn on a bank.

18.6   Consumer credit

The Consumer Credit Act 1974 was passed following the Crowther Committee Report – Report of the Committee on

Consumer Credit (Cmnd No 4569 1971). It offered greater protection to persons buying on credit, removing the distinction between purchases on credit, hire purchase and cash. It has repealed and replaced, for the most part, the Hire Purchase Act 1965. A wide variety of transactions are now within the remit of the Act eg loans, credit card agreements, bank overdrafts, credit sale agreements, hire purchase agreements et al which are the most common form of credit agreement. The Act also introduced a wide range of terminology which needs to be explained before other aspects of the legislation can be considered.

Creditor	The person/body who supplies the credit/finance.	18.6.1	The terminology
Debtor	The customer, borrower/the person who is obliged to repay the finance.		
Credit	Includes a cash loan or any other form of financial accommodation (s 9(1)).		

Debtor-creditor-supplier agreements are restricted use consumer credit agreements where the creditor and supplier are either the same person eg retailer financing purchase by customer, or there are pre-existing arrangements between the creditor and supplier eg credit card transactions; in addition, there can be unrestricted use debtor-creditor-supplier agreements where the creditor has pre-existing arrangements between himself and the supplier, with a view to financing transactions between the debtor and the supplier.

18.6.2 Debtor-creditor-supplier agreements

Any agreement not falling within the above category are debtor-creditor agreements. In some circumstances where an agreement falls within more than one category as defined by the Act, it will be known as a *multiple* agreement and each divisible part will be regulated accordingly. The distinction between this type of consumer credit agreement and a debtor-creditor-supplier agreement is based on the existence of a business connection between the creditor and supplier which may result in both the creditor and supplier being liable to the debtor for defects in the goods.

18.6.3 Debtor-creditor agreements

A restricted-use credit agreement is an agreement whereby the debtor has no control over the use to which the credit is put.

18.6.4 Restricted-use credit agreement

An unrestricted-use credit agreement is an agreement whereby the debtor has control over the use of the finance even where the contract itself states that the money must be used for a specific purpose (s 11(3) Consumer Credit Act 1974).

18.6.5 Unrestricted-use credit agreement

| 18.6.6 | Fixed-sum credit |

Fixed-sum credit is where the actual amount of the loan is fixed from the start of the agreement subject to the statutory limit for regulated agreements. The relevant figure is the actual amount of the sum being loaned excluding the amount payable as interest or deposit. It is irrelevant that it may be repaid or received by instalments.

| 18.6.7 | Running-account credit |

Running-account credit is where credit is fixed up to an agreed limit eg credit card agreements, bank overdrafts. Again such agreements will be regulated agreements within the Act as long as the credit limit does not exceed the current specified figure (s 10).

| 18.6.8 | Regulated agreements defined |

A regulated *consumer credit agreement* is defined as:

'... an agreement by which the creditor provides an individual (the debtor) with credit not exceeding a specified figure (at present £15,000). Obviously, where the debtor is a company or other body corporate an agreement is not a consumer credit agreement' (s 8). However, a partnership is to be regarded as an individual.

A regulated *consumer hire agreement* is defined as:

'... an agreement made between a person and the hirer under which goods are hired, leased bailed which is capable of lasting more than three months and does not require the hirer to make payments exceeding £15,000' (s 15).

Again an agreement where the hirer is a body corporate is outside the Act because the hirer must be an individual. Furthermore, a hire purchase agreement is not within the definition since this type of agreement falls within the definition of a consumer credit agreement.

| 18.6.9 | Small agreement |

A small agreement is either a regulated consumer credit agreement or a regulated consumer hire agreement where, with respect to the former, the amount of credit does not exceed £50 and with respect to the latter, the hire/rental charge does not exceed £50. The rules for determining whether the credit exceeds the limit are explained above by reference to fixed-sum and running-account credit.

| 18.6.10 | Exempt agreements |

Certain types of agreement are exempted from the provisions of the Consumer Credit Act 1974, for example, mortgages or any loan made by banks, building societies, local authorities etc for the buying or developing of land; credit agreements in respect of the export and import of goods; normal trade credit – where credit is provided in the sale of goods and services but the 'bill' is to be paid as one single instalment eg milk and paper bill and the hiring of meters/equipment from the essentials services and telecommunications companies.

Businesses which provide facilities for regulated agreements must be licensed by the Office of Fair Trading. These include not only businesses where their main activity is the supply of credit, but also businesses where credit is ancillary to its main activity eg debt-collecting, debt-counselling, credit reference agencies, credit brokerage. If the licence is refused then an appeal may be made to the Secretary of State for Trade and Industry. Unlicensed trading is an offence under the 1974 Act (s 39) and the unlicensed trader will have no legal means of enforcing his agreement (s 40). In addition, licences may be withdrawn, varied or suspended.

18.6.11   Licensing

The Consumer Credit (Advertisements) Regulations 1980 provide for control over the form and content of advertisements for credit. The spirit of the regulations is that any advertisement should contain a fair and reasonably comprehensive indication of the nature of the credit and hire facilities offered and their true cost or, at the very least, indicate that such information is available. Failure to comply with the regulations is a criminal offence. Additionally, it is an offence to advertise goods or services on credit where they are not available for cash (s 45).

18.6.12   Advertising and canvassing

Further offences include sending someone under the age of 18 years a document inviting him to seek information about credit or to obtain credit (s 50); issuing an unsolicited credit-token other than as a renewal or replacement; infringing regulations as to the content and form of a quotation of credit terms; such quotations must include prominent reference to the APR (s 52); failing to comply with regulations as to information to be displayed at the premises of credit businesses (s 53).

Specific offences have also been created concerning canvassing debtor-creditor agreements off trade premises; this is illegal unless the canvasser is responding to a written request (s 49). However, it is not unlawful to canvass debtor-creditor-supplier agreements provided that the creditor has a licence to trade in this manner. Note canvassing involves making oral representations about the agreements ie trying to verbally persuade people to enter into the agreements by making comments about it.

There are certain rules affecting regulated agreements which if they are not complied with prevent the creditor or owner from enforcing the agreement ss 60-65):

18.6.13   Form of the regulated agreement

- The terms of the agreement must be in writing and must be legible (s 61).

- The cash price of the goods must be stated in the agreement.

- It must provide for payment of equal instalments at equal intervals and must include reference to the method of payment.

- It must include a description of the goods sufficient to identify them.

- The agreement must contain certain statutory notices eg rights to terminate or cancel the agreement where that is applicable (s 64), plus rights over 'protected goods'.

- There are certain regulations about the written format of the agreement eg it must be typewritten and the hirer/debtor must sign in a box outlined in red which has a printed warning that the hirer/debtor must only sign this if he intends to be legally bound by it; the creditor/owner must also sign the agreement. Contravention of these provisions results in an agreement becoming unenforceable.

    The hirer/debtor is entitled to copies of the agreement. If the creditor or finance company signs at the same time as the hirer/debtor, then the hirer/debtor must receive a copy immediately (s 62). If, however, there is a time lag and the dealer/supplier has to send the forms off to a finance company for agreement then the hirer/debtor must receive:

- A copy of his offer on the spot (known as the first statutory copy);

- A subsequent copy of the concluded agreement within seven days (known as the second statutory copy (s 63)).

18.6.14 Breach of the regulations relating to formation

All copies must comply with the regulations as to form and content. Any breach will render the agreement improperly executed so that in effect it is unenforceable except through a court order. The courts can grant an 'enforcement order' and in so doing can vary the terms of the original agreement. However, the courts tend not to do this if the agreement does not comply with the regulations or the correct notices were not served or copies given. The correct copies must be given to the hirer or debtor before the court proceedings. If the agreement does not give notice of cancellation rights where they are appropriate, the courts will not issue an enforcement order.

18.6.15 Cancellation

If the agreement is signed off trade premises (eg on the front doorstep), it is cancellable and there must be a notice in the agreement about the right of cancellation and how it can be exercised, including the names and addresses of persons to whom cancellation can be sent (ss 67-73). The purpose of these requirements is to allow the customer a cooling off period so that he has an opportunity to think about whether he actually wants to enter into the transaction. An essential element must be personal contact between the debtor/hirer and the salesman including antecedent negotiations which include oral representations made by the creditor or owner in the presence of the customer.

The cooling off period commences when the customer signs the agreement and lasts until the fifth clear day after he receives the second copy (s 68). To cancel the agreement the customer must give written notice within this period to the creditor/owner or dealer.

Where the agreement is a debtor-creditor-supplier agreement for restricted-use credit or a consumer hire agreement, the customer is entitled to recover any payment he has made. He must, however, return the goods although this allows him to await collection of the goods by the creditor/owner/dealer (s 72). He must take reasonable care of the goods for 21 days after serving the notice cancelling the agreement.

Where the agreement is a debtor-creditor agreement for unrestricted-use credit, the debtor must repay any credit received with interest, although he does not have to pay interest on credit which he repays within one month of cancellation (s 71).

In addition, the Consumer Protection (Cancellation of Contracts concluded away from Business Premises) Regulations 1987 provide that any agreement by a consumer to buy goods or services from a trader during an unsolicited visit to their home or place of work shall be subject to a seven day 'cooling off' period, during which agreements covered by the regulations can be cancelled without any penalty to the consumer.

The effect of cancellation is as follows: 18.6.16   Effect of cancellation

- The agreement is erased and there is no liability under it;

- All sums cease to be payable and all sums paid out are recoverable;

- The hirer is not obliged to return the goods but must hand them over if the owner calls at a reasonable time.

- The hirer has a duty to take care of the goods for 21 days after notice of cancellation.

- The hirer has a lien on the goods for the repayment of sums paid under the agreement;

- Any part-exchange goods can be recovered within 10 days or a part-exchange allowance must be given to the hirer.

18.7   Default

Default occurs where the debtor or hirer fails to meet the repayments. The goods would normally be repossessed. This is, however, subject to the rules for protected goods.

18.7.1   Protected goods

Where there is a hire-purchase agreement, the hirer or debtor is protected from repossession of the goods after he has paid one third or more of the price of the goods. Section 90 of the Consumer Credit Act 1974 specifies three requirements for the goods to become protected goods:

- A debtor is in breach of a regulated hire-purchase or conditional sale agreement relating to the goods.

- The debtor has paid to the creditor one third or more of the total price of the goods;

- The property in the goods remains with the creditor.

Under s 90 the owner of the goods which are protected (normally the finance company) cannot enforce his right to repossess the goods, other than by action in the courts. This normally means obtaining a court order even though the creditor may wish to terminate the agreement because of the hirer's default.

This section does not apply if the hirer wishes to terminate the agreement himself and probably does not apply if the hirer has 'disposed of' or abandoned the goods.

In *Bentinck Ltd v Cromwell Engineering* (1971) a car was the subject of a hire-purchase agreement. The car was involved in an accident. The hirer took the car to a garage for repair; he then failed to pay any more hire purchase instalments or to collect the car. The finance company traced the car and repossessed it. They sold the car and sought to recover depreciation costs from the hirer. He claimed that they had repossessed the car without consent. It was held that when a hirer has abandoned goods and his rights to them show that he no longer has any interest in them, then the owner has a right to repossess even if the goods had been 'protected' goods. The defendants were found to be liable for damages.

18.7.2   Effect of repossession without a court order

If the owner does try to repossess the goods without a court order after the goods have become protected, the following will ensue:

- The hire purchase agreement is terminated.

- The hirer's responsibility is at an end and he can claim back anything he has paid under the agreement.

- Any guarantor/indemnifier is released from liability and entitled to recover any security given.

Note: a guarantor is someone who guarantees that the creditor will receive payment due to him from the hirer/debtor. It is a secondary responsibility based solely on the responsibility of the hirer to pay. An indemnity is a promise to pay the creditor for any loss suffered on the contract and is a primary responsibility to indemnify loss suffered by the creditor as a result of his contract with the hirer. Thus, an indemnity may have to be paid when the hirer could avoid responsibility, whereas a guarantor can only be asked to pay where the hirer should have paid.

In *Capital Finance Co Ltd v Bray* (1964) Bray acquired a car under a hire purchase agreement. He fell behind with the repayments and an agent of the finance company repossessed the car without obtaining Bray's consent or a court order. The finance company realised it had made a mistake and the car was duly returned to Bray. Unfortunately, Bray continued to default on the repayments and the company sued for repossession. It was held, on granting a repossession order, that Bray was entitled to recover all the money he had previously paid to the finance company.

The Consumer Credit Act 1974 gives the County Court exclusive jurisdiction over all actions relating to hire-purchase contracts within the Act ie personal credit agreements under £15,000. All parties concerned including any guarantor or indemnifier must be made party to the court action and the court can make various orders:

18.7.3 Action to recover possession of protected goods

- Return order

  The hirer is asked to return the goods to the owner/creditor. If the hirer fails to return the goods, the only fall-back position is to send in the bailiffs.

- Suspended return order

  This is awarded when the hirer has a reasonable excuse for default eg redundancy or ill health. The court can vary the terms of the original agreement to enable the hirer to meet his obligations. It can reduce the amount of each instalment and extend the period of time to pay if this is deemed necessary. These are known as time orders. The effect of a suspended order can therefore be summarised as follows:

(a) The agreement continues but with a variation in terms.

(b) The owner cannot claim extra interest for the longer period of time.

(c) If the hirer breaks any terms as specified in the agreement it is possible for the court to make an order that the creditor can repossess without going back to court ie implement the suspended order.

(d) The court can vary the time order upon application from the hirer or the owner, if the hirer's financial circumstances get better or worse.

(e) The hirer may avoid the suspended order by paying off the unpaid balance and becoming the owner of the goods.

• Transfer order

This order gives part of the goods back to the owner and allows the hirer to retain part of the goods and become owner of them. The hire purchase agreement is at an end.

18.7.4	Notice of default	Whenever the owner/creditor on the default of the hirer/debtor wishes to terminate the agreement, repossess the goods etc he must serve a 'default notice' (s 87). The notice must give the hirer/debtor seven days to pay or remedy the default, state the total amount due plus the consequences of non-payment ie termination and how the breach can be rectified if at all possible. If the hirer/debtor pays in time, the contract will continue as if there has been no default. Notices of default must be issued whenever the debtor/hirer is in breach of any term of the agreement, before the agreement can be terminated.
18.7.5	Time order	The debtor/hirer having been served with a default notice or in the event of any other action being taken to enforce a regulated agreement, may apply to the court for a time order allowing him extra time to make payments or rectify the breach. Such orders can be varied, extended or revoked by the court.
18.7.6	The dealer as agent of the finance company	The dealer/supplier is often regarded by statute as the agent of the finance company. He is agent in the following circumstances:

• For notice of cancellation;

• To receive the goods;

• To receive notice of withdrawal of offers;

- To receive notice of the rescission of the contract;

- To receive notice of termination.

The debtor can terminate at any time provided he gives notice to the finance company or its agent. He may be required to pay up to 50% of the price of the goods (or less if specified in the contract) as well as all sums due. The hirer will be liable for any damage caused by failure to take reasonable care of the goods.

The creditor cannot terminate for any breach of contract without serving a seven day notice of default (above).

A consumer credit agreement may contain an acceleration clause providing for immediate payment of the whole of the outstanding balance on default of payment. This is valid, provided it is not capable of being interpreted as a penalty clause. (Note: this can be achieved by providing for an appropriate rebate on early payment.) Such an acceleration clause cannot be operated without at least seven days notice in writing.

18.7.7 Termination of a regulated agreement

The 1974 Act gives the court power to reopen a credit agreement and take action if it finds that a credit agreement is extortionate (ss 137-140). A bargain is defined as extortionate when payments imposed on the debtor are grossly exorbitant or grossly contravene the ordinary principles of fair dealing. The court will take into account the prevailing interest, the age, capacity and experience of the hirer/ debtor. The court can rewrite the agreement or set aside the contract. They can, however, seem to be reluctant to intervene on some occasions.

18.7.8 Extortionate credit bargains

In *Ketley v Scott* (1981) Mr Scott had negotiated a loan for which he was paying interest at the rate of 48% per annum. He had an overdraft at the bank and the loan was negotiated in a hurry without full enquiries being made. He defaulted on the loan and the plaintiffs sued him. Mr Scott claimed the interest rate was extortionate. It was held that there was a high degree of risk involved in the loaning of money and therefore the interest charged was not disproportionately high.

Lawyers have speculated that the courts would be reluctant to intervene using this section of the Act. Perhaps the *caveat emptor* principle has left its mark on the judiciary.

To reflect the growth in the number of credit reference agencies and to provide protection and redress for those persons who are incorrectly rated as to their creditworthiness, ss 157-159 allow someone who has been refused credit to request the name and address of the credit reference agency

18.7.9 Credit reference agencies

from the creditor/owner. The customer is then entitled to make a written request to the agency for a copy of his file (subject to a small fee). The customer can then take the necessary steps to have the file amended if necessary (s 159).

Negotiable Instruments and Consumer Credit

Bills of exchange are governed by the Bills of Exchange Act 1882. A bill of exchange is defined by s 3(1):

- Unconditional order in writing.
- Addressed by one person to another.
- Signed by the person giving it.
- To pay on demand or at a fixed or determinable future time.
- A sum certain in money.
- To the order of a specified person or bearer.

The parties to a bill are the:

- Drawer.
- Drawee/acceptor.
- Payee.
- Holder/for value/in due course.

Bills of exchange

Depending on the type of bill, negotiation is either by delivery or by delivery and endorsement.

- Bearer bill – is negotiated by delivery.
- Order bill – is negotiated by instruction and signature.

Negotiation

Endorsements

These can be as follows:

- Blank.
- Special.
- Conditional.
- Restrictive.

Presentment for payment

The payee must present the bill for payment within a few days of the date stipulated. Failure to do so may release the parties from their liabilities (*Yeoman Credit v Gregory* (1963)).

Failure to pay on presentment of the bill amounts to dishonour. Notice of dishonour must then be given by the holder or dishonour can be 'protested'. To protest a bill, it must:

Notice of dishonour

- Be signed by a notary.
- Name the person 'protesting'.
- Enclose a copy of the bill.

Acceptance for honour

Acceptance for honour occurs where liability is accepted by a person with no liability on the bill which must be indicated on the bill in writing.

Forged signatures

No person can acquire rights where there is a forged or unauthorised signature on the bill (s 4), unless the following exceptions apply:

- Estoppel (*London Joint Stock bank Ltd v Macmillan & Arthur* (1918)).
- s 55 – holder in due course.
- Fictitious or non-existent payee – bill may be treated as a bearer bill.

Discharge of a bill

A bill may be discharged by:

- Payment in due course.
- Cancellation.
- A material alteration.

Cheques

Cheques are defined by s 73 Bills of Exchange Act 1882 as follows:

- A bill.
- Drawn on a bank.
- Payable on demand.
- Not 'accepted' – drawee is the bank.
- Has crossings.
- No need for notice of dishonour.
- Banker's protection for forged or unauthorised signatures.
- Delay in presentment does not discharge the drawer (*Wheeler v Young* (1889)).

Crossings

- A bank must pay in accordance with the crossing. The following crossings are recognised:
- General.
- Special.

- 'Not negotiable' (*Wilson & Meeson v Pickering* (1946)).
- 'Account payee' (*House Property Co v London County & Westminster Bank* (1915)).

The customer must:

Duties of the customer

- Not draw up cheques carelessly (*London Joint Stock bank Ltd v Macmillan & Arthur* (1918); *Tai Hing Cotton Mill Ltd v Liu Chong Hing Bank Ltd* (1986)).
- Inform the bank of forgeries (*Greenwood v Martins Bank* (1933)).

The bank must:

Duties of the bank to the customer

- Pay money to the order of the customer (*Rae v Yorkshire Bank* (1988); *Curtice v London City & Midland Bank Ltd* (1908)).
- Keep the affairs of his customer secret subject to:
  - (a) statute
  - (b) public duty
  - (c) bank's interests
  - (d) express or implied consent.
- Keep the customer correctly informed about his financial position.

Paying bank

Protection of bankers

The bank is liable where it pays the wrong person subject to:

- s 59 – payment in good faith and without notice of defect in title.
- s 60 where there is a forged endorsement, payment in good faith and in the ordinary course of business (*Charles v Blackwell* (1877)).
- s 1 Cheques Act 1957 – where the cheque is drawn on the bank who pays in good faith and in the ordinary course of business.
- s 80 where payment is in accordance with the crossing, in good faith and without negligence.

Collecting bank

Where payment is collected for anyone other than the true owner, the bank may be liable in conversion, subject to:

- s 2 Cheques Act which allows the bank to hold the cheque as a holder in due course.

s 4 Cheques Act where the bank receives payment in good faith and without negligence (*Lloyds Bank Ltd v EB Savory & Co* (1933); *Marfani & Co Ltd v Midland Bank Ltd* (1968)).

Other duties of the collecting bank are:

- To check references and enquire into identity;

- To be alert to potential misappropriations (*Thackwell v Barclays Bank Ltd* (1968); *Underwood Ltd v Bank of Liverpool & Marins Ltd* (1924)).

Consumer credit

The types of agreement are:

- Debtor-creditor-supplier agreement.

- Debtor-creditor agreement.

- Restricted-use credit agreement.

- Unrestricted-use credit agreement.

- Fixed-sum credit agreement.

- Running-account credit agreement.

The following are regulated agreements:

- Consumer credit agreement.

- Consumer hire agreement.

- Small agreement.

- Exempt agreements.

Licensing

Businesses which provide finance for regulated agreements are to be licensed by Office of Fair Trading.

Advertising and canvassing

The form and content of advertisements are controlled by Consumer Credit (Advertisements) Regulations 1989.

It is an offence to:

- Send an unsolicited credit-token.

- Canvass debtor-creditor agreements off trade premises.

- Solicit a minor by use of circulars.

Form of the regulated agreement:

- Must be in writing.

- State cash price.

- Describe the goods.

- Include information on rights to cancel or terminate; protected goods.

- Comply with statutory format.
- Comply with rules on copies.

Where the agreement is signed off trade premises, it is cancellable and the debtor must be given notice of his rights to cancel.

Cancellation

- There is a cooling-off period until five days after the second copy is received.
- Written notice must be given within this period to the creditor/owner/dealer.
- In a debtor-creditor-supplier agreement the debtor can recover money paid and await collection of the goods.
- In a debtor-creditor agreement the debtor must repay any money received with interest.

Goods are protected from repossession under a hire purchase agreement when:

Default

- One third or more of the price has been paid.
- The debtor is in breach of the agreement.
- The property in the goods remains with the creditor.
- *Bentinck v Cromwell Engineering* (1971).
- Notice of default must be given to the debtor.

    Repossession can only take place with a court order which can take the form of a:

- Return order.
- Suspended return order.
- Transfer order.
- Debtor may apply for a time order.

A debtor can terminate on giving notice to the creditor or his agent; will be subject to payments having to be made. A creditor can only terminate following default notice.

Termination of a regulated agreement

The court has power to reopen a credit agreement if it finds that the payments are grossly exorbitant with reference to:

Extortionate credit bargains

- Current interest rates.
- Age, capacity and experience of the debtor (*Ketley v Scott* (1981)).

A person who has been refused credit is allowed to request copy of his file from the credit reference agency.

Credit reference agencies

Index